Poverty Reduction that Works

Experience of Scaling Up Development Success

Edited by Paul Steele, Neil Fernando and Maneka Weddikkara

publishing for a sustainable future

London • Sterling, VA

11546661

First published by Earthscan in the UK and USA in 2008

Copyright © United Nations Development Programme, 2008

Asia Pacific Millennium Development Goals Initiative
UNDP Regional Centre in Colombo
23 Independence Ave, Colombo 7, Sri Lanka
Tel: +94 11 4526 400
Fax: +94 11 4526 410
www.undprcc.lk
Email: rcc@undp.org

The views expressed in this publication are those of the authors and do not necessarily represent
those of the United Nations, including UNDP, or their Member States.

ISBN   978-1-84407-601-7   hardback
        978-1-84407-602-4   paperback

Typeset by Composition & Design Services, Belarus
Printed and bound in the UK by MPG Books, Bodmin
Cover design by Susanne Harris

For a full list of publications please contact:

Earthscan
Dunstan House
14a St Cross Street
London EC1N 8XA
UK
Tel: +44 (0)20 7841 1930
Fax: +44 (0)20 7242 1474
Email: earthinfo@earthscan.co.uk
Web: **www.earthscan.co.uk**

22883 Quicksilver Drive, Sterling, VA 20166-2012, USA

Earthscan publishes in association with the International Institute
for Environment and Development

A catalogue record for this book is available from the British Library

Library of Congress Cataloging-in-Publication Data
Poverty reduction that works : experience of scaling up development success / edited by Paul
Steele, Neil Fernando and Maneka Weddikkara.
    p. cm.
  Includes index.
  ISBN 978-1-84407-601-7 (hbk.) -- ISBN 978-1-84407-602-4 (pbk.) 1. Poverty--Developing
countries. 2. Economic assistance--Developing countries. I. Steele, Paul. II. Fernando, Neil. III.
Weddikkara, Maneka.
  HC59.72.P6P687 2008
  362.5'6091724--dc22

                                2008015754

The paper used for this book is FSC-certified and totally
chlorine-free. FSC (the Forest Stewardship Council) is an
international network to promote responsible management
of the world's forests.

Mixed Sources
Product group from well-managed
forests and other controlled sources
www.fsc.org Cert no. SA-COC-1565
© 1996 Forest Stewardship Council
FSC

Contents

PART I – Employment Generation and Participatory Area Development

PART II – Local Economic Development

PART III – Agriculture and Rural Development for Poverty Reduction

PART IV – Localization of Millennium Development Goals and Monitoring

PART V – Social Safety Nets and Microfinance

PART VI – Community Mobilization and Advocacy for the Millennium Development Goals

List of Figures, Tables and Boxes

Figures

Tables

Boxes

Foreword

This compilation of global experience examines twenty examples of innovative targeted poverty reduction interventions from 15 countries – Afghanistan, Bangladesh, Cambodia, China, Egypt, India, Indonesia, Malaysia, Mexico, Nepal, Paraguay, Philippines, Sri Lanka, Thailand and Vietnam. The key questions asked are: what makes good practice for targeted poverty reduction, and how can this good practice be scaled up? What has worked and why? The book concludes that there are five inherent tensions limiting the impact of intervention design and implementation, and contains case studies where most of these challenges have been addressed. This has enabled micro-level initiatives to reduce poverty.

This book has come out of a process that lasted over a year, involving extensive consultation with colleagues around the world leading to an exciting participatory conference on MDG localization in Sri Lanka. Local poverty initiatives play a significant role in a continent where inequality is rising as fast as national incomes. Obviously this does not deny the critical significance of a poverty-reducing macro-environment. High growth and reasonable levels of equity are the foundation of poverty reduction. These pillars, however, leave some communities in the shadow of prosperity. Targeted micro-interventions throw light on the marginalized and build just societies.

This MDG localization initiative was led by Juan Mayo Ragragio, Paul Steele, Neil Fernando, Maneka Weddikkara and Sanath Manage of the UNDP Regional Centre in Colombo (RCC). We would like to thank all the development practitioners who shared their experience in the case studies presented here, and Earthscan publishers who efficiently brought this to publication.

The lessons of this book are carefully crafted to warn against over-simplistic replication models. The conference focused on a dialogue among practitioners on how to apply lessons learned pragmatically under diverse environments. This is a publication of the Millennium Development Goal Initiative at RCC, which is a programme designed to assist countries in accelerating progress towards their MDG attainment.

Omar Noman
Chief of Policies and Programmes UNDP Regional Centre in Colombo

List of Acronyms and Abbreviations

ACHR	Asian Coalition for Housing Rights
ADDCN	Association of District Development Committees
AI	artificial insemination
ANDS	Afghanistan National Development Strategy
ANR	Asociación Nacional Republicana
ASEAN	Association of South-East Asian Nations
ASHG	artisan self help group
BAPPENAS	National Development Planning Agency
Basin	Building Advisory Services and Information Network
BLDC	Balkh Livestock Development Centre
BPL	below poverty line
BRAC	Building Resources Across Communities
BSHIIP	Bindoy Social Health Insurance Indigence Program
CA	conservation agriculture
CBET	Chambok Community-Based Ecotourism
CBMIS	community-based monitoring information system
CBO	community-based organization
CCBEN	Cambodian Community Based Ecotourism Network
CDB	commune development board
CDD	community-driven development
CDF	community development fund
CDP	commune development plan
CEMA	Committee for Ethnic Minority Affairs
CFPR/TUP	Challenging the Frontiers of Poverty Reduction/Targeting the Ultra-Poor
CHC	city health centre
CMAC	Cambodia Mine Action Committee
CMS	content management system
COGENT	International Coconut Genetic Resources Network
COM	Community Operations Manual
CPLTC	Community Professional Learning and Training Centre
CPN(M)	Communist Party of Nepal (Maoist)

CSC	community score card
CSR	corporate social responsibility
CVC	community voice card
CVT	community voice tool
CWMB	community's civil work management board
DARD	Department of Agriculture and Rural Development
DDC	district development committee
DFID	Department for International Development
DPCU	district project coordination unit
DRM	Disaster Risk Management
DRRO	District Relief and Rehabilitation Officer
DTF	Development Technocrats' Forum
DWMA	Distributed Work Management Application
EGPRSP	Economic Growth and Poverty Reduction Strategy Paper
EOC	emergency operation centre
ERSAP	Economic Reform and Structural Adjustment Program
FAO	Food and Agriculture Organization
FNCCI	Federation of Nepalese Chambers of Commerce and Industry
GO	Government Order
GoI	Government of India
GoN	Government of Nepal
GoSL	Government of Sri Lanka
GoTN	Government of Tamil Nadu
HEPR	hunger eradication and poverty reduction
HRDC	human resource development centre
HRDP	Ha Tinh Rural Development Project
IAY	Indira Awaas Yojana
ICT	information and communications technology
IDP	internally displaced person
IDS	integrated dairy scheme
IFAD	International Fund for Agricultural Development
IFPRI	International Food Policy Research Institute
IGVGD	Income Generation for Vulnerable Group Development
IPGRI	International Plant Genetic Resources Institute
IPM	integrated pest management
IRDA	Insurance Regulatory and Development Authority
KDU	Kabul Dairy Union
KPEL	Kemitraan Pembagunan Ekonomi Loka
LED	local economic development
LGU	local government unit
LPA	local public administration
MAIL	Ministry of Agriculture, Irrigation and Livestock
MBN	minimum basis needs

MC	management committee
MCC	milk collection centre
MDG	Millennium Development Goal
MFI	microfinance institution
MLD	Ministry of Local Development
MNBEID	Ministry of Nation Building and Estate Infrastructure Development
MoF	Ministry of Finance
MOLISA	Ministry of Labour, Invalids and Social Affairs
MOWCA	Ministry of Women and Children Affairs
MPCS	milk producers' cooperative society
MPDF	Municipal Partnership Development Fund
MPI	Ministry of Planning and Investment
MuAN	Municipal Association of Nepal
NCCM	National Council for Childhood and Motherhood
NGO	non-government organization
NHIA	National Health Insurance Act
NPC	National Planning Commission
OVOP	One Village One Product
PC	people's company
PCA	Philippine Coconut Authority
PCF	production centre functionary
Phil-Health	Philippine Health Insurance Corporation
PMCDB	Project Micro-Credit Development Board
PMDP	Participatory Municipal Development Planning
PPA	participatory poverty assessment
PPCU	Provincial Project Coordination Unit
PPP	public–private partnership
PRSP	poverty reduction strategy paper
PSU	project support unit
RCF	revolving credit fund
RHU	rural health unit
RMC	rural market centre
RoI	returns on investment
RRD	Relief and Rehabilitation Directorate
RUNET	Rural–Urban Linkage Network
RUPP	Rural Urban Partnership Programme
SDC	Swiss Agency for Development and Cooperation
SEDEMA	Socio-economic Development Programme for Ethnic Minority Areas
SEWA	Self-employed Women's Association
SHG	self-help group
SME	small and medium enterprise

SRA	Social Reform Agenda
TA	technical assistance
TDU	technology demonstration unit
THF	Tibet Heritage Fund
TLO	tole/lane organization
UIC	urban information centre
UNDP	United Nations Development Programme
UNICEF	United Nations Children's Fund
UNTRS	United Nations Team for Recovery Support in Tamil Nadu
UNV	United Nations Volunteers
VCSG	village credit and savings groups
VDC	village development committee
VDF	Village Development Fund
VDP	village development programme
VFU	veterinary field unit
VGD	Vulnerable Group Development
VGF	Vulnerable Group Feeding
VO	village organization
VSCO	Village Savings and Investment Organization
VSHLI	Village Self Help Learning Initiative
WFP	World Food Programme
WSCG	women's saving and credit group
WSHG	women's self help group
WUA	water users' association
WTO	World Trade Organization
YAPD	Youth Association for Population and Development
YSDF	Youth Skill Development Fund

Overview

Paul Steele, Neil Fernando and Maneka Weddikkara

Targeted poverty reduction efforts

The Asia-Pacific region is home to more than half the world's population and over 60 per cent of the world's poor people (UNESCAP/ADB/UNDP, 2007). Rapid progress in poverty reduction in the region is crucial if the world is to make significant progress toward meeting the Millennium Development Goals (MDGs).

To ensure that countries are able to achieve the MDGs by 2015, macro-policies to generate growth are crucial. In many countries, especially in Asia, macro-economic policies are relatively stable and the economy of Asia as a whole is growing at over 6 per cent per year. Many countries such as China and India are growing by over 8 per cent per annum (World Bank, 2008b). The ideological battles between the role of the market and the state have diminished – often constrained by the imperatives of globalization and competition for both domestic and foreign private capital.

Millions have been lifted out of poverty by this rapid economic growth – especially in China, India and, to some extent, Bangladesh. But rapid growth has still left many poor people behind. Major pockets of poverty remain. Across Asia, over 70 per cent of poor people live in rural areas (World Bank, 2008b), although they often depend on non-farm incomes through remittances or other financial transfers. There are also increasing numbers of poor people living in slums; Asia is the world's most rapidly urbanizing region. Reduction of poverty in urban slums is a specific MDG target (Target 11). In China, the inland western regions remain much poorer than the booming coastal belt. Some Indian states such as Bihar and Orissa have much higher poverty levels than the national average. Some groups in society – the elderly, children, the disabled, female-headed households and people marginalized by caste, religion and displaced by conflict – are particularly vulnerable to poverty (World Bank, 2008b). To lift these people out of poverty, more than stable macro-economic policies may be needed. It is vital that pro-poor macro-economic policies are complemented by targeted poverty reduction interventions.

In addition to Asia's rapid economic changes, there have been major changes in Asia's political context. Asia has made remarkable progress in democratization. The majority of Asian countries are now democratic for the first time in history. Nonetheless many countries across Asia are struggling with political pluralism. Often these struggles are based on class and religion, but also on ethnicity, caste and clan loyalties to certain political patrons. The struggles can manifest themselves as tensions between central and local decision making, devolution of power and minority rights. Aspects of the struggles can be seen across Asia in countries such as India, China, Pakistan, Nepal and Sri Lanka.

This book reviews how innovative, targeted poverty reduction initiatives have arisen in Asia's dramatically changing economic and political context. Such targeted poverty reduction approaches need to be thoroughly analysed and documented to reveal why some have succeeded and others failed. The book provides valuable lessons on the nature of targeted poverty reduction initiatives and the factors that explain a successful initiative. What worked and why? How can mistakes be avoided and more effective approaches introduced? What are the lessons of these initiatives for improving development outcomes?

Targeted poverty reduction programmes need to be scaled up if they are to have a significant poverty impact. Local 'pilot' projects need to expand beyond their cocoon if they are to be taken seriously. There are many examples of targeted poverty reduction that support a single village or group of villages. There are many NGOs that have targeted poverty reduction programmes, but these remain isolated islands of success. The challenge is to scale up and ultimately support thousands and even millions of poor people to raise themselves out of poverty. How to address this challenge of scaling up is at the heart of the book.

In the following chapters, 20 case studies from around the world – with a main focus on the Asia-Pacific region are analysed using a standard approach to identify what makes good practice for targeted poverty reduction and how can such good practice be scaled up. The book concludes that there are inherent challenges and tensions in intervention design and implementation – which is why scaling up is inherently difficult and there is no standard blueprint. However there are certain lessons that can be learned and when certain challenges and tensions are resolved, scaling up is possible. It is by broadening poverty reduction efforts from primarily a macro-economic and national emphasis to also include targeted poverty reduction interventions that all of Asia's poor people will eventually be lifted out of absolute poverty.

Case studies

To understand scaling up of targeted poverty reduction, it was decided to review existing good practice. A call for good practice in targeted poverty reduction was issued in early 2007 and solicited almost 100 case studies from more than 20 countries spanning Asia, Africa and Latin America. Twenty of the most illuminating abstracts were selected based on agreed criteria including their recognition as a good practice by a third party and their demonstration of scaling up. These case studies were then invited for presentation and discussion at a conference held in Colombo, Sri Lanka in October 2007. The 20 studies were selected from 15 countries, with 17 studies from Asia (including South, South East and East Asia), and 3 from outside Asia (Mexico, Paraguay and Egypt) (see Table 0.1). Contributions came from a range of practitioners working in civil society, government and donor agencies.

Table 0.1 *Case studies and their themes*

THE CASE STUDIES	COUNTRY	THEME/MAIN FOCUS
Part I – Employment Generation and Participatory Area Development		
Chapter 1: Good Practice of the Chambok Community-Based Ecotourism Project in Cambodia	Cambodia	Community-based ecotourism, focusing on environmental conservation and the provision of income generation alternatives
Chapter 2: Promoting Social Mobilization and Appropriate Housing Technologies for Disaster Mitigation and Poverty Reduction in Orissa	India	The use of cost-effective disaster-resistant housing technologies using sustainable artisan self help groups. Linking habitats with sustainable livelihood opportunities
Chapter 3: Upgrading Housing as a Strategy for Poverty Reduction: The Case of Old Lahsa, Tibet	China	Demonstrates how the upgrading of housing and infrastructure can be combined to promote preservation in a participatory way
Part II – Local Economic Development		
Chapter 4: Poverty Reduction through Local Economic Development: 'Pathway out of Poverty' in Indonesia	Indonesia	Creating economic opportunities and growth at sub-national levels
Chapter 5: Poverty Reduction through Rural–Urban Linkages: The Case of Rural–Urban Partnership Programme in Nepal	Nepal	People's participation and enterprise development activities for livelihood options; rural–urban linkages for balanced development and ICT
Chapter 6: One Tambon One Product, Thailand	Thailand	Poverty reduction of the local community through the generation of employment and income
Part III – Agriculture and Rural Development for Poverty Reduction		
Chapter 7: Dairy Projects in Afghanistan	Afghanistan	Innovative approaches for increased milk production, processing of value added products and marketing involving formation of cooperatives

Table 0.1 *(continued)*

THE CASE STUDIES	COUNTRY	THEME/MAIN FOCUS
Chapter 8: Information Communications Technology for Poverty Reduction: Bringing the Technology to Rural and Disadvantaged Communities in Western China	China	Demonstrates an innovative 'multiple-step flow model', involving school teachers, to diffuse on-line agricultural information among rural farmers who do not have access to the internet
Chapter 9: How Joint Action Can Increase Production while Contributing to Poverty Reduction: The Case of Frutika in Paraguay	Paraguay	Public–private partnership
Chapter 10: Poverty Reduction and Millennium Development Goal Localization: A Case Study of Ha Tinh Rural Development Project in Vietnam	Vietnam	Decentralized participatory planning and implementation of community development plans, the development of community-based organizations and the community-implemented Village Infrastructure Development Fund, and social microfinance through the development of women's saving and credit groups
Chapter 11: Good Practice for Poverty Reduction in Coconut-Growing Communities in the Philippines	Philippines	How four good practices associated with coconut farming can reduce the poverty of coconut farmers
Part IV – Localization of Millennium Development Goals and Monitoring		
Chapter 12: Community Driven Development to Improve Livelihoods: The 'Gemidiriya' Project in Sri Lanka	Sri Lanka	Employment generation and rural poverty reduction based on the Community Driven Development strategy
Chapter 13: Recent Experience with Community Voice Card: An Innovative Tool for Assessing Service Delivery for the Millennium Development Goals	India	Important lessons from the piloting experiences of a participatory report/score card method
Chapter 14: The P135 Programme for Socio-economic Development of Communes Facing Extreme Difficulties in Ethnic Minority and Mountainous Areas in Vietnam	Vietnam	Targeted budget support for localizing the MDG achievement
Chapter 15: Empowering Women through Home-Based Income Earning Opportunities in Malaysia	Malaysia	Shows the tenacity and innovativeness of homemakers in building a grassroots e-community that promotes information technologies, self-help and economic self-reliance

Table 0.1 *(continued)*

THE CASE STUDIES	COUNTRY	THEME/MAIN FOCUS
Part V – Social Safety Nets and Microfinance		
Chapter 16: Poverty Reduction and Millennium Development Goal Localization: A case study of the Income Generation for Vulnerable Group Development Programme in Bangladesh	Bangladesh	Food relief programmes linked to income generating activities supported by microfinance
Chapter 17: Beating the Odds: How Progresa/Oportunidades Became Mexico's Major Poverty Alleviation Programme	Mexico	Substituting food transfers for cash transfers for the extreme poor
Chapter 18: The Phil-Health Indigent Program: A Locality-Based Health Insurance Programme for the Poor in the Philippines	Philippines	An innovative approach employed by several local government units in the Philippines to extend the health insurance coverage to the poor
Chapter 19: VimoSEWA Self Employed Women's Association Microinsurance Programme in India	India	Shares the experiences of a successful microinsurance programme operated by an organization of poor self-employed women workers
Part VI – Community Mobilization and Advocacy for the Millennium Development Goals		
Chapter 20: Sailing the Nile for the Millennium Development Goals: A Yearly Festival of Development, Human Rights and Volunteerism in Egypt	Egypt	An innovative joint initiative with UN Agencies in Egypt aiming to raise awareness, trigger local action and bring United Nations agencies together around the MDGs.

Good practice in targeted poverty reduction

The examples that are showcased in this book illustrate many aspects of good practice in targeted poverty reduction as reviewed below.

Targeting poor people

One important characteristic is the emphasis on identifying or targeting poor people. The case studies demonstrate that aggregate economic growth does not necessarily benefit all of the poor, especially those living in areas or groups still burdened with the consequences of conflict and geographical isolation. Initiatives to address these 'pockets' of severe poverty and directly reach out to the socially excluded can include direct support targeted at the geographical area, at particular groups (for example the elderly) or at sectors where the poor can benefit most.

In this context, one of the challenges of poverty reduction is how to target effectively. Targeting has both advantages and disadvantages in terms of the economic cost of a programme, political acceptability and social inclusion. Sometimes attempts to target the poor can be undermined by 'leakages' when other people benefit through political interference or because a programme is badly designed. Targeting varies depending on what kind of benefits are being provided, such as cash and credit or in kind benefits such as food, training or materials. Self-targeting can be used as a way to reduce leakages, for example, setting wages at a level that would not interest non-poor people.

In terms of the case studies presented here, geographical targeting can be seen in some programmes that focus on certain poor areas, such as the P135 programme of Vietnam. Other programmes such as Progressa in Mexico target particular groups of poor people. Other programmes explicitly target young people, such as unemployed youth in the Lhasa housing programme. Many of the programmes provide a particular focus on women as they are often prone to poverty but when given some assistance may be the most effective in lifting themselves and their children out of poverty. Still other case studies illustrate programmes that target sectors where the poor can benefit most, such as labour-intensive construction in Lhasa, Tibet, or ecotourism in Cambodia.

In order to make sure that targeting works there is a need for effective assessments both at the start of the intervention to form the baseline and as the intervention takes place. There is also a need for accountability mechanisms to ensure that these results are used to reform programmes as required. Many of the case studies reviewed here are notable for the impressive datasets they use to monitor their results and impacts.

Improving the assets of poor people

Poor people are poor for many reasons but a common characteristic is their lack of different kinds of assets – physical, financial, human, social and natural, as set out by the so called 'livelihoods framework'. The obvious implication is that reduction in poverty involves an increase in their asset base in terms of these five key assets:

- *Physical* – many of the case studies focus on increasing the physical infrastructure of an area (the roads, market and storage facilities),such as the case studies for Nepal, Vietnam and Sri Lanka;
- *Financial* – many of the programmes focus on the provision of different types of finance – microfinance to start a business in Sri Lanka or insurance in times of need in India and Bangladesh, or health insurance in the Philippines;
- *Human* – many of the programmes seek to improve the skills base of the poor, often through training. Examples are the housing programme in Orissa, India and the dairy programme in Afghanistan;
- *Natural capital* – the poor are often the most dependent on natural capital and several programmes seek to make their use of nature more productive. This

includes the dairy programme in Afghanistan and the coconut programme in the Philippines

- *Social* – this refers to the networks and organizations to support poor people. Almost all the interventions include some aspect of increasing social capital, particularly the example from Malaysia focusing on group formation among home-based women workers, and the example from China on the role of information technology in creating networks among farmers. There are also interventions to develop market linkages such as the One Tambon One Product market development programme in Thailand.

In addition to directly supporting the assets of the poor, the livelihoods framework also identifies the importance of the broader context, or what some have called the enabling context, that can either advance or constrain poverty reduction. Several of the case studies identify interventions around information dissemination, advocacy and mobilization to increase the voice of the poor and highlight their concerns. The two most obvious examples are the use of 'voice cards' in the Indian case study, which allow poor people to express their views on service quality, and the MDG advocacy campaign in Egypt that seeks to highlight poverty issues in an innovative way.

Areas of intervention for poverty reduction

In summary, it is worth highlighting four major areas: employment, local economic development, agricultural development and social safety nets as instruments of micro-level poverty interventions. These are all areas that are increasingly receiving attention as key components of targeted poverty reduction efforts.

Employment generation

For most development practitioners, the creation of employment is central to poverty reduction.[1] Many of the case studies highlight the importance of increasing the availability of employment for the poor and their increasing labour productivity. This can be in a rural area as in the example of ecotourism in Cambodia, or in an urban area such as construction work in Lhasa in Tibet.

Local economic development

The Thailand case study of One Tambon One Product, the case from Indonesia and the case of Rural Urban Partnership Programme from Nepal are examples of local economic development (LED)[2] projects. The study from Thailand is a good example of using local competitive advantage to create sustainable employment.

Agricultural rural development for poverty reduction[3]

Agriculture as a tool for poverty reduction is not a new theme and it has its successes and failures. However given that it is a source of livelihood for an estimated 86 per cent of rural people and provides jobs for 1.3 billion smallholders and landless workers, it is of great importance and yet has been overlooked over the last decade. Of the developing world's 5.5 billion people, 3 billion live in rural areas (World Bank 2008b). The cases from Afghanistan, Paraguay, the Ha Tinh project in Vietnam, the information and communications technology (ICT) project in China and poverty reduction using coconut-based interventions in the Philippines address the theme of agriculture. The case from Vietnam reveals valuable experience on decentralized participatory planning and implementation of commune development plans. The case from Afghanistan presents the experiences of an integrated dairy development project that uses innovative approaches for increased milk production, processing for value added products and marketing involving the formation of cooperatives. The case from Paraguay illustrates how small farmers through a public–private partnership with Frutika, a Paraguayan fruit juice company, and regional government were able to reduce their poverty.

Social safety nets and microfinance[4]

Improved access and efficient provision of savings, credit, and insurance facilities can enable the poor to ease their consumption, manage their risks better, build their assets gradually, develop their microenterprises, enhance their income earning capacity, and enjoy an improved quality of life. Social safety net-based interventions are illustrated in this book by the cases of the Self Employed Women's Assocation in India, Progresa in Mexico, the Income Generation for Vulnerable Group Development Programme in Bangladesh and health insurance in the Philippines.

Decision making by poor people themselves

The 20 case studies reviewed here are consistent with other research that demonstrates that an intervention must be driven by the target group themselves – in particular recognizing the prime role poor people occupy in the development process (Gillespie, 2003). This may also require appropriate 'capacity', defined as 'the ability of individuals, organisations and societies to perform functions, solve problems, and set and achieve objectives in a sustainable manner' (Theisohn and Wignaraja, 2007). Creating the necessary conditions and providing the essential ingredients for poor people to help themselves is crucial when undertaking targeted poverty reduction.

So the success of a beneficiary driven development process or a targeted poverty reduction initiative depends partly on the group itself. The target group has to be involved from the outset of a project but with its role not limited to design but also including projecting outcomes, selecting interventions and so on.[5] The 'Gemidiriya' (meaning strength or courage of the village) Community Development and Livelihood Improvement Project in Sri Lanka is an example of decision making by the beneficiary poor themselves, while the crucial involvement of the target group in the planning and implementation process of the project is widely reflected in both Ha Tinh Rural Development Project in Vietnam and Rural Urban Partnership Project in Nepal.

The paradox of scaling up development success

A recurring dilemma surrounding successful micro poverty interventions is how they can be scaled up. One of the reasons why local or community-led development projects work is because the target beneficiaries are empowered to help themselves rather than creating a climate of dependency that many large-scale government- or donor-led projects create (Easterley, 2007).[6] But how do we keep the dynamism of the beneficiary-led approach while also allowing this to be scaled up and replicated? How can dynamism be institutionalized? Resolving this paradox, by reviewing a wealth of practical experience, is the aim of the book.

Scaling up is basically to take an intervention and apply it to a larger target group (Uvin, 1995).[7] Scaling up implies adaptation, modification and improvement and not just replication. Thus scaling up applies not only to a particular technology and techniques, but more importantly to principles and processes.

Much of the discussion of scaling up is focused on non-government organizations (NGOs), where distinctions are drawn between quantitative scaling up, functional scaling up, political scaling up and organizational scaling up (Uvin, 1995; Hooper et al, 2004). However these different types of scaling up are often difficult to distinguish in practice – and our scope here is not just single organizations but whole development processes. So here the term scaling up is used simply to mean impacting a larger target group.

Scaling up is necessary for increased impact of development practice. Where initial or pilot interventions have succeeded, scaling up is the logical next step. Successful pilots remain as islands of successes unless they are scaled up. However one should recognize that scaling up can rarely be done in one big bang at the national level. Moreover, any attempt to scale up successful initiatives needs to recognize the fact that what works at one scale is not likely to work at another scale; shifts in scale involve shifts in scope (Binswanger and Swaminathan, 2003). Simple replications of successful initiatives or an expansion of them may well produce 'diseconomies of scale' and render them unsuccessful (Binswanger and Swaminathan, 2003).

There are many factors that need to be considered when taking an intervention for scaling up. For example, logistically, is it possible to scale up a small project if the target groups are dispersed over a large geographic area or if the different groups have varying contextual challenges? What is the cost–benefit calculation?

Resolving the tensions that limit scaling up

Reviewing the 20 case studies illustrates that there are inherent tensions in many development interventions to target poverty reduction. Thus it is not surprising that so many fail – or are never scaled up beyond their initial focus. Resolving these inherent tensions is at the heart of successful scaling up. We identify eight key tensions and below examine how the case studies have successfully addressed these tensions:

- integration with government systems vs challenging anti-poor government structures;
- political ownership vs political interference;
- leadership vs dominance;
- realistic timelines vs quick wins;
- public–private partnerships vs monopoly by certain stakeholders;
- new technology and innovation vs indigenous knowledge;
- financial viability vs affordability; and
- flexibility vs predictability.

Integration with government systems vs challenging anti-poor government structures

Analysis of scaling up consistently emphasizes the need to link with existing government systems and receive political commitment (Uvin, 1995; Hooper et al, 2006; DFID, 2001). In many cases there is a need to integrate with these existing government systems rather than creating an antagonistic relationship from the start. The challenge is that often targeted poverty reduction can only be achieved by challenging some aspects of existing political and government structures. This can be overcome by ensuring that key government and political institutions are encouraged and coopted into supporting the programme.

The approach of the coconut project from the Philippines was to institutionalize the coconut-based farming systems poverty reduction approach. To do this, the programme collaborated with the Department of Agrarian Reform, the Department of Agriculture through its regional field offices, the Bureau of Agricultural Research, the Department of Trade and Industry, the local government units and the private sector suppliers of inputs (seeds and fertilizers). It conducted joint project planning with the Barangay Development Council to incorporate the project into the Barangay Integrated Development Plan and eventually into the Municipal Development Plan to make it eligible for funding by the municipal government. The project was also linked with local and international development organizations and donors to generate funding for replicating the project in other sites. The challenge of institutionalizing this project was overcome through aggressive advocacy that convinced the Department of Agriculture, the Department of Agrarian Reform and the Department of Trade and Industry to provide support to the project in cash and in kind.

The 'Gemidiriya' project in Sri Lanka faced the challenge of convincing the political and administrative cadres at lower levels to accept the 'community-driven' nature of the project. The case study illustrates several approaches to overcoming this challenge. First, the village organizations practiced principles of good governance by making the project model less threatening and more supportive to prudent political interests. Second, as the majority of leadership positions in the VOs are held by women, it has promoted inclusion of the poor and the youth while maintaining credit discipline and demonstrating results on the ground. As people have benefited from the project they have readily shown their gratitude and appreciation to the government. Third, bureaucrats have been involved as facilitators in order to experience the usefulness of including people in their own development activities. These bureaucrats have in turn become the guardians of the rules and principles of the 'Gemidiriya' project.

In some parts of Asia, integrating with government systems is made harder as these institutions are often weak or even non-existent. However this can be seen as an opportunity if the programme engages creatively to try to promote the kind of institutions that would be most supportive. For example for Nepal's Rural Urban Partnership Programme, the absence of elected representatives in local bodies created a major challenge to project implementation. The appointment of government employees in lieu of elected representatives hindered the programme's objective of improving good governance by making authorities (such as the mayor and other elected representatives) accountable for the delivery of public services, through the political empowerment of communities. To counteract this problem, a request was made to the Government of Nepal to form executive bodies with an all-party alliance in the local governments. The recognition and willingness to address the issue was in fact the first step to overcoming this challenge.

Political ownership vs political interference

Political commitment and ownership are important factors often cited by practitioners as being key to the successful scaling up of a project. By creating ownership not only among the beneficiaries and donors but also among political stakeholders, the likelihood of success in scaling up is increased. However at the same time there is a tension that comes with political commitment that is political interference. Although political commitment is necessary, it is important that the project beneficiaries are able to play a role in the design, development and implementation of the project without undue external influence. From the point of view of the donors, it is important that beneficiaries are selected based on need rather than influenced by political stakeholders. Here the challenge is to engage government without it taking over the project in ways that undermine its overall goals and objectives.

Political commitment cannot be created in a vacuum; it needs an enabling climate created by a lively and empowered civil society, free media, strong NGOs and so on (Binswanger and Swaminathan, 2003). The case study from Mexico is a good example of the ability of a programme to achieve political ownership without politicization of a project. Progresa started in 1997 with coverage of 300,000 families in the poorest rural areas and a budget of almost US$59 million. After three presidential terms, it is now the largest targeted social programme in Mexico both in coverage (benefiting 5 million families or 25 per cent of the total population) and in budget (reaching US$3.3 billion in 2007). What were the critical elements for policy change and continuity of Progresa in Mexico? First was President Zedillo's political will and his support to the Ministry of Finance, specifically to the Deputy Minister for Budget Mr Santiago Levy, who was one of the main architects and the champion of the programme since its beginnings. Second was the fact that the Ministry of Finance proposed and conducted the design and implementation of the programme and the change in the poverty alleviation strategy. This ministry had both legal authority and access to information to monitor all ministries and agencies of the federal government.

Indonesia's LED programme demonstrates that for an approach to be successful, an optimal level of engagement by the government needs to be determined. In some locations excessive involvement by the government proved to be counterproductive, making many feel that the government wanted to set the agenda, thus undermining the participative nature of the fora. Although this issue was not completely addressed, the incremental approach of this project enabled improvements and corrective action to be taken during implementation.

The Income Generation for Vulnerable Group Development programme in Bangladesh provides another example of the tensions that exist between political ownership vs interference. Differences between the key partners occasionally challenged the programme. These differences included views about the proper objectives of the programme. While WFP and BRAC emphasized the developmental aspects of the programme's partnership, local government representatives tended to emphasize the food aid aspects, as distribution of government food aid is an important feature of the role of local politicians. Differences between partners over the purpose and management of the savings component and problems relating to leakage and corruption also emerged over time. These partnership challenges were addressed through the development of closer interaction and dialogue between partners, and initiatives to improve transparency in food grain distribution and savings management.

Leadership vs dominance

Civil society leadership or championship of a programme by a single key indi-vidual is often vital to many interventions – particularly at the outset. However once a programme starts to mature and needs to be scaled up, this dominance by a single individual or leader can be counterproductive, leading to dominance rather than leadership. This is why dynamic civil society leadership, which can be crucial for catalyzing lackadaisical government systems, can ultimately undermine sustainability if it prevents a broader institutional arrangement from developing. The problem of dominant leadership has plagued many local poverty initiatives and is often a key reason for initial success, but it is ultimately unsustainable. Several of the case studies highlight the role of dynamic civil groups and NGOs in driving the interventions, but where these organizations are a 'one person show', overly dependent on a single individual, then this may endanger their institutional sustainability.

Realistic timelines vs quick wins

This challenge requires balancing the need for long lead times to allow effective implementation with the need to ensure quick wins and rapid visible results in order to encourage the participation of poor people. Poor people often have little free time and value the present more than the future (known as a high discount rate). So programmes need to avoid focusing excessively on long-term planning and capacity building without a tangible improvement in the human develop-ment of the poor.

The LED project in Indonesia is a case in point. Here the dichotomy between building institutional frameworks over the long term and the quick delivery of economic services in the short term was a challenge. Although, the development of institutional frameworks and capacities takes a long time, the producers who were the primary beneficiaries of this project naturally wanted rapid economic gains. The programme had to be flexible to respond to both these demands with some initial gains, while also focusing on longer term strategic planning.

The 'Gemidiriya' project in Sri Lanka also balances long-term improvements with short-term grants and loans. The project started as a 12-year programme in 2004 with a grant from the World Bank of US$51 million for the implementation of the first four-year phase. The Government of Sri Lanka's contribution is US$11 million and the contribution of the local communities is US$7.8 million. Is such a large-scale project financially viable? In terms of achievements, the 'Gemidiriya' project is impressive. Over a period of two and a half years during 2004–2007, the 'Gemidiriya' model was scaled up to 850 villages and 850,000 people; 210,000 people have road access and 80,000 people have drinking water facilities. The project has also provided opportunities for skills development and income genera-tion for nearly 80,000 people and trained more than 25,000 members on the preparation of village development plans, financial management, procurement procedures and so on.

Public–private partnerships vs monopoly by certain stakeholders

Partnerships between the government and private sector in what are often called public–private partnerships (PPPs) have grown exponentially in recent years. However there is a need to get the balance right. In some cases, these partnerships are overly dominated by government while in other cases there may be excessive control by a single company or group of private sector representatives. This balance is not easy to achieve and yet it is crucial to many types of targeted poverty reduction.[8]

The factors contributing to a successful PPP are a favourable political and statutory environment, a clear revenue system and detailed business plan/contract, among others. Even with these factors in place, PPPs can be faced with tensions between different stakeholders especially when one or two monopolize the partnership. The cases of One Tambon One Product from Thailand and Frutika from Paraguay are good examples of PPPs that have largely overcome these challenges.

The Frutika PPP gradually developed from a technical assistance project for soil recovery, initially implemented by GTZ (German technical cooperation agency) in 1998. This project did not have a concrete project design. Instead, it started with a soil recovery programme with the idea of fruit production as a suitable alternative to traditional crops, especially given the opportunity of exporting the products through the PPP. It was a process that grew slowly over a period of ten years. Although not all institutions were included in the planning process, they were aware of its activities and the central and local governments provided their support by convincing farmers to participate in the project and through the Caazapá 2013 Development Plan. The fact that public and private sector stakeholders were involved in developing this plan was crucial for the future success of Frutika PPP, as it brought all relevant stakeholders to the same forum and made them work toward a common goal. However although Frutika is a successful PPP, historically PPPs in Paraguay have been difficult to establish and seldom have successful outcomes. The GTZ-Frutika experience shows that PPPs can work and that it is possible to create a win–win alliance. However, in the case of GTZ-Frutika, this is as a result of a sequence of years of previous work concentrating on soil recovery and environmental agriculture, combined with participatory strategic planning processes resulting in the Caazapá 2013 plan.

One Tambon One Product is another example of a successful PPP with a close partnership between the government, banks and entrepreneurs. In 2001, the Government of Thailand announced the establishment of the project to respond to the Five-year National Economic and Social Development Plan for poverty reduction. In the same year, the National Committee on Administration of the

One Tambon One Product Project, chaired by the Deputy Prime-Minister was established. Strategies and action plans for the project implementation were set up by the Prime-Minister's Office. This ongoing project has been one of the most successful PPPs in Thailand.

The Partnerships for Local Economic Development Project (Kemitraan Pembagunan Ekonomi Lokal) implemented in Indonesia demonstrates a successful case of a PPP creating economic opportunities for the poor. With a view to improving access to larger markets, more than 60 partnerships were established around key business sub-sectors that had a concentration of micro and small enterprises. Among others, the sectors included coffee, horticulture, fish processing, lobster and shrimp farming and handicrafts. In a number of provinces, partnerships were officially formalized and received financial support from local government budgets. These partnerships created an institutional framework to address multidimensional problems affecting the region's competitiveness. Furthermore, the programme facilitated the partnerships to remove their constraints, to seek new ways of regulating businesses and assist in formulating policies for pro-poor development. The programme contributed towards stimulating local economic activities by empowering local producers, improving their access to markets, introducing improved production techniques and implementing pro-business policies thereby boosting incomes.

New technology and innovation vs indigenous knowledge

One of the key factors that contribute to the success of targeted poverty reduction is the transferability of knowledge and the ability to apply the principles of success elsewhere. It is often important to bring in new technology and innovation but also important to use existing indigenous knowledge. This creates ownership and expertise within the community from the outset and provides the opportunity for indigenous knowledge to be shared and preserved. The challenge is that often new technology and knowledge may be resisted or seen as expensive or high risk.

There are examples where new technology and knowledge have been innovatively used. Two case studies from Malaysia and China highlight the innovative role of the internet. In the case study from Western China, the use of the internet together with traditional methods of distribution of information has allowed farmers in a remote area to learn new farming techniques and adapt their own techniques to obtain maximum benefit in their farming practices. One of the unique findings of the case lies in the significant role that rural schools play in the extension of the internet. In Jinta, village schools served as an important link to relay web-based content to the farmers. This is a real example of how one village managed to overcome the digital divide through traditional methods.

However there are also examples where new technologies and knowledge were initially resisted. The case studies from the construction sector in India and China provide good examples of this type of tension and show that in construction, habits may be especially resistant to change. In Orissa, people initially resisted new disaster resistant technologies until they saw local masons apply them to their own homes. In the case of Lhasa, there was similar resistance to new forms of construction and maintenance until people had seen them with their own eyes. This shows the importance of demonstration to change behaviour.

Financial viability vs affordability

Financial viability is often key for programmes to keep going. While funding can be sought from donors and government, there is an increasing focus on part contributions by poor people. This not only generates funds but can also put in place incentives for poor people to demand effective programmes. However the challenge is that while the financial contribution by the poor seems to have some institutional benefits, it may also be counterproductive if it marginalizes the very poor.

Many of the programmes featured in this book were faced with this tension. For example it arises in the case of Mexico and some of the microfinance projects such as in Bangladesh. Through stringent beneficiary targeting, the projects were able to ensure that the benefits were worth the expense. However it is important to also consider sustainability when looking at financial viability. Is the project sustainable without external funding? These are questions that most projects are faced with when significant donor funding is a necessary component of the project. The success of the 'Gemidiriya' project would suggest that despite the high cost of the project and the project methodology that requires participants to contribute to the community fund, some part contribution is affordable by the community members.

One of the early challenges faced by the insurance project of the Self Employed Women's Association in India was negotiating the systems of the insurance company for claims eligibility and processing. Another was the difficulty in balancing the affordability of the insurance product and the protection that it offers. As the membership increased and became more geographically dispersed, ensuring regular contact with members became difficult. While financial viability is the goal of the insurance project, it is also a major challenge as the costs of administering a micro-insurance programme have to be balanced while keeping the product affordable to the poor. Despite claims to the contrary, the programme clearly demonstrates that the poor are willing to pay for insurance in order to protect themselves from unexpected losses. Educating members about health and economic security benefits of the insurance scheme was a crucial factor to ensure the success of the programme.

Flexibility vs predictability and focus

The ability to adapt to a changing local context is crucial. This is often a common factor that most practitioners emphasize as important to successful scaling up. Adaptation is needed for scaling up in different contexts (Binswanger and Swaminathan, 2003). This requires a 'learning by doing' attitude and being flexible and open to change. However the challenge is that programmes need clear goals and objectives to monitor progress and achieve results. This creates tension between flexibility and predictability.

The case from Cambodia is a case in point. Chambok is a unique example of a successful community-based ecotourism project in Cambodia that has enabled people to generate income from tourism and convinced them to protect their natural resources. The low level of education among villagers was a major obstacle to project implementation. The flexibility of the project was such that the Mlup Baitong was able to spend a significant amount of time in building capacity of the Management Committee members. This often involved repeating training sessions several times to ensure that members are able to take responsibility for implementing activities under the project. It was difficult for the project to persuade villagers, Committee members, local authorities and tourists to adapt to the innovative approaches and procedures. The project initially had difficulty in protecting the forest in and around the site from logging, hunting, forest fires, forestland encroachment, and clearance, but owing to the persistent efforts of Mlup Baitong to raise awareness of nature conservation through the cooperation of all stakeholders, effective mechanisms were established to address these challenges. Although the project ensured predictability and focus by keeping to its original aims, it was flexible in adjusting activities to address new difficulties.

Conclusions and recommendations

This Overview has identified certain tensions that determine whether a targeted poverty reduction intervention works and can be scaled up. During the design and implementation of an intervention, these tensions need to be addressed. The recommendations below summarize the lessons drawn from the case studies on ways to resolve each of the eight tensions:

- *Integration with government systems vs challenging anti-poor government structures* – coopt key government and political authorities into the programme through joint planning and design, training, ultimately institutionalizing the programme.
- *Political ownership vs political interference* – dialogue, publicity and an incrementalist approach are necessary to develop political ownership while limiting interference.

- *Leadership vs dominance* – dynamic individual leadership especially at the start must be balanced with shifting to more broad-based support as the programme matures.
- *Realistic timelines vs quick wins* – while many programmes seek to develop more strategic longer-term interventions, there is a need to also have at the start interventions that produce some quick tangible results to avoid planning fatigue.
- *Public – private partnerships vs monopoly by certain stakeholders* – equitable PPPs require a favourable political and statutory environment, clear systems for managing revenues and a detailed business plan and contract.
- *New technology and innovation vs indigenous knowledge* – new technology can build on existing knowledge and be viewed more receptively if it is disseminated by trusted channels (for example, masons who use new construction techniques on their own homes) and in ways that people can see with their own eyes.
- *Financial viability vs affordability* – beneficiary contributions are important and close dialogue with poor people can identify ways to design a programme so that it becomes affordable.
- *Flexibility vs predictability* – it is necessary to show flexibility in programme activities, but the overall goals and objectives of the programme should be kept fixed to ensure predictability.

These recommendations are not straightforward, which is why targeted poverty reduction often remains an elusive challenge. But when these challenges can be resolved, as in the case studies showcased in this book, poverty reduction can work.

Acknowledgements

We wish to acknowledge the helpful comments provided on this overview by Omar Noman and other RCC colleagues, Niloy Banerjee and Ashley Palmer (UNDP RCB), Neera Burra (independent researcher), Xinan Hou (UNDP China) and Bill Tod (SNV).

Notes

1   Decent work involves opportunities for work that is productive and delivers a fair income, security in the workplace and social protection for families, better prospects for personal development and social integration, freedom for people to express their concerns, organize and participate in the decisions that affect their lives, and equality of opportunity and treatment for all women and men (ILO, 2008).
2   'Local Economic Development (LED) is a practical concept to strengthen the economic capacity of a locality and focuses on local competitive advantages' (ILO, 2008). Others suggest LED to be a process that helps communities work together to achieve sustainable economic growth that enables increased employment, prosperity and quality of life (Swinburn, 2002).

3 The 2008 *World Development Report* states that 'In the 21st century, agriculture continues to be a fundamental instrument for sustainable development and poverty reduction. Three of every four poor people in developing countries live in rural areas' (World Bank, 2008b).

4 Social safety nets are transfers that are non-contributory in nature and target the poor and those vulnerable to poverty from shocks (World Bank, 2008a). The FAO (2003) defines social safety nets as cash or in-kind transfer programmes that seek to reduce poverty through redistributing wealth and/or protecting households against income shocks. Food safety nets are a subset of social safety nets and aim to assure a minimum amount of food consumption and/or protect households against shocks to food consumption (FA0, 2003). As ADB (2007) defines, microfinance is the provision of a broad range of financial services such as deposits, loans, payment services, money transfers and insurance to poor and low-income households and their microenterprises. Microfinance can be a critical element of an effective poverty reduction strategy.

5 Dongier et al (2003) contend that so-called 'community-driven development' (CDD) gives control of decisions and resources to community groups. CDD treats poor people as assets and partners in the development process, building on their institutions and resources. In other words, the target group determines the outcomes of the project and benefits. This focus on the poor themselves is a recommendation of the controversial book by William Easterly (2007) who focuses on the need to have feedback from poor people themselves.

6 In Easterly's analysis, top-down planners are contrasted with bottom-up seekers.

7 However, there are several more nuanced definitions. Some authors (IIRR, 1999) draw a distinction between *vertical* movement of experience, knowledge and impact that affect the higher level organizations of a sector or society, and *horizontal* spread within a sector or locality (for example, among farmers only without involving other stake-holder groups up the ladder).

8 UNDP's South–South unit defines PPPs as a contractual agreement between the public sector (government) and the private sector (for-profit companies). Under these agreements, the resources and risks of both are shared to meet a specific public need. This contractual relationship may include non-profit groups (either NGOs or special purpose organizations created by government action). In all cases, however, at least one for-profit entity (thus the 'private' in public–private partnership) is included. PPPs may be developed by a single government partner or through technical cooperation between two or more countries (NCPPP, 2008).

References

ADB (Asian Development Bank) (2007) *Microfinance Development Strategy*, ADB, Metro Manila, http://www.adb.org/Documents/Policies/Microfinance/microfinance0100.asp?p=policies

Binswanger, H. P. and Swaminathan, S. A. (2003) *Scaling Up Community Driven Development Theoretical Underpinnings And Program Design Implications*, Policy Research Working Paper No. 3039, Washington DC, World Bank

Devarajan, S. and Kanbur, R. (2005) 'A framework for scaling up poverty reduction with illustrations from South Asia', overview contribution to an edited volume prepared by the South Asia Region of the World Bank, from case studies commissioned for the

Shanghai Conference on Scaling Up Poverty Reduction (May 2004), available at www.arts.cornell.edu/poverty/kanbur/DevarajanKanburAug05.pdf

DFID (2001) Sustainable Livelihoods Guidance Sheets, www.livelihoods.org/info/info_guidancesheets.html

Dongier, P., Van Domelen, J., Ostrom, E., Ryan, A., Wakeman, W., Bebbington, A., Alkire, S., Esmail, T. and Polski, M. (2003) 'Community-Driven Development', in *World Bank Poverty Reduction Strategy Paper*, The World Bank, Washington, DC

Easterly, W. (2006) *The White Man's Burden: Why the West's Efforts to Aid the Rest Have Done So Much Ill and So Little Good*, Penguin, London

FAO (Food and Agriculture Organization of the United Nations) (2003) 'Safety nets and the right to food', Rome, FAO, www.fao.org/DOCREP/MEETING/007/J1444E.HTM#P33_1585

Gillespie, S. (2003) 'Scaling up community driven development: A synthesis of experience', Washington DC, World Bank, www-wds.worldbank.org/external/default/WDSContentServer/WDSP/IB/2005/06/02/000090341_20050602134253/Rendered/PDF/316310Synthesis0CDD0Scaling.pdf

Hooper, M., Jafry, R., Marolla, M. and Phan, J. (2004) 'Scaling up community efforts to reach the MDGs', in D. Roe (ed) *The Millennium Development Goals and Conservation*, London, International Institute for Environment and Development

IFAD (International Fund for Agricultural Development) (2008) 'Scaling Up Poverty Reduction: A Global Learning Process, and Conference Using community-driven approaches to reduce rural poverty', IFAD, Rome, www.ifad.org/events/reducing-poverty/vietnam.htm

IIRR (International Institute of Rural Reconstruction) (1999) 'Scaling up sustainable agriculture initiatives', Highlights and synthesis of Proceedings of the CGIAR NGO Committee workshop, 22–23 October, Washington DC

ILO (International Labour Organization) (2008a) 'Employment Promotion', Geneva, ILO, www.ilo.org/global/Themes/Employment_Promotion/lang--en/index.htm

ILO (2008b) 'Local economic development: A participatory development process to create decent jobs and stimulating economic activity', Geneva, ILO, www.ilo.org/dyn/empent/empent.portal?p_prog=L

NCPPP (The National Council for Public Private Partnerships) (2008) 'Guidelines for public–private partnerships', www.ncppp.org/undp/guidelines.html

Swinburn, G. (2002) *Local Economic Development in the World Bank: Next Steps*, Urban Forum, available at www1.worldbank.org/wbiep/decentralization/library8/swinburn.pdf

Theisohn, T. and Wignaraja, K. (2007) 'Capacity Development Practice Note September 2007', New York, UNDP, www.capacity.undp.org/indexAction.cfm?module=Library&action=GetFile&DocumentAttachmentID=1507

UNESCAP/ADB/UNDP (2007) 'The Millennium Development Goals: Progress in Asia and the Pacific 2007', available at www.mdgasiapacific.org/node/160

Uvin, P. (1995) 'Fighting hunger at the grassroots: Paths to scaling up', *World Development*, vol 23, No 6, pp927–939

World Bank (2008a) 'Safety nets and transfers', World Bank, Washington DC, www.worldbank.org/safetynets

World Bank (2008b) *World Development Report, 2008, Agriculture for Development*, Washington DC, World Bank, http://siteresources.worldbank.org/INTWDR2008/Resources/WDR_00_book.pdf

PART I

Employment Generation and Participatory Area Development

1

Good Practice in the Chambok Community-Based Ecotourism Project in Cambodia

Va Moeurn[1], Lay Khim[2] and Chhum Sovanny[3]

Introduction

Cambodia is situated in Southeast Asia. It covers an area of 181,035 square kilometres and has a total population of 13.66 million. The national population growth rate was 1.9 per cent per annum in 1998–2005 (National Institute of Statistics, 2005), the highest in Southeast Asia. Around 83 per cent of the population lives in rural areas. The GDP per capita per annum is US$385 (National Institute of Statistics, 2006) with the GDP growth rate at 13 per cent in 2004. More than 50 per cent of the annual national income is generated from donor assistance (around US$500 million to US$600 million per year). The average monthly household expenditure (estimated in 1999) is around US$95. The proportion of the population living under the poverty line (below US$0.50 per person per day) is 34.7 per cent. The literacy rate is 67.1 per cent, representing 74.4 per cent for men and 60.3 per cent for women (National Institute of Statistics, 2005).

After nearly three decades of civil war, Cambodian social and economic infrastructure has been seriously damaged, particularly in remote areas. Transportation and communication systems, school buildings, health care centres and other public and private facilities were cut off, damaged or abandoned. Human resources and public and private assets were seriously affected. There were also declines in solidarity, conservation, education, social tolerance and law enforcement, while poverty, crime, disorder, and ideological and political discrimination increased. In addition, natural resources, especially forests and wildlife, have declined due to uncontrolled exploitation. The nation's forested land covered 73 per cent of the country's land area before the 1970s, but decreased to only 40 per cent by 1992 (Dennis and Woodsworth, 1992). The situation was worsened by millions of land mines being left in rice fields and forests, rendering thousands of hectares uncultivable and leaving hundreds of people dead or disabled every year.

Kampong Speu province is located to the west of the capital Phnom Penh and hosts the Kirirom National Park, previously characterized by dense forests. Owing to low yields from rice and vegetable cultivation, limited available agricultural land and the danger of land mines, most of its people make their living from forest resources. Interestingly, around 94 per cent of households are engaged in a wide range of forest extraction activities in this study's area of interest, the commune of Kampong Speu (Mlup Baitong, 2003a). These activities include timber cutting, charcoal and fuel-wood production, non-timber forestry product collection and wildlife hunting. Frequently, these activities are uncontrolled and have led to rapid deforestation and severe degradation of wildlife resources. Consequently, the livelihoods of the villagers have been greatly affected and many (66 per cent) are very poor and in debt (Mlup Baitong, 2003a). Predictably, unemployment has also been increasing.

Project formulation

Realizing the need to protect and best utilize natural resources, an environmental organization, Mlup Baitong, has been working in the case-study area through the Chambok Community-Based Ecotourism (CBET) project. Mlup Baitong began this project by assessing the feasibility of attracting tourists to the area based on the existence of a 30-metre waterfall (see Figure 1.1), a bat cave with three bat species and the beauty of the remaining forest. Mlup Baitong started providing informal training on several related environmental topics, especially on the useful-ness of the forest and its resources to villagers, and then introduced the idea of an ecotourism project to the Commune Development Council, which enthusi-astically embraced it. Several workshops were conducted to explore the possible impacts of the project and to clarify the difference between ecotourism and typical commercial tourism. Another step was to support villagers' election of a manage-ment committee (MC) from among the nine commune villages. A committee of 13 representatives was elected, including 2 advisory positions for representatives of the Commune Council and National Park. The by-laws also mandate that at least three of the seats on the MC are reserved for women. Following the elections, clear goals and specific objectives were defined.

One of the most important hurdles for Mlup Baitong and the community was convincing the Ministry of Environment to cooperate in this project, since approximately half of the project site's area is located within the National Park, under the Ministry's jurisdiction. Fortunately, the Ministry was mindful of the need to support villagers' livelihoods to ensure protection of the park and, conse-quently, in August 2002, Mlup Baitong signed a two-year renewable agreement with the Ministry of Environment for a 'Community Conservation Area' of approximately 70 hectares in the park.

Figure 1.1 *A 30-metre waterfall uphill from the Chambok ecotourism site*

Source: Mlup Baitong

Rules and regulations for the site were drafted, as were by-laws for the govern-ance of the organizing committee (see Figure 1.2). Various stakeholders, including officers from the Provincial Department of Tourism, Provincial Department of Environment, Kirirom National Park and the Provincial Governor, were invited to a series of meetings to obtain consensus and final agreement on these crucial documents governing the site.

The practicalities of establishing the site were organized by the villagers themselves, but supported and facilitated by Mlup Baitong. First, Mlup Baitong arranged for Cambodia Mine Action Committee (CMAC) to conduct an assess-ment of the site. Once the site was declared safe, the construction of nature trails began. Villagers organized themselves to build the trails and other necessary facili-ties, while Mlup Baitong supported the villagers with 'food for work' in accord-ance with the standards of the World Food Programme. Finally, training on basic ecotourism services skills were provided. The Chambok community-based ecot-ourism site was officially opened on 4 January 2003 with the participation of district, provincial and ministry officials.

Figure 1.2 *A community meeting to establish community regulations*

Source: Mlup Baitong

Project goals and objectives

The project aims to empower Chambok community members to actively partici-pate in the sustainable management of natural resources in their community, to reduce poverty and improve livelihood. To achieve this goal, three main objectives were: 1) protection of forests and natural resources; 2) provision of income gener-ating alternatives to poverty-stricken and forest product-dependent communities; and 3) education of local people and visitors about environmental conservation.

Project description

Site geography and coverage

The CBET project is located in the remote jungle area of the northeastern border of Kirirom National Park in Chambok Commune, Phnom Sruich district, Kampong Speu province. Most of the site lies on the eastern slope of the Kirirom highland, which is part of Cambodia's southwest Cardamom mountain ranges. Traveling to the city of Sihanouk Ville along National Road No. 4, visitors must

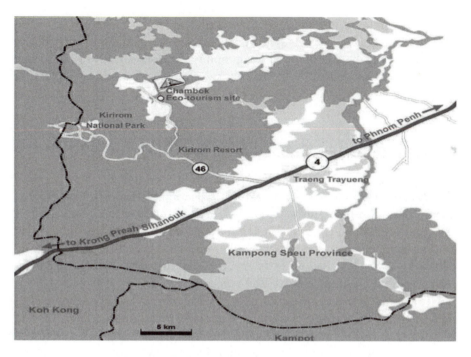

Figure 1.3 *Map of Chambok ecotourism site*

Source: Mlup Baitong

turn right at the small town of Treng Troyeng, approximately 88km from the capital city of Phnom Penh (see Figure 1.3). Continuing the journey on gravel roads for about 20km, one reaches the Chambok commune. An old forest trail was built when Kirirom served as a popular hillside resort for the wealthy during the 1950s and 1960s, and still connects the commune center to a 30m waterfall about 4km away. The project site covers 161 hectares of forest bordering approximately 750 hectares of forested community protected areas and 300 hectares of community forest.

Project beneficiaries

The target beneficiaries of this project include around 500 households of the 9 villages of Chambok commune. The beneficiaries can be divided into three main categories of MC members, service providers and community members. The MC is made up of 13 elected members, while the service providers include entrance fee collectors, tour guides, ox-cart drivers, homestay owners and coordinators, restaurant workers and souvenir vendors. The last two of these have been separately supervised by the Women's Association, which is composed of 13 women's self help groups (WSHGs). About 100 men and 200 women from 300 households have been employed in ecotourism services on a voluntary and rotational basis. The service providers get a daily wage according to regulations. The remaining community members benefit from community development activities through a community fund raised by the ecotourism project and from better access to non-timber forestry products, which have been well protected and successfully controlled by this project.

Implementing and coordinating agency

Mlup Baitong, literally translated as 'green shade', is a dynamic and respected national NGO. It was first established in 1998 as a project of a British NGO to address the problems of deforestation in Cambodia, with a focus on educating the general public on conservation of natural resources. In January 2001, Mlup Baitong became independent, established its own board of directors and drew up a set of by-laws. Mlup Baitong is the initiator and the implementing and coordinating agency for the Chambok CBET project.

To effectively manage this project, Mlup Baitong has dispatched some of its staff, including a programme coordinator, a project officer and a project assistant, to handle the work on the site. A counterpart from the Ministry of Environment is also contracted to coordinate communications between the project and the Ministry. Other staff of Mlup Baitong, working in the same area but on different projects, also may serve as support staff. Volunteers may occasionally join the team. Mlup Baitong sometimes contracts with external experts to deliver training or other required work that is beyond its capacity.

Besides being the project implementer, Mlup Baitong also acts as coordinator linking the local community to other institutions such as governmental agencies or NGOs. It also coordinates during conflict resolution between communities or between community and public authorities in some instances.

Project components and activities

To run this project successfully and to achieve all the above objectives, Mlup Baitong has divided the project into components. This division guarantees smooth and effective management, better implementation and easier follow-up and monitoring. There are five main components, each containing several supporting activities.

The first component of the project is the construction or renovation of infrastructure and facilities. This includes building forest trails, trail stairs, small bridges, an entrance fee ticket-sales booth, an entrance gate, rest shelters, a 96m^2 information centre, a 380m^2 botanical nursery with water supply system, ox-carts, toilets, 20 homestays, a 40m^2 restaurant, a car parking lot and vending kiosks.

The second component is building the capacity of MC members and service providers. In this component the project has provided training on general environmental knowledge and on project planning, implementation and management. The project also organized a visit for MC members and the Commune Council Chief to several ecotourism sites in Thailand and Cambodia to improve their understanding of ecotourism implementation.

The establishment and marketing of income generation services make up the third component. This includes establishing systems for entrance fee collection, car parking, ox-cart riding, tourist guiding, food preparation, souvenir vending, traditional dancing performance and homestays. The project has actively participated in the Cambodian Community Based Ecotourism Network (CCBEN) and contacted several tour companies for tourism product advertisement.

The next component involves keeping the ecotourism site environmentally friendly. Several key activities have been implemented to support this component. The project assists the community in setting up rules and regulations for waste management and educates villagers, service providers and visitors on relevant environmental topics. The MC regularly supports activities such as cleaning of the site, installing garbage bins and educational signs, and patrolling the forest to prevent fires and illegal forestry activities.

The last component is the establishment and support of the Women's Association to improve the livelihoods of its members. In this component, the project introduced the WSHGs, supported their formation and provided the groups with support for microenterprises, including souvenir selling, preparing guest meals and renting bicycles to visitors. These activities have been carried out through a savings group approach.

Key technical inputs

To ensure the success and sustainability of the project, technical inputs are provided to MC members and service providers. Inputs include training on environmental issues, facilitation skills, problem solving, report writing, micro-project/business design, project implementation and management, implementation of relevant laws, forest protection methods, and tourism service techniques and management. The last of these includes teaching community-based ecotourism concepts, bookkeeping, accounting, financial management, tour guiding, first aid, hygiene and sanitation, basic English conversation and computer skills. In addition, the concept of self help groups was also introduced to the Women's Association.

In particular, techniques of micro-project/business designing, implementation and management have been critical inputs provided to MC members. They have been trained on how to plan, implement and manage all sub-projects of CBET, and have been supported in implementing small projects by themselves (see Figure 1.4). The objective of this approach is to strengthen the capacity and ownership of MC members in project planning, implementation and management to strive towards community-based organization (CBO) establishment and to ensure the sustainability of CBET after Mlup Baitong withdraw (scheduled for 2009).

Figure 1.4 *Micro-project training given to the management committee*

Source: Mlup Baitong

Project timeframe

The Chambok ecotourism project can be divided into three main phases. The first phase, or *project establishment*, was completed in 2002. In this step, Mlup Baitong mobilized resources, searched for experts, promoted and explained the project to relevant stakeholders, with a special focus on community members and government institutions, and enlisting their support to establish this innovative project.

The second phase from 2003 to 2006 was *project improvement* in which all activities were focused on developing infrastructure, facilities, tourism services, marketing and capacity building for MC members and service providers. The aim of this step was to achieve natural resource protection and income generation for the community members.

The last phase, from 2007 to 2009, is *project graduation* in which the responsibilities for managing project activities, including planning and implementing, which were previously done by the project staff, are gradually being passed on to MC members through the micro-project approach. This is the transitional period towards CBO establishment. However, project improvements achieved in the second phase will continue to enhance the quality of the project.

From 2010 onwards there will be a period of self-management. Mlup Baitong plans to assist the MC in establishing a CBO, through which MC members will manage all project development activities. From this time, the income generated from the CBET is expected to be adequate to support the project expenses and to contribute to community development.

Total project cost

The total cost of the project from 2002 to 2009 is US$226,000. This cost has been broken down into five main components (see Table 1.1). Overhead costs constitute all administration costs and a small portion for the salary of supporting staff. Project staff costs include staff salaries and benefits. Productive input costs contain all expenditures for materials, equipments, community capacity building and infrastructure. Project operation costs account for expenses of communication, transportation, food and sundries for project planning, monitoring and evaluation. Project staff development costs consist of staff training and exposure visit expenses.

All project costs have been funded by foreign donors including Oxfam Novib, Scottish Catholic International Aid Fund, Oxfam Great Britain, Keidanren Nature Conservation Fund, Asian Development Bank, Blacksmith Institute, Canada Fund, McKnight Foundation and UNDP/Economic Commission. There was no direct financial support from the Cambodian government or private companies. However, the government contributed some support to the building of roads and land mine clearance, while tour companies assisted with advertising.

The yearly CBET project activity planning and budgeting are regularly conducted before project implementation. Usually several consultation meetings with representatives from the project beneficiaries are conducted to collect ideas and comments as inputs for the project plan. In addition, a mid-year-planning review is also conducted to revise some project activities and allocate the budget to respond to the project situation and external influences.

The CBET MC conducts monthly meeting to share the activities accomplished and the problems encountered. Minutes of each meeting are written and submitted to the project staff. Project staff include a project officer, a project assistant and, intermittently, a counterpart from the Ministry of Environment and a volunteer. The staff regularly monitor the CBET activities during working days

Table 1.1 *Project cost breakdown*

Cost Categories	Overhead	Project Staff	Productive Inputs	Project Operation	Staff Development	Totals
Cost US$	$20,340	$65,540	$101,700	$31,640	$6,780	**$226,000**
Percentage	9	29	45	14	3	
On-Site Expenses	0%	70% $45,880	100% $101,700	60% $18,980	0%	**74% $166,560**

and take turns observing activities during weekends and holidays. The project is supervised by the programme coordinator who visits the site once a week on average. Besides regular communication by phone with the project staff, the executive director has come to Chambok and met with CBET committee members an average of six times per year, usually on weekends.

Monitoring is also done through monthly programme meetings, organized by the programme coordinator at the field office. Several ad hoc meetings with relevant stakeholders have also been conducted with staff from other related projects working in the same or nearby areas. Monitoring information is documented in monthly activity reports, which are written by the project officer and edited by the project coordinator before being submitted to the executive director. Besides this, incidental reports on any illegal activities are also submitted by the coordinator to relevant local authorities, including the commune council and the director of the Kirirom National Park. In serious cases, the incidental reports must be submitted to the executive director so that he can take further action.

A project progress report is submitted to each relevant project sponsor according to its specific requirements. Each month or two, the executive director submits a consolidated report to the board of directors. Also an external project evaluation is conducted every three years, and an evaluation report is submitted to all project sponsors and some of the main stakeholders.

Impacts and outcomes

The project's efforts to raise environmental awareness have resulted in service providers, villagers and local visitors participating in keeping the ecotourism site clean, green and sustainable. For example, waste and water pollution issues, which frequently happen in tourism sites, have not happened in Chambok. The success of this project, especially in terms of raising environmental awareness and sustainable practices among visitors, has been frequently cited as good practice by guest speakers on radio, TV shows and panel debate programmes.

The conservation efforts have resulted in the prevention of forest fires and illegal logging and hunting inside the ecotourism site. More than 1100 hectares of forest have been properly managed. Illegal activities, which often happen in those areas, have largely stopped, with most villagers previously involved in logging or hunting becoming farmers, tour guides or tourism service providers. Of particular interest is the complete elimination of 72 charcoal kilns that operated in the project site before the establishment of this ecotourism project (see Figure 1.5). These charcoal kilns, which consumed hundreds of trees every day, were responsible for severe destruction of forest. Also, no major destruction of natural resources has occurred in the surrounding forest areas connected with the Chambok CBET site, thus allowing the forest a proper chance to regenerate.

Mlup Baitong plans to gradually phase out its support for the Chambok Ecotourism site by 2009. The graduation plan involves handing over responsibilities

Figure 1.5 *A typical charcoal kiln operating in Chambok prior to the introduction of ecotourism*

Source: Mlup Baitong

of managing the site to MC members step by step. Training on related topics has been provided to MC members including formal training, coaching and exposure visits. A micro-project approach in which the MC members are trained to design and implement activities for the management, maintenance and improvement of the site has been used since 2006 to strengthen their capacities and owner-ship, and to familiarize the MC members with the management and ownership of the project. As a result, most MC members can develop and implement a plan to improve facilities at the site without assistance. Currently, around 60 per cent of project activities, previously done by the project staff, are planned and implemented by MC members. The improvement of MC members' capacity is an invaluable element of sustaining the project.

In 2006, the total benefits generated by the community from all tourism services amounted to more than US$10,000 (Mlup Baitong, 2006) (see Table 1.2). A substantial part of the income from the ecotourism services goes directly on the daily wages of the workers and the remaining income is saved in the local bank as a community fund that will be used to support very poor families, construct and repair infrastructure, and support the WSHG members in creating small businesses. By mid-2007, the fund savings had accumulated to US$5000 (Mlup

Table 1.2 *Project costs and benefits*

Costs		Benefits	
		Tangibles	
Overheads	$20,340	1100ha forest land preserved/managed	$1,100,000
Project Staff	$65,540	Revenue of $10,000/year in 2006 (total to date)	$25,000
Productive Inputs	$101,700	Information Centre	$20,000
Project Operation	$31,640	Roads and trails	$35,000
Staff Development	$6780	Equipment	$5000
Total	**$226,000**	Total	**$1,185,000**
		Intangibles	
		Community cooperation and social solidarity	
		Environmental understanding of residents and tourists	
		Non-destructive ownership of forest land and project	
		Increased capacity for management and leadership	
		Improved reputation for Chambok, Kirirom National Park, Mlup Baitong, protected areas and community-based ecotourism	
		Understanding of dispute resolution processes	
		Structure and participation among council	
		Changed attitudes towards forest land	
		Opportunities for sustained income generation	
		Potential for duplication and scaling up throughout Cambodia	
		Improved English skills	
		Establishment of sustainable forest nursery	

Baitong, 2007). About 500 households directly benefit from this project through increased access to non-timber forest resources, including bamboo, bamboo shoots, mushrooms, raisins and rattan, and through the sale of agricultural products, including coconuts, bananas, vegetables, chicken and other livestock. Furthermore, 300 people have been employed in ecotourism services on a rotational basis, improving their livelihoods. Lastly the emigration of young villagers to cities has significantly declined.

Figure 1.6 shows the development of the project's outcomes over the past four years. It should be noted that the number of visitors in 2005 fell due to bad road conditions.

To date, ecotourism activities have had positive impacts on food security as well as environmental appreciation and awareness. In addition, the project has enabled a number of people to change their jobs to more environmentally sustainable occupations, giving the forest and wildlife a chance to regenerate.

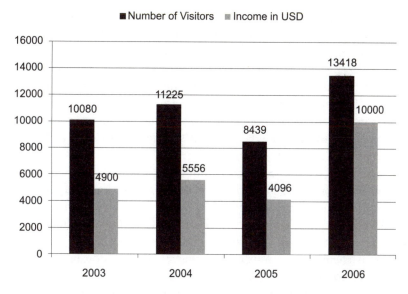

Figure 1.6 *Progress of project 2003–2006*

Source: based on Mlup Baitong, 2003b; 2004; 2005.

Challenges faced and how they were overcome

Behind all the successes mentioned above lie a number of challenges to the running of this project. The low level of education among villagers is a major obstacle to project implementation. At the start of the project in 2002, no one in Chambok commune had completed primary education. Mlup Baitong has spent a large amount of time building capacities of MC members. Sometimes Mlup Baitong had to teach skills repeatedly in order to enable MC members to take responsibilities in running projects. But even though slower than desired, progress has been made.

Since community-based ecotourism is a new concept for villagers, it has been difficult for Mlup Baitong to convince villagers, MC members, local authorities and tourists to adapt to the innovative approaches and procedures. The difficulties include limited awareness of biodiversity protection and conservation, and the protection of the site from litter. Mlup Baitong also gets many complaints about prohibiting car or motorbike travel in the site, instead making tourists walk on long forest trails. Yet Mlup Baitong continues to work hard to raise awareness of nature conservation and waste management.

Mlup Baitong faces big difficulties in protecting the forest in and around the site from illegal cutting, hunting, forest fires, forest land encroachment and clearance. It has cooperated with relevant government institutions and other stakeholders to set up effective mechanisms to deal with these issues. Sharing related information, cooperating in banning illegal activities, setting up clear internal regulations for community forestry and community protected areas, and participatory patrolling are the best solutions to these difficulties.

Mlup Baitong is challenged by the lack of expert project staff, which considerably limits the project's successes. During the project establishment phase in 2002, Mlup Baitong, aware of the lack of experts, invited a young Japanese expert in ecotourism to assist in designing and establishing the project for one year. This gave an opportunity for some Cambodian staff involved in the project to gain experience through practice.

Despite these challenges, the community-based ecotourism project holds great potential for developing community solidarity, improving livelihoods, protecting resources and relieving poverty in an equitable and sustainable way. There are encouraging results in the Chambok Commune, including a strong sense of community ownership of the project, increased confidence and solidarity and active participation in protecting resources they previously felt helpless to protect. In addition, the stable income from the project supplements daily living for many families, while tourists can appreciate the beauty of nature and the local indigenous knowledge of plants and animals. Villagers report that wild animal sightings have significantly increased during the patrols, they are all becoming supporters of conservation.

Lessons learned

Natural resources, including forests and wildlife, are the core of ecotourism. Mlup Baitong has combined the establishment of community forestry and community protected areas with the CBET project. In addition, the community has acquired the rights to manage forest resources in the project area. Mlup Baitong has developed good cooperation with relevant government institutions from the beginning of the project and has consequently received good support from them in return. These are critically important factors in the success and sustainability of the Chambok CBET project.

The CBET project belongs to community members. An appropriate community management committee and by-laws have been clearly established through a participatory approach. Equitable involvement and benefit sharing among community members was carefully taken into account during project implementation. This approach has encouraged community members' participation, support and cooperation in avoiding internal conflicts. The approach of WSHGs has been combined with women's income generation through tourism services such as food preparation, souvenir selling, bicycle rental and ox-cart rides. This combination is viewed as an effective way to promote gender balance between men and women.

Mr Touch Morn has been the head of Chambok CBET's MC since the start of the project. He is the only MC member with sufficient understanding and capacity to manage the project and to explain the project implementation and achievements to visitors and delegations visiting the site. During the past three years, most CBET committee members have come to rely heavily upon him. This situation results in problems with the project implementation and an over-reliance on him. If Touch Morn decides to resign from his position or is not selected as the head of the MC for the next mandate, this will have serious consequences for the sustainability of the project. Mlup Baitong seeks to encourage and support Touch Morn's continued success, but is training others to enable them to take over his responsibilities.

Mlup Baitong plans to gradually phase out its support for the Chambok ecotourism site by 2009 through the micro-project approach, which appears to be an achievable objective. Although this approach only began in 2006, it appears an appropriate mechanism to strengthen MC members' ownership and to sustain the project.

Good practice

CBET's MC members have gradually improved their management competencies, which is a major factor in the sustainability of the ecotourism attraction. Community-based ecotourism has been demonstrated to be an appropriate approach for Cambodia to contribute to environmental conservation while improving community livelihoods.

Because of the reputation of Chambok as a successful and unique model of community-based ecotourism in Combodia, 47 delegations visited the site between January 2006 and June 2007. These include national and international NGO workers, university students, researchers, government officials and international delegations. Some visits were arranged by travel agents; some were coordinated by Mlup Baitong partners; some were facilitated by government ministries; and others were organized by individual groups.

This project has been recognized by the Ministry of Tourism as a good model of pro-poor community-based ecotourism in Cambodia. In early 2006, the Chambok CBET project was given an award for its successful efforts to involve the Chambok Commune Council in its activities by the Commune Council Support Project, which works closely with the Ministry of Interior. In July 2006, the Cambok CBET project received a bronze medal from the prime minister through the Ministry of Environment for best practice in natural resource protection and community livelihood improvement.

Potential for scaling up or replication

One significant result of sharing the best practice in CBET is that the Ministry of Tourism has recently requested Mlup Baitong replicate the concepts of this project in other Cambodian provinces. Currently Mlup Baitong has decided to replicate this successful model in Steung Treng province by establishing community-based ecotourism in O'Reusey Kandal, Sieng Bok District. In addition, Mlup Baitong has also submitted a project proposal to establish another project in Kosh Sampeay in the same district.

Recently, Mlup Baitong has been invited by the Ministry of Tourism to apply for a grant for CBET establishment in Ratanakiri province. Mlup Baitong also plans to facilitate the community in Kosh Kong province to establish a project in O'Back Rotes commune.

Besides this, best practice and the experiences of Chambok CBET have been disseminated to many groups of visitors from other interested organizations through presentations by Mlup Baitong staff or the head of CBET's MC.

Conclusions

The Chambok CBET project has been implemented successfully and the CBET committee members have gradually improved their management capability, which is a necessary factor for the sustainability of any ecotourism attraction. Chambok CBET has been viewed as a best practice CBET model in Cambodia and is ideal for scaling up or replicating its practices throughout Cambodia. However, the Chambok CBET MC has also been viewed as sometimes weak and it requires further support in capacity building for financial management, management structure, English communication, marketing, planning and problem solving.

Community-based ecotourism can be considered an appropriate environmentally friendly approach for community livelihood improvement while natural resources are protected and conserved for sustainable development. However, ecotourism alone could not generate enough revenue to support the basic needs of all community members. Improving environmentally friendly agricultural techniques and other businesses are other aspects that must also be integrated to maximize total community benefits.

Acknowledgements

The authors would like to express their greatest thanks to all of Mlup Baitong's staff for their hard work in developing this ecotourism project from a concept into reality. Great appreciation also goes to all community members who have strived hard to protect and conserve their natural resources. Extended thanks are dedicated to all project sponsors, both governmental and non-governmental, for their support. Together, we continue to make an impact.

Notes

1 Executive Director, Mlup Baitong Cambodian NGO.
2 UNDP-Cambodia.
3 UNDP-Cambodia.

References

Dennis, J. V. and Woodsworth, G. (1992) *Environmental Priorities and Strategies for Strengthening Capacity for Sustainable Development in Cambodia*, Phnom Penh, UNDP

Mlup Baitong (2003a) *Mlup Baitong 2003 Report on Natural Resource Utilization and Food Security*, Mlup Baitong, Phnom Penh

Mlup Baitong (2003b) *Mlup Baitong 2003 Annual Report*, Mlup Baitong, Phnom Penh

Mlup Baitong (2004) *Mlup Baitong 2004 Annual Report*, Mlup Baitong, Phnom Penh

Mlup Baitong (2005) *Mlup Baitong 2005 Annual Report*, Mlup Baitong, Phnom Penh

Mlup Baitong (2006) *Mlup Baitong 2006 Annual Report*, Mlup Baitong, Phnom Penh

Mlup Baitong (2007) *Mlup Baitong Final Report to McKnight Foundation*, Mlup Baitong, Phnom Penh

National Institute of Statistics (2005) *Cambodia Socio-Economic Survey 2004*, Phnom Penh, National Institute of Statistics, Ministry of Planning

National Institute of Statistics (2006) *Statistical Yearbook 2006*, Phnom Penh, National Institute of Statistics, Ministry of Planning

2

Promoting Social Mobilization and Appropriate Housing Technologies for Disaster Mitigation and Poverty Reduction in Orissa, India[1]

Anindya Kumar Sarkar and Pradeep Jena

Introduction

The State of Orissa in India suffers from large-scale housing deprivation in rural areas, primarily due to acute poverty and lack of technical knowledge on house construction among the households and construction workers. Most of the poor either do not have a dwelling unit or live in unserviceable *kutcha* (mud and straw) houses.

In addition, Orissa is prone to multiple and recurring hazards in the form of cyclones, floods and tidal surges in the eastern delta region and droughts in the western parts, all of which aggravate the shortage of housing. About 2 million houses were damaged by the super-cyclone of 1999, while another 275,000 houses were affected by the flash floods in 2001. Consequently in the years 2000–2001, the housing shortage became so acute that about 60 per cent of all households suffered in one way or another. Of the total rural housing stock of about 6.8 million dwelling units, 10.3 per cent are in a dilapidated condition and as much as 67.5 per cent are barely in liveable condition (Census of India, 2001).

A detailed analysis of the structural condition of these houses reveals that about 70 per cent have mud floors while nearly 50 per cent of houses have grass, thatch, bamboo, wood or mud roofs. Similarly, 55 per cent of walls are of mud and unburnt bricks. This makes those who live in *kutcha* houses highly vulnerable to natural disasters.

Rationale

In the aftermath of the recent disasters, the Government of India (GoI) planned to rehabilitate 0.6 million homeless under Indira Awaas Yojana (IAY), a GoI rural housing scheme that gives a grant of Rs22,000 (US$540) to households that fall below the poverty line (BPL). However, this amount has proved to be insufficient for a family to undertake even the construction of a one-roomed *pucca* (brick and concrete) dwelling unit.

An assessment carried out by the Panchayati Raj Department (Department of Local Government) and Government of Orissa, with the help of United Nations Volunteers (UNVs) revealed that progress in reconstruction of housing was poor due to the following reasons:

- The price of building materials and the transportation costs had escalated after the super-cyclone.
- Most BPL families who were allotted an IAY grant had diverted part of the first instalment for livelihood consumption due to acute poverty caused in the aftermath of the super-cyclone. This prevented them from receiving the subsequent instalment.
- Since many of the local masons were unskilled and poorly educated, funds were not used optimally.
- Many of the beneficiaries were ambitious and initiated construction of houses with more than one room that then proved impossible to complete with the limited grant available.

UNDP joined the partnership to facilitate construction of the IAY houses through support from the Swiss Agency for Development and Cooperation (SDC) and this marked the launch of the SDC-UNDP Rural Housing Project in Orissa. A 29 member team of young and enthusiastic UNVs (who were technically qualified as architects, civil engineers and planners) was constituted to promote appropriate cost-effective disaster-resistant technologies, build capacity within the communities and facilitate the process of safe and affordable habitat development.

Project formulation

Perhaps the most important lessons acquired through the post-cyclone reconstruction efforts of UNDP in Orissa during 2000–2001 was that local masons act as architects, engineers and builders, all rolled into one, and so they are the crucial actors in the rural housing delivery system. The project thus focused on building the capacities of the informally trained or untrained construction workers so that they could become 'catalysts of change' for technology transfer and support the promotion of disaster-proof housing. It was also essential to create an institutional set-up that could help generate alternative or improved livelihood opportunities for the construction workers as well as address issues of their savings and social security.

The project implementation strategy and activities were planned in a project planning workshop in July 2002 in which concerned government and non-government agencies, technical agencies, bilateral and UN agencies, UNVs, *panchayat* (local government) leaders and trained masons participated.

Project goals and objectives

The goal of the Rural Housing Project launched in July 2002 was to promote appropriate, cost-effective and disaster-resistant housing technologies for safe and affordable shelters for all, and to link habitat with sustainable livelihood opportunities.

The project was based on the hypothesis that housing on a mass scale could assume the shape of a movement by addressing the factors that make housing affordable and safe:

- promoting of local building materials and appropriate housing technologies;
- improving the capacity of the community to access house building options and choices;
- developing self-supporting systems and institutions for entrepreneurship;
- building the capacity of local institutions and communities; and
- networking and promoting learning platforms at macro and micro levels.

Key elements of the project

Target beneficiaries

The main groups to benefit from the initiative were:

- households (about 4500 primarily from the BPL category) enabling them to build their houses using disaster-resistant technologies;
- construction workers and artisan groups, giving them access to training, both technical and non-technical (for example, accounts), leading to an increase in income levels; and
- women construction labourers, enabling them to upgrade their skills.

Area covered by the project

The project started initially in 8 districts of Orissa and was subsequently extended to cover a total of 16 districts in the state. Intense networking and partnerships on habitat development with government, civil society and voluntary organizations helped expand the movement to other disaster-prone states such as Uttaranchal, Karnataka, Bihar, Uttar Pradesh, Andhra Pradesh, tsunami-affected Tamil Nadu and Nicobar Islands, and the northeastern states of India and West Bengal.

Project activities

The key components of the project are:

- institution building;
- training and capacity building;
- documentation, creation of learning platforms and networking for knowledge management; and
- housing and habitat development.

Institution building

The emphasis was on upgrading the skills of the individual masons, and, as the number of trained masons grew, they were clustered with other artisans connected with the construction industry such as bricklayers, bar-benders, plumbers, electricians and carpenters. About 150 such artisan self help groups (ASHGs) are functioning in 8 districts of Orissa.

The ASHGs were further supported through skills-based training on the management of construction projects, such as construction of community centres, *anganwadi* centres[2] and water and sanitation activities, as well as on the development of microenterprises.

The training included bookkeeping, project management, market survey methods, negotiation and networking skills. The ASHGs were also trained to deliver better quality services and production of building materials. Further, the ASHGs were supported in applying for loans from local and national banks to start microenterprises, such as for the production of better quality building materials using local resources, concrete block and tile production, sanitaryware production and the renting of steel shuttering sets. Steps were also initiated to federate these groups at the district level into artisans' federations, which could coordinate the work of the ASHGs and liaise with the district administrations for taking up new construction projects.

A noteworthy development was that to institutionalize this movement, the UNVs who had spearheaded this initiative joined together and formed a registered society called the Development Technocrats' Forum (DTF) with its own memorandum, article of association and mission related to housing and habitat development. DTF is currently working in collaboration with the ASHGs and artisans' federations on housing and habitat related works within and outside Orissa. The

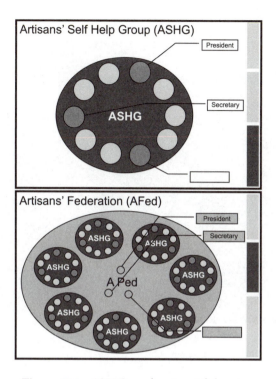

Figure 2.1 *ASHGs and artisans' federations*

Source: chapter authors

most competitive masons, artisans and leaders are shaping themselves as a rural construction consultancy to technically support the ASHGs and federations.

Capacity building

The capacity building efforts were led by the UNV team, which, in the aftermath of the recent natural disasters, had gained considerable expertise in the field of appropriate housing, disaster mitigation and social mobilization.

The masons were trained on the use of alternative construction technologies, both in theory and through hands-on exercises. They were sent on exposure visits to observe building construction so as to dispel the notion that these technologies were meant only for the poor and to clarify that the rich were also adopting them. Seventy-two *anganwadi* centres serving as technology demonstration units (TDUs) were constructed at vantage points with the help of trained masons to demonstrate the efficacy of these alternative technologies to the community. Each of the TDUs was unique in the sense that specially formed village development committees known as Nirmiti Samitis were actively involved in their design to suit community needs and local conditions.

Figure 2.2 *Masons visiting buildings in Bhubaneswar constructed using appropriate technologies*

Source: chapter authors

Figure 2.3 *Homemakers becoming breadwinners:*
Training of women in Dhenkanal district to make concrete blocks

Source: chapter authors

The Nirmiti Samitis also oversaw construction management. Participation of the village community was facilitated through advocacy activities such as village meetings, screening of video shows and distribution of leaflets. To ensure widespread technology transfer, government agencies were brought on board and 152 government engineers were trained in the use of alternative technologies. The district level administrators such as collectors and project directors were also exposed to the technologies.

The capacity building activities, focusing on good construction practices and on multi-hazard resistant building technologies, have been expanded to cover a much broader target group. This has been possible through a partnership with the Ministry of Home Affairs, the State Governments of Uttar Pradesh, Bihar and Nagaland, various NGOs and corporate groups such as HOLTEC (P) Ltd. Under the GoI-UNDP Disaster Risk Management Programme (DRM), the training of masons was undertaken in the states of Uttaranchal, Bihar, Karnataka, West Bengal, tsunami-affected Tamil Nadu, Nicobar Islands, Uttar Pradesh and the northeastern states of India.

More than 500 women construction labourers have been trained in several districts of Orissa. The Women and Child Development Department of the Government of Orissa organized their training in partnership with NGOs.

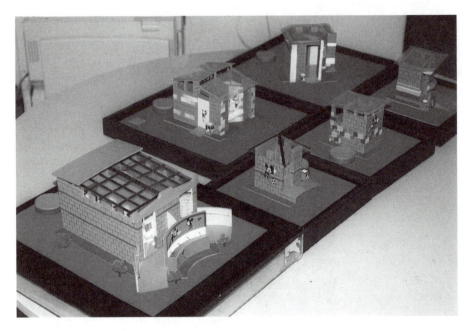

Figure 2.4 *Models of proposed buildings for school and anganwadi toilets*

Source: chapter authors

Training of women in partnership with unicef

The United Nations Children's Fund (UNICEF) was entrusted with the task of preparing appropriate architectural drawings and designs, including 3D models, and with the training of women ASHG members in the production of cement concrete blocks in different production centres. As a pilot project, the training programme started in Dhenkanal and Angul districts where 382 women production centre functionaries (PCFs) were trained. During the second phase of training, 64 PCFs were trained in Rayagada district.

Child-friendly and barrier-free toilets in schools and *anganwadi* centres were also designed and constructed. These structures were designed with special features to attract children so that they got used to using toilets. The features included small height swing doors, provisions for adequate light and ventilation, use of colourful translucent roofing (to bring in more light), ramps, special fixtures for the differentially abled children and small-sized pans for defecation.

Networking for knowledge management

Efforts were directed at large-scale information dissemination and the creation of learning platforms. Institution-building efforts and best construction practices were documented in detail for replication of the project by other stakeholders. Village, block and district level meetings and workshops were organized for sharing local know-how and indigenous technology practices.

Figure 2.5 *Child-friendly, barrier-free, cost-effective toilets
at a children's park in Koraput*

Source: chapter authors

Many bilingual reports, manuals and materials for sensitization were prepared
and published. These included the manual on 'Good practices in Building
Construction Technologies' in the Oriya language, ASHG manuals (in bilingual
formats) and data collection formats to help ASHG members keep track of the
work going on. Modules were also developed to sensitize *panchayat* leaders on
habitat issues, including water and sanitation.

Efforts were also made to sensitize the students of various schools of architecture and engineering. This included Jadavpur University (Kolkata), School
of Planning and Architecture (New Delhi), Indian Institute of Technology
(Kharagpur), ABIT (Cuttack), CET (Bhubaneswar) and the Institute of Town
Planners India. The Eastern India Zonal Workshop on Appropriate Disaster-
resistant Building Technologies was organized at Bhubaneswar with a two-fold
objective: orienting the students and advocating for the inclusion of the technologies in the course curricula of architecture and civil engineering. Twelve
young graduate architects from Tasmania University, Australia visited Orissa
and participated in the programme for a few months to derive on-site experience. Similarly, research scholars from Switzerland and the US visited the
project. The experience has also been disseminated to countries such as Cuba
and France. One of the senior architect-planners participated in a sponsored
study visit to the 'Architects in the Community Programme' in Cuba in May

Figure 2.6 *Anindya Sarkar speaking to housing programme managers in Havana, Cuba, May 2003*

Source: chapter authors

2003. The visit and subsequent experience sharing has inspired the team and guided the movement.

Association with learning platforms

The team has been associated with many national and international organizations working in the housing and habitat sector and is an active member of various networks, including the Habitat Forum-India. The project team has contributed to the editorial page of the *Basin Newsletter* (vol 2, November 2005) and also contributed an article: 'A New Thrust in Housing from Technology Transfer to Artisan Guild'.

The project team has technically supported Development Alternatives, an NGO, in a project entitled 'Greening of the Brick Industry'. This venture is not only useful from ecological and pollution perspectives, but also helps increase the brick stock, which is facing a serious crisis due to increasing industrial construction work. The project provides scope for the utilization of industrial waste as one of the ingredients in brick making. An important result has also been the generation of employment throughout the year for the labourers working in this sector.

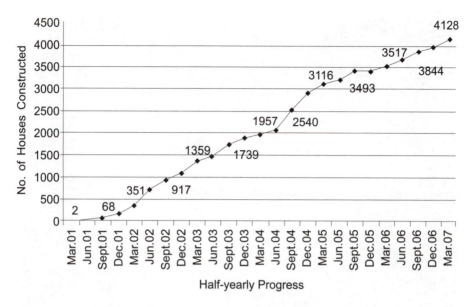

Figure 2.7 *Building movement progress in Orissa*

Source: chapter authors

Housing and habitat development

Committed to the transfer of appropriate housing technologies, the project aimed to develop a building movement, and to date, about 4500 houses have been constructed by communities using appropriate technologies.

Housing and habitat development for the tribes of rayagada

The Dongaria Kondha tribe of Rayagada was under stress as they faced difficulty in building traditional houses due to depletion of natural resources in their area and lack of access to masonry construction materials and skills. The government grant under IAY for these vulnerable communities remained unutilized. The team's intervention and some guidance helped these communities to build their houses themselves. Within a few years, 945 houses were built. One of the major aspects of this intervention was redesigning the traditional designs. The traditional houses were basic 'shacks' – igloos with a hearth in the middle where animals and humans shared the same space. In the redesigned house, although animals continued to remain visible, they stayed apart from the members of household.

Key technical inputs

An important component of the project has been the transfer of appropriate, safe and affordable technologies. These technologies are selected and finalized locally

Figure 2.8 *Inauguration of an anganwadi centre*

Source: chapter authors

in each region based on an intense resource mapping exercise conducted by the project team. Technical inputs have also been directed towards setting up and managing microenterprises.

Impact

Social

The project period was from July 2002 to June 2007 and during that time the institution building process empowered the construction artisans to work in groups, and their capacities were strengthened both technically and managerially. According to one project beneficiary, a construction worker involved in community centre construction in Jagatsinghpur district, 'Earlier we were definitely skilled masons prior to commencement of this project, but after the completion of this building construction, we have developed an intense understanding of the finer aesthetic appeal that a building ought to have'.

As ASHGs, the workers can network and negotiate in the market towards cost-effective construction management. Further, it has been found that the ASHG groups have begun saving, allowing them to take advantage of better educational opportunities for their children and to access health care for their families when necessary. Moreover, as construction work brings the threat of accidents, an informal insurance system has been developed within these groups. Further, the families have been inspired to first save and then invest their savings to build and own at least a one-roomed *pucca* house. This *pucca* room, when integrated with other rooms in mud and thatch, helps these families to seek refuge and save their essential belongings in case of any disaster.

The communities at large have benefited immensely from the project as they have now better access to information regarding ongoing rural housing schemes sponsored by the government as well as to the appropriate technologies. This has enabled them to construct their houses. They now use the services of ASHGs starting from soil excavation to completion of houses and need not wait anymore for masons, labourers, electricians and painters.

The project gave the families scope to design their houses with better use of space. Each homeowner is manager of her or his own funds (mobilized either through individual savings/loans or through the IAY programme wherein the funds are transferred directly by the government to the owner in instalments depending on the progress of work).

Mainstreaming gender in the construction sector

Mainstreaming gender was one of the focus areas of the project. Hence skill development programmes for women construction labourers to graduate them into masons were undertaken in many districts. The project also involved the women's ASHGs in income generation activities such as the production, thrift and trade of building materials. The creation and empowerment of *nirmiti samitis* to understand habitat issues and evolve as community contractors have also yielded results.

The women voiced their opinions in village meetings held in Saintal village of Jagatsinghpur district. The habitat planning exercises generated great interest

---

BOX 2.1 TRANSFORMATION FROM HOUSEWIFE TO MASON

Basanti is a housewife living with her husband in Ulba village in Balangir district, western Orissa. Her husband became blind during a welding accident and the family lost its income. Maa Pataneswari ASHG group immediately decided to substitute Basanti in place of her husband, who was a member of the group. She was then guided by the team, and today she is a master mason and involved in various construction projects in the locality.

Through her determination she became a construction labourer and then a mason in a very short time. Her family regained normalcy and her children joined school once again. During the lean period in construction work, she is engaged in the production of sanitary items in a sanitary workshop run by the ASHG.

Figure 2.9 *Training of women in a production centre at Rupkona,
Rayagada district, Orissa*

Source: chapter authors

among villagers to improve their immediate habitats. Even the children demanded
that their school building be made according to their design.

Environmental

The technologies promoted are not only cost-effective and disaster-resistant but
also environmentally friendly as the consumption of building materials is reduced
and the houses offer pleasant living conditions inside. Notwithstanding all the
cost saving measures, care is also taken that elements to ensure structural stability
and disaster-resistance are incorporated. For example, the rat-trap bonded cavity
walls and filler slab roofing with air gaps provide the necessary insulation desirable
for the hot and humid tropical climates. At the same time they are also designed to
be resilient. The consumption of earth is also reduced as fewer bricks are utilized
in rat-trap walling systems. Similarly, in the case of filler slab roofing, substantial
amounts of steel, cement and chips are saved. Brick arches that form a major part
of the vernacular style of architecture (used in temples, mosques and churches)
have been incorporated to eliminate reinforced cement concrete lintels.

During the construction of 50 *anganwadi* centres in Rayagada district, local
stones were used for foundation work and fly-ash bricks for the walls. Besides being

cost-effective and eliminating the use of cement plaster on the outside façade, this generated an overall awareness among the communities, local construction artisans and civil society organizations of the use of these environmentally friendly bricks in construction.

The project has also trained masons to get involved in a vertical shaft brick kiln project that involves production of bricks in a highly environmentally friendly process. Under this process, the consumption of coal is reduced thereby reducing emissions of carbon monoxide and carbon dioxide. Also, provision exists for adequate use of industrial wastes. This project has brought benefits to the entrepreneurs through the World Bank Community Development Carbon Fund.

Economic

Making housing affordable and improving accessibility

The technologies promoted under the project use local building materials and were designed for cost optimization without compromising structural strength. Thus, safe housing was made affordable. These houses have withstood the fury of the floods of 2001 and 2003. The role of technical facilitation initially taken by UNVs and the DTF is now fulfilled by the trained ASHGs. Cost reductions of 20–25 per cent have been achieved by using appropriate technologies.

Addressing income generation issues

The ASHGs have been able to increase their incomes as they can work more days as well as receive higher wages. Simultaneously, they have also been able to start producing and selling building materials. This has been possible because ASHGs were trained not only to offer better quality services but also in the production of building materials (such as brick kilns, sanitary ware, production of pre-cast door/window frames, skylights, staircase balusters and in the renting of concrete mixer machines and shuttering sets).

Data on the income levels of the ASHGs were compiled for the district level and state level and are shown in Figure 2.11.

Towards policy changes

The project team facilitated the fixation of the grant element for IAY houses, raising it to Rs25,000 (US$614) in many areas and Rs27,500 (US$675) in hilly and disaster-prone areas. It also facilitated the designing of emergency operation centres (EOCs) under the GoI/UNDP National Disaster Risk Mitigation Programme. In collaboration with the Government of Tamil Nadu (GoTN) and the United Nations Team for Recovery Support in Tamil Nadu (UNTRS), the team facilitated the development of the Housing Technical Reconstruction Guidelines in the tsunami-affected areas. Suitable manuals, brochures, leaflets,

Figure 2.10 *Livelihood opportunities for construction artisans: a) rural sanitary mart in Rayagada district; b) brick kiln in Puri district*

Source: chapter authors

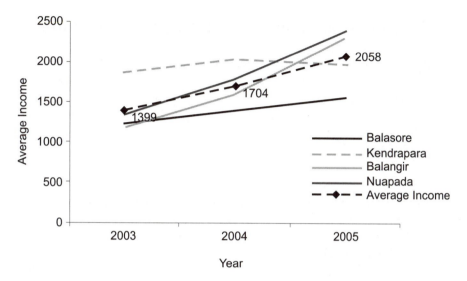

Figure 2.11 *Growth in average monthly income of ASHG members in Orissa*

Source: chapter authors

flyers, wall posters and hangings on multi-hazard resistant construction practices and reconstruction and retrofitting were also prepared by the team.

As a Governing Council member of the INHAF (Habitat Forum – India) and Basin-SA (Building Advisory Services and Information Network), the project team actively advocates for the causes of social housing and disaster mitigation. Efforts to organize the Eastern India Zonal Workshop on Appropriate Disaster-resistant Building Technologies and get these technologies included in the course curricula of architecture and civil engineering at the state level have been followed up at a national level, and presently the course curricula is being reviewed for inclusion.

Project cost

The project was implemented by UNDP with funding support from SDC, costing approximately Rs24,678,000 (US$580,000) from 1 July 2002 to 30 June 2007. The housing movement had a multiplier effect. Peoples' direct investment in housing using appropriate disaster-resistant building technologies is approximately Rs210 million (US$4.7 million). The project has generated benefits and savings (due to investments in affordable housing technologies) of the order of approximately Rs53 million (US$1.2 million over a period of approximately six years.

Project management, monitoring and evaluation

UNDP's office in Bhubaneswar has been managing the project and monitoring the day-to-day activities through a project coordinator and project officers. SDC has also been closely monitoring and guiding the process. The project has been reviewed regularly and project areas have been visited by many government officials, NGOs and Orissa Legislative Assembly Members.

The key indicators for the success of the project are:

- number of house constructions facilitated;
- number of masons trained and practising appropriate technologies;
- number of master trainer masons trained;
- number of ASHGs formed and linked to deliver better services and for the production of building materials;
- increase in the income of ASHG members observed after every three months;
- the spread of the movement within the state and beyond;
- the partnerships crystallized;
- the documents prepared, especially guidelines and manuals related to the field of housing, training course curricula and so on; and
- the number of links established and memberships gained with national and international information and knowledge management networks related to habitat.

Challenges faced and how they were overcome

The 'schedule of rates' formulated by the Public Works Department, Government of Orissa is based on conventional technologies and has hardly any scope to accommodate innovative appropriate technologies. In reality, it stands as a major bottleneck for the adoption of appropriate technologies on a large scale. Personal conviction of engineers and administrators is not enough if the schedule of rates is not altered.

The housing movement was driven by the work of the UNVs who were paid voluntary living allowances that were insufficient and thus staff turnover was high. Despite all these hurdles, the movement continues with peoples' support. However, the shortage of building material, lack of institutional finance, prevalence of masons with low skills and low literacy levels continue to act as the barriers.

Any innovative approach requires mustering support from the prevailing administrative system. With all the efforts made at the grassroots through cadres of trained masons – the true catalysts for technology transfer – the movement is as yet confined to some geographical regions. It is the approval and acceptance by the government system through official adoption that can lead to policy impact and widespread proliferation of the movement. This task has been partially successful.

Lessons learned

Any process of housing requires the mobilization of resources such as land, building materials, technologies, finance, human resources and organizational involvement. In this project, efforts were directed towards human resource development and technologies. Persistent efforts on these fronts guided the movement. A comprehensive approach with a focus on human resource development is essential to bring about the much-needed social and economic linkages. For example, material production centres run by construction artisans or their families do not have marketing difficulties as the artisans are trusted by rural households to build their houses. However, it has also been observed that most of these construction artisans, who play a major role in shaping the house, lack the minimum skills for construction of a masonry house. There is a dire need for guidance to be offered to them through training and orientation programmes.

Peoples' mindsets have changed mainly in those areas that have been affected by natural disasters. In these areas people now want to own a *pucca* house of brick and mortar instead of a house of mud and thatch. However, the families do not have the ability to pay back loans and so most households build houses in a casual fashion without a systematic plan. Drawings and estimates are alien to this process and permission is rarely sought, other than for the land. Therefore, most houses remain incomplete for years and end up poorly designed. The lack of involvement in housing by the family members, particularly that of women is a serious omission.

The training of construction artisans was widely welcomed and admired throughout India.

The innovative project developed in its own way with different strategies adopted in various regions of Orissa based on the local socio-economic profile,

---

BOX 2.2 CHALLENGES TO THE PROJECT

In Parsali Gram Panchayat of Kalyansinghpur block, Rayagada district, two men's ASHGs and one women's ASHG (comprising the kin of the men folk) are jointly networking and constructing small projects within appropriate cost, quality and timeframes. The challenge now lies in identifying such supportive male masons and artisans who would be ready to raise the skills and social prestige of the women in their families. It becomes easier for these men and women together to accomplish such works not only due to the nature of the various physical tasks involved but also because the recognition of trained women as masons in rural societies cannot be accomplished overnight. Together through a jointly led project, both find improved livelihood opportunities.

local culture, climatic conditions and so on. The most important champion of the project was UNDP, which helped the project to develop partnerships with government departments at state and national levels, network with various NGOs and leverage funds for the sustainability of the movement. The Women and Child Development Department of the Government of Orissa has been particularly supportive. The motivation and advice received from time to time from retired engineers and planners in the state government helped to direct and increase the pace of the movement. Visitors from far and wide and academics from eminent institutions also visited the project areas and forwarded their comments. The construction artisans, in particular, and the families whose houses were built, were the greatest motivators for the team in the field.

Key innovative features

Catalyst of the housing movement

Housing delivery is quite different from product delivery concepts. Convincing the rural people of the possibility of constructing a core house with a meagre government grant through the IAY is a great challenge in itself. Local communities need to be equipped with adequate technical know-how of house construction that meets the budget constraints. To motivate and inspire people to construct houses using appropriate and affordable technologies, the UNVs and DTF staff lived with the village communities to make them aware of the benefits of affordable and safe housing.

Also innovative is the way the project promoted institutional development to sustain the housing movement and its development of the concept of the ASHG as a one-stop shop. Also innovative were its efforts to formalize the construction sector. Finally, the process by which UNDP formed a composite multi-disciplinary team of local young professionals and graduated them into a team of entrepreneurs is an example worth emulating.

The capacity building of stakeholders

Equipping the construction labourers with adequate skills to perform as masons using good practices was not an easy process. Unlike the university certified courses of engineering and architecture, there are no formal institutions for training masons. To overcome this shortcoming, the team developed various tailor-made and needs-based course curricula for the training and capacity building of masons and construction artisans based on their skill levels. Different training modules were designed and these are being imparted to the local construction workers to graduate them from one level to the next (see Table 2.1).

Table 2.1 *Skills training*

	Skill Level	Training course content
Level 1	Construction labourers (men and women)	Basic construction practices (foundation, wall, openings, roof etc.)
Level 2	Semi-skilled masons	Good construction practices (layout, foundation, wall, openings, roof etc.)
Level 3	Skilled masons	Cost-effective and multi-hazard resistant construction technologies, reading drawings and designs
Level 4	Master masons	Multi-hazard resistant construction technologies, basic designing and estimation
Level 5	Master trainer masons	Skills on imparting training programmes

The learning platform

The learning platform is an innovative idea wherein academic institutions such as colleges of architecture and engineering and leading forums of the country participate. Brochures and leaflets both in English and local languages were developed and circulated. It is not a one-time event but a platform that promotes interaction for the wider propagation of the approach and technologies.

Good practice

Improving housing affordability and accessibility as well as addressing the issue of income generation were the twofold aims of this innovative housing project. The technologies promoted are not only technically designed to be disaster-resistant but are also cost effective and environmentally friendly. This inspires and enables the communities living in Orissa, which is one of the poorest and most hazard-prone states in the country, to build and dwell in a safe and affordable *pucca* house. The resultant impact on family life and health has been significant.

The initiative has demonstrated that a well-designed housing project can address the issue of employment generation. Housing is a social need and a housing project can be effectively designed to reduce the vulnerabilities of the communities to disasters as well as help generate local individual and group incomes related to the construction sector, strengthening its backward and forward linkages to the markets.

The tremendous impact of the project on the ground has helped in winning recognition through awards and citations from various quarters. These include the following:

- A 'good practice' award at Dubai by UN-Habitat in 2004.
- First prize for the best design concept for 'Hazard (tsunami) resistant house design' along with a cash award of Rs50,000 (US$1,200) organized by Gandhi Gram Rural Institute, Tamil Nadu in partnership with national and international

organizations (the design had to conform to the 'Guidelines for Reconstruction of Houses Affected by Tsunami in Tamil Nadu'. The house design evolved after conducting field studies to understand lifestyles of the local fisher folk. Besides allotting spaces within the house and homestead for the various activities that these households engage in throughout the day, it also incorporates appropriate, cost-effective and multi-hazard resistant technologies).

• Finalist for the World Habitat Award 2006.

Transfer and replication

The trained ASHGs have undertaken varied and diverse projects for improved and safe habitats, thereby acquiring additional livelihood opportunities. The fact that habitat and livelihoods are integrated and can be addressed concurrently has become enforced by the movement. The team continues to network and cement partnerships for affordable housing and habitat development, training of artisans, promotion of vernacular architectural styles and utilization of indigenous construction practices with government agencies, civil society organizations and voluntary agencies. In the post-tsunami reconstruction phase, the team extended technical assistance to the UN in various studies and the preparation of recovery frameworks in Tamil Nadu. It has also worked in partnership with the Ministry of Home Affairs and the Andaman Public Works Department on the planning and setting up of intermediate shelters through active community participation in the Nicobar Islands.

As part of the long-term tsunami reconstruction programme, the team has proactively supported the Government of Tamil Nadu in designing tsunami-resistant houses and in developing the technical guidelines for housing and habitat plans. It has also supported various local partners, NGOs and bilateral organizations in the reconstruction of housing and habitats.

Conclusions

The SDC-UNDP Rural Housing Project in Orissa has had far-reaching consequences. Its ripple effect in the course of time will yield significant results. The emphasis of the movement has been on housing, infrastructure development, integrated habitat planning and development, the environment and the promotion of livelihood opportunities. The long-term vision of this housing movement is to integrate habitat development with livelihood opportunities that directly contribute towards the well being of the society.

The majority of the construction sector in India is highly informal, but contributes greatly to the national and local economies, yet there is hardly any scope for a construction artisan to enter training programmes to learn and increase her or his technical knowledge. There is no formal classification of masons based on their skill-sets. This project has helped to design and develop different course curricula for the various identified grades of construction workers. The movement initiated by the project has been striving to bridge the gap between the rural construction artisans and professional architects, engineers and planners through capacity building and developing standardized course curricula and certification mechanisms. Enabling and empowering the construction workers with knowledge helped realize the project's vision of a better built environment free from disaster and accessible to all.

A construction labourer earns as little as Rs50 (US$1.2) and suffers from acute poverty. His or her family leads a life that has no income security for the next day and is deprived of social security benefits, including accident insurance. The success of the project lies in the institutional framework created where the masons and construction workers have been grouped into sustainable ASHGs. This attempt to formalize the construction sector through local artisan training and groupings, to help each artisan grow in knowledge and augment his or her income while constructing safe, affordable houses and homes for all, can be considered an exemplary initiative towards disaster mitigation and poverty reduction.

Notes

1 This chapter is based on the authors' experiences gained from the project in the field, supported by periodic reports, primary surveys, compiled data, success-stories and competition entries the team prepared and submitted to government departments, donors and UN agencies from time to time during the project period.
2 *Anganwadi* centres provide access to schooling for village children aged 2–5 years.

References

GoI (2001) *Census of India,* 2001, New Delhi, Central Statistical Agency, Government of India

3

Upgrading Housing as a Strategy for Poverty Reduction: The Case of Old Lhasa, Tibet, China

André Alexander, Pimpim de Azevedo, Lundup Dorje and An Li

Introduction

The city of Lhasa, historically the cultural centre of the Tibetan-Buddhist civiliza-
tion that has influenced the entire Himalayan plateau, today is the capital of the
Tibet Autonomous Region of China. The past 50 years have sometimes seen tumul-
tuous development, resulting in a great loss of historic structures and the exodus
of some of the religious and business elites. China's 'open door policy' arrived
almost a decade later than elsewhere on the Tibetan plateau and Tibet remains one
of the poorest and most subsidized regions in China. In the mid-1990s, when the
project discussed in this chapter was initiated, the city of Lhasa consisted of three
starkly different parts: a bustling modern town dominated by traders and busi-
nessmen from other Chinese provinces, large industrial and administrative tracts
of land, and the historic Tibetan old town. Here, most buildings were nationalized in the 1950s and served as low-cost housing but the experience was similar
to that in other regions and cities with subsidized housing in the historic centre,
such as East Berlin, Moscow and Beijing: lack of private initiative for maintenance
caused a dramatic decline in building quality. The cheap rents also attracted poor
Tibetan migrants from the countryside, with many families sharing a flat origi-
nally designed to accommodate just one family. Because of the decline in living
quality and lack of infrastructure, wealthier people moved out of the old town so
that the area started to effectively become a slum.

China's housing reforms

In the early 1990s China launched a nationwide reform of its subsidized housing
policy, called Weigai. In effect this saw the large-scale demolition and redevelopment

of the old housing areas all over China.[1] The replacement buildings would no longer be available for subsidized rent rates but instead flats had to be bought before the start of construction, a policy long implemented in Hong Kong. Poor families had to leave the historic area. In the case of Lhasa, however, this policy began to worry local people because many important and beautiful historic buildings in one of the most architecturally unique cities in the world started to be pulled down. The NGO Tibet Heritage Fund (THF) was founded in Lhasa in 1996 with the aim of developing an alternative strategy. The founders were a small group of foreign experts, including André Alexander, Pimpim de Azevedo and Professor Heather Stoddard, as well as Lhasa officials such as the archaeologist Sonam Wangdu. The Lhasa mayor Lobsang Gyeltsen and vice-mayor Dekyi Dolkar lent their crucial support, as did the Lhasa City Cultural Relics Office.

Project activities and objectives

The founding group then began with a social survey of the old town. Over several months, almost 300 residential units in 20 historic residential areas of old Lhasa were visited and information was gathered on the problems and disadvantages but also the positive aspects of life in the old town. The buildings were also inspected for their structural defects. Finally, the interviewed families were told that in other countries a common alternative to demolition and reconstruction would be upgrading and rehabilitation of dilapidated historic housing. The residents of one building, Tadongshar in Lhasa Barkor Street, met to discuss this idea and then decided to approach THF. They said that everybody was ready to vacate their flats if THF wanted to do a model rehabilitation of a historic apartment building. THF gladly agreed and then assembled the last surviving artisans trained in traditional construction in the 1940s and 1950s and planned the intervention. For labour, poor residents of the building and of the neighbourhood were employed on a preferential basis.

THF set itself the following goals:

* to preserve the historic and cultural identity of old Lhasa;
* to provide employment and reduce poverty for impoverished residents;
* to preserve and upgrade low-cost housing;
* to keep alive traditional construction skills;
* to provide vocational training and create new generations of artisans;
* to improve sanitary conditions in the old town; and
* to do all these things with a participatory approach.

The project initially limited itself to only work in the Lhasa old town and surrounding regions but later was extended to cover other Himalayan areas.

Key elements of the project

Target beneficiaries

Based on the group's assessment of the situation, it was decided that the residents of the old town should be the prime beneficiaries of the project. The aim was to create a living historic city (conforming to the ICOMOS Charter on Living Historic Cities), rather than working primarily to restore monuments or to convert residential buildings for tourism use. Of the residents, we wanted to help particularly those dependent on low-cost housing by securing affordable housing for them. We also wanted to benefit unemployed and uneducated residents of the old town by involving them in the implementation and offering them training opportunities. We wanted to offer these opportunities to a third target group: poor, unemployed and uneducated residents of villages on the outskirts of Lhasa who come to Lhasa to look for work.

Project activities

The project decided to operate in a two-fold way: to concentrate most efforts on one particular neighbourhood, but also to have emergency funds for residential buildings in danger in all parts of Lhasa. For the model conservation neighbourhood, the Barkor area was chosen. This is the oldest part of Lhasa, centred on the 7th century Jokhang temple, one of the most venerated shrines in all of Tibet.

One of the key components of the project was regular meetings of the residential communities. Buildings for upgrading were chosen by the community not by the NGO – residential communities could apply only if all parties agreed and also would support the project and jointly apply at the THF office. Then THF would visit the building together with government counterparts and plan the intervention so that the residents' aspirations could be met as much as technically and financially feasible. During the upgrading activities, there would be weekly residents' meeting where at least one member of each unit had to participate.

Within this model, the key activities implemented by THF included structural rehabilitation of historic residential buildings, upgrading and modernization (putting in drainage and improving the traditional compost-type toilets). Another aspect was to revive traditional building skills, as well as generally increase local skills and help to generate employment. Therefore a key component was vocational training, conducted by the last old master artisans and western technical experts. More than 300 local Tibetans participated, and included carpenters, masons, restorers, plumbers and draftsmen.

The THF team, together with student volunteers from Beijing, Shanghai and abroad undertook survey and full architectural documentation of 100 of the most important historic buildings in Lhasa. The local team conducted social surveys. Foreign experts were hired to work together with the Lhasa Water Department to lay for the first time ever a piped water supply in some parts of the old town. This group, the water and sanitation working group, also improved drainage facilities and paved alleys.

Timeframe

The rapid success and expansion of the project was due to the fact that the founders were already familiar with the situation in Lhasa. During1993–1995 they carried out private research on Tibetan architecture and on the history and structure of the old town of Lhasa.[2] So when the project was founded in 1996, the group knew the city, its inhabitants and problems first-hand, and already had access to a network of officials, local experts and important community personalities. During 1996–1997 the group then carried out a systematic social survey of the old town target area, and began by carrying out architectural surveys. In 1997–2000 the project ran at full steam with the upgrading of the Barkor neighbourhood with 1000 residents plus 6 other residential and monastic buildings.

Impact and outcomes

In Lhasa, over 300 artisans have been trained and most are now employed. The training has now begun with a second generation. The Barkor neighbourhood of Lhasa is preserved and upgraded, low-cost housing for residents of 20 buildings has been secured (over 100 families), 93 historic residential buildings have been listed by government as protected buildings, and communities in other regions of Tibet Autonomous Region and Qinghai and Sichuan provinces of China have participated in resulting skills training and exchange programmes, creating more jobs and also more demand for traditional building skills. Since 2001, many of the Lhasa-trained artisans have travelled to remote and poor rural areas inhabited by Tibetans in China, such as Qinghai and Sichuan, to train artisans there. The project has in effect been scaled up to achieve poverty reduction through upgrading, restoration and new construction in many regions of Western China. Since 2003, the project has also been replicated across the borders, in the Indian Himalayan region of Ladakh, where the Leh old town project was started.[3]

Project cost

Local and national governments did not make any financial contributions, while the communities contributed less than 10 per cent of the costs, which were charged mainly as fees for upgrading of water supply and drainage, as well as contributions to renovations of individual residential buildings (the most contributions came for the restoration of one Buddhist monastery in Lhasa, the Meru Nyingpa, where a significant contribution of around 35 per cent was raised locally). Instead, most resources came from external overseas assistance, including GTZ (US$100,000), The Getty Foundation (US$50,000), MISEREOR (US$50,000), Canada Fund (US$12,000), the German embassy in Beijing (US$24,000), The Netherlands embassy in Beijing (US$20,000), the Finish embassy in Beijing (US$12,000), the Trace Foundation (US$250,000 over five years) and THF privately-raised funds (US$50,000).

Project management

To carry out the project, the founding group registered THF as a non-profit NGO in Germany, and this was officially recognized in China as the non-profit implementation partner. Since then THF has also registered official branches in India and Mongolia. To effectively implement the project, THF used as coordinating mechanisms two Chinese government departments, the Lhasa City Cultural Relics Office and the Lhasa Barkor Neighbourhood Community Office. The Community Office is legally responsible for organizing and holding residents' meetings, and this office served as a crucial interface between residents, the NGO and government.

Since the project received funding from several different donors rather than from a single source, most donor agencies have sent inspection teams to visit and monitor the project. Many ambassadors also visited the project, and the project also reported regularly to its counterparts and to the Lhasa government. Conforming to the nature of the local administration, the monitoring was officially carried out by the two main local counterparts, the Lhasa Cultural Relics Office and the Lhasa Barkor Neighbourhood Community Office.

Challenges and how they were overcome

With the aim of preserving old Lhasa and making it a place where the long-term low-income residents could find affordable, adequate housing and even employment, the project faced two main challenges. One was that in the Chinese system of government there is no official space for public participation in urban development. This challenge was overcome when we discovered neighbourhood community offices. These community offices exist all across China and they serve as links between government and community, and are also engaged in social work. Upon request they agreed to participate in the urban rehabilitation project as organizer of participatory residents' meetings.

The second challenge was that very few people believed the old buildings could be made fit for modern life. Therefore in the beginning there was a lot of scepticism and things moved very slowly. Only after the first demonstration project was completed, and the Lhasa Mayor Lobsang Gyaltsen visited and approved it, was there widespread belief and support for the overall aims of the project.

Lessons learned

The success of the project was mainly due to the fact that local needs and aspirations were incorporated into the design of the project from the beginning. These were identified through surveys and preparation – the time spent on research in Lhasa was, in retrospect, invaluable to the success of the project. There was also community participation in all the phases of the implementation. This led to widespread public support for the project throughout its duration.

The Lhasa City Cultural Relics Office and Lhasa mayor Lobsang Gyentsen made the project possible by giving strong personal support. The Community Office also worked beyond their official duties to assist the project. The residents gave very strong support throughout. THF was the spearhead to start processes and organize quick responses to the challenges faced.

The donors gave crucial support and the support of several European ambassadors was also important, even though this came only later after the project had achieved its first successes. Crucial early support came from the Lhasa Cultural Relics Office.

All parties, NGOs, residents, Lhasa officials and donors were united in their goal that the unique characteristics and heritage of Lhasa should be preserved, and that the residents should stay in the town and not be displaced by tourists.

Good practice

The centre of the old town of Lhasa was preserved and not redeveloped, a fact which has since found widespread acclaim but at the time was considered controversial. It was preserved not as a tourist theme park, which very often happens to historic cities in Asia when their tourism potential is being discovered, but as a living historic city inhabited by the same residents as before the project. Affordable housing for hundreds of families was created and preserved.

Tibet is a region suffering from structural deficits, such as lack of industry, infrastructure and facilities of higher education. Therefore, the fact that 300 mostly young people participated in the project through a vocational training scheme, and most of them are still practising the newly learnt skills, is one of the project's most important contributions. Hundreds of residents have found new employment and successfully made the conversion from living in the traditional economy to participating in the future development of Lhasa.

In Lhasa this training and employment scheme has made an important impact, which since then has been replicated in many other regions of the Himalayas. The project has also demonstrated how residents can be involved in all aspects of urban rehabilitation, in planning and in implementation, thereby contributing to the sustainability of the results by directly linking the results to the expressed needs of targeted beneficiaries. Finally, many people in Lhasa have learned to look at traditional skills and historic buildings from a new, more appreciative, perspective.

Potential for scaling up and replication

The project has been extended to cover rural areas where Tibetans in China live, such as Sichuan and Qinghai. In Qinghai province, the local administration of the Golok prefecture presented a follow-up project with an award for successful projects. For this project Lhasa-trained artisans came and trained artisans of the region to restore an 18th century monastery that is one of the most important social, cultural, educational and spiritual centres of the Qinghai region.

The Lhasa project has been replicated in Leh, the historic capital of the Ladakh region in India. This was a former Tibetan kingdom and so shares most geographical and cultural traits with old Lhasa. The Leh Old Town Project implemented by THF since 2003 has been awarded a Best Practice 2006 award and a UNESCO Asia-Pacific Heritage Award 2006.

In 2007, the model was applied to a central neighbourhood in historic Beijing, the Gulou area, where THF and the local government cooperated to upgrade three historic residential complexes. THF has also participated in exchanges with other Asian cities facilitated by the Asian Coalition for Housing Rights (ACHR) Bangkok, who despite their own considerable network of experts have invited THF several times to consult on urban upgrading projects. THF has carried out a study on the impact of conservation activities on urban poor communities in ten historic cities for ACHR and the results will be published in 2008.

Conclusions

The Lhasa Old Town project tried to achieve a lot in a short amount of time. Undoubtedly, some mistakes were made, particularly since in the beginning there was a lot of trial and error, however, if THF had not taken on and financed the upgrading of the historic building, their fate would have been demolition and the construction of new housing at expensive market rates carried out by large construction companies using migrant labour. The saving of so many buildings and training and employment of so many local artisans are still being appreciated by many people in Lhasa and in Beijing. Unfortunately, when the project was not able to be continued beyond 2000 due to changes in Lhasa, other neighbourhoods of historic Lhasa could not receive the same assistance.

In recent years the Cultural Relics Office of Lhasa, assisted by Beijing, have stepped up conservation and upgrading activities, but no longer with involvement of the Neighbourhood Committee Office meetings. Compared to cities like Lijiang in China and Luang Prabang in Laos, where tourism is threatening to overwhelm the locals, where affordable housing in the historic districts is disappearing fast and professional large-scale operators begin to dominate the tourism industry, the Lhasa project has offered a real alternative.

Notes

1 See Alexander et al (2006) Chapters 1 and 2 for more on Weigai reform.
2 This research was introduced by one of the authors (A. Alexander) at the 1995 Seminar of the International Association for Tibetan Studies in Austria.
3 The Leh Old Town Project, with the same components as the Lhasa project, has since received a UNESCO Heritage Award and also a 2006 UN Dubai Best Practice Award.

References

Alexander, A. (2005) *The Temples of Lhasa*, Serindia,Chicago
Alexander, A. (2007) 'Towards a management plan for the old town of Leh: Structuring a plan for the preservation of an endangered townscape and revitalization of traditional social structures', thesis for partial fulfilment for Master of Science degree in Urban Management, Berlin University of Technology
Alexander, A. and De Azevedo, P. (1998) *The Old City of Lhasa*, Tibet Heritage Fund, Berlin
Alexander, A., De Azevedo, P. and Harrison, J. (eds) (1999) *The Old City of Lhasa*, vol II, Tibet Heritage Fund, Hong Kong
Anzorena, E. J. (2000) 'Conservation of traditional districts (the Professor Maeno approach)', *SELAVIP – Journal of Low-Income Housing in Asia and the World*, October, pp55–60
Dolker, D. (2005) 'Leh old town social survey', unpublished report, Leh Old Town Initiative, Leh, available from THF
Fleischhauer, A. and Kammeier, H. D. (2006) 'International environmental law and the role of indigenous peoples in protected areas: Hope for creative solutions in a setting of established incompatibility', paper accepted for publication by the *International Journal of Heritage Studies*, quoted with consent of author
Galla, A. (1995) 'Authenticity: Rethinking heritage diversity in a pluralistic framework', in K. E. Larsen (ed) *Nara Conference on Authenticity in Relation to the World Heritage Convention*, http://rspas.anu.edu.au/papers/heritage/nara_conference_authenticity_1994a.pdf
Hasan, A. (2001) *Working with Communities*, City Press, Karachi
ICOMOS (2005) *Xi'an Declaration on the Conservation of the Setting of Heritage Structures, Sites and Areas*, adopted in Xi'an, China, by the 15th General Assembly of ICOMOS on 21 October, available at www.icomos.org/usicomos/Scientific_Committees/Landscapes/ICOMOS-Xian-Declaration-2005.pdf
Jest, C. (1991) *Man and His House in the Himalayas*, Sterling, New Delhi
Logan, W. S. (ed) (2002) *The Disappearing 'Asian' City: Protecting Asia's Urban Heritage in a Globalizing World*, Oxford University Press, Hong Kong
Lowenthal, D. (1995) 'Changing criteria of authenticity', Nara Conference Proceedings, UNESCO, Paris

United Nations Educational, Scientific and Cultural Organization (1972) *Convention Concerning the Protection of the World Cultural and Natural Heritage*, adopted by the General Conference at its seventeenth session Paris, 16 November, available at http://whc.unesco.org/en/convention

United Nations Human Settlement Programme (2004) 'Urban indicators guidelines: Monitoring the Habitat Agenda and Millennium Development Goals', www.unhabitat.org

PART II

Local Economic Development

4

Poverty Reduction through Local Economic Development: 'Pathway out of Poverty' in Indonesia

Owais Parray and Abdurrahman Syebubakar

Introduction

In 1997 the devaluation of the Thai baht triggered off one of the worst financial crises of the 20th century, which caused ripples even as far away as Russia and Latin America. Indonesia was one of the worst hit countries: the crisis resulted in a near collapse of the financial system accompanied by political turmoil. As the country was grappling with its economic woes, a number of regions witnessed separatist and social conflicts fought along ethnic and sectarian lines, thus further compounding Indonesia's problems. As a consequence of massive layoffs, bankruptcies and hyperinflation resulting from the financial crisis, the poverty rate in the country dramatically increased from 17.7 per cent of the population (around 34.5 million people) in 1996 to 24.2 per cent (49.5 million) in 1998.

Finally, in 1999, there were the first signs of an economic recovery and a transition towards democratic governance. Starting in 2000 the country went through what has been described as one of the most radical decentralization programmes in the world. Since the passing of Law 33, 2004 on regional autonomy and subsequent laws on fiscal decentralization, Indonesia has undergone a series of reforms that have devolved authority over a broad range of economic and social affairs to the districts. Concurrent to this reform, governments at the regional level now retain a greater share of their economic revenue and also grants through the transfer of payments from the central government.

The project

The Partnerships for Local Economic Development Project (Kemitraan Pembagunan Ekonomi Loka – KPEL) was jointly developed by the UNDP and UN-HABITAT in consultation with the National Development Planning Agency (BAPPENAS) to respond to the growing poverty resulting from the financial crisis in 1997. The project was implemented from 1998 to 2004, starting with a pilot phase (1998–2000) that was followed by a replication phase in selected provinces. BAPPENAS, until recently, pursued this replication but limited funds constrained further scale-up.

Although there is no clear definition, in programming terms LED is generally defined as a strategy to promote economic opportunities and growth at the sub-national level by addressing constraints and improving the overall business environment to encourage entrepreneurial behaviour and investments. The interventions to promote LED can therefore take various forms and its scope depends largely on the context. Support to promote LED strategies has not been limited to only developing countries. In fact, in a number of developed countries, LED has been implemented as a key intervention by sub-national governments.

LED is not intended to replace sectoral policies but rather to complement them while building endogenous capacities. It is particularly useful in addressing problems at the sub-national level in countries where regional disparities exist. In such situations, macro-economic instruments alone do not provide the policy space for stimulating employment, income generation and poverty reduction. The approach recognizes the limitations of macro-economic measures and therefore is expected to play a complementary role in addressing these problems.

KPEL in Indonesia was primarily designed to address the challenges of transition in public administration, support economic recovery, link poorer areas to the mainstream economy, and promote responsive policies and action at the local level to boost local economies. In Indonesia before decentralization, the economic sector was seen as the domain of the central government, which was expected to take the lead in formulating policies and economic development programmes. The role of the regional governments was limited to implementation and oversight on behalf of the national government.

Project formulation

The KPEL Project design evolved through a series of carefully planned activities and stages. An in-depth needs assessment including consultations with key stakeholders was followed by the extended pilot phase to test the appropriateness and applicability of the methodology. Full implementation of the project started in 2000 and, subsequently, the project expanded further with the merger of two other Government of Indonesia projects called Local Economic Development and Rural Community Economic Development. Once the methodology for setting up the institutional frameworks had been developed, implementation and expansion of the project in the regions was done through consultations initiated by BAPPENAS through invitations. As a general guideline, the selection of the regions was based on three main criteria: incidence of poverty, economic potential and willingness and commitment of the local government to implement KPEL recommendations.

Considering the political transition that the country was undergoing and the emphasis on the sustainability of impact from the project, it was critical that there was buy-in from the local government. The project relied on a consultative process to get commitment from local government, civil society and businesses who were the main beneficiaries of this project. There were some elements of this project that were preconceived to ensure that that the project goals were not compromised. These areas were technical in nature, such as the KPEL partnerships and institutional frameworks at the local level that were needed as an entry point for reviewing business and economic policies. By the time the project entered a full scale up phase in 2000, a number of instruments had already been developed as well as a handbook that provided guidelines on establishing partnerships, sub-sector analysis and planning.

Project goals and objectives

The KPEL Project aimed to pioneer a strategy that would promote economic development at the sub-national level in Indonesia, consistent with the country's decentralization and effectively putting local stakeholders in charge of managing their own economies in a way that ensured greater prosperity and participation of all.

In Indonesia the KPEL strategy was applied to promote the facilitation of partnership forums at each tier of government, the development of economic clusters as a means to promote income-generating opportunities, and the empowerment of producers and their organizations to participate in KPEL planning and policy formulation.

Key elements of the project

Target beneficiaries

The project targeted a wide range of actors both at the national and provincial levels. Direct beneficiaries of the project were the business or producers groups, staff of the local government and civil society institutions. The project also involved and indirectly benefited donor agencies, international development agencies and policy makers at the national level. On a regular basis information on the project and results were disseminated and feedback was sought at every stage of implementation.

Geographic coverage of the project

The project was implemented across 15 provinces in Indonesia, targeting over 50 districts. More than 100 districts/provinces in Indonesia applied for participation in the project, but with a limited budget not all the areas could be selected. Overall, more than 60 KPEL partnerships were established around key business sub-sectors that had a concentration of micro and small enterprises. Among others, the sectors included coffee, vegetables, fish processing, lobster, shrimps and handicrafts. The project covered a diverse set of provinces in the country targeting various ethnic groups from all the major islands of the archipelago. The diversity of target groups and geographical locations was a test in itself for replicability of this project, and with continuous fine tunings in the methodology, the project became more adaptable and versatile.

Project activities

Through a series of field testing exercises and replications in different geographical areas, the project was able to develop a 13-step process for the implementation that became a unique trademark for this project. These steps evolved from contextualizing of the LED approach in Indonesia and lessons learned globally.

The 13 steps were broadly divided into 3 main implementation stages. The first stage consisted of intensive consultations with the local stakeholders and field research to identify business clusters or sub-sectors that the project wished to develop. In the second stage activities focused on a diagnosis of the problem and conceptualizing an intervention that was agreed by all. The third stage of this process consisted of establishing and strengthening institutional frameworks to implement, as well as to take necessary action to remove barriers and create greater opportunities in the selected business sub-sector.

At each stage, technical inputs were provided by experts who were hired on a short-term basis under the oversight and management of BAPPENAS. Inputs included technical studies of potential business sub-sectors, facilitation on organizing multi-stakeholder forums, capacity development and institutional support to KPEL partnerships, and advisory support on monitoring, reviewing progress and measuring impact on the business sector.

The overall feedback from the field suggested that the methodology was simple to implement and encouraged local actors to work collaboratively. Besides technical inputs, the project also covered financial resources to initiate the process, but gradually it cut down its financial contribution that was then expected to be covered by the local stakeholders. In many cases, the local costs were increasingly borne by the government.

Once KPEL partnerships and institutions had been identified, a team of technical advisors guided producers to develop market networks, build organizational

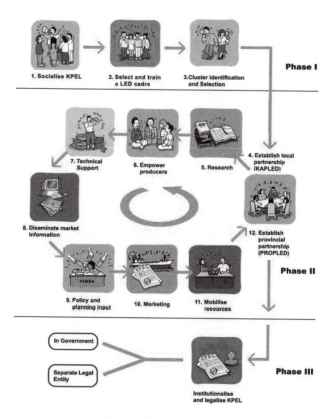

Figure 4.1 *KPEL steps*

linkages, improve products, explore diversification and create value along the production chain.

The timeframe for carrying out KPEL's 13-step implementation cycle varied across regions and business sectors. Normally, the process of identifying sectors, developing institutional frameworks and initiating actions took one year. Once appropriate strategies and action plans had been developed, it was expected that local stakeholders would continue to implement activities even in the absence of the project.

Impact and outcomes

More than 60 KPEL partnerships were set up across the country bringing greater opportunities to small-scale producers to access larger markets. In a number of provinces KPEL partnerships were officially formalized and received financial support from government budgets. These partnerships created an institutional framework to approach and address multidimensional problems affecting a region's competitiveness and economic growth.

The KPEL Project also facilitated Public–Private partnerships (PPPs), thus allowing a more holistic way of carrying out diagnostics, identifying barriers and seeking innovative ways of regulating businesses and formulating economic policies that are pro-poor in nature. The KPEL Project contributed greatly to stimulating of local economic activities in target locations, and, in particular, empowered local producers such as farmers in their standing as business partners, improved their access to markets and gave a boost to their incomes.

Producers were able to work in 'clusters', strengthening their bargaining position and enabling them to create economies of scale that, in turn, facilitated access to larger markets. A total of 30 business clusters or producer groups were established with the support of this project. Some of these groups went on to legally register themselves as cooperatives or business associations. Many benefited from that move. An association of coffee farmers in Lampung province after formal registration was able to demand and received a higher price for their coffee from Nestlé. Another group was able to access bank credit after getting registered as a cooperative.

Clustering of businesses also encouraged producers to improve the quality of their products and learn innovative marketing techniques. In North Sulawesi, within a period of two years a group of farmers was able to increase seaweed production from 310 to 1000 tons through better production techniques. Similarly in Southeast Sulawesi, with improved planting techniques the project enabled a group of cocoa farmers to triple their production. In another project location in Nusa Tenggara Barat, 1200 new jobs were created as a result of adopting better methods for growing and marketing lobsters in the province.

Besides testing and developing a set of tools and mechanisms for implementation, the project helped to accumulate very valuable field experiences and networks for the exchange of ideas, knowledge and experiences. A handbook for KPEL implementation was developed to assist facilitators in organizing partnerships and carrying out business sub-sector analysis. This handbook proved to be a very useful reference tool in the replication of this project in new locations.

Total project costs

The project provided financial inputs from 2001 to 2003 amounting to US$1.6 million, financed in equal parts by the Government of Indonesia and UNDP/ UN-HABITAT. The project provided a budget for international long- and short-term professional advisors (14 per cent of the total budget) and national personnel, and professionals for the management and coordination of project implementation (18 per cent). Through sub-contracts, the project managed the provision of consultants to support the implementation of the project at local, provincial and national levels (34 per cent). Substantial funding was also provided for training, study tours, for research and development of tools (19 per cent). The remaining budget was allocated for activities that included equipment, duty travel, reporting and miscellaneous.

Project management

The project was executed by BAPPENAS while its implementation was carried out by the respective provincial or district governments. UNDP, in partnership with UN-HABITAT, provided technical support to the executing agency as well as various implementing partners in the target locations. The project was implemented in 15 provinces, directly targeting over 50 districts.

A National Project Office in BAPPENAS was set up to provide secretarial support and project assurance. Administrative staff and advisors in this secretariat were provided by UNDP. Depending on the location, at the provincial and district level, project support units (PSU) were established to implement and manage project activities. At each tier, KPEL Partnerships were established to provide strategic direction and forums for identifying and solving local economic problems. Business groups or clusters were direct clients of this project, but capacity development support was provided at each level to strengthen institutions and improve policy frameworks for local economic development and poverty reduction.

Monitoring and evaluation of project activities

During the pilot phase, a number of monitoring tools were developed to review future progress against expected outputs. Primarily, the monitoring looked at the effectiveness and efficiency of delivering agreed outputs and focused on process indicators. In each project location, a PSU was set up to provide facilitation in establishing partnerships and also support in the implementation of the project. The PSU was responsible for providing regular reports to the National KPEL Secretariat who would then report to the Multi-stakeholder Forum.

Periodic reviews were also conducted that delved deeper to gauge outcomes arising from the project. These findings and lessons learned were then synthesized and incorporated into future plans. At the outcome level, the reviews looked at institutional frameworks, change in policies and income of the producers. After a business sector/cluster was selected, a detailed analysis was carried out to identify constraints and future potential for growth in that sector, which served as the baseline for future reviews. An online system that would have made it possible to share this information across KPEL partnerships in different locations was also designed, but could not be fully implemented due to connectivity problems in many districts.

A final evaluation of the project was carried out by an external evaluator in 2005. The evaluation showed that the project had played a key role in improving the business environment in selected locations. The findings from this evaluation

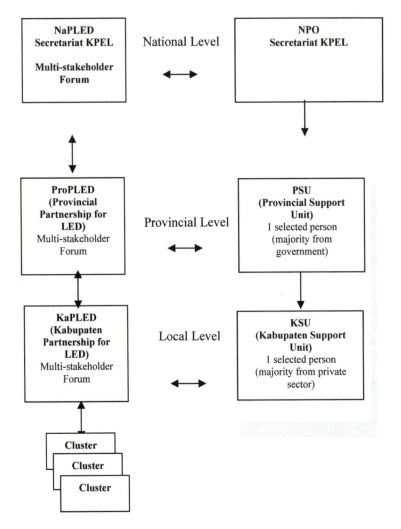

Figure 4.2 *Project structure*

suggested that, overall, the project was very successful in mobilizing action at the local level, and reiterated that the methodology that the project had helped to design was versatile and could be easily adapted in other locations. The evaluation highlighted a number of cases where the project had made significant contributions to improving household incomes. It did not, however, assess the macro impact on local economies as a result of this initiative, which would have been quite challenging as a variety of factors 'outside' the project would have had to be carefully studied and isolated for attribution. something beyond the scope of the final project evaluation. The evaluator underlined that the KPEL strategy was an important policy instrument to improve the local business environment and it could play a key role in attaining the MDGs locally.

The project was unrolled through a series of pilots and refinements in the design that somewhat delayed its implementation. However, these processes were needed for an effective iterative process to occur. The project involved a wide range of stakeholders in the design and implementation that again slowed down the project as decisions were reached through consultations and consensus was not always reached. From time to time, efforts were made to modify administrative and business processes to improve the turnaround time. Also, project locations were scattered across the country, which, at times, limited the provision of technical support from the national project office. The project tried to address this by hiring specialist staff from the targeted locations, but capacity was not always available.

Challenges and how they were overcome

The model posed challenges because of a tension between building institutional frameworks that have a long-term horizon and quick delivery of economic services to the recipients in the short term. Putting institutional frameworks in place and developing capacities takes a long time while producers who were primary beneficiaries of this project obviously expected immediate benefits from the project. Also, for the approach to be successful, an optimal level of engagement by the government needs to be determined. In some locations too much involvement of the government proved to be counterproductive as it affected the dynamics of the KPEL institutional partnerships making many feel that the government wanted to set the agenda, thereby undermining the participative nature of these forums. It is essential that partnerships are internalized in such a way that they offer everyone a chance to participate and the agenda reflects the needs of local businesses.

Another major challenge was to ensure that the focus remained on businesses rather than a broader agenda to include community development activities. In some locations, there was a tendency to move into those development issues that were clearly beyond the scope of KPEL. It is therefore important that from the very onset clear objectives are defined and agreed in a KPEL partnership.

Although all of these challenges were not fully addressed, they did provide important lessons that the project team tried to apply in the replication phase. Attempts were made to strike a balance in the structure of the KPEL partnerships to avoid domination by one group. The selection process was carefully scrutinized and members were transparently selected. Moreover, sufficient time was spent on explaining the KPEL objectives so that there was greater clarity and the project retained its focus on business and economic development, rather than making the objectives too broad.

Lessons learned

The success of this project is due to its relevance and adaptability. It was implemented at a time when Indonesia had just embarked on a massive decentralization programme that delinked the macro-economic policies of the country to economic development at the local level. The situation called for an intervention that could build and strengthen upward and downward linkages between macro-economics and LED.

At different stages of this project, key factors played an important role in determining the outcome of the project. In the preliminary stage, a capable facilitator who could motivate potential KPEL partners to work together was essential in the formation and consolidation of the organizational infrastructure. The role of champions in the overall implementation cannot be overstated. In most of the target areas where the project was considered a success, it was always the case that there was a person or a group of individuals who would take the lead to encourage others to participate and support the project. These champions set examples through their perseverance.

Related to the organizational structure, it was important that there was enough flexibility to allow for changes in the composition of the teams because there were some participants who dropped out or, in some cases, other relevant actors wanted to participate. Every effort was however made to ensure that the membership reflected the interests of all the stakeholders and there was a balance in the team. Furthermore, the project took the precaution of not rushing into establishing new institutional mechanisms. Working through existing institutions was the preferred choice, and new institutional partnerships were formed only when it could be demonstrated that they added value and could be sustained over the long term. This process also had to be carefully synchronized with the local annual budgetary process to ensure that the public resources needed were committed in advance.

At the producer level, one of the main lessons learned was the need to conduct a detailed value-chain mapping of the business sub-sector using various quantitative and qualitative tools. It was critical to bring a commercial or business-like approach to the process in order to avoid investing in sectors that had limited potential for growth or had already reached a stagnation point from where growth was too slow.

Good practice

The KPEL case study in Indonesia demonstrated that a local economic development approach is very effective in reducing poverty and it can serve as a critical pathway for people to improve the quality of their lives. As we have just passed the half-way stage before the deadline for reaching the MDGs, the approach has achieved even greater relevance now and can be a valuable tool for sub-national governments. In particular, in countries such as Indonesia that have decentralized, it offers an important strategy for reducing income poverty and achieving the MDGs locally.

Recent studies and reports suggest that at the national level Indonesia is likely to meet many of its MDG goals and targets, but there are disparities across the region. A number of poorer provinces are unlikely to meet most of their development targets including MDGs. Based on studies looking into impact on service delivery after decentralization, it is fair to conclude that the provision of social services has improved and that there are plans to further improve the delivery of these services. Although a major priority, an area that has received less attention is the local economic dimension in poverty reduction. Solutions need to be found and efforts need to be geared towards addressing problems of job creation and livelihoods. In the absence of decent work, progress in improving access to health, education and other services will have limited impact on the quality of life.

In the last two decades more and more developing countries have decentralized their public administrations. These changes should also shift economic development discourse from being simply a set of desired macro-economic policies and outcomes to a strategy that can be implemented at the local level to unleash economic potential and reduce inequalities. Prior to implementation in Indonesia, local efforts in economic development were often limited to ad hoc support to enterprise development, PPPs, business development services or agricultural extension. The KPEL Project took a much more holistic view of local economies as it was able to identify and strengthen upward and downward linkages with the macro-economic dimensions in the country. Also, the project took a pro-poor approach in LED that primarily looked after the interest of poor entrepreneurs who faced constraints to enter the mainstream economy.

Indonesia is also a unique case because the methodology was adapted and implemented at a time of a major political transition and economic chaos. It created a bridge between sub-national and national policies across a number of diverse geographical regions. Being subjected to such a test proved the versatility and potential for expansion of this approach within Indonesia and even replicability in other countries.

Potential for replication

In the current context, as decentralized governance seems to be finally finding its footing in national policy, the KPEL strategy and projects are particularly relevant and have huge potential for reducing poverty in Indonesia. If poor people are not able to engage in economically productive activities and have access to services, it is unlikely that they will be able to create their own pathways out of poverty. Increased resource allocation and provision of social services, which is gradually happening in Indonesia, without any or little improvement in livelihoods will make it extremely difficult for countries or sub-national governments to reach the MDGs. An LED approach that is inherently pro-poor is a critical input for reducing income poverty and improving overall quality of life.

Conclusions

KPEL in Indonesia demonstrates that an LED approach is a low-cost strategy with huge potential for unleashing business development and economic benefits for low-income households. It is an important stimulus for local economies and can be an effective tool in accelerating progress towards poverty reduction and achievement of MDGs locally. In a country as large and diverse as Indonesia, KPEL can minimize disparities and assist in the reduction of economic gaps between poor and rich provinces in the country. The project directly benefited many business groups by optimizing their potential and improved their incomes.

KPEL has even greater relevance now as decentralization in some countries seems to have widened the cleavages between the rich and poorer regions. The methodology provides a coherent action for addressing problems facing local economies. Although results from all the project locations were not uniform, the overall impact from the project was positive and the model itself proved to be versatile and replicable across the country.

Pro-poor economic growth will be one of the most important contributors in our efforts to reach the MDGs. Thus far, the debates on MDGs have mostly focused on the role of governments and how they can make social services available for poor people. These debates and actions on MDGs need to be further broadened to maximize opportunities for people to become economically empowered so that they can shape their own development. The KPEL strategy shows that it is possible to create these opportunities for those who are being excluded in a world that is globalizing on the one hand, but on the other hand is also localizing through decentralization.

References

Altenburg, T. (2007) 'Donor Approaches to Supporting Pro-Poor Value Chains', paper prepared for Donor Committee for Enterprise Development

Aziz, I. (2007) 'Disappointing Results after Six Years of Decentralization', paper presented at Decentralization Workshop, Jakarta, Indonesia, July 4–5

Bappenas (2004) *Indonesia Report on MDGs*, Bappenas (National Development Planning Agency), Government of Indonesia, Jakarta, Indonesia

International Finance Corporation (2007) *Doing Business – Removing Obstacles to Growth, Annual Review of Business Climate in Business Environment*, International Finance Corporation

Ishihara, Y. and Wallace, W. (2007) *Indonesia: Social and Economic Outlook*, Quarterly Country Updates, World Bank Indonesia, Indonesia

Lusby, F. (2002) 'Subsector/Business Service Approach to Program Design', paper submitted to Office of Microenterprise Development, Washington DC, USAID

Marulanda, L. (2004) 'Partnership for Local Economic Development", Final Substantive Report, KPEL, Jakarta, Indonesia

Meyer-Stamer, J. (2003) 'Why is local economic development so difficult and what can we do about it?', Mesopartner Working Paper 04/2003

Meyer-Stamer, J. (2004) 'Local Competitiveness – A Performance Measurement Tool for Territorial Development, Mesopartner Paper, September

UNDP, UN-HABITAT and KPEL (2001) *Revised Project Document*, UNDP, UN-HABITAT and KPEL, Jakarta, Indonesia

USAID DRSP (2006) *Stock Taking on Indonesia's Decentralization: Summary of Finding*, Assessment Report, Washington DC, USAID

Wiranto, T. (2002) 'Partnership for Local Economic Development (KPEL) – Experiences and Lessons for Poverty Alleviation', for Urban-Rural Linkages Workshop, UN-HABITAT and ESCAP, Cambodia

5

Poverty Reduction through Rural–Urban Linkages: The Case of the Rural–Urban Partnership Programme in Nepal

Ramesh Adhikari and Suresh Dhoj Shrestha

Introduction

Nepal is a landlocked country situated between India and China. It covers an area of 147,181 square kilometres with a population of about 26 million, which is growing at an annual rate of 2.1 per cent. About 16.2 per cent of the total population live in urban areas. It is an agriculture-based country where more than 31 per cent of the population lives below the poverty line and 78 per cent of households are dependent on agriculture (CBS, 2003a). Similarly, more than 60 per cent of the households own and cultivate less than one hectare of land, which, at most, acts as a means of survival for less than six months of the year.

In 2004, the economic growth rate was 3.6 per cent and the per capita GNP was inordinately low at US$269 (MoF, 2004). With a Human Development Index of 0.527, Nepal ranked 138th among 177 countries in 2004 (UNDP, 2006).

As per the 2001 census, there are 103 different castes and ethnic groups with different languages and dialects in Nepal. Nepali, written in Devnagari script, is the national language. The major religious groups in the country are Hindus (80.6 per cent of the population) and Buddhists (10.7 per cent). The overall literacy rate is 54.1 per cent: 65.5 per cent for men and 42.8 per cent for women (CBS, 2003b). Life expectancy at birth in 2006 was 63.3 years and infant mortality rate (under one year of age) is 56 per 1000 live births (UNICEF, 2006), whereas the total fertility rate is 3.5 children per mother. About 80 per cent of the population has access to safe drinking water, 39 per cent has access to sanitation and about 31 per cent of households have electricity connections (CBS, 2003a).

After a decade of armed conflict between the Government of Nepal (GoN) and the Communist Party of Nepal (Maoist) (CPN(M)), an interim government including the CPN (M) with eight different major political parties of Nepal has been formed. This interim government prepared for the elections of the Constituent Assembly held in November 2007, however, elected representatives are absent in local municipalities, district development committees (DDC) and village development committees (VDCs).

The project

The Rural–Urban Partnership Programme (RUPP) of the GoN and UNDP aims to improve the sustainable livelihoods of the rural and urban poor. Two realizations led to the formulation of the programme. First, most development projects and programmes in Nepal have strictly concentrated on addressing either rural or urban development problems or needs. They have encouraged an institutional culture largely associated with sectoral approaches to development. Sectoral approaches to development tend to direct resources towards development in isolation with little impact on people's livelihoods. Lack of focus on participatory planning, rural–urban linkages and the application of largely sectoral approaches to development have diverted development investments away from addressing priority problems at the local level. Second, the trend of rapid urbanization in Nepal, with an urban population of 16 per cent and sporadic growth of small towns and settlements all over the country, is evidence of the rural poor adopting rural–urban strategies to underpin their livelihoods. Thus, development efforts need to be directed towards: (1) strengthening rural–urban linkages, (2) empowering the poor so that they can access socio-economic development opportunities and potentials emanating from linkages, and (3) constituting an appropriate institutional mechanism that enables them to cope with the risks inherent in the rural–urban interactions and reduces their vulnerability.

Project formulation

GoN, through its strategies under the Ninth National Five Year Plan and in accordance with its commitments made during the HABITAT II conference, seeks to improve peoples' livelihoods and strengthen local economies by taking advantage of the social and economic development opportunities through improved rural–urban linkages. The programme was formulated in consultation with the UNDP in Nepal, line ministries, participating municipalities, major stakeholders such as the Municipal Association of Nepal (MuAN), Association of District Development Committees (ADDCN), Dalit Commission, Nepal Indigenous Peoples' Committee, civil societies, NGOs and the Federation of Nepalese Chambers of Commerce and Industry (FNCCI). The project developed in a participatory manner. Phases II and III of the project were formulated incorporating the previous experience gained in Phase I and the input received from community and local-level stakeholders.

Project goals and objectives

The main goal of the programme is to 'Secure the right to sustainable livelihoods of rural and urban poor'. It has set the following objectives:

- Livelihoods of the rural and urban poor are to be secured through social mobilization with the adoption of affirmative actions (with special emphasis on vulnerable groups – dalits, occupational castes, traditional tribes, indigenous groups and women).
- Economic and planning linkages between rural and urban areas need to be strengthened.
- Urban governance needs to be improved to provide efficient basic service delivery.
- National-level government and civil society institutions need to be strengthened to implement the issues of the National 10th Five Year Plan Urban Section.

Key elements of the project

Target beneficiaries

The primary beneficiaries of the programme are dalits, indigenous groups, other disadvantaged groups and the poor populace of the municipalities and rural market centres (RMCs). The programme implements its activities through TLOs (tole/lane organizations) – a community level grassroots organization, partner municipalities, VDCs where RMCs are delineated and with the private sector.

Geographic coverage of the project

The working area of the programme in Phase III is eight partnering municipalities mainly in Far Western, Mid-western and the Eastern Development Regions of Nepal (Ilam, Damak, Khandbari, Gularia, Dipayal Silgadhi, Dhangadhi, Tikapur and Mahendranagar). In addition, the programme provides technical support on the basis of demand to 12 Phase I and II municipalities (Dhankuta, Biratnagar, Hetauda, Bharatpur, Byas, Pokhara, Tansen, Butwal, Tribhuwannagar, Tulsipur, Nepalgunj and Birendranagar), and to an additional 15 municipalities (Itahari, Inaruwa, Lekhnath, Ratnanagar, Prithvinarayan, Kalaiya, Ramgram, Putalibazaar, Amargadhi, Mechinagar, Mdhyapur Thimi, Bidur, Baglung, Bhadrapur and Kapilbastu) replicated by the Ministry of Local Development (MLD) and the respective municipalities with their own resources. The programme is also implemented in 50 RMCs.

Project activities

Key components

The programme is contributing to the joint efforts of UNDP and GoN to meet the MDGs of halving the poverty level by 2015, promoting gender equality and empowering women, and reversing the spread of killer diseases, especially HIV/AIDS. It also helps reach targets of developing a global partnership for development in the country and providing secure livelihoods for the rural and the urban poor.

Information and communication

A participatory approach has been followed in the development of information systems that ensure the active participation of the partner organizations. The programme has introduced ICT as a development tool for strengthening good urban governance, poverty reduction and rural–urban linkages.

Social mobilization

Social mobilization is being carried out as an institutional base for implementing programme activities with the concept of sustainable development. It is also used for mobilizing resources for local development, decentralization and empowerment of the community. The social mobilization process has covered almost 100 per cent of households in the partnering municipalities and RMCs.

Social issues

RUPP is empowering the poor and disadvantaged people with a special focus on the women, dalits, ethnic minorities and the internally displaced persons (IDPs) for both equity and equality. With this inclusive approach, the programme is committed to ensuring their participation in all programme activities – both as participants in the decision-making process and as beneficiaries.

Institution building and management support to good governance

The managerial capabilities of the local institutions should be enhanced in order to strengthen good urban governance through participatory development efforts. The programme supports the enhancement of the professional capabilities of the municipal staff members and authorities to play a key role in planning, coordination and managing development activities effectively.

Linkage enterprise development

The development of linkage economic enterprises is concerned with the activities related to improving the livelihoods of the poor and disadvantaged by creating an enabling environment for undertaking economic initiatives based on rural–urban linkages. The communities in partner municipalities and RMCs are mobilized to form self-managed organizations to be engaged in the economic activities that help to improve production and enhance trading by taking advantage of local potentials and opportunities. The traditional tribes, occupational groups and artisans are trained, organized into enterprises to use their skills to produce intermediary goods or directly provide services to existing companies. Although the UNDP stopped supporting enterprise development, the partner municipalities have continued to support the poor and disadvantaged with livelihood opportunities through the Municipal Partnership Development Fund (MPDF).

Policy support

The main supporters at the national level include the MLD, Ministry of Physical Planning and Works, National Planning Commission (NPC) and MuAN in implementing the National 10th Plan's urban chapter. Support also comes from the MLD's decision to replicate the RUPP approach in non-RUPP municipalities as well as support to the NPC, High Level Commission for Information Technology, National Information Technology Centre and Nepal Telecom Authority in ICT for development policy.

Key activities

Information and communication

Apart from harnessing ICTs for strengthening information systems, crucial for municipal planning and rural–urban linkages, the resourcefulness offered by the ICTs has attracted RUPP attention in two specific areas. First, e-governance is being promoted as a means of strengthening tenets of good and inclusive local governance, and second, e-commerce and market information systems (compilation, processing and dissemination of daily agriculture price information) are being promoted as a means to complement RUPP efforts to support poverty reduction by enhancing rural–urban market linkages as well as regional economic linkages. Similarly, ICTs have been used to support poverty reduction by expanding access to market prices of agricultural commodities to farmers and traders living in the RMCs and municipalities in addition to business-to-business e-commerce-based implementation. These are the joint initiatives of partner municipalities, the local Chamber of Commerce and Industries, Afro Enterprise Center/FNCCI and the programme. While strengthening these activities, the demand for rural/

community telecenters as a means of bridging the digital divide has been felt and the programme has provided support in establishing community telecenters in the RMCs and some remote areas of municipalities to provide services to the poor by establishing two way communications and strengthening rural–urban linkages.

RUPP has continuously supported the partner municipalities in the establishment of urban information centers (UICs), preparation of socio-economic database of municipalities and RMCs, GIS-based resource/poverty maps and various other database software for planning and revenue generation. Preparation of municipal/ward/TLO profiles, HIV/AIDS profiles, situation analysis of IDPs and so forth of partner municipalities are some of the ICT-enabled implementations supported by the programme.

Social mobilization

Covering more than 230,000 households, 5530 TLOs have been formed across the programme locations (35 municipalities and 50 RMCs, covering 100 per cent of households). With the objectives of ensuring increased participation of the disadvantaged groups in development efforts, the programme has adopted a set of affirmative actions that ensure a significant representation of these groups in TLO leadership. Apart from ensuring appropriate representation of the disadvantaged groups, the affirmative actions adopted by the programme also guarantee the allocation of an appropriate amount of programme resources to these groups. The programme is successful in mobilizing the urban community (a mixture of migrants and locals) because of the opportunity provided to every household to participate in planning and decision making in community governance and poverty reduction activities. Similarly, the recognition of the TLOs as grassroots institutions aimed at the overall development of the community and the municipality is another important fact that has brought a shared purpose to diverse communities. In addition, the following activities also played a role in unifying and mobilizing the community.

Capacity development

Capacity remains central to the success or failure of entrepreneurial initiatives undertaken by the target beneficiaries. It is along these lines that structured economic enterprise development training and skills training are provided for entrepreneurs receiving support from the programme. In addition to these training programmes, several training initiatives for human resource development are also provided to enhance the capacity of TLO members and the staff/authorities of partner municipalities and VDCs. Training covers urban social mobilization, participatory municipal development planning, savings and credit mobilization, enumerators, local governance, information mobilization, gender, leadership, HIV/AIDS and inclusive development. So far, more than 70,000 participants have benefited from various training programmes conducted by RUPP, of which 56 per cent have been female.

Formation of internal capital (savings and credit schemes)

Savings and credit schemes are an important element that not only provide members with immediate access to financial resources but also brings them together as a group. Savings also help make the TLOs sustainable and effective in initiating and implementing development activities. Community savings have become a medium to attract outside resources. They boost community morale, promote financial discipline and empower the TLO members. Savings and credit schemes are mandatory for each TLO. The savings are invested among the TLO members.

Mobilizing the communities' resources for local development through seed grants

The RUPP has been assisting the TLOs with seed grants to support their community development initiatives, especially for the creation of pro-poor infrastructure and the strengthening of rural–urban linkages. Initially intended to complement the TLOs' efforts in local development, the seed grant interventions are fast developing proven capacity for mobilizing significant internal and external resources (non-RUPP resources). The programme mostly provides seed grants to those community infrastructure projects that enhance the local economy by strengthening rural–urban market linkages. For example, the programme supports the construction and management of link bridges, link roads, fruit and vegetable collection centres, milk chilling centres, periodic markets (haat bazaar), market outlets in the urban areas, slaughter houses and so on. These types of community projects constitute more than 80 per cent of total community infrastructure projects. The remaining 20 per cent of projects cater for social issues such as community building, drinking water supply and child welfare centres.

This is verified by the fact that resource allocation, while supporting a total of 2122 community-based projects was only 20 per cent of the total financial outlay, while communities themselves mobilized the remaining 80 per cent through varied sources.

Social issues

The programme has been engaged in a range of activities aimed at addressing pressing developmental issues relating to inclusive development, IDPs, combating HIV/AIDS, girl child education, and other issues of social importance. The programme is creating awareness of HIV/AIDS among every household of partner municipalities, providing livelihood options for HIV positive people, IDPs, sex workers and other disadvantaged groups, giving them easy access to credit through the MPDF. The programme is also providing support to these communities with vocational skills training, enterprise management, participatory planning, savings and credit mobilization and so on.

Institution building and management support to good governance

Ensuring sustainability through institutional development

Institutional strengthening of partner municipalities began with the creation and establishment of rural–urban partnership sections within each municipality's institutional structure for the purpose of carrying out development activities. It must be noted that these institutional entities are not ad hoc arrangements put in place to coincide with the duration of the programme but are permanent, thereby marking a process of institutionalization from the outset of the programme.

Ensuring financial and operational sustainability through MPDF

With the vision of ensuring financial and operational sustainability of programme activities, RUPP, when it started its activities in 1997 created the MPDF – located in each of the partner municipalities – to support poverty reduction activities by promoting enterprises that strengthen rural–urban linkages. The fund was jointly created with the contribution of the partner municipalities, the VDC of the particular RMC and the RUPP. The fund increases its size through an investment as credit to the poor populace of RMCs and to the municipalities to initiate linkage enterprises. With the significant amount of MPDF in every partner municipality and after a successful internalization of the RUPP and its activities, MPDF has been strengthened through the passing of by-laws. All the partner municipalities have adopted the by-laws, not only giving a legal status to the MPDF but also ensuring its sustainability by strengthening the municipal rural–urban partnership sections, cementing its mandate, and strengthening its management of personnel and resources.

Institutional strengthening of municipalities

With the objective of establishing an effective programme implementation structure within each partner municipality, especially for information management and the training of personnel, the programme has supported partner municipalities to establish UICs and human resources development centres (HRDCs). All the partner municipalities are adopting comprehensive guidelines prepared by the programme for the operation of their UICs and HRDCs.

Linking TLOs to municipal and village planning

The programme, with the intention of ensuring broad community participation in local development efforts and participatory planning, has introduced the Participatory Municipal Development Planning (PMDP) process in its partner municipalities. Partner municipalities have been linking the TLOs to the formation of their annual municipal plans. This is achieved through having ward-level TLO meetings, as per the Local Self Governance Act and its regulations. These meetings discuss local development issues, identify priorities and formulate development plans on a consensus basis, which are then included within the annual plans of municipalities and VDCs.

Linkage enterprise development

Giving a major thrust to poverty reduction, the programme has been reaching the poorest of the poor with its enterprise development plan, a comprehensive and integrated package of credit, training and technology transfer, by strengthening rural–urban linkages.

The TLO members, during their regular meetings, expressed their desire to undertake some entrepreneurial activities and form linkage enterprises. The programme supports only those enterprises that strengthen rural–urban linkages, such as agricultural marketing and service-oriented enterprises. The process centres on the formulation of an Enterprise Development Plan. The communities themselves identify the needy people and make recommendations to the municipality for credit support. Using the security of the TLOs, each municipality provides the technical and financial support to the linkage enterprises through the MPDF. To date, more than 31,000 entrepreneurs have benefited from credit support to initiate linkage enterprises. These entrepreneurs are successfully running their linkage enterprises and providing services and agricultural inputs to the rural areas and supply rural agricultural products, dairy products and a variety of industrial raw materials to the urban centres. To enhance their marketing capacity, these linkage enterprises are provided with easy access to daily agriculture price information of major markets of the country through bulletin boards, community FM radios and community telecentres. These enterprises are also linked up with business-to-business e-commerce for establishing rural–urban market linkages and regional market linkages. In addition, RMCs, established with the objective of strengthening rural–urban market linkages, also play a key role in the collection and marketing of rural products.

Similarly, the programme has been implementing a special and focused enterprise development package, namely Rural Labour Linkage to support occupational castes and traditional tribes as well as artisans to engage in some niche areas where their products and services would have tangible market potential. The skills of occupational castes and traditional tribes are enhanced and their products and services are linked up to urban market systems as well as industrial establishments.

Policy support

The best practices of RUPP have been incorporated in the 10th Five Year Plan of GoN as one of the processes to address urban poverty through rural–urban linkages. RUPP has supported the MLD to prepare the MPDF by-law, 'Guidelines for Municipalities on Integrated Property Tax' and 'Guidelines for Social Audit' to ensure the monitoring roles of communities in municipal development activities.

Furthermore, assistance is provided to tackle rapid urbanization. Based on extensive monitoring and research, the programme is providing data, information and recommendations to the ministries and line agencies to assist in the planning and policy formulation process to strengthen the capacity to deal with the rapid urbanization in the country and address the needs of the urban poor. The programme is providing support to MuAN for its advocacy and coordination activities to help build a stronger association of municipalities. Technical assistance is also provided especially to MLD with the aim of enforcing its pledge to replicate the RUPP approach to a minimum of five new municipalities each year. A total of 15 municipalities have replicated the RUPP concept and approach with the financial support of GoN and technical support through RUPP.

Key technical inputs

The programme provides technical inputs to municipalities and VDCs to identify new tools and techniques for urban development and poverty reduction through rural–urban linkages, providing training, preparing user-friendly guidelines, supporting social mobilization, participatory planning, decision-making and poverty reduction activities. The programme also provides inputs to local governments for the cross-jurisdictional planning of urban and rural areas.

Timeframe

Phase III of the programme ran from January 2004 to December 2007. Phase I was from September 1997 to December 2001 and Phase II was from January 2002 to December 2003.

Impact

RUPP impacts include:

- a sustainable mechanism for the promotion of good governance and poverty reduction through social mobilization and rural–urban linkages;

- increased awareness that 'development is not limited to physical infrastructure but covers overall social, economic and political empowerment of communities' (RUPP/UNDP, 2006);
- a bottom-up planning approach with the participation of the grassroots communities;
- people's direct participation in decision making;
- increased awareness on the issues of inclusive development, democracy, rights and duties;
- immediate access to cash through savings and credit, i.e. complete eradication of moneylenders;
- enhanced community ownership and initiatives in local development;
- enhanced resource mobilization capacity of communities;
- mainstreaming of HIV/AIDS, ICT and inclusion in municipal planning;
- increased awareness of ICTs as an effective development tool for poverty reduction and good governance;
- improved community access to information, markets and planning processes:
- generation of a local response to HIV/AIDS:
- institutionalization of community governance through a TLO coordination committee; and
- 23 per cent of entrepreneurs have been raised about the poverty line and 68 per cent have greatly increased their incomes.

Total project costs

From September 1997 to December 2007 the national government spent US$645000, while local government spent US$2 million (only cash contribution to salary and other benefits). Community groups contributed US$2,736,778 and other CBOs US$300,000. External assistance from UNDP amounted to US$7,015,371.

Project management

Implementing agency

The partners of the programme are at three different levels. At the macro level NPC, MLD and the Ministry of Physical Planning and Works, the national apex institution of other government agencies, the private sector and local authorities were all partners. At the meso level, the municipalities, DDCs, VDCs, NGOs and private sector organizations were the partners. Finally, at the micro level the partners were the local communities (organized through TLOs) and the RMCs.

Coordinating mechanisms used

RUPP has adopted a consultative approach with the partners for implementing activities. As Figure 5.1 shows, coordination is done at three levels of programme implementation – the macro, the meso and at the micro or community levels. Macro level coordination is achieved through the interactions at the Steering Committee and Coordination Committee meetings. Regular participation in field-level activities and monitoring visits by the members of those committees are the main tools for bringing synergy within and outside the programme spheres. The programme has also maintained good relations with other organizations by regular interaction and experience sharing meetings. Being a member secretary of the National Rural Tele Center Coordination Committee of the High Level Commission for Information Technology, it has established good relations with all the major players in ICT. Meso level coordination is maintained at the Management Committee meetings. In addition, two institutional mechanisms have been established to achieve coordination at municipal and RMC levels:

1   A Local Initiative Forum at the municipal level composed of all project/ programmes, NGO and international NGOs within the municipality has been established in all partnering municipalities. They meet monthly to share each other's experiences to avoid duplication in activities.
2   A network of partner municipalities called the Rural–Urban Linkage Network (RUNET) has been formed. It has proved to be an important platform for sharing experiences as well as mobilizing support to strengthen urban-based local development.

Finally, the micro-level coordination is established with the community of municipalities and RMCs (through the TLOs) through a social mobilization process. TLOs meet regularly and identify their needs and formulate plans and implement socio-economic development activities. They help support municipalities and VDCs in participatory planning and poverty reduction activities through enterprise development and service delivery. The municipal-level TLO Coordination Committees also make TLOs stronger and united in most of the partner municipalities.

Monitoring and evaluation of project activities

A comprehensive monitoring and evaluation system has been established to facilitate systematic monitoring of the RUPP activities at different stages of progress. The system is made in such a way that concerned personnel at different levels of programme implementation visit partnering municipalities and communities at regular intervals to observe. A computerized monthly progress reporting system is in place to monitor all project components. A separate computer package is also in

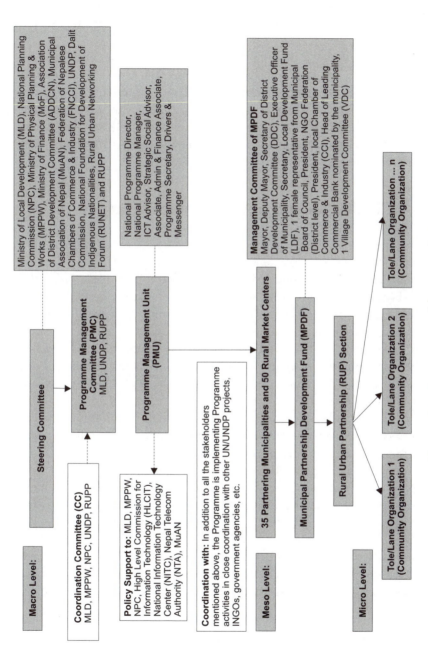

Figure 5.1 *Organizational structure of RUPP*

place to record and monitor credit and seed grant supports. All partner municipalities are connected through the internet and email. A computerized evaluation and impact assessment system has been developed and is being introduced.
Strategic planning, review and consultative meetings of the programme staff are
organized regularly.

A Steering Committee meeting and RUNET meeting is organized every
year. A programme Management Committee meeting with UNDP, ministry
and programme staff is organized every month. The management committees of
MPDF at partner municipalities chaired by their mayors also carry out regular
meetings. Similarly, monitoring of project activities in the field by stakeholders is
also ensured. In addition, a standard post-project evaluation will be carried out at
the end of the project.

Challenges and how they were overcome

Challenges include the following:

- The absence of elected representatives at local bodies remained a major challenge because the appointment of government employees in lieu of elected
  representatives significantly hindered the programme objective of improving
  good governance by making authorities (mayor and other elected representatives) accountable for public service delivery through the political empowerment of communities. A request has been made to GoN to overcome the challenge; the GoN is planning to form executive bodies with an all party alliance
  in the local governments.
- The frequent transfer of executive officers delayed decision making processes
  in project implementation at the local level as new executive officers needed
  time to understand the concept and modus operandi of the project. The issues
  have been conveyed to the MLD.
- Resources were insufficient because of the growing capacity of TLOs to implement infrastructure development projects and because of population growth
  putting extra pressure on services. More efforts have been given to resource
  mobilization.
- Although Nepal remained largely peaceful in 2006, frequent road blockades
  hindered staff movement, especially in the Far Western part of the country,
  thereby created challenges for smooth implementation. Now the situation has
  been improved.

Lessons learned

Success factors

RUPP was successful in strengthening good urban governance and poverty reduction and was recognized as the 'Urban Development Concept' by the GoN. GoN has replicated the programme in 15 additional municipalities through the MLD and respective municipalities using their own resources. Similarly, the internalization of the programme in all partnering municipalities by forming permanent partnership sections for carrying out RUPP activities is another major success of the programme. In conclusion, the complete ownership of RUPP by the GoN and municipalities for the overall development of the municipalities and RMCs is the major long-term achievement of the programme.

Role of champions

One of the major champions of this programme has been the UNDP, which helped it to develop partnerships with the GoN, network with various national and international NGOs, and leverage funds for programme implementation. Especially through the MLD, the GoN has led programme implementation and recognized it as an Urban Development Concept for good urban governance and poverty reduction, It has replicated the RUPP model in non-RUPP municipalities in a phased manner with its own resources. The GoN included the RUPP concept in its Poverty Reduction Strategy Paper and 10th Five Year Plan. The suggestions received from the partnering municipalities through the Rural–Urban Networking Forum helped in programme implementation and internalization of the programme within the national and local governments.

Support

The technical and financial support provided by the RUPP in partnering municipalities played a key role in the successful implementation of the programme. The components such as information systems, social mobilization, enterprise development, human resource development and policy support are some of the supports provided by the programme to the partnering municipalities and central-level government.

Motivation

The empowerment of communities socially, economically and politically in all partnering municipalities initiated a bottom-up approach for strengthening good urban governance and poverty reduction. Similarly, the concept of poverty reduction through rural–urban linkages motivated the programme.

Other innovations

The programme introduced public hearings and social/public auditing in municipalities and provided training of trainers to the TLO members on public hearings. This has resulted in greater participation, transparency and accountability in the municipalities, even in the absence of elected representatives. These activities have become significant innovations of the programme because they have created an open forum for discussion between people and the local government, which has helped people to interact and put their comments and grievances to those in power. It also helped the people in authority to further commit to greater transparency and accountability. The partner municipalities have now started to conduct social/public auditing, which has helped municipalities to gain the confidence of the public.

Similarly, the partnering municipalities are promoting enterprise development activities to support poverty reduction activities through MPDF even after UNDP's support was phased out (UNDP stopped supporting enterprise development from 2005). The poor and disadvantaged are still benefiting from easy access to credit for livelihood options from the MPDF.

Good practice

In a context where municipalities were focusing only on the infrastructure development, the emergence of the RUPP has changed the traditional concept of municipalities by introducing social mobilization, poverty reduction and good governance. Before the RUPP intervention, all the decisions were taken by a top-down approach and projects were implemented without people's participation. People were hesitant to visit municipalities and the authorities ignored them.

Now, after the RUPP intervention, people are socially mobilized by the TLOs (with one member per household). They are united, identify community needs, formulate plans and forward them to the municipality through ward offices for implementation. The bottom-up participatory planning and decision-making process has now been adopted by the municipality. The community organizations are actively involved in poverty reduction and development activities. With their internal savings, they mobilize credit to the needy community members. If the demand is high, with their recommendations, the municipalities provide credit support to the potential entrepreneurs without any physical collateral. Municipalities have established MPDFs to carry out poverty reduction activities. A study conducted by Murray (2003) shows that 23 per cent of entrepreneurs have successfully raised themselves above the poverty line and 68 per cent have increased their income significantly. Municipalities have initiated cross-jurisdictional planning between urban and rural areas, and mainstreamed ICT as a tool for development, HIV/AIDS and gender planning.

Potential for replication

As stated above, the GoN, realizing the effectiveness of RUPP has started replicating the programme in 15 additional municipalities with their own resources. There is a high demand from non-RUPP municipalities for RUPP implementation, but due to resource constraints the programme could not cater for the demand from the municipalities. Tribhuwan University, Purbanchal University and Public Service Commission and Urban Development Training Center of Nepal have incorporated RUPP in their curriculum. The programme also prepared a book on *Rural Urban Relations*. Apart from national agencies, Cambodia and Afghanistan have also shown their keen interest in RUPP replication.

Conclusions

In accordance with the Local Self Governance Act, municipalities in Nepal provide municipal services to their citizens. Most of the municipalities depend upon traditional systems and focus on physical infrastructure development. The planning is carried out through a top-down approach in many cases without active and meaningful people's participation. With the emergence of RUPP, the concept of urban development has taken a new dimension, for example, focusing on social mobilization, people's participation, enterprise development for poverty reduction and livelihood options, rural–urban linkages for balanced development, ICTs and affirmative action for IDPs and other disadvantaged people. The GoN has taken the ownership of RUPP by replicating it in additional municipalities with their own resources.

Partnering municipalities started a bottom-up approach to planning through social mobilization and PMDP. Municipalities covered 100 per cent of households through social mobilization processes, forming 5530 TLOs, including more than 230,000 households to support municipal development. With RUPP support, municipalities established and operationalized UICs, a municipal data bank and HRDCs to provide easy access for the community. Municipalities, with the objective of poverty reduction, established the MPDF to provide access to credit by the poor without the need for any physical collateral so that they could initiate linkage enterprises to strengthen rural–urban linkages. To date, the municipalities promoted more than 31,000 entrepreneurs that established market linkages through MPDF. RUPP's impact assessment (Murray, 2003) clearly states the success of RUPP in poverty reduction activities through strengthening rural–urban linkages. The municipalities have supported IDPs to improve their livelihood options and gain access to basic services. To strengthen and expand the linkage enterprises, municipalities started disseminating daily agricultural price information and supported rural–urban market linkages through the community-based infrastructure projects and through e-commerce services establishing virtual markets named '*Nepali e-Haat Bazaar*'. The effectiveness of rural–urban linkages for local development has been realized by the GoN and incorporated in the 10th National Plan. In addition to this, municipalities have also shown their commitment to participatory planning and transparency by introducing municipal e-governance. For easy access to information, municipalities established community-run telecentres in municipal as well as in the rural areas of the RUPP, and also set up RMCs. The programme has also mainstreamed HIV/AIDS awareness in municipal planning.

RUPP's objective is based on the targets of the MDGs, especially achieving the targets of halving extreme poverty and hunger, promoting gender equality and empowering women, combatting HIV/AIDS and developing a global partnership for development. Through social mobilization, the targets of achieving universal primary education, reducing child mortality and improving maternal health have also been covered by the programme.

References

CBS (2003a) *Nepal Life Standard Survey (NLSS)*, Katmandu, CBS

CBS (2003b) *Population Monograph of Nepal*, Volume I, NPC, Katmandu, CBS

MoF (Ministry of Finance) (2004) *Ministry of Finance Report*, Katmandu, UNDP/ UNCHS/NPC

Murray, J. (2003) *Impact Assessment of Rural Urban Partnership Programme's Linkage Enterprise Micro Credit Program in Nepal*, RUPP/UNDP, Lalitpur, Nepal

RUPP/UNDP (2006) *Annual Report*, RUPP/UNDP, Lalitpur, Nepal

UNDP (2006) *Nepal: Readings in Human Development*, Katmandu, UNDP Nepal

UNICEF, (2006) *Progress and Challenges in South Asia*, Katmandu, UNICEF

6

One Tambon One Product, Thailand

Chudatip Ritruechai[1] and Dr Chaivej Nuchprayoon[2]
with Octavio B. Peralta[3]

Introduction

The financial crisis of 1997 resulted in increased poverty in Thailand due to the fact that the majority of people affected were already at low income levels. In an effort to help the situation the Thai government created many projects. This included an initiative in 2001 to assist in the reduction of poverty and to develop community called the One Tambon One Product (OTOP) project (a *tambon* is a group of villages).

The 'Land of Smiles' is a well-known catch phrase applied to Thailand because Thai people are friendly and mindful. For all Thai people the nation, religion and King represent deeply held values and these three concepts, represented in the red, white and blue of the Thai national flag, have been the inspiration for many successful national projects of which the OTOP is one.

In 1994, the population of Thailand was 62.8 million, of which 7.08 million (12.4 per cent) were living below the poverty line of Bt838 (US$25) per month. The poverty line had increased to Bt1242 (US$38) by 2004, with most of the poor people located in the North Eastern region of Thailand (Chutimaskul, 2006). It is therefore a challenge for Thailand to alleviate poverty and to create well being for the majority of its people. In 2005, it was estimated that 94 per cent of the population were Buddhist and so Buddhist principles are deeply entrenched in all forms of national life. Willingness to contribute to the alleviation of poverty without expectation of reward is such a principle.

In the Kingdom of Thailand, Thai people consider themselves fortunate to have the Royal Family, who have devoted themselves to the country and people with their initiatives and support. The people's national focal point is their Majesties and the Royal Family. All activities implemented by the Royal Family, especially their 'sufficiency economy' philosophy, have a profound effect on the Thai people. The Royal projects have set an example for the Thai government and people to follow.

Thailand, as with other countries in the world, is a producer of agricultural products. Most people are classified as low income earners and live in rural areas. The Thai government is mandated to help its people avoid poverty and has indicated its mission for poverty alleviation in the current Five Year National Economic and Social Development Plan, plans that have been implemented since 1962.

The 10th plan for 2007–2011 clearly sets up the objective of poverty alleviation and community development by focusing on the development of a 'green and happy society' for Thai people. Goals include having leadership based on moral principles, having a better understanding of the outside world, being able to build a happy family, a strong community and a peaceful society with both quality and stability. By following these objectives Thailand is able to remain connected and in harmony with the world community.

Moreover, 98 per cent of enterprises are SMEs (small and medium sized enterprises), which are both stand alone and dependent suppliers. The financial crisis of 1997 made the government realize the fundamental importance of SMEs to the Thai economy. Subsequently, SMEs were recognized and targeted for promotion and development. To strengthen the economic growth of the country in accordance with the Five Year National Economic and Social Development Plans, the Thai government has initiated many projects such as the Fund Policy for Village and Urban Community, Debt Payment Suspension for Micro Farmers, People Bank, Health Guarantee for All People and OTOP for poverty alleviation and community development.

OTOP is an instrument that is capable of reducing poverty and enhancing community development and at the same time it can complement SME and micro-industry promotion and development.

The project

OTOP was inspired by the Japanese One Village One Product (OVOP) concept that focuses on the issues of local and global, self-reliance and creativity of local community wisdom including local human resources development. This concept was presented in Thailand by the Oita Prefecture. The OVOP concept also plays an important role in promoting rural economic growth, improving the livelihoods of people and contributing to poverty reduction. The OVOP concept was adopted in Thailand as OTOP.

OTOP became a priority project of the Thai government and has been the most popular instrument for poverty reduction and community development in Thailand. Through OTOP the government aims to create value added for good quality local products made from local materials combined with Thai expertise (expertise acquired through a learning process, selection and refined development, transferred from generation to generation). Thai expertise has its own character, which places value on culture and the Thai way of life. Apart from poverty reduction and community development, one of the highest aims is for OTOP products to be accepted by both domestic and international markets.

To implement the OTOP project is to apply community and local expertise to product development. At the same time, the government is ready to assist in areas such as modern knowledge systems and management. Moreover, the government can find both domestic and international markets for the products produced by the communities. This is to promote and support the local development process by building up strong communities and creating self reliance. People in the community can participate in income generation from quality products and services that have value added. The OTOP project also helps bring together people from the community to gain and share knowledge and experiences from other communities.

Project formulation

Before OTOP was launched, the OVOP concept was brainstormed in many forums and, in particular, the forum chaired by the prime minister. In 2001, the Government of Thailand announced the establishment of OTOP and in the same year, the National Committee on Administration of the OTOP Project, chaired by the deputy prime minister was set up to establish policies, strategies and action plans for the project implementation by the Prime Minister's Office. Issues such as standards and criteria for selecting and listing of 'products champions' of villages, *tambons*, districts and provinces were also regulated. Cooperation amongst public agencies, the private sector, technical organizations and financial institutions to provide effective support for implementation was urged. To this purpose other sub-committees were formed relating to such matters as management, manufacturing promotion, marketing promotion, standards development and product quality development as well as sub-committees on a regional, provincial and district/sub-district and *tambon* level. In addition, the Office of Coordination for the OTOP project was also established and experts on OTOP products were appointed.

Project goals and objectives

The goals are to enhance the capacity of the local community to generate income and community development as well as poverty alleviation (Ministry of Foreign Affairs, 2007). It aims to create jobs and income for the communities; to develop strong communities capable of independent thinking and execution at local level; to promote local expertise and human resource development; to encourage creative thinking by the community regarding product development that has been harmonized with the Thai way of life and local culture.

Key elements of the project

Target beneficiaries

Target beneficiaries include several groups:

- There were 38,740 entrepreneurs registered for community and local products in 2006. The products can be categorized into five categories such as utensil-decoration-souvenir products, food products, cloth and clothing products, beverage products and herbal products. Moreover, entrepreneurs can be categorized into 25,940 groups of community producers, 10,866 single-owner entrepreneurs and 1934 SME entrepreneurs. The producer group has good opportunities because of the demand for their products, both in the domestic and international markets. This is evidenced by the higher number of entrepreneurs who have begun operating since OTOP and by the fact that some of them have changed their status to that of exporters. OTOP can help the entrepreneurs to expand their market opportunities.
- One of the key indicators of success of OTOP is the increase in employment in the community, with 611,990 employees being recorded by the project in 2006. The group of local employees consists of housewives, seasonal workers and farmers. Most of them have achieved benefits from the project through increased incomes. Furthermore, they have gained experience by working for the community and they have participated in its development.
- Communities have benefited from their development as they enjoy better living standards derived from higher incomes. They also gain knowledge and experience by interacting with other communities from different parts of the country. Working within a networked system helps communities adapt themselves to modern methods and to respond to globalization.
- Both domestic and overseas consumers have benefited from OTOP because they are able to buy quality and high-standard products at a reasonable price.
- The nation as a whole has derived a benefit from poverty alleviation throughout Thailand, evidenced by the significantly higher sales of products since 2001. The OTOP mid-year fair held in July 2007 hit record sales to a value of Bt400 million (US$12 million) (data supplied in telephone call with OSMEP in 2007). This is in addition to sales from the Fifth OTOP City Fair in December 2007 and other fairs organized at other times of the year. This is clear evidence of OTOP success since its launch in 2001.

The project area

OTOP was initiated by cooperating bodies of both government and private agencies throughout the country after the first trial period began in eight provinces. In

2006, there were a total number of 38,740 entrepreneurs that were located nationwide. The largest number of 15,409 single-owner entrepreneurs were located in Northeastern region, the poorest part of the country.

Presently, OTOP, a key tool for sustainable growth of Thai communities, is implemented at national level and is well-known internationally. It also helps local communities in rural areas to strengthen and develop, as well as reducing poverty at grassroots level, which is the fundamental objective of the project.

Project activities

The success of OTOP is due to the cooperation of all parties concerned. The sustainable growth of the project is an outcome of the National Economic and Social Development Board for policy issues, the core and related government agencies and provincial networks for administering the project, committees at required levels for law and regulations for effective implementation, as well as private sectors and networks for assisting with business experiences, together with market direction. Moreover, financial institutions provide funding assistance while education institutions provide technical assistance regarding modern knowledge and experiences to enhance the local expertise and strengthen the production process. Communities, entrepreneurs, employees and consumers who are the human resources of the communities are required to develop their community through project implementation as they are the key beneficiaries.

All stakeholders play an important role in the success of the project through ethical team work and business management. OTOP has successfully been implemented throughout the country because all stakeholders work with patience, perseverance, diligence, wisdom and prudence under the philosophy of the Royal Family's 'Sufficiency Economy'.

Product development

OTOP products are continually developed through new product designs with the support of both training and advisory services as well as through a competition for 'Product Champion' selection. This competition assigns up to five stars to products depending on their standard; this motivates improved quality. One key tool for OTOP to gain consumers' trust is guarantees from standards institutions such as halal standard, industrial standards and various health standards. Entrepreneurs are required to reach the basic standard before submitting their products for Product Champion selection. Hence, the OTOP Product Champion selection is the key activity in the selection of top products for export and local sales.

In 2006, there were 14,520 products selected for Product Champion and these products were categorized into 1 to 5 star products of which 812 products were 5 star products suitable for export, 3728 were 4 stars products with potential for export, 4880 were 3 stars products that can be developed to a 4-star level, 4253 were 2 stars products that can be developed to gain 3 stars, and 847 products were 1 star products that are difficult to develop.

Financial support

Initial special financial assistance for OTOP was provided by the government in the amount of Bt5 billion (US$150 million) for two years, ending in 2004. The funds were provided through four banks, which helped OTOP producers manage their business and production processes through the OTOP Policy Loan Project, which provides a cheap interest rate scheme.

The SME Development Bank of Thailand (SME BANK) also helps OTOP customers through a non-financial assistance scheme for SME development called 'Marketing Arms', which provides market places, market knowledge and mass media. The three other banks are the Government Savings Bank, which provides funding for community development and personal requirements, the Bank of Agriculture and Agricultural Cooperatives, which provides funding for agricultural material resources, and the Export and Import Bank, which provides funding for OTOP exporters. Additionally the Department of Industrial Promotion under the Ministry of Industry also provides funding in terms of revolving funds that OTOP and micro-enterprises can access.

Human resources development

Many training courses have been conducted for entrepreneurs and employees to upgrade their professional skills. Community leaders are required to be trained in order to help lead their own community development. Other aspects that are an important part of business are ethics and professional codes of conduct, which are also required for human resources development to create trust and loyalty. It is very important for entrepreneurs to create trust and loyalty especially when conducting business with foreign customers at great distances.

Market place promotion

The added value of Thai expertise when combined with OTOP products has attracted the interest of both Thai and foreign consumers. The success of OTOP implementation can be seen at trade fairs and exhibitions, which are held to provide market places for producers who then have the opportunity to assess the needs of consumers. Trade fairs and exhibitions have been organized both locally and abroad.

In 2001, which was the first year that OTOP products were available to the public, there were 17 trade fairs held nationwide. There were also fairs and exhibitions held abroad by way of Thai embassies. There were four 'OTOP City Fairs' organized annually during 2003–2006 with many activities created alongside products sales. The first fair was initiated under the theme 'The City of Thai Wisdom'. The highlight of the second fair was the display provided by Oita Prefecture from Japan, affording Thais the opportunity to learn about the original concept of OTOP and in so doing, experiencing the same pride in their local expertise as the Japanese do. The latest fair was held in July 2007 and was called 'OTOP Mid-Year Sales 2007'. 1850 stalls of OTOP entrepreneurs joined the Mid-Year Fair and many activities were created to motivate the people to visit and purchase goods. It was expected that OTOP products would enjoy greater sales and provide more attractions at the 5th OTOP City Fair held in late 2007, particularly as it coincided with the celebration of the King's 80th birthday.

Another activity created by the private sector as a marketing promotion channel is a website (www.thaitambon.com), which was set up to distribute all information concerning the OTOP project. At present, details of 16,797 products from 5054 *tambon* have already been uploaded onto the website and sales are recorded of over Bt20,000 million (US$606 million) per year. This website effectively links domestic markets to international markets and also producers to consumers. In order to facilitate public relations, in line with marketing channels, a product information system is required nationwide. There is still a requirement to upload an additional 3500 products and services onto the website.

In addition, marketing channels for product gathering and distribution are planned to take the form of network distribution hubs. Thousands of product distribution places will be created in practical locations at the regional level, for example, in department stores, tourist attractions, petrol stations and education institutions. Also, 75 marketing networks are planned with at least one network per province.

Technical inputs

Most entrepreneurs of OTOP need to be supported with regard to technical knowledge. Normally, public agencies are the main support and provide facilities and techniques based on the entrepreneurs' and communities' requirements but particularly on the production process, marketing development or product design and environmental management, as well as business management systems. Most local manufacturers know only what they can produce from their local expertise but not from modern management techniques. There is also technical assistance provided for entrepreneurs by public, private and technical agencies such as education institutions, allowing constant updates.

Duration of the project

OTOP has been implemented since 2001 and the Thai government has decided to extend it indefinitely. It is assumed that the project will last a long time as it is beneficial to all stakeholders and it is a practical tool for the Thai government to use for poverty alleviation.

Funding for the project

Government

When the government launched OTOP, the seed fund it provided Bt1,500 million (US$45 million). Since implementation, funding has been provided by the government through government agencies throughout the years of budget allocation. For OTOP City Fairs, Bt80 million (US$2.4 million) was spent in the first fair in 2003, Bt200 million (US$6 million) on the second and third fairs in 2004 and 2005, and Bt100 million (US$3 million) on the fourth fair in 2006 (OSMEP, 2007). In addition, Bt80 million (US$2.4 million) was provided for OTOP Mid-Year Sales in 2007. Normally, the Department of Community Development is the key organization through which funding is allocated by the government for OTOP City Fairs.

Communities and corporations

A good example of private assistance to OTOP is the website creation. This website helps promote activities relating to the OTOP project including providing opportunities for entrepreneurs and customers to meet their need for sales. A further example of the private sector's help includes the support provided by such entities as The Federation of Thai Industries, Thai Chamber of Commerce, Association for the Promotion of Thai Small and Medium Entrepreneurs, and many other private associations.

External assistance

There has been assistance from Japan as the OTOP project developed the concept of the Japanese OVOP. Thailand has received assistance from Japanese agencies, for example, the Ministry of Trade and Industry assisted the project through Japanese experts, training in Japan for human resources development, and providing business opportunities such as exhibitions, trade fairs and business matching.

In 2006, OTOP products of Thailand were displayed in the Maekong Exhibition in Tokyo (Ministry of Economy, Trade and Industry, 2006). Thailand is learning from Japan's experiences and is gaining more knowledge from transferring methods, a key input for the OTOP project to reach its expected potential.

Project management

The management process of OTOP has two strands. The top-down management process is the line of management for issuing policies, strategies and action plans. The line of management runs down from the government cabinet to the National (Central) Committee and then to the Provincial Committee. The line then runs down to the District/Sub-district Committee and to the Tambon Committee. The National Committee on OTOP Administration was established and the deputy prime minister was assigned to be the chairman. The role of the Committee is to set up a management mechanism for OTOP and to issue standards and criteria of selecting and listing top products. The National Committee also scrutinizes the project operation. There are five sub-committees to support efficient implementation in the sectors concerned. Second, is the bottom-up line of management concerning OTOP product selection starting at the *tambon* level. The Tambon Committee explains concepts and arranges the meetings of communities to select the top products. After this, the selected products are submitted to the Amphor (group of *tambon* or District) Committee that prioritizes the product range and position of the top products from all *tambons* and then submits the list to the Provincial Committee. The Amphor Committee also integrates plans and allocates budget. The Provincial Committee then prioritizes products from the Amphor and submits them to the National Committee that has a key role in issuing criteria for Product Champions selection and listing of *tambon*. The Central Committee also ensures that products are in line with policies, strategies and action plans. The OTOP project management chart is shown in Figure 6.1.

Implementing agency

Implementation is undertaken by cooperating government agencies, which consist of the Department of Community Development under the Ministry of Interior, the Industrial Promotion Department and the Thai Industrial Standards Institute under the Ministry of Industry, the Ministry of Agriculture and Cooperatives, the Department of Export Promotion under the Ministry of Commerce, and the Ministry of Foreign Affairs. Some other organizations such as the Ministry of Science and Technology, the Ministry of Education, the Ministry of Public Health, the Ministry of Employment and Social Welfare, and the Ministry of Defense also give their assistance to OTOP. All agencies work together through

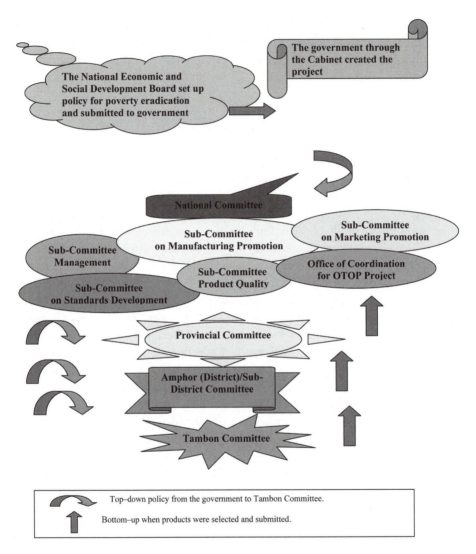

Figure 6.1 *OTOP management structure*

their networks at provincial level, and therefore information can be coordinated throughout the country. Private bodies such as the Foundation of Thai Industry as well as the Thai Chamber of Commerce are also key organizations in providing assistance to the government in developing OTOP products and communities through their networks at provincial level. Moreover, technical institutions assist with knowledge management and experience, while financial institutions lend support on financial fund management and some kinds of entrepreneurial development.

Coordination mechanisms

Committees are used as the management mechanism for OTOP. The committees assign management teams for each activity and to follow up and monitor work that has already been completed. Working through committees also draws out all view points and integrates problems or obstacles and often results in them giving recommendations to the project.

The committees are set up from national to *tambon* and community levels so that they can cover all activities required. Additionally, sub-committees are established to cover activities in sectors in order to cope with entrepreneurs and community development. The management team of OTOP uses both formal and informal systems for coordinating the agencies concerned in public and private sectors including education and financial institutions. Apart from this, there has been support from donor countries such as Japan and Germany, and from the UN. By this method of coordination, most of the necessary activities related to the project have been executed and evaluated for developmental progress in accordance with policy objectives.

Outcomes of OTOP

The number of entrepreneurs has increased from 7000 in 2001 to 38,740 enterprises in 2006 throughout Thailand. More than 1000 enterprises have become exporters. Employment data show the increasing number of employees as a result of the project reached 611,990 in 2006.

Another indicator of success is the OTOP City Fairs, organized annually, where sales revenue has increased significantly. The reputation of the project's success is not just confined to Thailand but it has also spread abroad through many foreign representatives visiting OTOP City Fairs to get experience and knowledge of OTOP project performance. The CEO Forum of the Association of Development Financial Institutions in Asia and the Pacific had its delegates visit the 5th OTOP City Fair in order to gain experience regarding OTOP success.

Sales of OTOP products had increased up to the Third Fair, as is shown in Table 6.1, however, in 2006, a coup d'etat took place and this negatively affected consumer confidence and sales.

In the first year that the OTOP project was launched sales reached only Bt216 million (US$6.5 million). In 2002 when the project was fully implemented sales rose to Bt23,987 million (US$726 million), much higher than the forecast of Bt10,906 million (US$330 million). In 2003, sales revenue was Bt33,727 million (US$1022 million) rising to Bt46,363 million (US$1405 million) in 2004. The value of revenue from sales was Bt55,105 million (US$1670 million) in 2005 rising to Bt67,859 million (US$2056) in 2006. In 2007 (October 2006 to May 2007), sales revenue was Bt38,749 million (US$1174 million) (OSMEP, 2007).

Table 6.1 *Revenue from sales at OTOP City Fairs and Mid-Year Sales events*

Year	Fair	Revenue from Sales (Bt million)	Fund Provided by Government (Bt million)
2003	1st OTOP City Fair	835	80
2004	2nd OTOP City Fair	1,138	200
2005	3rd OTOP City Fair	1,127	200
2006	4th OTOP City Fair	359	100
2007	OTOP Mid-Year Sales	400	80

Source: OSMEP, http://www.thaitambon.com

As the figures show, the project can generate sufficient income to lead to poverty reduction at a grassroots level, thus achieving the major objective of OTOP.

The successful outcome of the project is seen when communities, especially in rural areas, develop and become stronger as a result of the infrastructure and communications brought to the community. Well being is enhanced because families can remain together and earn more income without moving to Bangkok. Moreover, the government agencies and private sector, as well as other parts of society, have delivered on their pledges to the community, especially at the grass-roots level. Thai people are proud that their local expertise has met the modern needs of the markets and strengthened those markets.

Thailand, therefore, enjoys a good reputation for its ability to apply the concept of the OVOP of Japan to the OTOP of Thailand according to 'The Philosophy of Sufficiency Economy' of His Majesty the King. This has meant both growth and strength in Thailand.

Challenges and how they were overcome

Challenges that the project faced were how to make it sustainable and lead to poverty reduction and, secondly, how it could become nationwide and gain acceptance from the Thai people. These challenges have been overcome by the government by issuing policy, strategies and plans of action that have been distributed through the committees and agencies concerned, enabling the project to be wholly understood as both a concept and operating system. Using a networking cooperation strategy throughout the country, the policy has been implemented nationwide.

Another challenge was those communities that lacked opportunities to participate and make products that could meet the needs of the market. These producers have also faced problems from infringement and product copying. To deal with this challenge, the government has delivered knowledge and experience sharing through training courses for some of the topics required and set up a strategy concerning market opportunities through trade fairs and exhibitions, which have been organized throughout the year both locally and abroad.

Lessons learned from OTOP

Success factors

OTOP's success is due to three factors. First, the monarchy in Thailand is widely respected and inspires Thai people through its example of hard work and projects to improve the lives of poor people (Energy Information System Development Division, 2006). Second, most Thai people are influenced by the Buddhist concept of 'loving kindnesses'. The idea of help and cooperation to reduce poverty willingly and without reward is part of Buddhist teachings. Third, the Thai government together with all stakeholders put a great effort into running the project and can take satisfaction in the results. All beneficiaries are proud of their contribution to the development process of the nation brought about through the project's contribution to poverty reduction.

Role of champions

Entrepreneurs who are selected as 'Product Champions' are proud of their creativity and high quality products. They know that their products are trusted by their customers. Product Champion entrepreneurs set an example to other entrepreneurs in terms of their experiences of production together with participation in community development, especially employment building, local expertise and raw material utilization. They can share their experiences with others and can gain more knowledge through assistance from relevant organizations. Normally, five-star Product Champion entrepreneurs become exporters. The key role of Champions is as representatives of Thai products in the global market, bringing economic benefits to the whole nation.

Support

Support for OTOP comes from all stakeholders but especially from the government in terms of both financial and non-financial support. Communities have played a major role in terms of raw materials, human resources and local expertise to support the project.

Motivation

OTOP entrepreneurs are motivated by the desire to meet market needs. Previously they lacked the knowledge to tailor their products to the market and instead their products reflected their skills and available raw materials. They lacked knowledge of how to sell and manage their businesses. After OTOP was launched, local entrepreneurs started to learn more and gain more experience from other stakeholders. They also learned to know that market forces are important for them as well as the production process. The other motivation for OTOP entrepreneurs is the Product Champion Scheme, which can lead them into the global market.

Other innovations

The New Way

In 2006, the Thai government adapted, developed and expanded the scope of OTOP to become the 'Project on Community and Local Product Promotion'. Products in the expanded OTOP project are adapted and divided into two categories: 'community products' and 'local products'. In addition, there are five categories of product: food, beverages, cloth and clothing, ornaments and souvenirs and herbal products. Entrepreneurs are divided into three categories: community producer groups, community producers and SME producers. In 2007, the government established a new policy for promoting community and local products under the theme of the 'New Way of OTOP', which focuses mainly on the community instead of the product. A one-stop service is promoted under the 'New Way' and marketing has become the leading device to link consumers with producers (*Thairath* Newspaper, 2007).

The New Way has also seen the introduction of 'Prime Minister Awards for Honorable Persons of Community and Quality Producers'. These awards will be given to those persons who have shown extraordinary sacrifice and devotion in their key role in local community development. The 'New Way' provides guidelines to upgrade community economies in such a way that the community is the product creator and meets market needs through quality and efficiency.

Success cases

Jirapha Ceramic Company Ltd, Samuthsakorn Province: 'Benjarong'

An outstanding example of a five-star Product Champion is Jirapha Ceramic Company Ltd, located in Samuthsakorn Province. Jirapha Ceramic produces the high quality ceramic products called 'Benjarong', which are hand-made, carefully crafted and then hand-painted. The company sells worldwide and has competitive pricing. With regard to human resources, Jirapha has helped surrounding areas and the local community with employment and better living standards. Local people are trained and taught how to paint by the factory. They are then able to take the raw products back to their communities where they can work. The company has created both employment and income generation while increasing revenue from Bt8 million (US$242,424) per annum to Bt10 million (US$303,030) per annum after joining the OTOP project.

J. Angel Rice Company Ltd, Rachaburi Province: Skin care products

J. Angel Rice Company Ltd specializes in skin care products made of a Thai rice milk vitamin from rice grain germ. The company at first started business with raw materials from Thai rice 20 years ago in Rachaburi Province. The concept of using extracts from rice grain germ was registered as a sub-patent right at the Department of Intellectual Property, leading to certification of its standards. In addition, the skin care products are produced in the factory that has passed quality standard tests by Rangsit University. J. Angel Rice was selected as a five-star Champion Product at national level and has a good opportunity to become a Premium Grade A Product. In addition, the company has created employment by buying rice from farmers, while packaging is hand made by groups of people in Amphor Suanphueng. Additionally, various kinds of herb are ordered from groups of planters. The product stimulates the use of Thai rice products and is marketed internationally.

Songkla Golden Mermaid Company Ltd, Songkla Province: 'Mermaid' shrimp products

These products are produced in Songkla Province, which has a long history of traditional working practices being passed from generation to generation. In terms of product development, shrimp from Songkla Lake are solid, sweet and rich and pass manufacturing standards, including halal standards. After joining OTOP, the company was invited to attend marketing and packaging courses organized by the Community Development Agency in Songkla Province. At present, Mermaid shrimp crackers and crystal shrimp have been selected as four- and three-star products and are popular among consumers in both domestic and international markets. The company obtained assistance from the government to promote sales abroad in countries such as China, Lao, Malaysia and Cambodia. The products generate jobs and income for the local community and have received continuous support from OTOP.

Good practice

OTOP creates employment and generates income in local areas as well as contributing to local human resources development. Moreover, Thai expertise and local knowledge is utilized in combination with modern knowledge for value creation in the form of product development.

Setting an example

OTOP is a very good example to countries that require community development at grassroots level and poverty reduction in rural areas. The first step is dissemination of the project's concept so that its aims are clearly understood. A national policy framework is also necessary to create a project, its strategy and action plans. Cooperation at all levels is needed for project management and a core agency is required to urge all stakeholders to cooperate and work together towards the same goal. At present, Cambodia is an example of a country that has applied the OVOP concept from Japan and the OTOP concept from Thailand with Japanese assistance. Nepal has also adopted the approach.

Recommendations

Ethical standards and professional codes of conduct are essential for all stakeholders of the project and are important in the business world. Trust promotes strong team work, especially in the absence of robust consumer protection laws. Therefore, concentrating purely on product development is not enough to make project growth sustainable. Ethical and professional codes of conduct help all parties create the good reputation necessary for project growth and sustainability. Most importantly, a project of this scale and importance to the national interest must be driven by a government that is able to capitalize upon the strengths of the population.

Conclusions

OTOP was initiated by the Thai government as a tool for poverty reduction. It creates jobs, increases skill levels and increases income generation activities that benefit the community. Following Thailand's experiences with OTOP, it is clear that other countries could utilize most of the principles that have been successful in Thailand in an effort to reduce poverty.

Notes

1   Manager, International Relations Division, President Office, SME Development Bank of Thailand.
2   Hospital Director, Chulabhorn Cancer Centre, Chulabhorn Research Institute.
3   Secretary General, Association of Development Financing Institutions in Asia and the Pacific.

References

Chutimaskul, W. (2006) Thailand's eGovernment for Poverty Reduction and Helping the Disadvantaged Groups, School of Information Technology, King Mongkut's University of Technology Thonburi, *Handout for Capacity Building of Asia Pacific eGovernment Initiatives*, 24–25 April, Thailand

Energy Information System Development Division (2006) 'Thailand at a glance', Country Overview, Energy Information System Development Division, Bureau of Energy Policy and Plan, Energy Policy & Planning Office, Ministry of Energy, Bangkok, Thailand, available at www.eppo.go.th/indicators/country_overview.html

Ministry of Economy, Trade and Industry (2006) 'One Village, One Product Campaign', Tokyo, Ministry of Economy, Trade and Industry

Ministry of Foreign Affairs (2007) Kingdom of Thailand: OTOP Project, www.mfa.go.th/web/1146.php, Ministry of Foreign Affairs, Bangkok, Thailand

Thairath Newspaper (2007) 'New wave of OTOP', *Thairath Newspaper*, Bangkok, Sunday 8 July, p32

PART III

Agriculture and Rural Development for Poverty Reduction

7

Dairy Projects in Afghanistan

Lutfullah Rlung

Introduction

Afghanistan stretches over a total area of 652,000 square kilometres bordering with China, Iran, Pakistan, Tajikistan, Turkmenistan and Uzbekistan. The population was estimated at just over 25 million in 2006 with an annual growth rate of 2.03 per cent. Only 12 per cent (7.9 million hectares) of the land is arable and 4 per cent (2.6 million hectares) is irrigated. Rapid deforestation has reduced forest cover to only about 2 per cent of the land, which is under threat of being cleared. An additional 46 per cent of land is under permanent pasture and 39 per cent is mountainous. Geographically, about 75 per cent of the arable area is concentrated in three of the eight agricultural planning regions of the country – north, northeast and west. Of the total arable area, not more than half is actually cultivated annually, mainly because of a lack of water (FAO, 2005).

Landlocked and mountainous, Afghanistan has suffered from instability and conflict during its modern history, thus ruining its economy and infrastructure and leaving more than 3 million people as refugees, mostly in neighbouring countries. The country is also afflicted by natural disasters such as droughts, floods, earthquakes and severe frosts.

There is a very high level of micronutrient deficiency among children and the elderly that is caused mainly by the absence of a balanced diet, combined with a high prevalence of some diseases. Results from the 2003 National Rural Vulnerability Assessment (MRRD and WFP, 2004) show that 57 per cent of people have very little diversity in their diets.

In a country where 80 per cent of the population relies directly on the natural resource base to meet its daily needs, widespread environmental degradation poses an immense threat to livelihoods. More than two decades of conflict, military activities, refugee movements, collapse of national, provincial and local forms of governance, lack of management and institutional capacity, and over-exploitation have heavily damaged Afghanistan's natural resource base. The recent long drought

Figure 7.1 *Afghan dairy*

Source: FAO (2005)

has had an additional negative impact. As a result, the country's vulnerability to natural disasters and food shortages has increased.

In a low-income country like Afghanistan, food security is uppermost in the minds of the people and their government. Agriculture initially ensures food security by producing the basic food requirement for each family. As development occurs and generates income, food can be purchased both by the government and by individual families, and commodities can become more specialized and better suited to the natural resource base. For Afghanistan, the need is to produce staple food crops in a reduced area so that more land can be devoted to the high value commodities.

There are a large number of people with small plots of land that provide little income or employment. These people, often classified as farmers, are part of the rural non-farm population. Thus, massive increase in employment in the rural non-farm sector is needed. However, the goods and services of the rural non-farm sector almost all go to the local market. They cannot be sold in international markets as they do not meet processing and packaging standards.

The political situation

After two decades of civil war, Afghanistan is governed by the Islamic Republic of Afghanistan. Before that, Afghanistan was governed by the Islamic Transitional Government of Afghanistan, a government that followed the Afghan Interim Authority. The Interim Authority was inaugurated on 22 December 2001 and administered Afghanistan until June 2004.

In 2006, the insurgency, illegal narcotics, corruption and problems of governance, among others, all left their mark and, to some extent, damaged public confidence. The resurgence of violence, particularly the Taliban insurgency, is a major concern that could pose a serious threat to the ongoing process of reconstruction in Afghanistan.

The current parliament was inaugurated on 19 December 2005 and the president presented his cabinet to the Wolesi Jirga (Lower House of Parliament) in 2006.

The project

Livestock keeping is an important element of the Afghanistan economy both for home consumption and for sale of livestock products. For a large proportion of the rural population, cattle are the most important animal species and increase in milk production for sale and home consumption is seen by many farmers as an important development opportunity. With an increasing number of people living in the cities and having higher incomes, there is also an increasing demand for livestock products, offering a good opportunity to invest in the sector and produce for the urban markets. Increased milk production can primarily be achieved by increasing productivity through better feeding and management, improved genetic potential of the cattle and good animal health. For dairy development, establishment of efficient marketing facilities is another important prerequisite. The strong internal demand for dairy products provides a good basis for a viable commercial dairy sector.

Dairy appears to be a key source of household income, especially for women, and improved nutrition among rural families, particularly for poor households. Improving milk production and distribution could therefore be an excellent instrument to increase rural women's household incomes and household nutrition. The Afghan diet traditionally includes a substantial amount of meat and milk as a vital source of food and livestock provide wool, leather, manure, fuel and farm power too. Indeed, for many rural families, farm animals supply the household's only source of cash income. For dairy development, the establishment of efficient marketing facilities is another equally important prerequisite. The Afghanistan National Development Strategy (ANDS) states that the Afghan children suffer from widespread chronic malnutrition, and over half (54 per cent) of Afghan children between 6 and 59 months old have stunted growth (Islamic Republic of Afghanistan, 2005).

Over the last seven years, the Food and Agriculture Organization (FAO) has demonstrated in three locations the opportunities and successes of small-scale integrated dairy production schemes. In addition to dairy development, the FAO programme in Afghanistan has extensive experience in the field of animal health from establishing a network of community-based veterinary field units (VFUs) for eradicating Rinderpest following its most recent entry into the country (1995–1997), for strategic surveillance for transboundary animal diseases and for establishing a diagnostic laboratory for the continuous control of common endemic diseases. Through its development work for small-scale poultry production, FAO in Afghanistan also has broad experience in working with village women, enabling them to get involved and benefit from the development process.

The establishment of small dairy schemes is important in rural areas because:

- milk production is a very important part of the rural economy;
- most villagers have milk surpluses that they would like to sell as marketable surplus;
- there is demand for milk and dairy products in the markets close to villages;
- although the majority of cattle are of local origin, a larger number of exotic and crossbred cattle already exist around cities; and
- an increase in production requires improved management, feeding and development of the breeding stock.

German-funded dairy projects have been supporting the development of the dairy schemes since 2003. Their main components are as follows:

- Raising the quality of available fodder through the selection and distribution of new and improved fodder varieties, conducting demonstrations with

Figure 7.2 *Milk collection*

Source: MAIL (2005)

selected farmers and establishing producer groups to organize the production of seed of improved fodder types.

- Facilitating breed improvement through the provision of quality sires and imported semen at artificial insemination centres at strategic locations.
- Improving access to markets for milk and milk products by establishing milk collection schemes on the fringes of major cities, together with processing centres to ensure that the milk and milk products are hygienic and available to customers.
- Assisting in the formation of milk producer groups as a mean of raising knowledge, particularly in feeding regimes, animal husbandry and care, and coordinating milk collection.
- Raising knowledge of the impacts of animal parasites and disease and the actions to combat diseases (MAIL, 2005).

Project formulation

Most farmers have one or two cattle that, during the lactation period, can produce 5–10 litres of milk per day. Part of this is consumed by family and the surplus is supplied to the market. The rural market is very small and cannot absorb all the surplus milk of the farmers. The Project for Development of Integrated Dairy Schemes in Afghanistan identified this problem and, after discussions with milk producers, a milk producer group was initiated at the village level. This group made a collection point for milk, which was later called a 'milk collection centre' (MCC). The MCCs were expanded to different locations at district and provincial levels. In order to improve the management and marketing of the milk, the farmers established milk production cooperatives at district and provincial levels. After a time receiving financial and technical support from the project and benefiting from government policy to support the private sector, the cooperative members created a Dairy Union.

In the fight against hunger, the project strives to encourage voluntary farmers' participation and organization at village, community and national levels. Cooperatives as a means of encouraging peoples' participation provide not only opportunities for income generation through employment and enterprise development, but also can reduce the cost of inputs and other goods and services to farmers. Afghanistan has long recognized the role of cooperatives in its national development agenda. The project supported the government to create policy and legislative frameworks for the development of dairy sector cooperatives through mechanisms such as the Cooperative Law.

Seven milk producers' cooperative societies (MPCSs) have been registered under the Cooperative Department of the Ministry of Agriculture, Irrigation and Livestock (MAIL) under the Kabul Milk Scheme in the provinces of Wardak and Logar. In turn, these seven MPCSs have joined together and formed the Kabul Dairy Union (KDU), with 416 registered members and as per the newly-approved

Cooperative Law of Afghanistan. KDU was officially registered with MAIL on 29 November 2006; this is the first cooperative dairy union formed in Afghanistan. Kunduz Dairy Union, with 208 registered members, was also officially registered with MAIL on 13 January 2007.

The project has given technical and financial support to the Dairy Union's cooperatives to make linkages between rural and urban markets. The project helped the cooperatives to register with government. As registered organizations, cooperatives have attained the right to benefit from various opportunities available in the country. For example, Mazar Dairy Union received about US$500,000 of processing machinery and equipment from a USAID organization, which enabled it to produce and supply attractive products to the large market of Mazar.

The project built up the capacity of the Dairy Union to transport fresh milk to small processing plants in the big cities every day and, after processing, it is supplied to the consumer market. The cooperatives made contracts with the shopkeepers in populated areas of the cities to supply dairy products on a daily basis and meet the demand of the area. People prefer to purchase fresh local dairy products in the cities, despite the fact that the quality of local packaging is poor compared to imported products, because imported products are more expensive. The aim is that by the end of the project the ownership of all plants will be transferred from the government to the private sector (Dairy Union).

Encouraging the private sector's involvement has been the centrepiece of the idea behind the project. The project:

- supports the development of a private dairy industry in close cooperation with the public sector;
- has been instrumental in translating the commitments of the Government of Afghanistan to developing the livestock private sector with practical activities; and
- assists through policy development and the participation of all stakeholders in the further clarification of the responsibilities of the Afghan government in the field of livestock production.

Project goals and objectives

The goal of the project is to improve food security in Afghanistan by raising the productive capacity of the national dairy sector through the development of integrated model dairy schemes. The immediate objectives of the project are to:

- increase the consumable and saleable products from cattle;
- develop processing and marketing structures for milk and dairy products;
- develop cooperative organizational structures for the management of the three dairy schemes in Kabul, Mazar and Kunduz; and
- assist with the development of policies and strategies for the dairy sector.

Key elements of the project

Target beneficiaries

The intended target beneficiaries of the project will be around 2000 village families from the targeted areas. Unintended beneficiaries, who include government officials, institutions/organizations and consumers, are numerous.

Project area

This project covers Mazar and Kunduz Provinces and Kabul Region in Logar and Wardak provinces. The project's intervention in fodder production and extension activities for cattle over the past year has shown that Kunduz Province is potentially a suitable location for the development of dairy production. It is therefore planned to extend the approach, which was developed in Kabul and Mazar Provinces to Kunduz Province. Efforts to further develop the dairy sectors in Kandahar and Nangarhar Provinces did not progress as anticipated, primarily due to the precarious security situation in these provinces.

Project activities

Key project components are:

- raising the quality of available fodder;
- promoting the use of concentrates and minerals as feed;
- raising knowledge on animal health issues, improved management and hygiene;
- facilitating breed improvement through artificial insemination (AI);
- assisting in the formation of milk producer groups that include processing and marketing groups; and
- improving access to markets for milk and milk products.

Key activities

Three milk processing facilities operating on a commercial basis

Milk processing facilities are operating on a commercial basis. The three integrated dairy schemes (IDS) have reached the maximum capacity of milk handling and processing, based on currently available equipment and facilities.

Animal health services

Animal health services include:

- monitoring and control of the zoonotic diseases of dairy cattle;
- providing regular vaccination for the cattle against common infectious diseases (FMD, HS, BL and anthrax);
- monitoring the reproductive performance of the cows and providing veterinary services; and
- training farmers (men and women) in animal health.

Fodder crop and feeding

This includes:

- propagating the cultivation and proper use of improved fodder crops for dairy members;
- introducing seeds of improved varieties of fodder crops as per climatic condition of area for cultivation via demonstration plots;
- organizing the production and marketing of improved fodder seeds;
- arranging the commercial production and marketing of concentrate and mineral feeds through the dairy scheme; and
- practically training farmers.

Cattle housing activities

Cattle housing activities include:

- surveys to investigate cattle keeping problems;
- increasing farmers' technical knowledge regarding proper keeping of cattle in stables;
- introducing improved cattle stables as demonstration projects at village level; and
- providing necessary items for stables as a bonus or incentive.

Artificial insemination

The AI process includes:

- procuring semen straws and equipment for AI;
- supporting AI technicians to implement AI activities for the member farmers of the dairy scheme;
- monitoring the result of the AI activities and advising and assisting the farmers in the proper management and feeding of resulting livestock offspring; and
- training farmers in proper breeding times and selection of bulls for breeding.

Figure 7.3 *Training technical staff*

Source: MAIL (2005)

Training programme

The training programme involves:

- training farmers (women and men) on animal husbandry and animal health fields and livelihood issues;
- training leaders of cooperatives and associations on leadership skills, management and accounting; and
- training technical staff (project and government staff) on planning, management and policy issues.

Processing and marketing of milk and dairy products

The processing and marketing of dairy products involves:

- establishing and developing village MCCs and providing the necessary tools and equipment for measuring quantity and quality of milk;
- regular collection of daily milk from member farmers and inspection of quantity and quality of the milk;
- proper recording of milk collection and weekly payments according to quantity and quality;
- establishing proper processing and storage facilities for milk, yoghurt and cheese with the capacity of 8792 litres of milk per day in three processing plants in Kabul, Kunduz and Balkh Provinces;
- procuring and installing the necessary equipment for processing, storage and packing;

- producing hygienic pasteurized milk and dairy products for public consumption in two main centres;
- making sales agreements with agents in different areas;
- creating awareness among consumers about hygienic and quality dairy products; and
- generating income for the development of the milk schemes.

Establishment of MPCSs at village level

This involves:

- promoting their membership to village MCCs among dairy farmers;
- holding regular meetings to inform member farmers about conditions and activities of the milk schemes; and
- distributing and selling of inputs through the village MCCs;

Establishment of dairy associations at province level

Establishing dairy associations involves:

- getting approval from the government for a legalized framework for the dairy schemes;
- developing farmers' representation for the management of the dairy schemes;
- developing independent staff and management structures for the dairy schemes including their processing centres;
- creating and developing financial management systems and performance monitoring of the dairy schemes; and
- the transferring of full financial and operational responsibility to the management of the dairy schemes.

Key technical inputs

Technical staff include a senior dairy advisor, national field manager, national consultants, field technicians and counterparts.

Timeframe

The project extended from 1 April 2005 to 31 March 2008.

Outputs

The project outputs have been achieved through a bottom-up approach and community participation throughout project planning, implementation and operation. The project has been implemented with close coordination and collaboration of MAIL and developed on the basis of community demands.

The first three outputs listed below take into consideration the cultural limitations of organized women's groups and involved the help of female staff of the project, and trained and emprowered women on livestock management and other related issues. Project outputs include:

- increased women's participation in livestock production through hiring female trainers to train women on livestock management-related subjects;
- increased decision-making powers for women through organizing women's groups;
- women receiving more than 80 per cent of income from dairy production; this is because women became empowered in terms of decision making and better management of livestock so they could participate in decision making within their households and gain more income;
- increased access to regular and dependable raw milk for raw milk producers in the market;
- increased household income from livestock production;
- increased level of employment at grassroots level;
- control of 95.33 per cent of foot and mouth disease and tick-born diseases and also of zoonotic diseases and mastitis in the targeted areas of the project;
- improved breeds of cattle for more than 45 per cent of selected farmers;
- cultivation of improved fodder crops by more than 70 per cent of selected farmers; and
- an increase in milk production from 1.22 litres to 5.14 litres per farmer per day from 2002–2007 (in 2007, data cover only the first six months), as shown in Table 7.1.

The increase in surplus milk production per farmer per day is due to an increase in the number of animals per farmer as well as increases in milk productivity. Milk productivity has steadily increased from 1 litre per cow per day in 2002 to almost 5 litres per cow per day in 2007 (see Table 7.1), reflecting a 4.5 fold increase. As shown in Figure 7.4, annual milk production from all the MCCs has dramatically increased from 32,530 litres in 2002 to 1,932,664 litres in 2006.

Table 7.1 *Increases in milk production and household income*

Description	2002	2003	2004	2005	2006	2007
Average milk production (litres) per day per community	232	1,795	3,522	4,112	5,414	6,274
Surplus milk (litres) per farmer per day	1.22	2.72	4.32	4.21	4.61	5.14
Milk yield (litres) per cow per day	1.11	2.49	3.68	3.71	4.28	4.96
Number of farmers	190	659	816	976	1175	1220
Number of milking cows per community	210	720	957	1107	1265	1265
Milk price (Afs) per litre	6.5 (US$0.13)	8 (US$0.16)	9 (US$0.18)	12 (US$0.24)	13 (US$0.26)	14 (US$0.28)
Income (Afs) per farmer per day	7.93 (US$0.15)	21.76 (US$0.44)	38.85 (US$0.78)	50.56 (US$1.02)	59.90 (US$1.20)	72.00 (US$1.45)

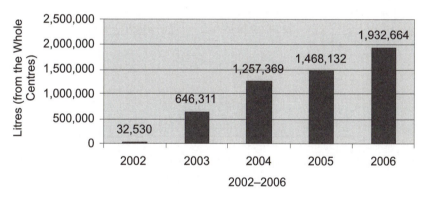

Figure 7.4 *Variation in milk production of all MCCs*

Total project cost

The total project cost is EU€1.5 million and the Government of Germany sponsors the project through its German Trust Fund.

Project management

The overall management of the project is the responsibility of the national field manager based in Kabul, while a senior dairy advisor visits and assists the implementation of the project in close coordination and collaboration with the Department of Animal Husbandry of MAIL.

A Letter of Agreement was signed with Balkh Livestock Development Centre (BLDC) in August 2006, handing over the operational and business responsibility of Mazar Dairy Scheme to the BLDC. Technical subject matter assistants are also transferred to the BLDC under that agreement. These assistants help the cooperative dairy farmers in Mazar to operate and manage the business in a sustainable way.

Implementing agency

The implementing agency is the FAO of the UN.

Coordination mechanisms

There are three steering committees organized in Kabul, Kunduz and Mazar-e-Sharif by the Department of Animal Husbandry of MAIL (also acting as Chair), FAO project staff and Dairy Union representatives and held on a monthly basis to discuss planning, management, policy issues and marketing aspects of the project, see Figures 7.5 and 7.6.

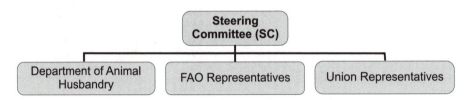

Figure 7.5 *Organization of steering committee*

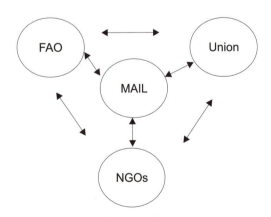

Figure 7.6 *The coordination mechanism among the stakeholders*

In particular, the project assists the coordination of different dairy development activities including a dairy programme recently started by USAID and the promotion of intensive dairy production. The current project focuses on smaller farmers and the production of various dairy products in processing units with a capacity up to 10 million tonnes per day. Establishing cooperative management and ownership structures is part of the project, while it also promotes private ownership of the processing plants by individual entrepreneurs. Figure 7.7 illustrates the organization of the Kabul Dairy Union, similar in structure to the other unions.

Monitoring and evaluation of project activities

The FAO's regional offices in Afghanistan have the capacity to provide on-site daily monitoring, supervision and technical guidance. External monitoring and evaluation will be undertaken in accordance with the general rules of project cycle management. Moreover, government counterparts monitor the project at the central and provincial levels and provide feedback. A final project evaluation mission will be undertaken towards the end of the project, as agreed by donor, Government and FAO.

Challenges faced

The project has faced numerous challenges:

- inadequacy of the processing facilities in terms of size of the schemes and the technology in the processing centres;
- competition from dairy imports (including those produced locally from imported milk powder);
- inadequate profit margins to maintain the schemes;
- scarcity of qualified staff;
- change from aid to development mode;
- deteriorating security situation due to presence of Al-qaida and Taliban mostly in the rural areas; and
- insufficient financial resources.

Lessons learned

Success factors

The development of successful dairy schemes is a complex process involving not only various technical aspects of milk production, milk processing and marketing

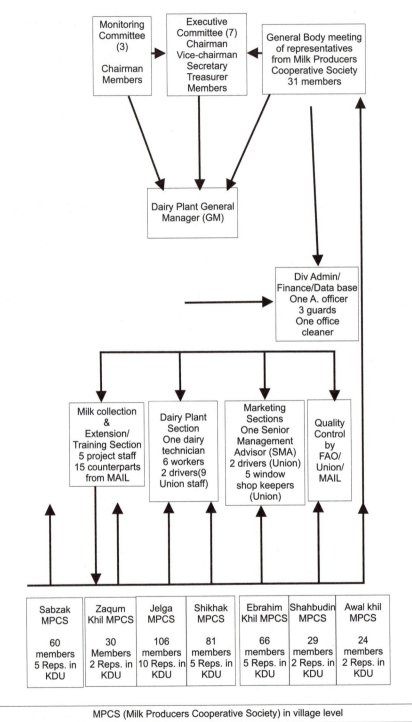

Figure 7.7 *Organizational structure of Kabul Dairy Union*

but also a variety of organizational and policy issues. Therefore, the project may need further support after completion. The general attitude towards dairy products, low purchasing power of the population and the influence of imports of dairy products are also factors to be considered. The initiatives taken during the project period could be valuable to other countries whose geographical and socio-economic status are similar to those in Afghanistan. Success factors are:

- the participatory and bottom-up approach of the project encouraged community participation that led to the setting up of cooperatives and unions by the communities themselves;
- close coordination of activities with the relevant departments of MAIL;
- use of efficient and easy technology, for example, machinery for milk processing and animal food processing;
- creation of the MCCs as a key facility to encourage beneficiaries to bring milk on a daily basis that resulted in the daily production and processing of dairy products; and
- hiring of dedicated and committed staff at the managerial and professional levels; this acted as a crucial factor for the success of the project.

Motivation

During the initial periods, farmers were motivated to participate in the dairy business by their understanding of its importance. Having raised their daily incomes from the sales of fresh milk, they are requesting that the project help set up a processing facility. The dairy cooperative societies at producers and processor levels are also popular.

Support

Farmers are committed to participating in the establishment, operation and management of dairy cooperative societies and farmer-owned milk processing plants in terms of providing land and manpower.

Good practice

The Integrated Dairy Development Project has successfully demonstrated the possibility of local farmers effectively responding to the domestic market demand for milk and milk products through improved knowledge, appropriate farmer-friendly tools, market linkages and the formation of producer and processor groups. These findings enabled some specific recommendations to be made on the development of the dairy sector, forming a key component of the recently approved 'Master Plan for Agriculture' (MAIL, 2005) in Afghanistan.

The project has also demonstrated how a locally available resource (dairy resource) could be better used to lift rural farmers out of poverty, for example, the poverty of 2000 village families was reduced by 19 per cent, consumers were able to purchase high quality and hygienic milk and milk products at a relatively low price and the nutritional status of consumers has improved by 2 per cent in the target area. The demonstration effect of the project has stimulated the Afghan dairy sector as a whole, with a tendency to replicate similar models in non-project locations by other organizations.

Potential for scaling up and replication

The current project approach for dairy sector development was included in the 'National Agricultural Master Plan' in Afghanistan, which reflects the potential for scaling up of the model. Based on the successful achievements and outputs of the FAO dairy project, in 2006 the Government of Italy gave US$2 million to replicate the project with FAO and started a three-year project in Herat Province under the name of 'Integrated Dairy Development Schemes in Herat'.

In 2006, the World Bank invested US$50 million in the two sectors of horticulture and livestock, which are the primary priorities of the Master Plan; the project is named 'Emergency Horticulture and Livestock Project'.

Traditionally, rural Afghan farmers rear just one to two cattle. A recent Livestock Census Survey (MAIL, 2003) has further revealed that about 57.5 per cent of rural families raise cattle. These factors positively influence the chances of replication of the project model. Integrated dairy development that encompasses several components in the milk value chain, namely production, processing and marketing (as opposed to focusing on a single component such as production alone) proved to be effective and a further positive factor for scaling up.

Conclusions

Milk production in Afghanistan has traditionally been practised by individual farmers with very small herds, precluding a sizable supply base for milk. This project has introduced/strengthened the producer cooperative groups concept coupled with MCCs, enabling the collection of a sizable supply of milk. The MCC model avoids the transaction costs of procuring small quantities of milk from a large number of individual farmers. MCCs also perform the function of input sales and livestock services and this cooperative approach has demonstrated the possibility of reducing the cost of inputs and livestock services to farmers.

Afghan farmers keep animals including cattle for numerous purposes. Usually the villages have one or two shops that provide different food stuffs to the villagers. The purchasing power of farmers is very limited because there is very little cash in the villages. The farmers also purchase food items at specific periods of the year, therefore, farmers use dairy products as a central food stuff, reducing malnutrition in the rural areas. For example, if a farmer's wife does not have enough breast milk to feed a new-born baby, she will feed the baby with cow's milk or other dairy products. The farmers do not have access to fresh meat to feed their young children regularly and the main source of animal protein for most of the rural children is dairy products. Families without cattle or access to animal products in rural areas are facing malnutrition problems (MAIL, 2005).

The project impact clearly demonstrates that it can contribute towards Afghanistan achieving its MDGs. Thse state that 'By the end-2010, the proportion of people living on less than US$1 a day will decrease by 3 per cent per year and the proportion of people who suffer from hunger will decrease by 5 per cent per year'. One of the priorities of the Agricultural Master Plan is to increase livestock production.

The dairy project has income generation potential for rural people in particular. The project has supported women's socio-economic status at the household and community level. In addition, the project plays a pivotal role in the economic status of rural society and communities. The success of the FAO's dairy activities has encouraged other institutions to start similar initiatives for dairy development. Furthermore, synergy, planning and coordinated efforts for dairy development are necessary.

The farmers should be exposed to all opportunities that are available from the government, private sectors and civil society groups. In addition, the project helps farmers to develop realistic business plans and project management is open and honest with the farmers regarding the failure and success factors of the project. The model is useful for countries where the institutional capacities of governments to provide services such as extension support and input supply are not yet developed and where the private sector is also undeveloped.

References

FAO (2003) *National Rural Vulnerability Assessment*, Food and Agriculture Organization of the United Nations, Kabul, Afghanistan

FAO (2005) *Project Document for Development of Integrated Dairy Schemes in Afghanistan*, GCP/AFG/040/GER, Food and Agriculture Organization of the United Nations, Kabul, Afghanistan

Islamic Republic of Afghanistan (2005) *Afghanistan National Development Strategy (ANDS)*, Islamic Republic of Afghanistan, Kabul, Afghanistan

MAIL (2003) *Livestock Census Survey 2003*, Kabul, FAO and Ministry of Agriculture, Irrigation and Livestock, Kabul, Afghanistan

MAIL (2005) *National Agricultural Master Plan, 2005–2009*, Ministry of Agriculture, Irrigation and Livestock, Kabul, Afghanistan

Information and Communications Technology for Poverty Reduction: Bringing Technology to Rural and Disadvantaged Communities in Western China

Zhao Jinqiu

Introduction

After a modest beginning in the mid-1990s, China now boasts the world's second largest population of internet users,[1] which stood at 137 million people by December 2006, a big jump from 620,000 users in 1997 (CNNIC, 1997; CNNIC, 2007). The internet penetration in China, however, is basically an urban phenomenon that excludes the majority living in rural and remote regions (Wacker, 2000). The number of rural internet users is about 0.5 million, accounting for approximately 0.4 per cent of China's total internet users (CNNIC, 2007). Poor communication infrastructure and low levels of knowledge and incomes have put rural people at a disadvantage, resulting in a huge digital divide between the urban and the rural, the more developed coastal areas in the east and vast rural areas in the west.

Despite its low penetration in the vast rural areas, the internet is generally perceived as a new engine for rural empowerment and quite a number of experimental projects have been started in different parts of China in recent years to test such an assumption. With the aim of indentifying practical solutions to bridge the gap between the urban and rural areas, and exploring the potential that internet adoption and usage could have in helping rural people improve economic conditions, education, healthcare, gender equality and political participation, a case study on an ongoing internet project was conducted at Jinta County, Gansu Province.

Jinta County is located in the northeastern part of Jiuquan City, Gansu Province (see Figure 8.1). As one of the outposts on the ancient Silk Road, Jinta is a rural oasis bordering the Badain Jaran Desert of Inner Mongolia. Around 138,000 rural people live in the county in 123 villages under 13 townships within an area of 18,800 square kilometers, 1.4 per cent of which is arable. Jinta is rich in natural resources, especially in land, underground water, heat energy and minerals. In addition to the arable land, there are more than 1000 square kilometers of unused land suitable for cultivation and grazing. Since ancient times, Jinta has been famous for its irrigated agriculture thanks to 2 rivers running through the county and 14 reservoirs. Jinta also enjoys 3193 hours of sunshine per year and rainfall of 59.5mm. Sharp temperature differences, limited precipitation and quick evaporation render Jinta an ideal base for breeding seeds and growing grain, cotton, corn, sugar beets, cumin and forage crops (Jinta gaikuang, 2005).

Despite the favorable natural conditions that Jinta enjoys, the local farmers remained relatively impoverished before the ICT project was introduced to the county. As Jinta is not within easy reach of any of the national highways, its farmers constantly face the problem of finding potential buyers, even when they have high quality farm produce. Due to limited channels of communication, it is difficult for the farmers to either adjust their farming plans in accordance with market trends or establish business contacts with the outside. The county government hopes to enhance the livelihoods of the rural poor with the aid of ICT such as the internet.

Figure 8.1 *The location of Jinta County, Gansu Province*

The project

China's accession to the World Trade Organization (WTO) poses great challenges to self-subsistence agriculture in the county, which has been managed as part of a planned economy for decades. The opening up of the rural economy makes it more subject to the influences of the market as the supply and demand of farm produce tends to fluctuate with market changes both at the national and the global levels. The inland location and the less developed economy put Jinta farmers at a disadvantage when adapting themselves to market mechanisms and trying to gain an edge over their competitors. The local economy has undergone setbacks resulting from the lack of updated market information. It is not uncommon that farmers' incomes decrease even when output is higher. Therefore, keeping farmers informed about agricultural technologies as well as changes in the prices of farm produce is critical for them to get accustomed to the rules and practices of the market economy, which, in turn, may contribute to the transformation of county economic structures.

Project formulation

The county government started to set up websites in 1999. However, until Shen Juntao became the county head in 2001, no effort was made to meet the information needs of the 110, 000 farmers in Jinta, who form the overwhelming majority of the county population. Changes in the rural economy system and the shifting role of the local government in terms of agricultural production activities served as catalysts for Shen's initiatives of networking the rural households. When Jinta farmers are trying their best to cope with the changes brought about by the market economy, the local government had to shift its role from issuing administrative orders to providing services and consultancy to help farmers make informed production decisions. The new county head, Shen, realized that the old practice of bureaucratic interventions would no longer work under the market mechanism and farmers could suffer huge losses due to production plans prescribed by the government. Shen believed that as the level of risk and uncertainty involved in agricultural production and management tends to be much higher under the impact of market forces, decision making should be left with the individual farmers, letting them be responsible for the possible losses or gains.

When studying rural information, Shen noticed that with networked computers the government agencies at the municipal or county levels were in command of large amounts of up-to-date agricultural information. However, farmers, who made real decisions on production and management, were ill-informed due to their poor economic status, low knowledge levels and geographic isolation. Shen believed the county government could serve the farmers better by setting up a rural information network. After conducting door-to-door surveys in four villages near the county centre, Shen and the staff at Jinta Information and Network Center decided to carry out an ICT project called 'Networking the Villages and Informing the Farming Households' in 2001. The goal of the project was to provide farmers with vital information over the internet.

Key elements of the project

Target beneficiaries and project area

The target beneficiaries of the project are 138,000 rural people living in 123 villages under 13 townships within Jinta County in Western China.

Project activities

During the course of implementing the project, great effort was made to minimize the cost and lower the knowledge barriers that internet technology poses to its rural users. Instead of making huge investments in purchasing servers and other network facilities, the Information and Network Center adopted the concept of virtual servers and set up its websites through renting the server at Lanzhou Telecommunications Bureau. The virtual server helps the centre avoid the possible expenses of technical maintenance of real servers and becomes a cost-effective solution to the extension of internet technology. With US$120 as the annual rental fee, the 13 government websites run by the centre can enjoy the same network quality as users in big cities.

Instead of connecting every rural household, the Information and Network Center uses an innovative way to let agricultural information reach the local farmers. The centre launches a biweekly e-newspaper titled *Jinta Jingji Xinxi Daobao (Jinta Economic Development Herald)*. The content of the paper is compiled by two information technicians with one in charge of information collection and editing, and the other responsible for typesetting and finalizing the paper into an online version. As locally born college graduates, both editors are quite familiar with agricultural production and farmers' information requests for different farming seasons.

Much of the content in the e-paper comes from the national or local agricultural websites. It focuses on information about farming skills, fertilizers, seeds as well as the market supply and demand. According to its chief editor, Li Fagang, the frequently visited websites include *Zhongguo Xingnong Network* (http://www. cnan.gov.cn/), managed by China Meteorological Bureau, which has branch websites in over 34 provinces and municipalities in China. Its branch in Gansu Province, *Gansu Xingnong Network* (http://www.gsnw.net/), supplies the *Herald* with large amounts of information on farming technologies, pest and disease control, fertilizers and pesticides, and current prices of farm produce, which bear close relevance to local agriculture. Information on market analyses and trends can be obtained from Beijing Agricultural Information (http://www.agri.ac.cn/) and

Oriental Agricultural Information (http://www.dfagri.com/, based in Zhejiang Province). Government circulars and documents targeted at farmers serve as another source of information for the *Herald*. Before the existence of the e-paper, the information on farming and government policies from the local agricultural organizations such as the Animal and Husbandry Bureau and the Forestry Bureau had to go through various bureaucratic channels to reach the farmers. This often resulted in delayed transmission and also possible loss of information. The *Herald* now provides the government with an alternative way of spreading its messages among the rural people.

Feedback from readers is also taken into serious consideration when the editors are making preparations for a new issue of the *Herald*. While most of the responses come from phone calls, some are sent by the village information centre via e-mails. When an issue of the *Herald* is ready for publication, the online version is uploaded onto the county government website (www.jtxnet.com). By clicking the hyperlink, one can either read the newspaper online or download it. However, the objective of delivering updated online information to the farmers cannot be achieved simply by putting an e-paper onto the government website. Unlike the traditional method of agricultural extension channeled through government administrations, Shen and his staff succeeded in persuading the village schools to play an active role in disseminating the information.

There are several advantages for the project to situate its information centres at the village schools. First, by circumventing the administrative channels such as the township government and the village committees, the Information and Network Center can greatly speed up the time it takes for the *Herald* to reach the farmers. The majority of the local leaders are still clinging to the old thinking about governance[2] and therefore do not see the need for bringing information to the rural households. This would greatly hinder the effective diffusion of online information among the farmers. Second, as computer literacy is high among school teachers, they take the responsibility of downloading the online newspaper. This not only eases the shortage of qualified technical personnel but also helps to save on outsourcing and hiring costs. Third, many of the local elementary schools have existing networked computers as part of the nationwide distance education programme for rural areas sponsored by the Ministry of Education. By employing the hardware (networked computers) and the brainpower (teachers) at the village schools, the county government can easily promote the extension of online information at the village level without putting extra financial burdens on the local farmers. With a printer and a mimeograph machine, the teachers can download the *Herald* from the government website and print it in hard copies according to the number of village households. Then students can hand deliver the papers to their parents and neighbours.

In addition to its role of distributing the e-paper, the village information centre is also responsible for soliciting feedback from the rural readers. It keeps a log book recording the dates and number of newspapers distributed as well as farmers' responses. If a villager shows interest in a particular piece of information, he may call the Information and Network Center directly or let a student bring his request to the teachers in charge of the operation, who, in turn, email the feedback to the county centre. The village information centre also helps the Information and Network Center conduct surveys to monitor the information requests of the farmers and evaluate the relevance of the information in the *Herald* to the local agricultural production.

Impact and outcomes

From April 2001 to October 2005, 114 issues of the *Herald* were published by Jinta Information and Network Center. Our field observations suggest that the printed copies of the *Herald* have resulted in vast diffusion of the online information on agriculture and the rural market. The *Herald* has become one of the main sources of information for local farmers to make production decisions. To better understand the reasons behind the rapid diffusion of the e-paper, a content analysis was conducted by the researcher on the accessible issues at Jinta government website. The results of the analysis suggest that the *Herald* has been finely attuned to the local information requests as conditioned by seasonal and geographic characteristics. Altogether 1254 information items (as measured by the headlines) were covered within almost 5 years of circulation, with each issue carrying 11 information items, on average.

The most popular categories include farming technologies (744 items, 59.3 per cent), market analysis (271 items, 21.6 per cent), supply and demand posted online (150 items, 12 per cent), public health (59 items, 4.7 per cent), government policies (18 items, 1.4 per cent) and weather forecasts (12 items, 1 per cent). With respect to farming technologies, the skills and tips on livestock raising, disease control, greenhouse cultivation and fertilizers and pesticides carry much more weight than those on crops, cotton, fruit cultivation and new breeds (see Figure 8.2). The variation in coverage reflects the transitions taking place in the county economic structure. As the crop yields have almost reached the maximum after hundreds of years of cultivation, farmers start to turn to sidelines such as livestock rearing (sheep, cows, pigs or chickens) or greenhouse vegetable growing for more income.

The 21st, 22nd and 23rd issues of the *Herald* in 2003 were special editions related to the raising of sheep, pigs and cows. The sheep edition told farmers the problems they should be aware of if they wanted to raise sheep on a large scale. Farmers were also taught how to tell the age of a new breed of sheep and help lambs put on weight after suckling. The pig edition discussed eight kinds of diseases easily contracted by pigs and provided details about symptoms and methods of treatment. The cow edition was mainly about disease control using medicinal herbs.

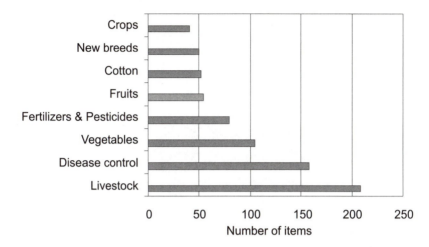

Figure 8.2 *The allocation of subcategories under farming technologies*

With the overall improvement of people's living standards, there has been a great surge in the demand for fresh vegetables in winter. More and more Jinta farmers are engaged in producing off-season vegetables. Instead of resting themselves and their land for almost three to four months in the winter season, the northern farmers are able to break with climate constraints and work all year round, provided that they are equipped with modern farming techniques. The adoption of new ways of farming involves skills acquisition so as to reduce the level of risks and uncertainties associated with the investment ventures. Therefore, the *Herald* devotes much space to advanced greenhouse cultivation technologies, such as biological pest control as well as temperature and humidity management.

Moreover, the *Herald* offers farmers advice about disease control for plants as well as animals. Because of a shortage of agricultural experts in the countryside, farmers often suffer great losses if diseased cotton plants or animals do not receive timely treatment. Based on the agricultural websites containing detailed descriptions of recently discovered diseases and the most effective treatment, the *Herald* helps farmers make accurate diagnoses and take appropriate steps to manage the problems.

In addition to exposing farmers to updated agricultural technologies, the *Herald* also keeps farmers informed of the price fluctuations as well as the market trends. The results of the analysis suggest a high weightage has been assigned to reports on cotton, sheep and other crops. This slant of coverage coincides with the local development needs as cotton and meat sheep production serve as two major revenue-generating sectors for the local economy. One third of market analyses are about cotton prices or the supply and demand in either domestic or international markets (see Figure 8.3). The market information is indispensable to farmers making farming decisions and adapting to market changes. In 2001, the *Herald* reported that the cumin harvest in India and Pakistan suffered huge losses due to

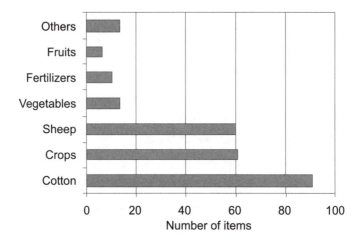

Figure 8.3 *The allocation of subcategories under market analysis*

an earthquake. The county farmer association quickly collected cumin at a higher price and sold directly to an Indian company dealing in agricultural products. This helped local farmers earn an extra RMB8 million (US$1.13 million).

The *Herald* acts not only as an information provider and advisor but also as a communicator by establishing a business platform where local farmers and enterprises can exchange product information and establish contacts with potential business partners. The information about agricultural products is categorized into supply and demand when it is posted online. Of 150 posted items, 81 are for sales, 60 for purchases and 9 seek local partners. Generally speaking, the advertised products include cotton, crops, vegetables, livestock and medicinal herbs.

Jinta Information and Network Center does not charge local farmers or external parties for publicizing their agricultural products in the *Herald*. Besides a detailed description of the products, the *Herald* also provides contact information of farmers or traders. For example, many villagers of Sanwangou Village were interested in a piece of information about a special breed of Han sheep in distant Shandong Province. Many previous reports in the *Herald* advised the local farmers to adopt the breed because weather conditions in Gansu are suitable for raising sheep. However, the farmers remained sceptical about the information. Only after they saw the pictures of the sheep farm over the internet were they convinced. Using the contact information printed in the *Herald*, the village managed to buy 180 sheep from Shandong, which turned out to be highly profitable.

Though the *Herald* devotes much of its content to information related to agricultural production, it is also responsible for propagating government policies and health information to rural people. The *Herald* often runs columns on national and local policies closely related to rural life, such as taxation reform, subsidies for grain planting, tax relief for natural disasters as well as welfare packages for households with no male offspring. Prior to the existence of the *Herald*, television was the only medium for such a purpose. However, during the high farming season, villagers are too busy to watch TV programmes, which were also lacking in detail. To meet the farmers' needs, the *Herald* often carries speeches by government officials and government documents of relevance to the farmers in their entirety, thus opening an additional channel of information on rural policies and improving the transparency of the government.

During the outbreak of SARS in 2003, the April and May issues of the *Herald* carried large amounts of information about the prevention of the epidemic. The farmers learnt not only the various transmission modes of the disease and its typical symptoms but also the necessary precautionary measures. The paper warned local people not to take traditional herbs without consulting doctors. The 11th issue of the *Herald* in the same year was a special edition aimed at creating awareness of family planning. The reports ranged from the appropriate uses of contraceptives and government birth control policies to the newly founded family planning association. Despite its infrequent coverage, the health information can supplement the existing channels of communication and help to disseminate public health messages and disease prevention techniques as well as promote healthy lifestyles among the farmers.

In order to make the *Herald* better serve the development needs of local agriculture, Jinta Information and Network Center tries its best to make sure that the coverage in the *Herald* matches the farming calendar and the cycle of crop growth under the climate of northwestern China. Despite being a so-called bi-weekly publication, the issuing of the e-paper does not actually follow the timeline rigidly and enjoys much flexibility to cater to the farming cycles. Jinta farmers receive the *Herald* more frequently at the sowing and harvest time, whereas the non-farming seasons show an apparent fall in terms of the number of issues. Therefore, the publication of the e-paper is seasonally based rather than monthly based (see Figure 8.4).

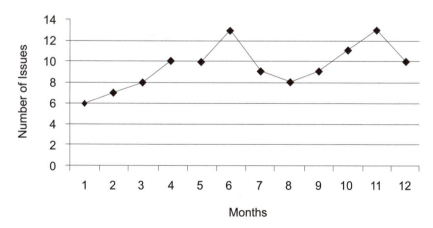

Figure 8.4 *The issuing of the* Herald *on a seasonal basis*

Table 8.1 *Analysis of the* Herald's *content on a seasonal basis*[3]

Categories	Spring	Summer	Autumn	Winter
Market information	Least		Most	
New breeds	Most	Least		
Disease control	Least	Most		
Fertilizers and pesticides	Most			Least
Vegetables	Least			Most

Much of the information in the *Herald* is selected to synchronize with the changing farming seasons. This has been supported by the analysis of the spread of various information categories on a seasonal basis (see Table 8.1). During spring sowing, farmers read most reports on new breeds of crops, livestock and fertilizers, while market information is at a minimum. In summer farmers are more often informed of disease control methods for their livestock. In autumn when produce is ready to go to market, the *Herald* often carries most information on the prices of various farm products at major markets. In winter farmers are taught about the preservation of grains and vegetables and the operation of greenhouses.

The positive impact of the *Herald* on the farmers' lives can be easily observed. The advanced farming skills and the updated market information help farmers raise crop output and livestock yields, which bring them better income levels. A farmer named Wang Qing in Jinda Village reported that the warning of severe weather changes in the *Herald* helped him avoid damages caused by windstorms and frost to greenhouse vegetables. Zhu Xuming, a farmer in Hongguang Village, secured a high output of cotton by planting a quality breed recommended by the *Herald*. As the new breed was more suitable for the local climate and geographical conditions, Zhu ended up producing a bumper harvest way ahead of other cotton producers.

Jinta County has witnessed much social and economic progress with the implementation of the Networking the Villages and Informing the Farming Households project. There has been a consistent growth in the annual per capita income for the local farmers, rising from US$435 in 2001 to U.S$520 in 2004. On average, Jinta farmers' personal income is 2.3 times that of the farmers in the province. According to the county statistics, 12 towns in Jinta County secured business transactions of over RMB1 billion (US$140 million) by posting sales information in the *Herald* as well as the local government websites in 2003 (Shen, 2004).

Total project cost

Except for the investment in computer hardware, the cost-sharing operation allows the county government to pay less than US$100 a year for each village to receive

Table 8.2 *Cost breakdown of the Jinta project[4]*

Level of Administration	Category	Cost (Yuan) (= US$0.1408)
County Network Centre	Establishment of centre (computer hardware, renting of servers, etc.)	1,230,000
	Yearly running cost	100,000
Village Information Centre	Establishment of centre (computer hardware, printing machines, etc.)	10,000
	Yearly running cost	800

the relevant information from the internet (mainly for the cost of paper and ink). With the initial success at 4 pilot villages in 2001, the operation soon spread to 75 villages, covering 90 per cent of the rural households within 6 years. Table 8.2 shows a cost breakdown of the project.

Project management, monitoring and evaluation

The chief government agency promoting internet diffusion is Jinta Information and Network Center, which was set up as a branch under the County Bureau of Statistics in 1999. After the successful implementation of the Networking the Villages and Informing the Farming Households project in four pilot villages, Shen felt that the county needed an agency dedicated to rural networking. As a result, the centre was separated from the Bureau of Statistics and reports directly to the county government.

The institutional change has not only granted the centre more authority over the township and village administrations but also helped to break the institutional barriers. Instead of serving a single government section, the centre is responsible for providing information services to all government organizations, private enterprises as well as individual farmers. The Jinta Information and Network Center, directly affiliated to the county government office, became the chief agency responsible for not only carrying out the project at the county level but also supervising, coordinating and evaluating the implementation work at the village level. On the one hand, the information centre serves as a technical institution by selecting and compiling online information and uploading the *Herald* onto the internet. On the other hand, it is a government agency with administrative power over the town and village administrations.

Jinta Information and Network Center has set up a reward and punishment system to ensure the implementation of the project and established role models to exemplify best practice. The project evaluation in Table 8.3 shows the progress achieved by each town concerning the distribution of the *Herald*, the household coverage rate, the training of information technicians and the investment in building local information networks in 2003.

Table 8.3 *The 2003 project evaluation of Jinta County*

| Towns | Number of issues | Distribution of the Herald | | Households sampled for survey | Personnel Training | Investment (10,000 Yuan) | Evaluation grade |
		Number of copies (10,000)	Household coverage rate (%)				
Jinta	68	21	95	350	66	18	98
Zhongdong	34	12	98	240	180	62	97
Gucheng	32	5	80	50	27	13	98
Xiba	24	6.48	90	120	5	6	95
Sanhe	24	3.5	70	60	18	11	94
Dongba	36	10	95	100	25	22	98
Dazhuangzi	23	5.4	98	100	27	3	96
Dingxin	36	12	90	100	19	30	99
Shuangcheng	28	4.2	91	130	25	51	98
Jiji	15	1.2	80	–	13	4	88
Tiancang	25	2.5	90	20	14	4	95
Yangjingziwan	28	1.05	100	20	7	28	97
Total	–	84.33	90	1290	426	252	–

Challenges and how they were overcome

Jinta has achieved satisfying results from internet extension given the relative costs spent in extending the online information to over 90 per cent of rural households in the county. The adoption of the virtual server, the transmission of the *Herald* over the internet, the employment of the existing network facilities and teachers at village schools, the selection of print media as the information carrier, and the recruitment of students for hand delivery have tremendously reduced the potential costs involved in extending online information to the vast rural population. With the number of project villages reaching 75 by the end of 2004, the county government spent no more than US$100 a year covering the costs of internet access, printing paper and ink for each village.

To the rural population in China, the digital divide is not only a reality today but also seems to be an unbridgeable gap in both the near and distant future. It is unrealistic to think such a digital divide will be automatically reduced with the passage of time. As the Chinese economy is increasingly becoming knowledge-based, disadvantages in communication and information exchange will certainly make the rural areas lag even further behind the urban areas. Though the existing environments are not favourable towards the wide expansion of the internet in the rural areas, experimental projects and isolated attempts should be encouraged to create awareness and provide rural people with opportunities using the technology.

In the rural areas, where the overall education level is inadequate to cope with advanced communication technology such as the internet, schools as the power-house of knowledge naturally help to fill in the gaps. As the central hubs of the technological extension process, rural schools have not only increased teachers' and students' exposure to the internet, but also facilitated the dissemination of advanced agricultural technologies and innovative farming and marketing ideas. One of the unique findings of the present study lies in the significant role that rural schools play in the extension of the internet. In Jinta, village schools served as an important link to relay web-based content to the farmers.

Lessons learned

Many factors contributed to the rapid growth in the use of internet technology and the widespread adoption of online information among Jinta farmers. First, the Jinta project is mainly a result of the government's initiative. The diffusion of the internet was included by Shen in the development agenda of the county government from the very beginning, which led to the subsequent planned and organized extension efforts both at the county and village levels. When local economic development and rural telecommunications infrastructures are inadequate to allow for the use of technology like the internet, only a powerful institution like the government can mobilize social resources to push the technology to its rural users. The multi-million yuan investment in installing computer and network facilities and covering the maintenance fees and the printing costs at the county and village information centres could only come as a result of the commitment of the government. If it were not for Shen as the county head, the village schools would not have agreed to play a part in the project, as it adds extra workload to the school management.

Second, the change agency has made wise use of internet technology to diffuse online information from the county to the villages. Instead of going through the traditional agricultural extension channels such as the township government and the village committees, the transmission of the *Herald* can be completed within seconds by uploading and downloading information over the internet. The Jinta project has successfully bypassed the institutional hierarchies and greatly facilitated the diffusion process.

Third, the project has been carefully designed to minimize the costs and ensure its sustainability. The adoption of the virtual server at the county information centre greatly reduces the hardware expenses and makes up for the technical inadequacies. The pre-existing computer facilities and teachers with IT skills in the village schools also help the county government avoid the possible costs involved in the purchase of computer and network facilities as well as the employment of technical personnel. The students serve as the best messengers due to their natural links to the farming households. 'Last mile connectivity' is innovatively achieved without building telecommunication infrastructures catering to a limited population dispersed across large areas. With an annual expenditure of RMB60,000 (US$8,450), the county government manages to extend the updated agricultural and market information to about 90 per cent of the households in the county.

Jinta's experiences suggest that internet initiatives have to depend heavily on the strong commitment and support of local governments. The establishment of Jinta Information and Network Center signifies the importance local governments have attached to the development of the internet and its role in rural networking. By incorporating internet platforms into rural development strategies, the government administrations at various levels have mobilized social and financial as well as human resources under their control to ensure the implementation of the internet project as well as the achievement of the extension objectives.

Good practice

Several characteristics of the *Herald* contribute to its wide adoption and popularity among Jinta farmers. Rogers (1983) argues that an innovation tends to diffuse rapidly within a social system when it is of relative advantage, compatibility, less complexity and observability. The information needs of Jinta farmers are greatly enhanced as the county economy is increasingly market-oriented. The adoption of scientific methods of farming and new breeds of crops and livestock require advanced farming skills as well as changes in traditional farming. However, the existing communication channels such as TV cannot meet such information requests due to the shortage of programming content targeted at the rural people. The *Herald* has become an indispensable source of information for the local farmers to make decisions on agricultural production and management.

The *Herald* also manages to target its content at the local farming cycles. Not only the number of issues but also the content of the newspaper has been finely attuned to the varying information needs. Moreover, the transformation of the *Herald* from a digital medium into a print medium circumvents the requirement of IT knowledge, allowing Jinta farmers to access online information while staying offline.

Moreover, the *Herald* integrates the advantages of both the old media and the new media. The employment of the digital technology enables the fast collection and transmission of the agricultural information over the internet. Its conversion into the print format greatly reduces the cost and the knowledge barriers posed by advanced internet technology to its rural users. The printed words give farmers more leeway in terms of the time and venue to read the information. This has greatly enhanced farmers' exposure to the information. Its free access, easy readability and portability lead to the wide readership of the e-paper among the rural people.

The objectivity of the information source also helps to explain the sustained adoption of the *Herald* among Jinta farmers. According to the deputy Party secretary of Zhongdong Town, nowadays farmers no longer believe in the information from the government circulars. In the past, the local government often interfered in the cultivation decisions of farmers by issuing administrative orders. Consequently, the farmers' interests were sacrificed to meet the goals set by the local government. For example, in order to prevent a sugar factory from going bankrupt, some farmers were forced to plant sugar beets despite the low profit. Therefore, farmers are inclined to follow the *Herald* rather than government directives.

Potential for scaling up and replication

In Jinta, the innovative use of the traditional print media proved to be a more cost effective way for online information to reach the farmers, who otherwise would be excluded from such communication despite the technical availability of the internet. Although such an indirect method of online communication is far from ideal, it is the most practical way to allow rural farmers to find their presence in cyber space.

The success of Jinta enables the county to take the lead in diffusing internet technology in the province. Gansu Development and Reform Commission has decided to replicate Jinta's practices by setting up a rural information service network covering the whole province. The provincial government will invest RMB88.5 million (US$12.5 million) to build 87 county information centres and 15,000 village school information centres in the next 5 years (2005–2009), with each county having approximately 60 village information centres (GDRC, 2005). The State Council Information Office has taken Jinta's experience as one of the most cost-effective models of innovatively employing the internet to provide farmers with information services and started to investigate the possibility of extending the practice to other rural areas with relatively low levels of development (Shen, 2004).

Conclusions

The Millennium Declaration sees ICT as an important tool with the potential to help achieve the MDGs. Target 18 of Goal 8 calls upon the UN member states to cooperate with the private sector to 'make available the benefits of new technologies, especially information and communications' (UNDP, 2003). The corresponding indicators for the target are fixed telephone lines and cellular subscribers, personal computers in use and internet users. The case examined by this study has demonstrated innovative and successful practices, which have important implications for the achievement of MDGs with the aid of new ICT.

Without direct access to the internet, the printed copies of the electronic paper enabled 90 per cent of local rural households to obtain updated agricultural information from the internet at relatively low cost for six years (T. Zhu, personal communication, 8 April 2005). Jinta's experiences indicate that as internet usage involves a fair amount of technical know-how and the purchase of expensive computer hardware, online information is unlikely to flow to the farmers in one step. The additional steps in the flow of web content to Jinta farmers actually help to reduce the cost of internet access, overcome the technical barriers and facilitate the processing of information.

The experiences of Jinta suggest that, while the internet does not come to the rural people as a natural step in their social and economic development, the ways of deploying the technology are very much used by the change agencies. Since farmers depend on the financial and technical support provided by the government to be introduced to the internet, the change agency is obviously shaping their internet usage through the extension initiatives. From the very beginning of their interaction with the technology, the internet is perceived by farmers as a useful tool to improve quality of life.

Another conspicuous feature of internet usage at the project site is the mediated usage. The interaction between farmer users and the internet is accomplished through a different information channel (the e-paper). This is largely due to rural users' low level of computer literacy and lack of capabilities to process online information. As a social phenomenon specific to the rural settings covered in the study, the mediated usage is in effect a product moulded by the social contexts of the rural areas. The usage patterns have been adapted to suit the local conditions and needs. On the one hand, it helps to overcome the knowledge barriers posed by the internet to its rural users. On the other hand, the mediated usage acts as an efficient information gate-keeping process, which facilities farmers' processing of web content and assists them in arriving at informed farming decisions.

Since agricultural production is very much influenced by natural conditions such as weather and soil, there are strong regional differences in terms of the applicability of farming skills and products. Rural users are confronted with high levels of risk when making farming decisions on the basis of online information. The change agencies and information technicians play the important roles of information gatekeepers to help farmers locate web content most relevant to local farming and reduce the uncertainties involved in adopting the information.

The majority of Jinta farmers also do not need to bother about acquiring computer literacy to access online information. The online information is disseminated among rural households in the form of a newspaper. The conversion of bits and bytes into printed words greatly facilitates farmers' information processing as the print media are less skill-dependent compared with the digital media. Most of the content of the e-paper was selected from agricultural websites both at the country level and the local level by the editors at Jinta Information and Network Center. The content analysis of the published issues of the *Herald* suggested that both the selection of the online information and the issuing of the newspaper were finely attuned to local farming cycles and farmers' information needs. Therefore, the *Herald* helped farmers arrive at sound production decisions by providing updated information on farming technologies, market trends and rural policies.

The experience of accessing online information in the rural setting of Jinta force us to broaden our understanding of internet usage. Rural people have come up with an adapted and pragmatic way of using the internet as the current social, economic and technological environments in rural areas are unfavourable to the adoption and use of the technology. Through the mediation of the popular traditional mass media that farmers feel most comfortable with, they can still enjoy the benefits derived from the internet without personally operating the computers.

The innovative practices of Jinta have had important implications for narrowing the digital divide between the urban and rural areas. With the overall economic and infrastructure contexts unfavourable to the wide diffusion and adoption of the internet in rural areas, the multiple-step flow model can allow rural people to access updated online information on market trends, advanced farming technologies, education and healthcare without going online. This will contribute significantly to reducing the widening socio-economic disparities between the information rich and information poor.

Notes

1   China Internet Network Information Center defines the internet user as a Chinese citizen who uses the internet at least one hour a week.
2   Despite the transition to market economy, the rural leaders still feel reluctant to shift their roles from issuing administrative orders to providing services and consultancy to help farmers make informed production decisions.
3   According to the local calendar, spring is from March to May, summer is from June to August, autumn is from September to November and winter is from December to February.
4   The cost breakdown does not include the expenses incurred from personnel training and other activities held at the town level to create awareness of the project.

References

CNNIC (China Internet Network Information Center) (1997) 'Statistical Report on the Development of Chinese Internet', www.cnnic.net.cn/develst/9710/e-9710.shtml, accessed 14 April 2003

CNNIC (2007) 'The 19th Statistical Survey Report on Internet Development in China', www.cnnic.cn/uploadfiles/pdf/2007/2/14/200607.pdf, accessed 11 March 2007

GDRC (Gansu Development and Reform Commission (2005) 'Gansusheng nongcun xinxi gonggong fuwu wangluo gongcheng shishi fang'an', [The implementation plan of rural information service network in Gansu Province'], Gansu, GDRC

Jinta gaikuang (2005) 'The overview of Jinta County', www.jtxnet.com/jtgk/jtgk/jtgk.htm, accessed 23 October 2005

Rogers, E. M. (1983) Diffusion of Innovation, 3rd Edition, New York, The Free Press

Shen, J. (2004) Zuihou yigongli: Jingji qianfada diqu jianshe nongye xinxi fuwu wangluo shiyong zhinan [The Last Mile Connectivity: A Handbook on Establishing Agriculture Information Services in Less Developed Areas], Lanzhou, Gansu People Publishing House

UNDP (United Nations Development Programme) (2003) Human Development Report 2003, New York, UNDP

Wacker, G. (2000) 'Behind the virtual wall', www.swp-berlin.org/biost/ber2000/b2000_06.htm, accessed 3 June 2006

How Joint Action Can Increase Production While Contributing to Poverty Reduction: The Case of Frutika in Paraguay[1]

Ramiro Rodriguez Alcala and Thomas Otter

Introduction

Paraguay is a small landlocked country in South America located between Brazil and Argentina. Over half of its GDP consists of primary and agriculture production, or is at least directly dependant on them. Approximately half of the entire population still lives in rural areas, in spite of the accelerated urbanization process in recent years. Overall, approximately 40 per cent of the population lived in poverty in 2006, while extreme poverty affected around 18 per cent of the population, made up of some 6 million people (DGEEC, 2006). Extreme poverty used to be higher in rural areas, however, this trend has reversed since 2005. Although extreme poverty is now higher in urban areas, this is the result of rural poverty that has pushed poor people to migrate to towns and cities.

Historically, Paraguayan agriculture was characterized by a considerable number of small-scale farmers (some 300,000 families), cultivating mainly for self-consumption and cash crop farming. On average, these properties were between 5 and 10 hectares in size, however, there were also a considerable number of farms less than 5 hectares (some 35,000 families). During the 1970s and 1980s, agricultural growth was determined by an expansion of the agricultural frontier (deforestation), but small farmers did not benefit from this shift since almost all newly cleared land was dedicated to large-scale mechanized soya bean plantations or livestock farming.

Cotton, the traditional cash crop for small farmers, entered a price and health crisis during the 1990s. Nevertheless, the government kept insisting that cotton farming was the best solution for small farmers and proceeded to set up an inefficient and corrupt subvention system, which far from improving cultivation results and improving the livelihoods of cotton farmers, sentenced them to dependence and poverty.

The basic structures of small-scale farming remain the same to this day. Cotton farming still remains important, despite its poor results with respect to farmer welfare and interests. There have been a number of efforts focusing on diversification and alternative products, but with limited success. To date it has not been possible to upscale any of the alternative products to cotton to more than 10–15 per cent of farmers. To increase this number would require new crops and updated and improved technical and financial assistance.

Poverty is a complex historical phenomenon in Paraguay; wide sections of the population are used to being poor and this widespread poverty has created a fertile ground for political and/or social instability. During the period of 1998 to 2002, Paraguay went in to a deep economic recession and poverty rates rose from 32 per cent in 1997 to more than 41 per cent of the population in 2003 (DGEEC, 2003). Despite economic recovery, beginning in 2003, there was little or no reduction in poverty because growth was limited to sectors such as telecommunications, livestock and mechanized farming. Poverty reduction through the trickle down of growth to poor households via social policies has not been successful in Paraguay. Short-term assistance programmes and long-term structural reform processes have also been unsuccessful in reducing poverty, despite being successful in other contexts, due to deficiencies in terms of scale and efficiency.

Even after returning to a democratic government in 1989, after 35 years of dictatorship, the same political party that set up and supported the dictatorship since the late 1940s, the ANR (Asociación Nacional Republicana), is still in charge of the government. In spite of the ANR losing influence and popularity over the years, it has always managed to remain in power, even under a democracy, mainly as a result of a disjointed opposition. In 2003, the ANR won the last presidential and parliament elections with only 38 per cent of the votes. The next elections are to be held in 2008.

The combination of rising poverty and the sense of injustice due to the economic recovery benefiting only a few people in the country has created a sensation of social discontentment which, this time, appears to have evolved into a more unified opposition preparing for the 2008 elections. Although social and economic protest is growing, there is not yet an unstable situation in the country.

The project

The Frutika PPP has grown slowly out of a technical assistance project for soil recovery, at first implemented in the department of Caazapá in 1998 by the GTZ. In addition to searching for alternative products to replace cotton as the principal cash crop, small farmers are heavily affected by soil degradation and the lack of appropriate and sufficient technical and financial assistance. According to the household survey results (DGEEC, 2001), only about 10–15 per cent of all farmers are reached by any kind of technical or financial assistance (either public or private).

Caazapá is one of the poorest departments[2] of Paraguay, also historically characterized by small-scale farming. As a result of its geographic location, it is threatened by the upcoming soya bean frontier advancing from the east (from Brazil). During the late 1990s, Caazapá was selected by GTZ for technical assistance with the aim of poverty reduction. From the start, project implementation concentrated on direct technical assistance at a local level to small farmers. Although the project was agreed with and approved by the central government, neither the Ministry of Agriculture nor any other related central government institution, such as the Ministries of Planning or of Industry and Commerce, participated initially.

Soil recovery through green manure and ecological and conservation agriculture (CA) programmes were the first steps implemented in Caazapá during the late 1990s. The basic idea was to recover the soil's fertility and improve cultivation efficiency of any future crops, considering poor farmers' limited means of accessing new or additional farmland. The basic recovery process took between two and three years and was first implemented with some 800 families. Soil recovery, using conservation techniques such as green manures and direct drilling, results in harvest improvements of anywhere between 40 and 200 per cent, depending on the initial soil conditions and on the crop (see Tables 9.1 and 9.2).

Table 9.1 *Comparison of yields of cotton, maize and manioc on farms with and without CA and with more than two years of CA*

	N	Cotton (kg/ha)	Maize (kg/ha)	Manioc (kg/ha)
With CA	17	1,087	1,090	13,879
Without CA	60	788	720	11,200

Source: GTZ (2005)

Table 9.2 *Comparison between family income of farms with and without CA*

	With CA (US$, annual)	Without CA (US$, annual)
Monetary income from agriculture	1075	875
Non-monetary income from agriculture	430	221
Monetary expenditure	257	180
Non-monetary income	1000	1000
Family income	2248	1916
Per capita income	450	383

Source: GTZ (2005)

CA in Paraguay consists of four basic elements:

1   crop planting is carried out by direct seeding/planting/drilling, which means that the fields are not tilled;
2   crop rotations are applied, which means that no monoculture system is used;
3   a permanent soil cover or mulch is used resulting from crop residues left on the surface that improve soil humidity content and reduce the effects of erosion; and
4   green manure cover crops are planted with the purpose of providing soil cover and additional nutrients to the soil through decomposition and nitrogen fixation.

Once successful results in terms of soil fertility were attained, GTZ started involving district and departmental governments in their project under a second stage, inviting them to participate in a joint local and regional development strategic planning process, with GTZ acting as a facilitator. The initial success of soil recovery proved to be one of several possible means of development in the initial planning process. The departmental development plan of Caazapá, a joint product of local and departmental governments and civil society, set up development objectives and goals.

Soil recovery was the first step towards supporting the agricultural production process. Additionally, the project also worked on diversification (self consumption and cash crops) and the way to combine these agricultural activities with forestry activities on the same plot of land, generally of no more than 2 hectares. Initially, planting native tree species for wood production was combined with farming activities, however, any surplus production and harvest had to be sold.

It was at this time that Frutika, a semi-industrialized enterprise for fruit and fruit juice production, achieved high profits from their juice sales. Traditionally, due to quality reasons and standards, Frutika only used fruit from their own farms, however, commercial success forced them into purchasing fruit from outside producers and so devising ways to ensure product quality from the external farmers. This created an opportunity for small-scale farmers in Caazapá to produce fruit.

Frutika is located in Caazapá's neighbouring department, Itapúa, so there is a strategic advantage in terms of location and short travel distances. The enterprise agreed to invest in planting new fruit trees with smallholders and guaranteed the purchase of these plantation's future production, once market access via export was assured by a PPP facilitated by GTZ.

Project formulation

There was never a concrete project design as such. The project began after the soil recovery programme with the idea that fruit production could be an interesting alternative to traditional products in a crop diversification process, especially since there was the opportunity to link this new production to export via the PPP. It was a process that grew slowly over almost ten years. Although not all institutions were included in these processes, they were at least aware of what was going on. The central government was aware of the project's activities and supported the relevant local governments (logistics, convincing farmers to participate and the formulation of the Caazapá 2013 development plan). When the project advanced successfully, more and more institutions joined the process.

Initially, GTZ was convinced that soil recovery, diversification processes, market access and political support for this process would increase incomes (and result in reduced poverty), assuring environmental sustainability and future production. This was formulated as a goal once the PPP was to be set up. More importantly, incremental participatory planning and an ongoing planning process based on the results and outcomes reached are both part of the success story. This step-by-step philosophy allowed the involvement of different and additional agents and stakeholders. New stakeholders widened the support for the process and generated alternatives and different opportunities for future project activities.

Project goals and objectives

The specific goal for the PPP itself was to assist farming families and plant different kinds of fruit. These would be produced within an 'agri-fruit-forestry' farming approach. Total production was to be absorbed entirely by Frutika for increased juice production and export to Germany.

This project is part of a wider assistance programme by GTZ with the main goal of reducing poverty through increased income, the creation of new opportunities and improved governance, regarding international cooperation. At the sub-national government level, these activities are part of the Caazapá 2013 development plan with an overall goal to reduce poverty and improve living conditions.

Key elements of the project

Target beneficiaries

The main target group is comprised of the small peasant farms in the Caazapá department. The project aims to assist up to 2000 farms, each of which should plant between half and one hectare of citrus crops for the PPP, of which two thirds of this area should be planted with orange trees and the remaining third with grapefruit trees. Overall farm sizes are between 2 and 5 hectares. The fruit production is to be combined with cash crops and crops for home consumption, as well as silvicultural and reforestation activities. This is the agri-fruit-forestry approach, which requires qualified and permanent technical assistance. By mid-2007, approximately 700 hectares of fruit production had already been set up by the project.

Project area

The PPP is being implemented in the Caazapá department, specifically within the districts of San Juan Nepomuceno, Tavaí and Buena Vista. Meanwhile, the fruit juice producer Frutika is currently purchasing fruit from other departments, including San Pedro, Concepción, Ñeembucu, Misiones and of course from Itapúa itself where the industrial plant is located. Overall, Frutika purchases approximately 70 per cent of all fruit required to meet their own production; the remaining 30 per cent is covered by their own internal production from farms owned by the Frutika Company. Buying fruit in a manner that contributes towards poverty reduction in geographical areas within the vicinity of the firm's centre of operations is new. Doing this within a PPP is an important factor that has allowed the project to build up its scale, assisting up to 2000 farms.

Project activities

Key Components

Key components can be divided between the contribution of each of the principal agents and stakeholders in the project, namely the GTZ and the Frutika Company.

The contribution of GTZ consisted of financing costs for technical advice for the project coordination between the involved institutions (Departmental Government, Ministry of Agriculture, Frutika, Capiibary Corporative Society and the Institute of Agricultural Research of National University). GTZ also contributed considerable support towards technical assistance (additional fees and logistics, such as vehicles, maintenance and fuel) offered by the Ministry to the farmers.

Frutika's contribution consisted of the purchase of 80,000 orange and 40,000 grapefruit tree seedlings (starting trees) and additional equipment. A 'tree starting kit' in Paraguay has a unit cost of US$3 and includes the tree itself, fertilizers, pesticides and pruning tools. The tree seedlings for oranges are grown in Frutika's tree nursery, while the grapefruit seedlings come from the tree nursery of an agricultural cooperative society in the Capiibary district. The Capiibary cooperative society receives technical assistance from Frutika to make sure that the tree seedlings are of good quality and free of viruses, in order to ensure future high quality yields.

Key activities

The project's key activities are: permanent technical support to small farmers; total absorption of costs for starting trees and their cultivation kit by Frutika; and the production of high quality fruit on small farms with guaranteed market access via Frutika and the PPP to international markets via the export of fruit juice concentrate.

These three activities are core components of the project and could not be successfully carried out without the input of the agri-fruit-forestry cultivation model, which requires a planning exercise and is based on ecological agriculture and soil recovery. Finally, the PPP is built upon the successful implementation of a previous process of some five to seven years, which included setting up the production model of associated plantations and an institutional process of strategic planning for departmental development, including municipalities, departmental government and regional offices of the Ministries of Agriculture and of Industry and Commerce.

Key technical inputs

Key technical inputs were the provision of citrus starting trees of high genetic quality and free of viruses to small farmers, accompanied by the necessary fertilizers, pesticides, tools and permanent technical advice.

Timeframe

The GTZ project began in 2003 and ended in late 2006, focusing on planting the trees and offering technical support during their early growth period, however, the PPP is ongoing. Technical support from Frutika to the farmers will continue until the trees start to fruit (between four and five years after planting under Paraguayan climatic conditions). GTZ's support to the PPP came to an end in late 2006.

Impact and outcomes

The project's main outcome has been an overall increase in incomes, and through this an increase in wealth of farmer households (all considered poor by official standards) derived from higher productivity (resulting from soil recovery and CA programmes), and a combination of self-consumption and cash crops with secure market access for the cash crops. To date there is no measurement of the exact level of poverty reduction among the families that participated in the project. However, since family incomes have increased, even if not to a level where households rise above the poverty line, they are without doubt better off than they were before the project was implemented.

An additional outcome has been the adoption of soil recovery and environmentally sustainable cultivation techniques, as well as the generation of real and empirical evidence that small-scale (family) agriculture can be the object of a successful and sustainable development project. These outcomes are also important as they form part of the successful implementation of the Caazapá Plan 2013 departmental development, namely the implementation of local and regional projects with public and private participation for poverty reduction, growth and development. Additionally, small-scale and family agriculture brings increased opportunities for women and can enhance gender equality.

Project costs

The total approximate project cost between 2003 and 2006 was US$600,000, of which 60 per cent was funded by Frutika and the remainder by GTZ.

Government participation

The central government's participation in the project consisted of technical assistance to farmers via the Ministry of Agriculture, inputs for technical assistance from the Agricultural Research Institute of the National University and the provision of starting trees for all kinds of reforestation activities (except fruit trees) through the National Forestry Service.

Local governments' activities prior to the PPP consisted of defining the Caazapá 2013 development plan. This plan was set up in a participatory manner, including the local offices of the Ministries of Agriculture and of Industry and Commerce in this participative strategic planning exercise. These activities prior to the beginning of the PPP were crucial in later developing the partnership and project.

Private sector participation

Apart from the Frutika Company itself, the cooperative society of Capiibary has also been involved in the project providing the grapefruit trees mentioned earlier.

Project management

According to the agreement between GTZ and Frutika in the PPP, Frutika is in charge of the project management, while the project was monitored by GTZ with methods and approaches set up by the German government for monitoring the use of funding and its outputs and impacts.

Challenges and how they were overcome

The PPP broke with commonly held beliefs that small farmers could not success-fully implement farming activities that included silviculture or reforestation components. The project's success shows that not only is the cropping of trees and cash crop a success, but that the trees also contribute to soil recovery and act as (climatic) protection for other crops too. The project proves that the challenge of diversified cropping systems goes far beyond the basic idea of combining self-consumption and cash crops, and it shows that all this can be achieved on very small farms (up to 5 hectares) and even with economically viable results.

The challenge of overcoming traditional ideas of what can be done on small farms, and what can be achieved in terms of agriculture at a household level, had to be overcome in the minds and opinions of small farmers themselves. This was achieved through the free provision of starting trees and their growing kits, as well as guaranteed market access via Frutika.

Finally, public–private cooperation in Paraguay has historically been diffi-cult. The GTZ-Frutika experience shows that this kind of activity can work and that it is possible to create a win–win alliance. However, such alliances cannot be achieved randomly and at no expense, and in the case of GTZ-Frutika it was the result of years of previous work concentrating on soil recovery and environmental agriculture combined with participatory strategic planning processes, resulting in the Caazapá 2013 plan.

Lessons learned

Success factors

There are several important success factors for the PPP:

- previous successful experience with soil recovery;
- existence of the Caazapá 2013 development plan;
- proximity of Frutika as an exporting company; and
- opportunity for market expansion.

In addition, GTZ's support concentrated on building up a development process based on 'what already exists'. This includes working with farmers who have their own land, building up a PPP with an existing enterprise with international market access, and finally, including existing institutions such as Capiibary Cooperative Society.

The development strategy did not seek to convert farmers into industrial workers or implement any other major structural changes. All parties involved continue working under more or less the same scheme. Farmers remain farmers, while the project searches for ways to increase their income and improve the consistency of income over the year. Income increases with increased production, but increased production requires technical assistance. Agents for technical assistance existed by working in an uncoordinated manner before the PPP was implemented.

Role of champions

Perhaps the agent or institution with the lowest profile, but the most important contribution, was GTZ itself, since their knowledge of how to design projects, facilitate and create alliances and partnerships made the project happen. The support of GTZ was crucial and the agency was able to assume this function because of its credibility. The financial support of GTZ was also important, as it served as starting capital.

Other innovations

The agri-fruit-forestry approach is a paradigmatic change. Previous projects and technical cooperation never crossed the line in terms of basic ideas of product diversification or carrying out agricultural or forestry activities that help to increase small farmer's incomes. For years it was believed that there was no scope for forestry activities on small farms. The basic ideology was to cut down all trees and open up the land with a plough for cultivating a limited and undiversified cropping system. The shift to soil recovery and then CA programmes and then to the agri-fruit-forestry approach required a great deal of 'soft assistance' to convince very traditional and conservative small farmers, most of them with only a limited number of schooling years who were very wary of innovation and new technologies, to do something different. Convincing farmers was a slow process of implementing activities step-by-step in order to prove to the participants that such methods work.

Good practice

The Frutika PPP is good practice because of its positive impacts on farmers' incomes. These positive impacts can be guaranteed for at least a certain period of time by ensured access to external markets via the PPP. It is considered good practice because all the important agents are involved in the process, including the public sector, and all parties are doing more or less what they are intended to do. In a sense, this is a win–win alliance because farmers increase their incomes, Frutika increases its production and exports, governance increases in the department because the development plan is being implemented, and the central government obtains higher tax revenues as a result of increased production. Finally, this project has contributed to the environmental sustainability of the region as a result of all these activities being carried out under a CA system.

Potential for scaling up and replication

In theory there is great potential for scaling up, however, such efforts depend on sustainability and increased access to international markets. Replication in other parts of the country is possible but considering all the work that was put in before setting up the PPP, replication would not be possible in a short space of time.

Perhaps a better sort of scaling up opportunity would include exploiting positive tradeoffs, such as the work of the Capiibary Corporative Society, which is selling starting trees to producers who are external to the PPP (and who were not assisted by the structures set up by GTZ). These farmers sell their fruit to Frutika, however, the difference between them and the farms included under the PPP project is that they are usually slightly better off. Consequently, they have their own financial capital and access to loans and are able to buy the starting trees themselves and maybe even to pay for technical assistance. In this sense, the PPP is indirectly offering production and marketing opportunities even to better off farms outside the project.

Conclusions

The core element of the Frutika PPP is the 'know-how' of GTZ that led to the setting up of the project based on the outputs and outcomes of previous project activities and that brought agents and stakeholders together to work towards a common goal or benefit. The Frutika PPP has many special aspects and consequently it will not easily be replicated, even within Paraguay, however, it is far from being perfect. For example, additional fees for Ministry of Agriculture technical assistance staff were paid for by GTZ, but it would have been preferable to set up an incentive structure (such as a surplus to monthly income based on harvest success) to be paid by Frutika itself. However, there are some lessons to be learned about the structures the PPP has developed, such as the importance of working step-by-step, working with what exists without trying to create new institutions and the importance of foundations built by previous years of work, all of which made the project a success.

Notes

1 This case study was prepared for the Human Development Office of UNDP Paraguay as an input for the *National Human Development Report 2008*.
2 Paraguay is a centralized state divided into 17 departments with very low political independence.

References

The following list includes material that is not directly cited within the chapter but may be of interest as further reading.

Areco, E. (2001) "Ladrones y Señores. Los Dueños del Cartel del Algodón. Causa de la Extrema Pobreza Campesina y del Desastre Económico del Paraguay", El Lector, Asunción (Paraguay)

Derpsch, R. (1998) "Implicaciones Económicas de la Adopción de Practicas Conservacionistas en el Paraguay con Énfasis en el Sistema de Siembra Directa", (n. publ.)

Derpsch, R. (2005) "Area under No-tillage in different countries", www.rolf-derpsch.com

DGEEC (Direccion de Estadistica, Encuestas y Censo) (2001) *Encuesta Integral de Hogares 2000/1 [Comprehensive Household Survey 2000/1]*, DGEEC

DGEEC (2003) *Encuesta Permanante de Hogares 2003 [Permanent Household Survey 2003]*, DGEEC

DGEEC (2006) *Encuesta Permanante de Hogares 2006 [Permanent Household Survey 2006]*, DGEEC

Dietze, E. (1997) "Diagnostico de Sistemas de Producción de Pequeños Productores Asociados a la Cooperativa Colonias Unidas, Ubicados en tres Compañías de Departamento de Itapúa", Tese de Grado, Universidad Nuestra Señora de la Asunción (UNA), Hohenau, Paraguay, 1997 (inpublished.)

Dixon, J., Guliver, A., Gibbon, D. (2001) "Farming Systems and Poverty", Improving Farmers' Livelihoods in a Changing World, FAO/World Bank, Rome/Washington D.C.

Duarte, R. & Kawamura, P. (2002) "Situación actual de la agricultura de precisión en el Paraguay", in: *Tercer Taller Internacional de Agricultura de Precisión del Cono Sur de América* – Argentina 17–19 Diciembre 2002, Carlos Paz, Córdoba, Argentina. Organizado por PROCISUR (Programa Cooperativo para el Desarrollo Tecnológico Agroalimentario y Agroindustrial del Cono Sur) www.agriculturadeprecision.org/cursos/IIITallerInternacional/indice.htm

Florentín, M. A., Peñalva, M., Calegari, A., DERPSCH, R. (2001) *Abonos verdes y rotación de cultivos en siembra directa. Pequeñas propiedades*, Proyecto Conservación de Suelos MAG – GTZ, DEAG, San Lorenzo (Paraguay)

Glas, M. Van Der (1998) "Gaining ground. Land use and soil conservation in areas of agriculture colonization in South Brazil and East Paraguay", in *Nederlands Geografische Studies* 248, Utrecht

Glatzle, A. & Stosiek, D. (2001) "Country Pasture/Forage Resource Profiles", El Lector, Asunción (Paraguay)

GTZ (2005) Estudio de Línea de Base del Programa: Buen Gobierno a Nivel Descentralizado y Reducción de la Pobreza', Asunción, STP/GTZ

Lange, D. (2005) "Economics and Evolution of Smallholdings' Conservation Agriculture", *Mid-term Experiences,* FAO/GTZ/MAG, Asunción (Paraguay)

Lange, D. & Moriya, K. (2004) *"Conservation Agriculture Cotton for Smallholder Farmers", Experiences from Paraguay*, FAO/GTZ/MAG, Asunción (Paraguay)

Masi, F., Penner, R. & Dietze, R. (2000) *"Evaluación de Rol de las Regiones Fronterizas en el Proceso de Desarrollo Económico del Paraguay"*, Banco Central de Paraguay, Asunción

Molinas, J., Cabello, C. & Otter, T. (2004) "Paraguay: crecimiento, exportaciones y reducción de pobreza y desigualdad", in: Ganuza, E., Morley, S., Robinson S., Vos, R. *¿Quien se beneficia del libre comercio?*, Alfaomega, Bogotá (Colombia), p.423–452

Sorrenson, W., Duarte, C. & López Portillo, J. (1998) "Economics of No-till Compared to Conventional Systems on Small Farms: Policy and Investment Implications ", GTZ/MAG, San Lorenzo (Paraguay)

UNDP (2003) *"Informe Nacional sobre el Desarrollo Humano"*, UNDP, Asunción (Paraguay)

UNDP (2007) "Innovación productiva y reducción de la pobreza", Cuaderno de Desarrollo Humano # 1, Asunción

Vallejos, F., Kliewer, I., Florentín, M. A., Casaccia, J., Calegari, A. & Derpsch, R. (2001) "Abonos verdes y rotación de cultivos en siembra directa", *Sistemas de producción tractorizados*, Proyecto Conservación de Suelos MAG – GTZ, DEAG, San Lorenzo, (Paraguay)

10

Poverty Reduction and Millennium Development Goal Localization: A Case Study of Ha Tinh Rural Development Project in Vietnam

Tran Dinh Hoa and Nguyen Thanh Tung

Introduction

Ha Tinh Rural Development Project (HRDP) is considered a successful project in Vietnam as it not only helped many households in Ha Tinh province to escape from poverty, but also generated a number of innovative poverty reduction approaches that have been widely replicated by the government and donors in other provinces. For example, the project successfully introduced the new approach of community self-implementation of infrastructure schemes. Instead of subcontracting out the civil works to construction companies, the project enabled groups of poor households to sign implementation contracts with the Commune Development Board for the construction of small-scale roads and irrigation schemes. The project also prioritized the poorest households in the commune to get additional work under the schemes, such as land levelling or construction materials transportation. Therefore, the civil works not only raised the incomes of the poor, but also improved the sense of ownership and empowerment of local people, and the sustainable maintenance of infrastructures. Today, the approach of directly using community groups to implement civil works has been replicated by the National Poverty Reduction Programme in other provinces.

Another impressive model of community empowerment that HRDP demonstrated is the development of community based organizations (CBO). Water user associations, introduced by the International Fund for Agricultural Development (IFAD) in Tuyen Quang province and replicated under HRDP, have also been institutionalized by the Government's National Strategic Framework for Participatory

Irrigation Management in 2004. Ha Tinh is one the leading provinces in the development of participatory water resource management thanks to the outcomes of HRDP.

HRDP also incorporates successful and innovative microfinance services. These do not use local banks but the Vietnam Women's Union, the largest social women's organization representing the interests of women in political discourse in the country. Continuation of the women's saving and credit groups (WSCGs) set up by the HRDP was assured even after the end project through the Ministry of Finance's decision to transfer the management of the credit funds for a further 14 years to the Vietnam Women's Union in Ha Tinh. Today, more than 3000 WSCGs are working well and have doubled the initial capital provided by IFAD two years after the end of the project in 2005.

Due to its remarkable achievements, the Government of Vietnam and IFAD have extended HRDP to another project in Ha Tinh. The on-going or follow-up IFAD-funded Improving Markets for the Poor Programme since early 2007 is progressing on the foundations established by HRDP. It also introduces another innovative poverty reduction approach by enabling the poor to benefit from greater access to markets since Vietnam's links to the World Trade Organization (WTO).

Context

Ha Tinh is a coastal province located in the central region of Vietnam and has 8 districts covering 605,574 hectares. In 1999, the total population of Ha Tinh was 1.3 million with a growth rate of 1.58 per cent per annum. Women represent 51 per cent of the population and 99.9 per cent of people belong to the majority Kinh group. Fifty-two per cent of all households in the province were classified as poor households in 1999 (based on the equivalent income per capita per month of VND20,000 (US$9)), and almost all households in Ha Tinh earned their living from agriculture. The main causes of poverty were inadequate productive resources due to small farm size, very poor soil quality (a vast area of coastal sand) and lack of capital and limited access to knowledge and skills to increase its productivity, poor infrastructure to facilitate access to markets, and excessive exposure to risks, particularly natural disasters such as typhoons, floods (almost every summer) and droughts (winter). The main constraints to development expressed by the communities were lack of access to credit, lack of irrigation and lack of knowledge and skills to increase the productivity of their meagre land holdings or to invest in livestock and other enterprises that would provide additional sources of income. In addition, the top-down approach to development programmes in the past and the lack of participation of the poor in planning and implementing government programmes limited the effectiveness of poverty alleviation initiatives.

The project

The rationale for selection of the project was the very high rates of poverty in Ha Tinh and the absence of substantive donor-funded poverty initiatives in the province. At the same time the IFAD area-based participatory poverty reduction approach had proved very successful in Quang Binh province, which was close to Ha Tinh and faced similar development constraints. With benefits from the experience gained in other on-going IFAD-funded projects in the three provinces of Tuyen Quang, Ha Giang and Quang Binh, this project provided opportunities to further improve the approach to decentralization and participation, and better focus on acheiving a greater level of self-reliance of the poor, which could be replicated by government and other donors.

How the project was formulated

The project was formulated through a participatory approach. The overall concept of the project was developed through missions and reviews in 1998, with IFAD working in close collaboration with local stakeholders. Prior to a project formulation mission, an in-depth socio-economic assessment was carried out and the province developed its own project proposal based on results from consultations with stakeholders at the commune level. Moreover, discussions were also held with relevant stakeholders at all levels with technical departments, local government authorities and farm households. Consultative workshops were held at both the beginning and the end of the mission to discuss the project design. The project design also drew on the experiences of three international NGOs (Oxfam UK, Save the Children UK and Action Aid in Vietnam), who were assisting Ha Tinh in poverty alleviation at the same time. The project design also benefited from the lessons learned in three previous IFAD projects, which recommended this project be more geographically focused and integrated, while the participatory and gender aspects be much more mainstreamed. HRDP was appraised by IFAD in February 1999 and approved by the IFAD Executive Board in April 1999. A loan agreement was signed on 18 June 1999 and became effective on 17 September 1999. Project implementation was complete by the end of 2005.

Project goals and objectives

The development objective of the project was to improve the incomes and living standards of poor rural households and increase their participation in the development process. These objectives were to be achieved through:

1   the sustainable operation of microfinance schemes providing access to credit for the poor;

2   improved rural infrastructure; and

3   improved technical support in crop and livestock services.

The key feature of the project strategy was the participation of project beneficiaries in the selection of investment activities, the direct responsibility of communities for the implementation and maintenance of the rural infrastructure schemes, and the provision of regular feedback for adjustment and improvement of the project.

Key elements of the project

Target beneficiaries

The project target groups were poor and very poor households and women in the eight (subsequently increased to nine) rural districts in Ha Tinh province. It was estimated that 200,000 poor people could benefit from the poverty reduction initiatives of the project.

Geographic coverage of the project

The project covered 137 communes classified as poor communes, out of the total 265 communes in the province. The primary focus of the project was 48 of the poorest communes, which received a full range of assistance including a Commune Development Fund for improvement of small-scale infrastructure, small-scale irrigation and rural roads. Microcredit and agricultural production activities were implemented in all the 137 communes.

Project management

The project was implemented by the Province Project Coordination Unit and the provincial line-departments as the co-implementing agencies.

At the provincial level, the Province Project Steering Committee and, at the district level, the District Project Steering Committee were established by the local government to coordinate relevant technical agencies, community organizations and other stakeholders at all levels for the purposes of integrated project implementation.

Key components

The project had 4 components and 11 sub-components, namely:

• Component 1 – Participatory Development – focusing on participatory planning and a demand-driven approach to the selection and implementation of small-scale rural infrastructure schemes through the mechanism of the Community Development Fund (CDF);

- Component 2 – Income Generation and Diversification – covering small-scale irrigation, support to crop and livestock production, veterinary services, community forestry, financial services and rural markets;
- Component 3 – Rural Roads and Bridges – improving a number of key district-level roads and bridges;
- Component 4 – Project Management.

The project design also included provision for a Development Initiatives Fund, equivalent to 20 per cent of the total project base cost, to provide flexibility to move funds to areas of demand as expressed by the participatory planning procedures following the project's mid-term review. Following the review two new components were added, namely: aquaculture covering the rehabilitation of fish hatcheries, rehabilitation of farmers' ponds and training; and plant protection covering capacity building of technical staff and farmers. In addition, the coverage of the credit component was reduced from 137 to 97 communes to avoid overlap with international NGO credit schemes operating in the other 40 communes.

Key activities

Participatory development

The project introduced the concept of bottom-up planning of development priorities for the 48 poorest communes eligible for the full range of project activities. Participatory planning exercises were used to assist the communities to assess their development needs and draw up a commune development plan (CDP). The process evolved and improved over time as the benefits of participation were better realized and the staff became more skilled in embracing a wider representation of the population through a series of village meetings, which eventually covered 36,099 participants in the 48 poorest communes, representing, on average, around two-thirds of the households in the commune and involving 72,653 person-days. 54 per cent of the participants were poor and 57 per cent were women. HRDP subsequently involved the beneficiaries for 42,130 person-days for annual development planning exercises in which the commune development plans were updated and new activities identified for implementation. The poor and women represented 55 per cent and 54 per cent respectively of the participants in these annual planning exercises.

The project contributed significantly to enhancing the participatory management capacity at the commune level through capacity building of commune development boards (CDBs), elected by the communes with representatives from the villages and mass organizations to oversee the implementation of the commune development plans. The project also developed various CBOs, such as water users' associations (WUAs), market management boards and school management committees, established to manage the operation and maintenance of the specific schemes.

The CDF, allowing communities to prioritize and select rural infrastructure investments, enabled community members to have direct control over resources and this led to a sense of ownership. The 109 schemes selected by the communities for implementation under the CDF in the 48 poorest communes comprised 39 schools with 246 classrooms, 19 inter-village roads with a total length of 58km, 14 bridges totalling 264m in length, 4 markets, a drinking water supply system and 28 irrigation schemes. The investments in irrigation, markets, roads and kinder-gartens are acknowledged to have made the most direct contribution to poverty reduction. The emphasis placed on the upgrading of schools reflects the fact that communities value education highly for its long-term contribution to poverty reduction and as the ultimate route out of poverty for the next generation.

Income generation

Small-scale irrigation

The project rehabilitated 29 schemes with a total command area of 2,849ha, established 43 WUAs – including 20 WUAs for irrigation schemes implemented under the CDF – and trained 5,359 WUA members in scheme operations. The WUAs were established immediately after the schemes were selected and the WUA members participated in every step, i.e. feasibility study, design, construc-tion, supervision, final inspection and operations and maintenance. The WUAs were trained in maintenance and they were allowed by the Provincial People's Committee (PPC) to retain the water use fees for their own maintenance.

Support for crop and livestock production

This sub-component comprised a range of activities to strengthen various agricul-tural extension programmes, improve the supply of inputs for intensive farming and diversify agricultural production activities.

Seed/seedling production

Support for the establishment of a Rice Seed Production Station resulted in 54ha under seed production annually involving 1840 farmers as contracted growers producing around 195 tonnes of seed annually. In total the station was able to provide farmers annually with 1770 tonnes of rice seed of several varieties and of good quality. Farmers were trained and could produce a wide range of good quality, high yielding varieties of rice seed on their own land. Improvements under the project of the Provincial Fruit Tree Production Station enabled it to supply 83,200 seedlings of fruit trees of various varieties and 480,000 seedlings of forest trees to farmers throughout the province with high survival rates of 87–92 per cent.

Extension programme

The project improved the extension services in the province through capacity building of the provincial and district staff of the Department of Agriculture and Rural Development (DARD), (194 participants for 4909 person-days including 51 per cent women), providing them with access to new technologies and equipping them to train at the grassroots level. Subsequently, 36,551 key farmers in 137 communes were trained for 88,781 person-days including 59 per cent women. Using the farmer-field school mechanism, these key farmers have trained thousands of other farmers. The training of key farmers has proved a very cost effective way of rapidly transferring modern production techniques to farmers, with around 60 per cent of the key farmers being very active. The project developed and distributed 62,000 training manuals to the key farmers and 8000 manuals to extension staff.

Demonstrations

The project implemented 550 on-farm research studies, 17 demonstration plots on improved rice production and integrated pest management (IPM), 12 demonstration plots on improved groundnut production and IPM, 9 demonstration plots on agro-forestry, 15 demonstrations on Mong Cai sow husbandry and other demonstrations for ducks and poultry production – the last of these not proving very successful. The project also established 367 household-based nurseries for fruit and forestry plants making seedlings widely available to the communities with a good response on uptake.

Pig semen station

With the support provided under the project for 7 pig semen stations with a total production capacity of 10,000 semen doses of hybrid pigs per year, the stations are now able to meet all the demand of farmers in the province. The total supply of semen since the start of the project has been 86,400 doses with a 76 per cent pregnancy rate achieved resulting in the production of 660,960 improved piglets to date.

Plant protection

As plant protection is a pressing need of farmers, the mid-term review agreed to allocate some budget for this new activity for 2004 and 2005, during which time the project trained 137 plant protection workers at the commune level, 84 plant protection officers at the provincial and district levels (including 49 per cent women), and trained 12,440 farmers in 137 poor communes for 24,688 person-days.

In addition, the project distributed 13,000 training manuals to staff and farmers. The training has helped farmers to appreciate the techniques of combining cultivation with plant protection.

Animal health support

The project has contributed significantly to improving veterinary services and the control of animal diseases through upgrading the provincial Disease Diagnosis Centre, establishing 3 new district level veterinary stations and training 345 provincial and district veterinary staff (25 per cent women) in improved practices for 6635 person-days. In addition, the project trained 274 veterinary workers from the community, of which 52 per cent were women, for 36,380 person-days.

Aquaculture

The project rehabilitated three fresh water fish hatcheries, which can provide 70 tonnes of fingerlings annually to farmers, rehabilitated 135 ponds covering 75ha assisting 250 poor persons, and providing 13,768 person-days of training for farmers in 55 communes of which 81 per cent were poor and women. The project also prepared and distributed 6000 booklets on fish culture techniques.

Social forestry and environmental protection

The project planted 903ha of acacia and pine on degraded forest land against the project target of 750ha, providing 460 poor households with the opportunity of leasing forest land and retaining 90 per cent of the income from the wood sold. The project has also strengthened the capacity of the forestry department through training 250 district and commune cadres on forestry development strategy, policies and laws, and forestry and environmental protection. It enhanced the awareness of communities to environmental protection through training 3633 farmers on forest ecology, and on tree planting and maintenance.

Financial services

A key component that underpinned the success of the project was the establishment of a microcredit scheme managed at the grassroots level by the Women's Union but under the overall guidance of the Project Micro-Credit Development Board (PMCDB), which was responsible for the management of the project's revolving credit fund (RCF). The Women's Union has established 2570 village credit and savings groups (VSCGs) in 97 communes with 26,852 members, of which around 67 per cent are from poor households (against the target of 80 per cent). The project provided regular training on various aspects of credit management for provincial and district level Women's Union staff for 952 persons and for 46,450 group leaders and 42,103 group members. Total lending reached VND82,682 million (US$5.2 million), involving 50,999 loans

Figure 10.1 *A meeting of a women's savings and credit group*

Source: HRDP

(63 per cent to poor households), with many women on their second or third loans.

Rural markets

The project has built/upgraded 57 rural markets (plus 4 under the CDF). These markets have generated jobs and extra incomes for about 3500 households through new trading and transport opportunities and through daily operations, maintenance and managerial work at the markets.

Roads and bridges

The project built/rehabilitated 8 inter-commune roads with a total length of 89.7km and 22 independent bridges with a total length of 457m. These roads service 115 communes of which 66 are poor communes, including the targeted 48 poorest communes. 59 communes have benefited from the new bridges, of which 22 are poor communes.

Project management

The project established the Provincial Project Coordination Unit (PPCU) and nine district project coordination units (DPCUs) to manage the implementation of the project. The Project Steering Committee was duly instituted and met very regularly. The project contributed significantly to building the capacity of the project management staff providing training for 940 staff for 3959 person-days covering such areas as planning, report writing, project coordination and management, and computer operations and ICT.

Project impacts and outcomes

Poverty reduction

HRDP made a significant contribution to lowering the rate of poverty in Ha Tinh. Data from the Provincial Department of Labour, Invalids and Social Affairs (DOLISA) indicate that the poverty rate in the 48 poorest communes where HRDP's activities have been the most intensive has decreased by 34 percentage points from 52 per cent in 1999 to 18 per cent in 2004, and by 31 percentage points for the 137 project communes from 46 per cent to 15 per cent over the same time period, higher than the overall rate of poverty decline in the province as a whole, as shown in Table 10.1 below. This has removed all but 6 of the 48 poorest communes from the category of poor commune (on the basis of the revised lower poverty threshold of 25 per cent). Under the old poverty criteria, whereby communes with 40 per cent poor households were classified as poor, all the 48 poorest communes would have been lifted out of the poor category.

The project has also contributed significantly to increasing the incomes and livelihoods of poor households. With reference to the key logframe indicators, the annual per capita income in the 137 project communes has more than doubled US$3.5 million or in rice equivalent from 280kg to 625kg. Food consumption per head for poor households has increased from 180kg to 300kg, greatly enhancing food security through increasing food consumption from 45 per cent

Table 10.1 *Changes in the poverty rate between 1999 and 2004*

| | Poverty Rate | | | | | |
| | 1999 | | | 2004 | | |
	Total number of households	Number of poor households	% poor	Total number of households	Number of poor households	% poor
48 poorest communes	49,162	25,354	52	52,924	9,458	18
137 project communes	139,715	63,878	46	153,287	22,995	15
Total for Province	266,833	95,720	36	311,555	36,949	12

Source: Ha Tinh Department of Labour, Invalids and Social Affairs

of the 400kg/capita required to attain full food security to 75 per cent of that required.

Intensification and diversification of income

A total of 5039ha of land has been brought under improved irrigation – 2849ha under the small-scale irrigation component and 2190ha under CDF irrigation schemes. Combined with improved access to quality inputs (seed, fertilizer and chemicals) and increased production skills brought about by the extension activities, yields have increased by between 15 and 50 per cent, and an estimated 20,000 tonnes of additional paddy is produced annually in the project area. The increased paddy production has resulted in increased staple food supplies for an estimated 86,250 households. The assured supply of quality seed is a major achievement of the project and in 2005, DARD estimated that 80 per cent of the paddy farmers in the province would have access to improved quality, certified seed. This is largely attributable to the upgrading of the Thien Loc Rice Seed Production Station and the improved distribution system of contract growers.

Households receiving increased incomes and food production from livestock have increased by over 50,000 in number and livestock numbers have increased on average by 5 per cent per annum. Disease outbreaks have been contained and through access to credit, livestock numbers have increased significantly. Improved roads and access to new markets have allowed the poor to maximize returns from production, reduce transaction costs and provide new job opportunities for an estimated 15,943 people. Data show that around 356,287 people use and benefit from the markets. The new roads and bridges have facilitated access to education for children as well as access to the market and to health services for farmers, particularly those living in remote communes. Initial assessments show that the project roads serve more than 125,000 people. The movement of vehicles has increased substantially with estimated increases of 2600 per cent, 600 per cent and 300 per cent for bicycles, motorcycles and pick-ups respectively, and an additional 3500 pick-ups and trucks have been purchased by the local people since the roads have been improved.

Capacity building

The emphasis given to capacity building at all levels from government staff to community institutions and farmers is widely acknowledged to have been a key factor in the success of the project. Through the provision of professional training, HRDP has made a significant contribution to enhancing the knowledge, skills and development orientation of a number of key government technical agencies (agriculture, irrigation, forestry, veterinary, etc) at the provincial and district levels, thereby helping to provide a solid foundation for promoting the future economic development of the province. Project management and implementing agency staff have also been exposed to modern management practices that represent a significant addition to the nation's organizational capital.

By setting up representative bodies at the village and commune level and linking them up with the existing social, political and developmental framework, the project has contributed towards the institutionalization of the processes as well as building up social, organizational and institutional capital. The training of key farmers, who have subsequently trained thousands of other farmers, has proved to be a very cost effective mechanism for the rapid transfer of modern production practices to farmers at large. The improved extension services and farmer training has proved valuable in increasing the capacity of farmers and promoting the adoption of new practices.

Participation

Through the introduction of participatory planning, HRDP entirely changed the approach to planning from top down to demand driven. Through the participatory planning process, HRDP effectively demonstrated how the poor and women can be effectively targeted, how they can be given a voice in decision making and how they can be made effective agents of change. The participatory planning processes have contributed significantly to realizing democracy at the grassroots level in the target communes. The participatory planning exercises involving community members, particularly the poor and women, have not only built their self-confidence but also enabled them to assess their household's economic status as well as the options for optimum utilization of their resource base and to actively participate in formulating the community's development plan. The CDF has enabled community members to have direct control over resources and a dominant voice in prioritizing development needs and this has led to a sense of ownership and their active participation in all the processes of implementation, operations and maintenance.

Decentralization

HRDP took bold initiatives on decentralization by allowing communities to fully implement and manage small infrastructure works, both physically and financially, and has thereby demonstrated that decentralized implementation is viable. By empowering communities through the decentralized implementation of rural infrastructure, significant improvements were achieved in terms of transparency, greater involvement of local people in construction providing more income, improved sense of ownership, enhanced capacity of the commune/village staff and community members, higher quality of work, and more effective use of budgetary resources. Indeed, the cost of works was 10–15 per cent lower resulting in savings that could be devoted to other development activities. By adopting the

Figure 10.2 *A road being built by commune members*

Source: HRDP

decentralized approach, the project encouraged the beneficiary communities to develop their own initiatives and innovations, and to promote democracy.

Gender equality and women's empowerment

The project has achieved good success in gender equality and gender mainstreaming in participation and training, ensuring that women comprised 57 per cent of the participants in the planning processes, 59 per cent of key farmers, 55–59 per cent of trainees for agricultural practices and managers of demonstrations, around 80 per cent of managers of pig breeding demonstrations, 30 per cent of the operators of household-based nurseries and 52 per cent of vet workers. More importantly, women have become involved in management, and comprise 25 per cent of the members of CDBs, 30 per cent of the members of the project management units established for implementation of the various civil works, and 37 per cent of the members of the WUAs.

Policy impact

Through taking bold initiatives on decentralization and community participation, HRDP made a significant contribution to the practical demonstration of the Government's Decree on Grassroots Democracy. Through the strong support of the provincial authorities, particularly in issuing the necessary legal and financial regulations in support of project activities, HRDP has been in the forefront of operationalizing and institutionalizing the broad guidelines from central-level government policy. Thus, the province responded to the government's support for participatory irrigation management by extending regulations for the strengthening of WUAs to all irrigation schemes in Ha Tinh.

Project cost

A summary of the final allocation of expenditures compared with the original financial projections is given in Table 10.2 below. This shows the significant increase in the proportion of project expenditure going to participatory development (mainly the CDF element) with smaller increases in rural markets, roads and bridges, and project management.

Table 10.2 *Summary of expenditure by component*

Project Component	Initial Projection		Mid-term Review		Final Expenditure	
	Amount (US$ thousands)	%	Amount (US$ thousands)	%	Amount (US$ thousands)	%
I Participatory Development	2252	11.8	4853	25.4	5082	25.4
II Income Generation						
– Small-scale irrigation	3242	16.9	3246	17.0	3404	17.0
– Vet services support	779	4.1	571	3.0	388	1.9
– Community forestry			281	1.5	236	1.2
– Crop and livestock support	1530	8.0	1310	6.8	1034	5.2
– Financial services	2965	15.5	2891	15.1	2451	12.2
– Rural markets	715	3.7	1466	7.7	1812	9.0
– Solar energy	60	–	83	0.1	54	–
Sub-total (income generation)	9291	48.6	9848	51.5	9379	46.8
III Roads and Bridges	2903	15.2	3075	16.1	3461	17.3
IV Project Management	1231	6.4	1355	7.1	2105	10.5
Decentralized Infrastructure Fund (DIF)	3452	18.0				
Total Project Cost	19,131	100.0	19,131	100.0	20,027[1/]	100.0

Source: IFAD (2005)

Challenges and how they were overcome

HRDP was the first IFAD project in Vietnam without a grant-funded technical assistance (TA) component and all TA requirements of the project were covered under the loan funds. It was expected that the TA would be provided by the national consultants who were involved in the other IFAD-funded on-going projects. In addition, Voluntary National Advisors were expected to provide regular implementation support to the project. The project faced difficulties in regard to both these sources of technical support.

There was a reason why the project could not mobilize TA from national consultants. The consultancy rates applied to the IFAD loan projects were stipulated by the Ministry of Finance and they were too low to attract the qualified national consultants to work in the challenging location. Therefore, the project very much needed donor-supported TA so that the consultancy rates applied to national consultants by the donor could be used.

On top of the lack of TA, the initial implementation was much more difficult than the project formulation expected, in particular, in the local capacity building efforts to implement a greater level of decentralization and participation. For example, the local regulations at that time did not allow the community groups to directly implement the civil works, which require legal entities with certified standards for implementation of civil works. To apply the pilot model of self-implementation of civil works by the communities, the project had to mobilize TA to study the legal framework and the formulation of a decision by the local government that could enable the community-led approach at a pilot scale. To make the pilot model successful, the project management and TA consultants had to work very hard to build capacities of the local communities to self-manage the complicated construction of roads and irrigation schemes.

Due to the lack of TA from a co-financing donor, the project had a very low implementation rate for the first year. In view of several recommendations from United Nations Office of Project Services (UNOPS) Supervision Missions for mobilization of additional, especially international TA support for the project, UNDP, on the request of the Ministry of Planning and Investment (MPI), agreed to extend TA support to HRDP under its MPI-based project – 'Technical Assistance to IFAD Programme'. The TA project became operational in July 2002 and since then the senior technical advisor to the project and a Ha Tinh-based United Nations volunteer helped the project in the areas of community participation, participatory planning, capacity building, decentralization, gender and microfinance. The UNDP also financed much needed national TA and training for participatory planning, participatory monitoring and evaluation, and microfinance.

The IFAD country portfolio manager always followed up closely and provided effective support and assistance to the project throughout the whole implementation process. IFAD staff participated regularly in the supervision missions and in the Mid-Term Review Mission. IFAD exercised flexibility in responding to the implementation needs of the project, such as increasing the authorized allocation to a special account to improve the overall liquidity of the project and approving simplified fund withdrawal procedures. In addition, IFAD was very responsive to modifying the project design to improve performance and effectiveness, for example, in agreeing to enhance the standard of roads to be funded under the project from gravel roads to tarmacadam surface. IFAD was also very responsive to the emerging needs of the target group, agreeing to the funding of two additional sub-components – plant protection and aquaculture – to meet concerns raised by farmers during the participatory planning exercises.

Government at the central level through the MPI and the Ministry of Finance (MoF) provided strong support to project implementation with active follow-up of issues. MPI and MoF assisted the project in raising recommendations and proposals to the Government of Vietnam, IFAD and the Cooperating Institution (CI) to resolve constraints and difficulties faced by the project during the implementation process. MoF performed well in submitting withdrawal applications in a timely manner, facilitating prompt processing of replenishments to the special account. The Government of Vietnam also provided its contribution in a timely manner as scheduled throughout the project implementation period.

At the provincial level the project received excellent support from the provincial authorities, which facilitated and enabled the PPCU to comply with all the provisions of the Loan Agreement and the Project Appraisal Report as well as the recommendations raised by the UNOPS/IFAD annual supervision missions and the mid-term review. The provincial authorities were particularly supportive in issuing the necessary legal and financial documents in support of project activities. Pending the specific policies and guidelines on such areas as microcredit services, empowerment and simplified procedural steps to decentralize the implementation of civil construction to be officially introduced by the central government, the PPC of Ha Tinh took the initiative to promulgate a number of much needed regulations such as the implementation guidelines or handbooks issued by the PPCU. Due to these regulations and guidelines, the project could conduct its activities more easily, effectively and successfully.

Lessons learned

The experience of implementing the project generated a number of key lessons that can provide guidance for subsequent project design.

Participatory development

Project experience demonstrated that while the overall approach and methodology for participatory development was quite sound, it hinged on a number of necessary conditions that were not available during the initial phase of project implementation. These conditions include:

- the availability of sufficient numbers of key staff conversant with the participatory methodology;
- the existence of an enabling legal and institutional environment that allows the beneficiaries to become investment owners and to take financial and administrative charge of the project-funded schemes;
- sensitization of key decision makers to the objectives and processes of participatory development;
- ensuring that all project information is shared with the beneficiaries in a transparent and consistent manner; and
- the first year of the project should be devoted to capacity building of the concerned staff in the implementing agencies and the communities/beneficiaries so that everyone clearly understands the roles, responsibilities, rights and duties under the participatory implementation approach.

Grassroots empowerment

The project experience also showed that the achievement of democracy and grassroots empowerment requires the following conditions to be met:

- Policies and regulations are issued by the provincial and district authorities to ensure systematic targeting of project interventions to the poor.
- Meetings are held to ensure that the beneficiary community understands well the purpose, objectives and significance of all the provisions in the regulation.
- Complete transparency is ensured through making public all the information on the project criteria, economic and technical norms, and beneficiaries are helped to know what benefits they can expect from the project and what they must do to ensure such benefits.
- Empowerment must be commensurate with the recipients' capacity and must be accompanied by capacity enhancement and technical assistance.
- Systems and procedures should be in place that allow the grassroots level to take initiatives in implementation and full responsibility for physical and financial management; the roles and responsibilities of each level in implementing decentralized works should be clearly determined.

Potential for scaling up and replication

Overall, the project was very successful in developing models that have been replicated and institutionalized not only in the province but also under national programmes and projects. The project played a catalytic role in realizing certain key aspects of government policies and adopting innovative development approaches, particularly decentralized implementation of infrastructure works, decentralization of service delivery such as extension and livestock services, development of civil society organizations such as the CBOs. Particularly, the participatory planning approach introduced by the project has been recognized as a useful tool that national programmes for poverty reduction have institutionalized under their planning mechanisms.

In particular, the project in its final stage successfully implemented a new approach with community-self implementation of 17 infrastructure schemes in 17 of the 48 target communes. Instead of subcontracting out the civil works to construction companies, the project enabled groups of households (community's civil work management boards – CWMBs) to sign contracts with CDB on implementation of the civil works, including roads and irrigation schemes. The local government got agreements from relevant agencies to test this method under HRDP. CWMBs prioritized the poorest households in the commune to take works under the projects, such as land levelling and transportation of construction materials. Therefore, the civil works not only raised the incomes of the poor, but also improved the sense of ownership and empowerment of the local people for the sustainable maintenance of the infrastructures. Today, the approach of directly using community groups to implement civil works has been replicated by many projects in other provinces.

The model of WUAs, which was first introduced by IFAD in Tuyen Quang province and replicated under HRDP, was institutionalized by the Ministry of Agriculture and Rural Development (MARD) Strategic Framework for Participatory Irrigation Management in 2004. Consequently, the PPC in Ha Tinh, based on the strategic framework, institutionalized all the WUAs in the province, making this province the leader in the implementation of this policy. Continuation of the WSCGs was assured post-project through the MoF decision to transfer the management of the credit funds for a further 14 years to the Women's Union. Today, more than 3000 WSCGs are still working well two years after the end of the project. The on-going or follow-up IFAD-funded Improving Markets Participation of the Poor Programme started early in 2007 is progressing on the foundations established by the HRDP.

Conclusions

HRDP is a complex, multi-faceted project that aimed to reduce poverty by supporting irrigation and agricultural/livestock extension, providing access to credit and improving rural infrastructure (roads, bridges, markets and schools). The project made commendable progress in achieving its development objectives to improve the living standards and food security of poor rural households, and to increase their participation in the development process. It made a significant contribution to reducing the poverty rate in the 137 project communes from 46 per cent in 1999 to 15 per cent in 2004, and in the 48 poorest communes from 52 per cent to 18 per cent.

Through the participatory planning process, the project effectively demonstrated how the poor and women can be effectively targeted, how they can be given a voice in decision making and how they can be made effective agents for change. HRDP's effective implementation of participatory planning has been recognized at province, district and commune levels as a responsive, transparent and efficient approach to the allocation of development resources, while local people now consider community participation an essential requirement of the development process.

However, it was not easy to achieve the development goals expected. The project had to overcome many constraints to reduce poverty, demonstrating to national and local decision makers the importance of reforms for decentralization and participation. Lessons learnt from the project have contributed to developing the current Socio-economic Development Plan 2006–2010 in Vietnam as well as in Ha Tinh province.

Since HRDP was very successful, IFAD and the Government of Vietnam have decided to extend development cooperation for sustainable poverty reduction in Ha Tinh province. The new project, Improving Market Participation of the Poor, was formulated during 2006 and began in early 2007. While further consolidating the HRDP approach of participation and decentralization, it is promoting a quite innovative approach to poverty reduction that mobilizes a broader range of economic development opportunities through the inclusion of SME development, processing and marketing, and the development of linkages with the private sector. It is expected that Ha Tinh Province will continue to develop the market-based poverty reduction model applicable for wider replication in Vietnam.

References

IFAD (International Fund for Agricultural Development) (1999) *Ha Tinh Rural Development Project Appraisal Report No. 0936-VN*, IFAD, Rome, Italy

IFAD (2003) *Ha Tinh Rural Development Project Mid-Term Review Report No. 1479-VN*, IFAD, Rome, Italy

IFAD (2005) *Ha Tinh Rural Development Project Completion Report No. 1700-VN*, IFAD, Rome, Italy

IFAD (2006) *Improving Markets Participation of the Poor Programme in Ha Tinh and Tra Vinh Provinces, Appraisal Report No. 1777-VN*, IFAD, Rome, Italy

11

Good Practice for Poverty Reduction in Coconut Growing Communities in the Philippines

Pons Batugal[1], Erlene Manohar[2] and Maria Luz George[3]

Introduction

The coconut is considered a 'tree of life' as it provides many products such as liquid from the water and flower sap, cream, milk and cooking oil from the kernel, geotextiles and organic fertilizer from the husk, activated carbon and fashion accessories from the shell, baskets and brooms from the leaves and lately, medicinal, cosmeceutical and nutriceutical products and biofuel from the oil. In the Philippines, although coconut earns about US$1 billion annually from exports and about one-third of the population depend on the coconut directly or indirectly, coconut farmers still belong to the marginalized sector of society and most live below the poverty line. Despite its economic importance, the potential of the coconut has not been fully realized to help the poor coconut farmers. Over 90 per cent of coconut farmers are smallholders, tending four hectares or less; many work on land they do not own; are considered unbankable by the formal banking sector; and usually do not have political clout to influence government or private sector policy. Due to poverty, coconut farmers in general are not capable of or interested in improving their aging coconut farms, resulting in decreasing yields and exports. Unless poverty in coconut growing communities is effectively addressed in a sustainable manner, the situation will further worsen and lead to the demise of coconut, an important crop for the poor.

The project

The authors believe that coconut farmers need not be poor and that when a community-based sustainable coconut-based farming systems approach is developed and promoted at the community level, the quality of life of coconut farmers can be improved and the coconut industry can be sustained (Batugal and Oliver, 2005). In an effort to help reduce poverty in coconut growing communities, the Philippine Coconut Authority (PCA) collaborated with the International Coconut Genetic Resources Network (COGENT) to develop and implement a poverty reduction model to address the above-mentioned problems.

Project formulation

The project was formulated in a participatory manner. In order to better understand the basis of poverty in coconut growing communities, consultations were conducted with coconut farmers and members of their families in coconut-growing communities in the major islands of the country, namely Luzon, Visayas and Mindanao. Using focus group discussions, farmer participants were asked to identify their problems and opportunities and how these can be addressed in a sustainable manner. Participatory tools such as pre-ballot box, matrix ranking and SWOT (strengths, weaknesses, opportunities and threats) analysis were employed in gathering the data (Manohar, 2006).

The consultations revealed that coconut farmers are poor because:

- most farmers plant coconut commercially as a monoculture crop and mainly depend on a single commercial product – copra or the dried coconut kernel – whose price is low and unstable;
- only one member of the family (the farmer) is employed;
- they lack technology, appropriate village-level machinery, capital and access to markets; and
- they lack CBOs to assist members address their common problems and opportunities.

Based on the above findings, an initial research project was designed to test a four-pronged poverty reduction strategy to determine whether such interventions could effectively help poor people in coconut-growing communities to escape from poverty. The components of the strategy for generating income were: diversification of coconut products, intercropping, livestock integration and coconut seedling propagation and planting. The project developed and tested these interventions as good practice models.

The consultations with farmers also revealed that a support system needs to be in place to support the poverty reduction strategy and make a coconut-based farming system sustainable. Hence, the following agricultural development components of a community-based support system were incorporated into the project: (1) establishment and strengthening of CBOs in each project site; (2) access to appropriate technologies and efficient and affordable village-level equipment; (3) access to capital and markets; and (4) training and capacity building.

Project goals and objectives

The project goal was to reduce poverty in selected coconut growing communities, while its objectives were to develop good practice for increasing incomes and employment at the community level, and to develop support systems to make such good practice sustainable

Key elements of the project

Target beneficiaries

The target beneficiaries were coconut farmers and socially disadvantaged unemployed and underemployed women in poor coconut growing communities in four pilot coconut growing communities.

Project area

The project was implemented in four coconut agrarian reform communities in Malapad, Real, Quezon on the island of Luzon; Caliling, Cauayan, Negros Occidental on the island of Visayas; and on Linabu, Balingasag, Misamis Oriental and Old Poblacion, Maitum, Sarangani on the island of Mindanao. The strategically selected project sites will eventually serve as the nuclei for expansion of the project in these major islands of the country.

Project activities

Development and testing of coconut-based good practice for income generation

Diversification of coconut products

Various technologies for the production of high-value coconut products and by-products from the kernel (virgin coconut oil, '*bukayo*'), coconut husk (geotextiles, organic fertilizer), shell (shell handicraft and fashion accessories) and sap (coconut sugar, vinegar) were introduced and tested by CBOs to determine their technical feasibility, financial viability, social acceptability and environmental safety. The choice of product was based on a market survey conducted by trained CBO members and PCA technical personnel at the local, provincial and national levels using participatory rapid market appraisal techniques (Manohar and Sancha, 2005).

Crop diversification through intercropping cash, food security and medicinal crops

With about 50 per cent interspaces left unutilized in a coconut plantation, intercropping with marketable high-value crops was expected to generate additional income from the coconut farm. The choice of crop to grow was based on a rapid market survey conducted by trained CBO members and PCA technical personnel. In at least one community (Maitum), medicinal plants for common diseases and ailments were identified, characterized, propagated and conserved in a 'living pharmacy' or medicinal plant garden that was operated by CBO members. Establishment of nurseries for producing seeds of native crop varieties was also encouraged to sustain the availability of high-quality planting materials for the next cropping season. To lower the cost of fertilizer inputs and to protect the environment, organic fertilizer was also produced using vermiculture (earthworms) and fungus (*Trichoderma harziarum*) to aid decomposition of farm wastes. The high-potash coconut coir fibre pith was also used as organic fertilizer for the coconut and intercrops.

Livestock integration

Integrating livestock (i.e. chickens, ducks, pigs, goats and cattle) under the coconut-based farming system was included to provide cash and enhance nutrition. To augment the source of feeds for the ruminant animals, planting of fodder crops was also undertaken. The choice of livestock to be raised was based on the results of rapid market surveys and feasibility studies. The initial use of native breeds of animals was encouraged as these are more resistant to diseases and tolerant of hunger.

Coconut seedling propagation and planting

The existing stands of coconut in the community were evaluated by farmers and important varieties were identified and characterized with the help of PCA coconut breeders. Coconut 'diversity fairs' were conducted in each community in which farmers brought fruits of their coconut varieties. Performance of these varieties was assessed by the project participants in each village with the help of PCA breeders and important varieties were selected as a source of planting materials for the community nursery that was established through the project. Each project participant was required to plant at least five coconut seedlings per year to replace aging coconut palms and to conserve precious farmers' varieties.

Development of agricultural support systems to make good practice sustainable

Establishment and strengthening of CBOs

A CBO was established in each project site that was registered with appropriate government agencies, namely the Cooperative Development Authority and Department of Labour and Employment. CBO members elected their set of officers who developed policies and procedures for the implementation of various income-generating activities and the operation of their respective microcredit systems.

Access to appropriate technologies and affordable village-level equipment

The project encouraged the use of indigenous technologies and these were often improved to increase their efficiencies. Through COGENT, suitable village-level technologies and equipment from its 38 network member countries were identified and tested, and those found technically feasible and financially viable were introduced for further testing at the community level. Equipment financing from the microcredit system was provided for selected equipment.

Access to capital and markets

A microcredit system was established that was supported by a revolving fund. The fund was managed by the officers of the CBO who decided who should get a loan, how much interest to charge and the repayment period. It also linked the CBOs to other microcredit-providing agencies. This access to capital provided a rare opportunity for members to acquire non-collaterized small loans to invest in income-generating technologies. The project supported a marketing survey to identify current marketable products from coconuts and new product opportunities, and linked the CBOs with interested private sector users of their products and with the Department of Trade and Industry to help CBO members in product packaging and marketing.

Training and capacity building

The project trained CBO members on CBO and microcredit establishment and management and human values formation. It also provided training on the production of high-value coconut products such as virgin coconut oil, coconut sugar, fibrer-, shell- and sap-based products, on intercropping and livestock raising, and on community nursery establishment and management. Experts from various agencies of the government and the private sector provided training and technology transfer services. The project also encouraged CBO members and officers to conduct regular meetings to discuss common problems and opportunities.

Promotion

To encourage more community members of the four communities to participate, the project conducted 'farmers' field days' and intra-project and inter-project farmers' visits. To promote collaboration, adoption and replication of the project strategy nationwide, the project documented and published success stories, organized and participated in seminars, meetings and media campaigns through radio programmes and published scientific papers in refereed journals, and popular articles in newspapers.

Institutionalization

To institutionalize the coconut-based farming systems poverty reduction approach, the PCA collaborated with the Department of Agrarian Reform, the Department of Agriculture through its regional field offices, the Bureau of Agricultural Research, the Department of Trade and Industry, the local government units (LGUs), and the private sector suppliers of inputs (seeds and chemicals). It conducted joint project planning with the Barangay Development Council to incorporate the project into the Barangay Integrated Development Plan and eventually into the Municipal Development Plan, and to make the project eligible for funding by the municipal government. It also linked the project with local and international development organizations and donors to generate funding for replicating the project in other sites.

Key technical inputs

The key technical inputs were the high-quality seeds and animal breeds, village-level technologies and equipment, capacity building for CBO and microcredit establishment and management, training on coconut products and crop diversification, livestock integration and coconut nursery establishment and coconut characterization, on-farm conservation of coconut genetic resources and project monitoring and evaluation.

Timeframe

The project was implemented from 2002 to 2005 under the direct supervision of PCA, after which PCA only monitored the progress of the project and status of the microcredit funds.

Impact and outcomes

Adoption of income-generating technology interventions

Based on a feasibility study and market potential survey data presented by the project, CBO members had the option to choose the kind of income-generating interventions to undertake and which kinds of crops, livestock and products to produce that were appropriate to their farm conditions and their present economic situation. Table 11.1 shows the frequency with which the different options were chosen by the farmers.

Intercropping and livestock integration were the interventions adopted by most coconut farmers. Seventy-one per cent or 163 farmers out of the 228 farmer-respondents adopted intercropping; 65 per cent or 149 farmers adopted coconut-livestock integration. In the case of high-value coconut products, there were only 66 adopters or 29 per cent of the total respondents; while 13 per cent or 29 farmers adopted coconut nursery establishment as their income generating activity. Several families adopted up to four of these income-generating options depending on their capacity and socio-economic conditions.

Table 11.1 *Frequency and percentage of adoption of technology by coconut farmers in four project sites, 2005*

TYPE OF TECHNOLOGY	PROJECT SITES								TOTAL	
	Maitum		Balingasag		Real		Cauayan			
	No.	%	No.	%	No.	%	No.	%	No.	%
Coconut Nursery										
Adopted	0	0	15	27	11	22	3	9	29	13
Did not adopt	89	100	40	73	38	78	32	91	199	87
Total	89	100	55	100	49	100	35	100	228	100
Coconut High Value Products										
Adopted	17	19	21	38	14	29	14	40	66	29
Did not adopt	72	81	34	62	35	71	21	60	162	71
Total	89	100	55	100	49	100	35	100	228	100
Coconut Intercropping										
Adopted	79	89	33	60	31	63	20	57	163	71
Did not adopt	10	11	22	40	18	37	15	43	65	29
Total	89	100	55	100	49	100	35	100	228	100
Livestock Integration										
Adopted	65	73	31	56	26	53	27	77	149	65
Did not adopt	24	27	24	44	23	47	8	23	79	35
Total	89	100	55	100	49	100	35	100	228	100

Note: The farmer-respondents considered in this study were only those who had been interviewed before and after the implementation of the project.

Table 11.2 *Farm income structure at project start and project end in the four project sites*

PROJECT SITE	At Project Start (US$)		At Project End (US$)		
	Value	%	Nominal Value	Real Value[a] (2002=100)	%
Balingasag, Misamis Oriental (n=50)					
Total Farm Income	**353**	100	**840**	**761**	100
Coconut production/processing	212	60	78	70	9
Intercrop production	52	15	537	487	64
Livestock production	89	25	225	204	27
Cauayan, Negros Oriental (n=35)					
Total Farm Income	**114**	100	**416**	**378**	100
Coconut production/processing	57	50	161	146	39
Intercrop production	24	21	134	122	32
Livestock production	33	29	121	110	29
Real, Quezon (n=45)					
Total Farm Income	**275**	100	**605**	**572**	100
Coconut production/processing	173	63	354	335	59
Intercrop production	50	18	133	125	22
Livestock production	53	19	118	111	19
Maitum, Sarangani (n=85)					
Total Farm Income	**411**	100	**963**	**864**	100
Coconut production/processing	365	89	496	446	52
Intercrop production	41	10	427	384	44
Livestock production	5	1	39	35	4

Note: [a]Actual farmers' income adjusted to consumer price index. Errors in sums are due to rounding.

Increase in income as a result of income-generating interventions

The good practices tested such as coconut product diversification, intercropping, livestock integration and coconut seedling propagation and sale of planting materials increased incomes by about two times in Balingasag, Real and Maitum and by about three times in Cauayan (see Table 11.2).

Decrease in poverty levels in coconut-growing communities

With farm incomes having significantly increased at the end of the project, poverty in all project sites has declined dramatically within a period of just three years. Decreasing poverty due to the project interventions had its greatest impact

Table 11.3 *Poverty level at start and end of the project in the four project sites*

ITEM	Poverty threshold estimate[a]		At project start		At end of project	
	2002[b] (US$)	2004[c] (US$)	No.	%	No.	%
Balingasag, Misamis Oriental	203	232				
Below Poverty Threshold			22	44	6	12
Above Poverty Threshold			28	56	44	88
Cauayan, Negros Oriental	167	196				
Below Poverty Threshold			22	63	14	40
Above Poverty Threshold			13	37	21	60
Real, Quezon	252	292				
Below Poverty Threshold			27	60	15	33
Above Poverty Threshold			18	40	30	67
Maitum, Sarangani	234	226				
Below Poverty Threshold			15	18	2	2
Above Poverty Threshold			70	82	83	98

Note: [a]NSCB estimates; [b]NSCB provincial estimates; [c]2003 NSCB regional estimates used since estimates for 2004 were not yet available at the time data were obtained.

in Balingasag CBO (see Table 11.3). Its poverty incidence declined from 44 to 12 per cent or by 32 percentage points. Project sites in Real and Cauayan followed with a decline of 27 and 23 percentage points after the project, respectively. The project site in Maitum, Sarangani had the smallest decline with only 16 percentage points. However, it should be noted that it has the lowest poverty level at the start (18 per cent) and at the end (2 per cent) of the project.

Maitum had an existing cooperative that helped farmer members even before the start of the project, and already had a lower below poverty threshold level and a higher above poverty threshold level compared to the other project sites. Nevertheless, the incremental incomes from coconut production/processing, intercropping and livestock production as shown in Table 11.2 still improved the poverty reduction effect of the project (Table 11.3).

Equitable income distribution

In order to assess how the income-generating interventions addressed equity of benefit sharing, a comparison of the income distribution for both periods in the Balingasag project site (Manohar and Sancha, 2005) was studied (see Table 11.4). This analysis was done to test whether the project site that had the biggest reduction in poverty also resulted in an equitable distribution of income. Results showed that at the start of project implementation, 46.5 per cent (US$8672) of the total farm income (US$18,650) in the project site was shared by the lower 80 per cent of the

Table 11.4 *Income distribution analysis before and after the project in Balingasag, Misamis Oriental, 2002–2004*

Group of Farmers* by Income	Basic Data		Data for Lorenz Curve	
	Total Income (US$)	Percentage Share	Cumulative Percentage of Income	Cumulative Percentage of Farmers
Before the Project				
Lowest 20%	56	0.30	0.30	20
Second 20%	1136	6.09	6.39	40
Middle 20%	2928	15.70	22.09	60
Fourth 20%	4552	24.41	46.50	80
Highest 20%	9978	53.50	100.00	100
Total	18,650	100.00		
After the Project				
Lowest 20%	1765	4.64	4.64	20
Second 20%	4422	11.62	16.25	40
Middle 20%	6331	16.63	32.88	60
Fourth 20%	8850	23.25	56.13	80
Highest 20%	16,700	43.87	100.00	100
Total	38,069	100.00		

Note: Based on data set of 50 farmers.

farm income groups, while the remaining 53.5 per cent (US$9978) was shared by the upper 20 per cent of the farm income groups, indicating high income inequality among the farm households of Balingasag.

At the end of the project, farm incomes of coconut farmers in *Balingasag* had increased dramatically (see Table 11.2) from P17,629 (US$353) to P38,069 (US$761) and so did the total income by farmer income groups (lowest 20 per cent to highest 20 per cent). At the end of the project (see Table 11.4), the lower 80 per cent of the farm income groups now shared 56.13 per cent of total income, up from 46.50 per cent at the start of the project or an increase of approximately 9 percentage points. Also, the percentage share of total income by the upper 20 per cent decreased from 53.5 per cent to only 43.87 per cent at the end of the project. These observations indicate an improvement in income distribution among the farm households, which showed that the four-pronged poverty reduction strategy in coconut-based farming system could be used not only to increase incomes but also to reduce inequality of income distribution among poor coconut farmers.

Coconut genetic diversity conserved on-farm

In a period of 3 years, the 4 communities propagated 29,124 coconut seedlings from 4 local farmers' varieties and planted 22,689 seedlings while selling the rest

Table 11.5 *Coconut seedlings propagated and planted*

Project Site	Number of farmers managing the nursery	Number of seedlings propagated in the nursery	Number of coconut seedlings planted	Number of farmers who planted
Real	14 (all males)	Coconut: 6589	1735	39 (17 male, 22 female)
Cauayan	8 (6 male, 2 female)	Coconut: 1535	1617	47 (16 male, 31 female)
Balingasag	12 (7 male, 5 female)	Coconut: 16,000 Fruit and forest trees: 9699	18,672	91 (49 male, 42 female)
Maitum	5 (all males)	Coconut: 5000	665	14 (13 male, 1 female)
TOTAL	39	Coconut: 29,124	22,689	191 (95 male, 96 female)

Source: ADB-COGENT (2004)

to other communities (see Table 11.5). In effect, the four CBOs planted more coconut seedlings than they had over the previous ten years and also conserved precious coconut diversity.

Capacity building

One of the impacts of the project was the training of CBO members to provide them with skills for income-generating activities and support activities. In a period of 3 years, the project trained a total of 1146 participants on the 4 good practice models for income generation and support systems in coconut growing communities, with almost 50 per cent of the trainees being women (see Table 11.6). The training enhanced the capacities of poor coconut farmers to earn more income and escape poverty. The additional benefits to previously unemployed and underemployed women were their economic and social emancipation. As they started to earn incomes they enhanced their self-esteem and are now considered assets to their communities.

Total project cost

A total investment of around P500,000 (US$10,000) was made in each community, or a total of US$40,000 for the four communities. This consisted of 50 per cent from the ADB/International Plant Genetic Resources Institute (IPGRI), 45 per cent from the Government of the Philippines and about 5 per cent from the 4 communities.

Table 11.6 *Training conducted and participants by project site, 2004*

Training	Real		Cauayan		Balingasag		Maitum		Total Number of Participants	
	Male	Female	Male	Female	Male	Female	Male	Female	Male	Female
CBO and microcredit systems	31	35	38	90	87	74	108	14	264	213
High-value coconut products	20	44	20	30	21	17	55	38	116	129
Intercropping	54	73	31	53	12	5	NA	NA	97	131
Livestock production	37	28	36	38	0	0	NA	NA	73	66
Seedling production and nursery management	16	0	8	3	20	10	NA	NA	44	13
Total	158	180	133	214	140	106	163	52	594	552

Source: ADB-COGENT (2004)

Project management

The project was coordinated by the IPGRI through COGENT as part of its eight-country poverty reduction project in the Asia-Pacific region.

Implementing agency

The PCA served as the implementing agency and organized its national, regional, provincial and municipal technical staff to support the project.

Coordination mechanisms

The PCA municipal, provincial and regional teams compiled and analysed the data and submitted reports to the PCA national project leader. The PCA project leader visited the project sites at least every quarter to monitor progress and identify constraints and opportunities.

Monitoring and evaluation of project activities

COGENT developed an effective monitoring system consisting of work plans, target outputs and output deficit forms. These were submitted to COGENT twice a year by PCA. In addition, PCA participated in a COGENT-organized annual review and planning meeting involving eight countries. The ADB also conducted an annual review of the project and IPGRI arranged for an International Fund for an Agricultural Research Fellow to conduct a socio-economic evaluation of the project (Manohar, 2006).

Challenges and how they were overcome

The biggest problem was met at the start of the project when coconut farmers were cynical about what researchers could do for them because they had been living in poverty all their lives. This attitude changed when they observed that the project was participatory in nature and especially when CBO members were trained to identify their problems and solutions, and participated in making decisions on what income-generating activities to test and adopt. The other major problem was inadequate funding. This was overcome by aggressive project promotion by PCA, which convinced PCA, the Department of Agriculture, the Department of Agrarian Reform and the Department of Trade and Industry to provide support to the project in cash and in kind.

Lessons learned

Lessons from the project are as follows:

- The importance of the participatory nature of the project: When poor people were involved in making decisions, a sense of ownership was built into the project that significantly contributed to its support and sustainability.
- The importance of recognizing and rewarding successful CBO participants: This converted them into champions and they challenged others to also perform well.
- The importance of project support in the form of village-level technologies, equipment, access to capital and markets, all making significant contributions to the success of the project.
- The importance of supervision and monitoring: For example, in one site, a larger than average loan was obtained by the CBO president. Close supervision by PCA of the credit committee in each CBO had to be strengthened.
- The importance of early CBO training on project planning: For example, joint project planning with the Barangay Development Council took some time as there was a need to equip CBO officers early on with needed planning skills.

Good practice

Diversification of coconut products from all parts of the coconut increased income opportunities and spread the risk; intercropping and livestock integration increased incomes and enhanced nutrition while seedling nurseries increased incomes and conserved precious coconut diversity.

This case study has convincingly demonstrated the possibility of increasing the farm incomes of coconut farmers by up to three times and thereby reducing the poverty of marginalized coconut communities. The case has also demonstrated the successful micro–macro integration of the pilots by successfully institutionalizing this poverty reduction intervention approach into municipal development plans and into the national research and development agenda for coconut in the Philippines.

A paper describing the project, entitled 'Product diversification and biodiversity conservation: A community-based approach in overcoming poverty', won the 'Best Paper' award at the recent 2007 Annual Conference of the Federation of Crop Science Societies of the Philippines. The model has also been adopted in the Philippine Agriculture Plan 2020.

The CBOs continued to manage the project as their own even after termination of funding by ADB and without direct management inputs from PCA and IPGRI. They also made efforts to generate funds for additional activities of their members. In the case of Maitum, the CBO was able to generate P2,500,000 (US$50,000) from UNDP for income generation, environmental protection and medicinal plant conservation and use. In the case of the other three CBOs, they were able to generate financial support worth P50,000–150,000 (US$1000–3000) in cash and in kind from local government units.

Potential for scaling up and replication

Through joint planning between CBOs and Barangay Development Council, the projects were integrated into the Municipal Development Plan. Joint training also integrated the project with the provincial, regional and national programmes of the Department of Agriculture. The initial success of the project and the devolved administrative structure of Philippine agriculture provided opportunities for rapid scaling up of the project nationally. For example, the Philippine Bureau for Agricultural Research has funded an additional four communities to replicate the project in four provinces. Other government offices have also committed to fund nine communities in three other provinces of the country. Externally, IFAD has also funded an additional 3 communities in the Philippines and 25 more communities worldwide.

Conclusions

Four income-generating activities in coconut growing communities, namely coconut product diversification, intercropping, livestock integration and coconut propagation in seedling nurseries proved to be good practice models to increase the incomes of poor coconut farmers. Such good practice significantly reduced poverty and promoted the equitable distribution of income in coconut-growing communities. The provision of a support system consisting of CBO establishment and strengthening, access to capital and markets, and training and capacity building contributed to the sustainability of the good practice, in particular, and poverty reduction in general.

Notes

1   President, Farmers Community Development Foundation International.
2   Project Development Officer IV, PCA.
3   Coordinator, COGENT.

References

ADB-COGENT (2004) *Project Annual Report*, ADB-COGENT, International Plant Genetic Resources Institute, Regional Office for Asia, the Pacific and Oceania (IPGRI-APO), Serdang, Malaysia

Batugal, P. and Oliver, J. (eds) (2005) *Poverty Reduction in Coconut Growing Communities, Volume III: Project Achievements and Impact*, Serdang, International Plant Genetic Resources Institute, Regional Office for Asia, the Pacific and Oceania (IPGRI-APO),

Manohar, E. C. (2006) *Socioeconomic Assessment of the Poverty Reduction in Coconut Growing Communities Project in the Philippines*, IPGRI-PCA-CBO partnership, IFAR Fellowship report, Rome, International Plant Genetic Resources Institute (IPGRI)

Manohar, E. C. and Sancha, L. V. (2005) 'Impact assessment of the poverty reduction in coconut growing communities project in the Philippines', in P. Batugal and J. Oliver (eds) *Poverty Reduction in Coconut Growing Communities. Vol. III: Project Achievements and Impact*, Serdang, International Plant Genetic Resources Institute-Regional Office for Asia, the Pacific and Oceania (IPGRI-APO)

PART IV

Localization of Millennium Development Goals and Monitoring

Community Driven Development to Improve Livelihoods: The 'Gemidiriya' Project in Sri Lanka

Gamini Batuwitage[1] and Neil Fernando[2]

Introduction

Since independence in Sri Lanka, various programmes have been launched at national and sub-national levels to achieve poverty reduction and rural development. Under the first MDG, between 1990 and 2015, Sri Lanka aims to halve the proportion of people whose income is below the national poverty line.[3] In 1990, the proportion of the population below the national poverty line was 26 per cent and the target is to reduce this proportion to 13 per cent by 2015. As revealed by DCS (2006), the latest available related national publication, the proportion of population below the national poverty line fell from 26 per cent in 1990 to 22.7 per cent in 2002. However, given the present scenario, it is unlikely that the MDG of reducing the proportion of poor households from 22.7 per cent in 2002 to 13 per cent in 2015 will be achieved (DCS, 2006). This is largely due to various impediments to efforts to reduce poverty and to promote rural development in Sri Lanka.

Sri Lanka's social indicators, such as life expectancy, literacy and mortality rates are well above those in comparable developing countries and are on par with many developed countries (World Bank, 2005a). In terms of the Human Development Index, in 2004, Sri Lanka ranked 96th with an index of 0.740 among 177 countries (MFP, 2005). However, even after 58 years of independence, there has not been an appreciable reduction in poverty in the infrastructure-deficient least developed regions. In fact, there has been an increase in the inequality of consumption patterns (World Bank, 2005a), reflecting an increase in the disparity of income between high and low income groups. This has been attributed to the slow growth of the economy being inadequate to meet the demand for investment for development (MFP, 2005). The ethnic conflict in the northern and the eastern regions of the country has also drained resources for national security and the country has had to increasingly depend on external resources and foreign aid to balance the resource gap.

The limited development achieved has been concentrated in the Western Province, which contributes 51 per cent to the national GDP (DNP, 2005). The rural areas across the country have been largely deprived of the major infrastructure investment required for accelerated growth. Economic growth needs to be accelerated further to at least 8 per cent to alleviate poverty, reduce unemployment and raise the standard of living on a sustainable basis (CBSL, 2006). A domestic savings ratio of about 30 per cent would be needed to support such a rate of growth and the current ratio is only 19 per cent.

The largest ever welfare and social protection programme called 'Samurdhi', which has been in operation for the past ten years, distributes food stamps, offers credit for income generation and issues grants to build infrastructure for the benefit of the poor. This programme, which spends US$90 million annually, is failing to reach more than 58 per cent of households in the poorest consumption quintile, while more than 40 per cent of the benefits go to the richest 60 per cent of the population (World Bank, 2005b). The mis-targeting is basically due to the poor methodology adopted for the identification of the poor and lack of opportunity for the poor to drive the process.

The project

The new approach to development in the country proposes a major policy shift with an emphasis on pro-poor and pro-growth income and redistribution strategies. The main objective of the poverty reduction strategy in the country is to provide poor groups with income support to engage in income earning ventures, reduce the disparity in income between different social strata and minimize regional disparities in the incidence of poverty and development (MFP, 2005). The poor and other vulnerable groups are to be involved in the implementation of poverty reduction programmes, and to be made active partners in the overall development process.

In 2006, a budgetary provision of SLR46 billion (US$460 million) was made through 21 line ministries for rural development and poverty reduction. The government's dependence on public sector institutions to enhance service delivery and on private sector institutions to provide an impetus to growth will have to be validated by putting in place mechanisms to enhance productivity, accountability and improved governance (CBSL, 2006). However, supply-driven approaches depending on the public service structure alone to deliver development to the poor would not produce desirable outcomes. People must be made central to development by investing in their capabilities to enable them to take charge of their own development process (NCED, 2005). This calls for the adoption of community-driven development, as applied in the Gemidiriya[4] Community Development and Livelihood Improvement Project (hereafter referred to as Gemidiriya).

Project formulation

The Gemidiriya project design offers a very carefully thought out model backed by a wealth of experience in project implementation in many parts of the world. During its design, many leaders of major poverty alleviation programmes locally and abroad were involved in identifying impediments and risk factors in implementation. Gemidiriya was launched in October 2004 to assist the implementation of the poverty reduction strategy of the Government of Sri Lanka (GoSL). It has been recognized that the mere availability of funds for development in itself does not guarantee poverty reduction. Gemidiriya has accordingly been designed to address the five widely-accepted impediments to poverty reduction in South Asia. These are:

- the attitude of dependency and the resultant absence of self-help and self determination;
- the non-inclusion of women, who constitute more than 50 per cent of the population, but are not represented in the decision-making process of major poverty reduction programmes;
- the expectation that village development will take place through plans formulated outside the village, usually in urban centres, where there is limited knowledge of the ground realities, and which will be imposed from the top down on village communities;
- the lack of investment of village savings within villages to boost their economies as well as a decline in production and an increase in input costs resulting in inadequate insurance for village initiatives; and
- the absence of effective social mobilization.

Gemidiriya project addresses these impediments and facilitates the adoption of a comprehensive, holistic and integrated approach to community development. The project was designed on the principles adopted in a pilot called 'Village Self Help Learning Initiative' (VSHLI) carried out in three villages in the district of Polonnaruwa. Its design, formulation of rules and procedures, implementation, monitoring and evaluation were done using a highly participatory community-driven approach. During the pilot, the hypothesis was tested that if rural communities are provided with information, decision-making power and supplementary resource assistance to their self-help initiatives, they would be able to better manage resources for their development. With the pilot's successful results, the GoSL requested scaling up of this initiative. The design of Gemidiriya was the response, which started in March 2003 with further testing and refining of the VSHLI model in 24 villages in 3 districts.

Project goals and objectives

The objective of the 12-year programme is to enable rural communities to improve their livelihoods and quality of life by building sustainable local-level institutions elected and managed by empowered village communities. This will be achieved by building linkages with local authorities and the private sector and by increasing the size and diversity of economic opportunities for village communities through federated community organizations, business enterprises and convergence with other development programmes.

The programme adopts a CDD approach where communities establish a village-based institution and plan their own village development programmes (VDPs), mobilize resources, receive financing directly from government resources and undertake implementation and maintenance, ensuring benefits to the poor and disadvantaged members of the communities.

Key elements of the project

Target beneficiaries and project area

During the first four-year phase from 2004 to 2008, Gemidiriya aims to enable communities in seven selected districts (Moneragala, Badulla, Hambantota, Matara, Galle, Ratnapura and Polonnaruwa) in four provinces (Uva, Southern, Sabaragamuwa and the North Central) to build accountable and self-governing local institutions and to manage resources by: (1) devolving decision-making power and resources to CBOs; (2) strengthening selected local governments that demonstrate responsiveness and accountability to rural communities; and (3) working with federations of village organizations (VOs) (registered under the Companies Act), the private sector and NGOs to develop strategies for economic empowerment (of the village communities) to increase the scale and diversity of livelihood options (World Bank, 2004).

The expected coverage of the project in its first phase is 1000 village communities in the 7 districts, and by the end of the third and final phase, 4000–5000 villages or about 7 million people.

By design, the project focuses on a comprehensive, integrated approach to village development with the principles of inclusion of the poor, women and youth having priority.

Badulla and Moneragala are the poorer districts of Uva province while Hambantota and Ratnapura are the poorer districts of Southern and Sabaragamuwa provinces respectively. By the end of June 2007, the project had expanded to

58 divisional secretariat divisions, covering 835 village communities and aimed to cover 1000 villages by the end of 2007.

Project activities

The project has five major components: (1) village development, (2) institutional strengthening/capacity building, (3) an Innovation Seed Fund, (4) project management and (5) continuation of the VSHLI pilot.

Key activities

The unique features of the project are:

- gradual devolution of power to local governments;
- direct transfer of funds from the government to the communities;
- fixed budget envelope and milestone-based disbursement;
- devolution of operations and maintenance activities to the communities;
- community contribution of up to 30 per cent of capital cost;
- simple and transparent rules of engagement (non-negotiables);
- independence and autonomy of the 'guardian of principles'[5]; and
- participatory targeting of the poor.

Targeting

Communities are chosen through a self-selection process based on their poverty status and expressed willingness to follow the principles of the project. The building of village institutions is facilitated by the project so that after maturity these village institutions, registered as people's companies (PC) under the Companies Act, will be able to use their experience and capacity to access funds from other sources. Such sources include the Decentralized Budget, provincial council funds and donor funds and will allow for implementation of the remaining activities of their VDPs, which would continue to be revised based on new needs. The funds available to Gemidiriya are limited by an entitlement computed at the rate of US$60 per person for the population of the village.

The project assists rural communities to form PCs and register them under the Companies Act to obtain legal recognition. Village communities organize members of the community into small self-help groups (SHGs) of five to seven members, form clusters of small groups and form a Village Savings and Credit Organization (VSCO) from cluster representatives within the company but as a separate sub-system. The members of the community elect a board of directors, form a financial committee, social audit committee, procurement committee and sub-committees based on the need. PCs work to have more than 80 per cent of households as shareholders without any discrimination by sex, race, religion or caste. The poor, women and youth are given priority. More than 50 per cent of the decision-making positions are held by women and about 30 per cent of youth representation is maintained with youth groups formed in all VOs. All important decisions are made at the general assembly with more than 50 per cent of participating being women.

The communities undertake a baseline survey, formulate a VDP using participatory rural appraisal techniques and allocate the entitlement of the Village Development Fund (VDF) for capacity building, social and community infrastructure and livelihood improvement. They allocate about 5 per cent of the VDF to award one-time grants to the poorest of the poor to provide social protection, saving them from misery. The communities allocate about 10 per cent of the VDF to a Youth Skill Development Fund (YSDF) to issue loans to the unemployed youth of the community to acquire skills, get a means of living and pay the loan back. The balance of 85 per cent of the fund is for providing credit to the members of the community through the VSCO, which is the microfinance subsystem of the PC. The communities contribute 30 per cent (10 per cent in cash and 20 per cent in labour) to all infrastructure sub-projects and reduce costs of the projects by using local materials and applying community procurement methods. The model focuses on community savings, investment and proper insurance for livelihood activities, which ensure that village savings are reinvested within the village economy.

The conditional transfer of funds for the implementation of the VDPs directly to the community takes place when the VO reaches certain agreed milestones. These milestones reflect completed stages of Community Operations Manual (COM) procedures on the way to developing outputs and outcomes. The PC should be registered and a financial agreement has to be signed with the Gemidiriya Foundation to access funds based on the entitlement. While the milestones indicate the completion of activities in a particular sub-project of the VDP, there can be certain milestones that indicate the need for the completion of related activities in another project in the plan. For example, before claiming the second instalment of the Livelihood Support Fund, a community has to start at least one sub-project activity of community infrastructure to ensure efficiencies in the implementation of the holistic VDP.

Information on current events and success stories is published weekly through the National Broadcasting Corporation and regional community radio and through national TV at relevant events. Seventy-five-thousand copies of newspaper supplements carrying news from village communities are published bimonthly in a prominent daily newspaper. Copies of this publication are presented to all parliamentarians and are available in the Gemidiriya website (www.gemidiriya.org).

Key technical inputs

The COM guides the CDD process. There are several other manuals for technical aspects of planning sub-projects, social mobilization, savings, investments and loan tracking, community professional services and the social accountability process.

A team of project facilitators and support organizations assists the communities in building capacity. Communities are required to follow an ethical framework of the 'Ten Golden Rules' of unity, self-esteem, accountability, trust, realism, thrift, transparency, equality, consensus and sincerity to support the implementation of the CDD approach.

Timeframe

Gemidiriya was started in October 2004 and is a 12-year adaptable programme loan divided into 3 4-year phases.

Impact and outcomes

Over a period of two-and-a-half years from the second half of 2004 to 2007, the Gemidiriya model:

- scaled up to 850 villages with 850,000 people (535 community organizations have been formed as socio-economic organizations and registered under the Companies Act);
- provided road access to 210,000 people, drinking water facilities to 80,000 people and other types of infrastructure such as sanitary facilities, culverts, bridges, community information centres and multi-purpose buildings to 160,000 people;
- provided opportunities for skills development and income generation for nearly 80,000 people;
- trained more than 25,000 members on preparation of VDPs, financial management, procurement procedures and so on;
- trained nearly 10,000 youth on income generation activities and skills development, out of which 50 per cent are engaged in income generation;
- created partnerships for milk production and the marketing of fruits and vegetables;
- members of the VSCO of Gemidiriya VOs save at least one rupee per day – savings and initial assets of these members are now worth over SLR400 million (US$4 million);
- gemidiriya communities maintain a loan recovery rate of 98 per cent and most of them are covering their costs by investing in livelihoods, generating income and repaying loans on time.

By the end of June 2007, Gemidiriya had released SLR815 million (US$8.1 million) directly to village communities for capacity building, infrastructure sub-projects and livelihood improvement. Their entitlement/allocation for the four-year period was SLR2,715 (US$27 million).

VOs have demonstrated the capacity to carry out wealth ranking in all the 535 villages with registered organizations. They have categorized households into the poorest of the poor, the poor, the medium income group and the rich, and displayed the lists publicly. SLR9 million (US$90,000) has been allocated in one-time grants to 4880 of the poorest individuals to invest in appropriate income earning activities, demonstrating the ability to provide better social protection to the poorest from the community. Among the beneficiaries who were assisted by the VOs are the old, the blind, the disabled and mothers with disabled members in the family. There is evidence to show that if a sense of community protection is ensured even with a small grant, the poorest are able to come out of their social isolation under the protection of a small group and engage in activities to earn a living and live their lives with dignity.

The Gemidiriya PCs allocate a portion of the VDF to operate a Skill Development Fund for village youth. SLR24 million (US$240,000) has been offered as loans to youth to obtain training and secure employment opportunities over the two-year period.

Communities have been empowered to take leadership positions in the villages. Those who did not previously have a voice now have the opportunity to improve their leadership skills. In the 535 project villages with registered organizations, 13,831 committee members are participating in community resource manage-ment, and 4739 are members of 535 boards of directors, of whom more than 50 per cent are women and 30 per cent youth. Out of the 3745 decision making positions in the boards of directors, social audit committees, finance committees and procurement committees, 2166 positions (58 per cent) are held by women. All chairperson positions of the 527 VSCOs active in the 535 PCs are held by women.

Over a period of two-and-a-half years, communities have demonstrated the capacity to plan and implement at least one basic infrastructure sub-project to meet their basic needs such as drinking water, transport and/or communi-cation. By June 2007, 455 sub-projects were being implemented with funding. Communities hire TA following community procurement principles and under-take construction work such as causeways/bridges across streams, culverts, paving of roads, metalling and tarring of roads, and building irrigation canals.

All infrastructure projects completed have saved 30–50 per cent of the esti-mated cost due to communities undertaking the construction, procurement and community contribution. This has enabled some PCs to convince local political leaders to supplement their village development infrastructure projects with local development funds, accepting the cost effectiveness of the community-driven development (CDD) approach.

Community professionals are emerging from communities after having completed two years of implementation of VDPs. There are 1000 bookkeepers employed by communities for record keeping and accounting in microfinance. After being trained in communication, 155 volunteers are engaged in activities supporting the boards of directors, while 285 community professionals are engaged in 369 villages, training members of 8822 small groups. Four community professional learning and training centres (CPLTCs) and a national CPLTC have been formed and community professionals have taken part in periodic reviews undertaken by World Bank missions (Munshi et al, 2006).

Some Gemidiriya villages have become demonstration villages for the Gemidiriya model. For example, the pilot villages of Ethumalpitiya, Nissankamallapura and Pahala-Ellewewa have attracted many visitors and most of the Gemidiriya staff have visited these villages to learn about the project. Kabillegama village has attracted more than 100 visits from other villages and Perahettiya village has had 120 such visits. These model villages charge a fee for the training imparted.

Capacity building and infrastructure development promote expanding livelihood development activities, which, in turn, pave the way for poor Gemidiriya villages to enter into partnerships with private sector exporters and start exporting village products to other countries. Project villages demonstrated the ability of poor communities to learn practices to ensure quality, quantity, grading, storing, processing and delivery on time to meet exporters' demands.

Total project cost

The World Bank granted US$51 million for the implementation of the first four-year phase of the project. GoSL's contribution is US$11.0 million and the contribution of the local communities is US$7.8 million (World Bank, 2004). The breakdown of the cost under five major components is shown in Table 12.1.

Table 12.1 *Gemidiriya cost breakdown by component*

	Component	Allocation (US$ millions)
A	Village Development	
	A1. Development and Strengthening of VOs	7.5
	A2. VDF	49.1
B	Institutional Strengthening/Capacity Building	6.0
C	Innovation Seed Fund	1.5
D	Project Management	4.7
E	VSHLI Pilot (continuation)	1.0
	Total	**69.8**

Source: World Bank (2004)

Project management

Implementing agency

The project is placed in the Ministry of Nation Building and Estate Infrastructure Development (MNBEID). Gemidiriya Foundation was created and registered under the Companies Act as an autonomous body to be responsible for the implementation and management of the project. A board of directors, chaired ex-officio by the secretary of the MNBEID, consists of six other members (secretary to the Ministry of Small Industries, two senior representatives from the Ministry of Finance, the CEO of Gemidiriya Foundation, a practitioner of community development, and a representative of a national level private sector agribusiness institute).

Coordination mechanisms

The project management works with the district and divisional development administrations for coordination. There is a district team with a team leader, civil engineer and facilitators for capacity building, livelihood development and bank linkages. They attend the DDC meetings held monthly with all district and provincial political leaders and officials of government agencies in the district. The team leader reports progress to this meeting and gets relevant problems resolved.

The same mechanism works at the divisional level. A field operations unit operates with a chief facilitator and facilitators for capacity building, microfinance, livelihood development, technical aspects, gender and youth, and finance and social accountability. The chief facilitator attends monthly coordinating meetings chaired by the divisional secretary who is the representative of the district secretary.

At the village level, monthly progress review meetings take place with the participation of the heads of the VOs in a given area. The head of the local government institute and the divisional secretary attend this meeting.

At the Gemidiriya Foundation, a two-day coordinating workshop is conducted once every two months with the participation of all the district team leaders and field operations unit leaders and the senior project management at national level. Representatives of the CPLTC are also invited to attend this workshop where progress is reviewed and issues are discussed and deliberated.

Monitoring and evaluation of project activities

Monitoring and evaluation are conducted as follows:

- A web-based management information system and monitoring and evaluation (MIS/M&E) system operates for project monitoring and evaluation.

- The VOs prepare a progress report. And the chairpersons of the boards of directors of the VOs and the savings and credit organizations in each area get together every month to review progress. Each village hosts this meeting. The progress information collected is uploaded onto the Gemidiriya website and at the Gemidiriya Foundation this information is checked and published on the internet.
- Monthly and quarterly progress reports covering the whole project are produced by the Gemidiriya Foundation and presented to the relevant stakeholders.
- Each village has a baseline survey that could be used for future evaluations.
- World Bank missions have reviewed the implementation status of the project once every six months.
- A mid-term review was conducted by an independent consultancy firm, which included a survey of 2600 households and focus groups in 90 village communities. Sixteen World Bank mission members completed the mid-term review with 21 community professionals also as members of the team probing into details of all aspects of empowerment, governance, fiduciary and adherence to principles.

Mid-term review of Gemidiriya

The mid-term review found that:

- investments made in Gemidiriya villages reflect 100 per cent of the needs of the community;
- the community members reported that they make 90 per cent of decisions on their priority needs, that the community is engaged in development activities decided by themselves and maintenance activities are being carried out by the community itself and they are empowered to do all such activities;
- more than 50 per cent of inhabitants reported that their economic and living standards had improved; and
- more than 80 per cent of families believed that they received such benefits through Gemidiriya because of the government.

Challenges and how they were overcome

The community-driven approach that involves giving decision-making power to communities and directly giving them funds, thus empowering them, is a new model. The most obvious challenge was to make the political and administrative leaders and bureaucrats accept this 'community-driven' approach. This challenge was, however, overcome by the following strategies. First, VOs are supported to encourage the emergence of a new leadership practising principles of good governance and so making the model less threatening and more supportive to prudent political interests. Second, the majority of the leadership positions are held by women promoting inclusion of the poor and the youth in decision making, maintaining credit discipline and demonstrating resources and results on the ground. Community members attribute the benefits of the project to the work of the government. Third, bureaucrats are involved as facilitators, letting them experience the need and the usefulness of a different approach that asks them to become the guardians of rules and principles while communities run the project.

The communities are traditionally rooted in supply-driven project interventions with free goods, ignoring cost-sharing principles. Shifting them from this traditional supply-driven project approach to demand-driven and CDD was very challenging and necessitated additional time and facilitation efforts. Intensive social mobilization helped to overcome this challenge.

Local interest groups/individuals whose livelihoods were threatened by the collective enterprises of the communities posed a challenge at the beginning. This problem was overcome by better sharing of increased income, opportunities and benefits through collaboration.

Lessons learned

Success factors

Results on the ground produced by the community are the key to attract political and bureaucratic leadership. The trust of the community is built up when its members have access to and control over resources.

Early provision of support to internalize principles, rules and norms within communities is necessary to ensure speedy action, fast mobilization of community contributions, savings and investment.

Finally, it was also found that community professionals play a more effective role than external professionals in scaling up, increasing acceptance and adherence to principles and rules, and in accessing and managing resources by communities.

Support

The project staff and the community members have access to very highly respected resource persons and also to communities with numerous social forces for learning, training and orientation. They learn through exposure visits, best practice models and participation in knowledge sharing events. The project staff as well as the community organizations have access to capacity building funds to advance their interests in filling capacity gaps.

Role of champions

The champions who emerged in the implementation of this project represent different groups and different roles. First, project staff at different levels, who won the acceptance and the praise of the communities, working as facilitators of change in the villages and of CDD are the champions. Their role was to help communities remove negative attitudes, accept change and create positive attitudes towards project principles of participation, inclusion, transparency, accountability and cost sharing for self-development.

The second group of champions emerged from the village communities as community professionals who have now formed the national CPLTC and four district centers. They became professionals who learned from the communities when forming and managing legally accepted VOs, managing resources for village development, training SHGs and community members in financial management, community procurement, social audits, infrastructure building and livelihood development, savings and investment. Their role is to share learning with the new villages adopting the Gemidiriya project model.

The third group of champions emerged from the federated PCs and the government and local government staff whose roles and contributions have been supportive of CDD in their respective areas, setting examples to others.

The fourth group of champions comes from the World Bank Task Team and members of project support missions who are members of the 'Gemidiriya Family' and are not just donor and supervisors, but participants and collaborators, adding value with experience and understanding of local realities to the process of reform and change in governance and development.

Motivation

The motivation behind the project is the CDD approach, where the community receives decision-making powers and funds directly in order to acheive the desired development. Performance of all stakeholders is also on the basis of actual progress made on the ground. The bottom-up governance structure paves the way for better representation so that motivation to act to receive benefits quickly occurs. Also, motivation is generated by community obligations, such as cash and labour for capital works. Social auditing and community assessment of accountability practised by the communities also provide a motivating factor to work hard to achieve results.

Other innovations

Two major innovations have emerged from the project. The first is the emergence of community professionals from the implementation process of Gemidiriya in the villages. They are highly motivated people who have acquired knowledge and skills of managing VOs and PCs, giving social mobilization training to SHGs, registering and entering into business agreements, receiving funds, record keeping and accounting, building infrastructure including drinking water schemes, roads, irrigation works, mobilizing community contributions, managing microfinance, social auditing and community assessment of performance. The national CPLTC and four district CPLTCs are in operation providing services to existing and new Gemidiriya communities. The second innovation is the community radio pilot, which is currently being tested and developed to be a truly community-managed communication chanel to produce economic and social benefits to communities.

Good practice

The Gemidiriya project is regarded as a model of good practice for several reasons.

Ability to provide the necessary conditions for poverty reduction and community empowerment

Gemidiriya, by its design, addresses the widely-accepted impediments to poverty reduction in the country by providing the necessary conditions to achieve the expected outcomes. The project facilitates the process of moving away from dependency, promoting self-esteem, community contributions and community ownership. It provides communities with access to information and encourages them to make decisions, promote savings and to access supplementary resources to enable CDD. The village institution ensures full participation of the community and a minimum of 50 per cent of the decision-making positions are held by women. The community is thus empowered to undertake village development planning, set priorities, allocate resources and implement plans, maintaining transparency and accountability.

Setting up community-based institutions as implementing agencies

Gemidiriya helps communities to set up PCs as implementing agencies of development activities for poverty reduction and income generation by the communities. Since PCs receive direct funding and they are empowered to plan and mobilize TA and utilize the funds received for investment, they become implementing agencies themselves at low cost when compared to the public sector implementing agencies. Their legal recognition facilitates the public sector and private sector institutions to enter into mutually beneficial partnerships for effective and productive ventures bound by the law of the country. PCs provide access to local markets and have entered into export markets through various partnerships, for example, through the signing of a Memorandum of Understanding with the National Dairy Development Board of India for a major partnership to improve livelihoods.

The Gemidiriya project demonstrates the potential strength of communities that can be mobilized for poverty reduction through village institutions to supplement the service delivery of responsive public institutions. Mature VOs, once federated at a higher level, have the potential to undertake development work at a larger scale and handle larger volumes of production responding to demand from the organized private sector, having the potential to scale up activities successfully.

Practice of principles of good governance

Gemidiriya communities demonstrate, with results on the ground, the application of the five non-negotiable principles of full participation, inclusion of the poor, transparency, accountability and cost sharing and the ten golden rules (see above) as a viable ethical framework that gives the community the capability to manage resources and resolve conflicts by themselves. This allows all the households of the community to graduate to a higher level of economic and social well being. Full participation is assured without any discrimination on the basis of race, caste or religion, and ensures inclusion of the poor, with an emphasis on women and youth. Gemidiriya communities mobilize human resources, promote self-help, and adopt cost-effective mechanisms for resource utilization, setting an example of local resource use and the application of the principles of good governance.

Mobilizing the economic power of the community for holistic development

While savings are normally deposited in a commercial bank, the Gemidiriya microfinance system allows small groups, who contribute one rupee per day to the group, to use these savings to meet the instant credit needs of their members. Small groups access these savings for emergencies such as buying medicine or meeting unexpected expenses. The additional savings are deposited in a commercial bank. Communities can access funds received from the project for improvement of livelihood opportunities up to ten times of what has been saved. This guarantees that savings are reinvested in the village economy, creating economic opportunities for the poor.

Ability to provide social protection

Gemidiriya communities identify the extent of poverty in the village, undertake the ranking of households in terms of wealth, categorize and select beneficiaries, decide on social protection norms, and the type, amount and method of grant and disbursement to the poorest of the poor. As decision making is at the community level, communities manage the resources for the holistic development of the village.

Promotion of devolved decision making

Gemidiriya offers a mechanism to devolve decision-making power to communities to improve their quality of life. The communities are empowered with direct financing to make decisions on identifying needs, prioritizing, resource allocation and investment. The boards of directors give the control of the village savings and investment system to women representatives of the small groups. Infrastructure sub-projects are managed by separate sub-committees maintaining their own bank accounts. Community procurement is handled by a separate committee, allowing many community members to hold leadership positions and responsibilities.

At the same time, the project develops the necessary skills in the community and provides investment to help improve conditions in the village by investing in infrastructure and expanding economic activities beyond the village by entering into export markets. Such opportunities can be used to raise income levels leading to a more satisfying life with additional physical and financial assets, access to capital, better health and social protection.

People of different ethnic identities are often found in the PCs due to the golden rules that ensure equal opportunities and the practice of principles of good governance. With these objectives and preconditions, the model offers a sustainable mechanism for CDD and, at the same time, demonstrates the viability of the model for ethnic integration, peace and harmony among diverse groups in rural communities.

Potential for scaling up and replication

Producing results on the ground, Gemidiriya has created a demand at the highest level of the government for scaling up. The design of the project, its institutional aspects and method of implementation in Sri Lanka have been studied by specialists from various fields such as microfinance, communication, infrastructure development, livelihood improvement, gender and youth, financial management and procurement. As part of the bi-annual review process of the World Bank, results were presented to the government and a decision has been made to adopt Gemidiriya principles in the major government rural development programmes.

A team of 17 non-government support organizations have been acquainted with the Gemidiriya model through assisting the VOs. These organizations provide a resource pool for scaling up.

The project is implemented in all the three major agro-ecological zones in the country, i.e. the dry zone, wet zone and the intermediate zone, and in both flat and hilly terrains in remote infrastructure-poor areas. The principles of CDD are acceptable and attractive to multi-ethnic villages. The COM and other communication materials are available in the two major languages, Sinhala and Tamil. The North-East Irrigated Agriculture Project[6] has decided to adopt Gemidiriya principles. The application of the ten golden rules attracts multi-ethnic communities to work in harmony, demonstrating the potential acceptance of the model in the plantation sector and conflict areas.

The Ministry of Poverty Alleviation and the Samurdhi programme started testing the methodology adopted by Gemidiriya for the participatory identification of the poor, with a view to selecting recipients for the Samurdhi programme, which spends about US$90 million a year. The president of Sri Lanka directed a presentation on the performance of the Gemidiriya model at a project review session in November 2006.

Two project teams from the Social Development Fund of Bangladesh and from the Rural Poverty Reduction Project in Tamil Nadu, India have studied Gemidiriya and decided to include its major elements in their project design.

Conclusions

Livelihood development efforts in poor rural communities need many enabling conditions to get off the ground. Savings and credits, microenterprises and skills development form necessary conditions but not sufficient to trigger off investments to improve livelihoods.

Poverty reduction initiatives share common general objectives of reducing poverty, increasing income and improving quality of life of the poor. However, they differ in what they do to achieve those objectives. The strategy and activities undertaken reflect the strength of the particular initiative in contributing to the desired economic and social change. It is in this scenario that *Gemidiriya* set the pace during the two-year period of its implementation to reach its first objective of helping rural communities form and establish village-level institutions that are formally organized and empowered to exercise decision-making power and manage available resources.

Of the 1000 communities to be covered during the first phase of 4 years, at the end of the second year, the project had already reached more than half (535 village communities). Capacity building has been planned, with the conditional transfer of development funds direct to the communities. As a result, communities have invested funds in village economies, maintaining a 98 per cent repayment rate.

A relatively simple definition considers poverty as a condition of a society where some of its members are unable to attain a level of social and material well-being considered as an acceptable minimum by that society (Nanayakkara, 2005). The application of the CDD approach reflects the ability of the community to identify the conditions that keep people in poverty both in the economic and social status in their community, identify development priorities and assist targeted disadvantaged groups to improve their situation.

The identification by almost all of the VOs of the poorest of the poor, providing them with the required social protection to undertake activities and earn an income, reflects a satisfactory level of realization of commitment to this ethical framework. The leadership of women and youth, who hold positions that influence decision making, social mobilization, the generation of social capital and an emerging social workforce of community professionals who undertake extension of the model to new villages, all indicate that these efforts are appropriate, sustainable and can be replicated.

The investment in village economic and social infrastructure to provide unfulfilled basic needs such as drinking water, transportation and communication, and investment capital to tap income earning opportunities indicate that poverty reduction will be achieved.

The project has resulted in increased savings and investments in livelihoods within the village economy by village households. Repeated disbursements of loan funds indicate that the households are earning a satisfactory income to continue investing even higher amounts. The project management team has made a moderate estimate of 15 per cent of such households having crossed the poverty line during the two-and-a-half year period, although this figure could be higher in some communities.

Notes

1   Chief Executive Officer, Gemidiriya Foundation, Gemidiriya Community Development and Livelihood Improvement Project
2   Programme Analyst, UNDP Regional Centre in Colombo
3   For the year 2004, the official poverty line, which is the real per capita monthly total consumption expenditure, was SLR1423 (US$12).
4   In Sinhala, '*gemidiriya*' means courage/strength of the village.
5   The Gemidiriya community development model adopts a rule-based approach founded on five non-negotiable principles and ten golden rules to be observed and practised by the communities who, with those who facilitate, coordinate, appraise and supervise for compliance, become the guardians of principles. They should be free from undue influence. The five non-negotiable principles are:

  • participation for all without discrimination on race, cast creed, religion or political affiliations;
  • priority to the poor, to women and to youth;
  • transparency;
  • accountability; and
  • cost-sharing.

  The 10 golden rules are: unity; self esteem; accountability; trust; realism; thrift; transparency; equity; consensus; and sincerity.
6   This project, which expands from 2004 to 2011, aims to help conflict-affected communities in the North East Province and adjoining areas to restore livelihoods, enhance agricultural and other production and incomes, and build capacity for sustainable, social and economic reintegration.

References

CBSL (Central Bank of Sri Lanka) (2006) *Annual Report 2005*, Colombo, Central Bank of Sri Lanka

DCS (Department of Census and Statistics) (2006) *Millennium Development Goals in Sri Lanka: A Statistical Review: 2006*, Colombo, Department of Census and Statistics, Colombo

DNP (Department of National Planning) (2005) *Mahinda Chinthana: Vision for a New Sri Lanka: A Ten Year Horizon Development Framework 2006 – 2016*, Discussion Paper, Colombo, Department of National Planning

MFP (Ministry of Finance and Planning) (2005) *Sri Lanka New Development Strategy Framework for Economic Growth and Poverty Reduction*, Colombo, Ministry of Finance and Planning

Munshi, M., Hayward, N. and Verardo, B. (2006) 'A story of social and economic empowerment: The evolution of 'community professionals' in Sri Lanka', in World Bank (ed) *Social Funds Innovations Notes*, Vol 4, No 2, Washington DC, World Bank

Nanayakkara, A. G. W. (2005) *Income and Expenditure disparities and Poverty in Sri Lanka*, Colombo, Department of Census and Statistics

NCED (National Council for Economic Development) (2005) *Millennium Development Goals Country Report 2005 Sri Lanka*, Colombo, National Council for Economic Development

World Bank (2004) *Project Appraisal Document on a Proposed Grant in the Amount of SDR 34.2 Million to the Democratic Socialist Republic of Sri Lanka for a Community Development and Livelihood Improvement 'Gemidiriya' Project in Support of the First Phase of the Community and Livelihood Development 'Gemidiriya' Programme*, Washington DC, World Bank

World Bank (2005a) *World Development Report 2005: A Better Investment Climate for Everyone*, Washington DC, World Bank

World Bank (2005b) *Attaining the Millennium Development Goals in Sri Lanka*, Washington DC, World Bank

13

Recent Experience with the Community Voice Card: An Innovative Tool for Assessing Service Delivery for the Millennium Development Goals

Neela Mukherjee

Introduction

The community voice card (CVC) is a tool that enables people to assess in a structured way the services they receive (whether from government, non-government or private agencies). The tool is applied through a range of discursive formats such as focus group discussions and interviews. It captures people's views and this information can then be used to strengthen the services they receive. The scope of CVC (also termed community score card (CSC) and, community voice tool (CVT)) for assessing MDG-related performance from people's perspectives holds great potential in the absence of appropriate tools for measuring people's satisfaction with how the MDGs are progressing in developing countries.

The tool has been applied in at least four countries to achieve different objectives (as described below). CVC was first applied as a tool for institutional assessment during a participatory poverty assessment (PPA) study at a sub-national level in 2004–2005 in West Bengal, India. Realizing the potential of the tool and the community response, it was refined within an institutional framework of good governance, which helped to evolve a set of criteria for assessing delivery of services by different institutions. In late 2005, it was further developed as a tool for participatory monitoring systems for poverty reduction strategy papers (PRSPs) and MDG-related indicators in Nepal and was applied in 2006. From August to September 2006, the tool was piloted in Moldova to see its applicability in terms of monitoring MDG-related indicators under PRSPs by civil society. In 2007, the tool was further refined and is being applied for long-term monitoring of institutional performance in a poverty reduction project in South China, covering three provinces.

CVC has thus come a long way since 2004 though it is still evolving through cross-country experiences. The remainder of this chapter provides an account of the context, objectives, key elements of the projects, implementation strategies, costs, challenges faced and how they were overcome, lessons learnt, innovative features, replication possibilities and other dimensions of CVC.

Context

India (West Bengal)

India's GDP grew at the rate of 6.2 per cent per annum from 2000–2004 and is one of the fastest growing economies in Asia. Situated in the Eastern part of India, the state of West Bengal covers an area of 88,752km^2 with 12 agro-ecological zones and, in 2001, had a population of 82 million, which accounts for 7.8 per cent of the country's total population. The state has a literacy rate of nearly 70 per cent. West Bengal, a forerunner in the implementation of agrarian reforms with a three-tier system of decentralized planning and governance, has emerged as having the highest rate of growth in agricultural productivity, coupled with a rapid decline in rural poverty since 1977. However, despite the declining trend in rural poverty, some studies have observed that the state's initiative to promote social opportunities in the rural areas has been 'mixed'. While land reforms and minimum wage-related policies have been given priority by the Marxist government, social development services such as health and education have been comparatively neglected and the state's achievements in these sectors are only 'modest'(Drez and Sen, 2002).

Nepal

The Human Development Index of Nepal is 0.527 and it is ranked 138th out of 177 countries (UNDP, 2004). Nepal's economy, after prolonged conflict, has been promising since 2006 due to the successful conclusion of the historic peoples' movement in April of that year. Though still in a fragile situation due to the uncertainty of political coalitions and other socio-economic bottlenecks, Nepal's situation is gradually improving after more than a decade of conflict, political stalemate and lack of local governance. Despite the conflict, poverty in Nepal has been gradually declining 42 per cent in 1995–1996, to 38 per cent in 2001–2002 and to 31 per cent in 2003–2004 (United Nations, 2007). With 90 per cent of its poor living in rural areas and engaged in subsistence farming, it is important to mention that poverty in Nepal results from a complex combination of low human development, weak capacity, conflict, weak governance, political instability, skewed economic growth and high levels of social exclusion.

Moldova

The Republic of Moldova, a low-income economy in transition, has made continuous progress in terms of recording steady growth since 2000 and achieved GDP growth of 6.8 per cent at the end of 2004 (United Nations, 2007). Faced with many challenges as part of the ex-Soviet bloc, Moldova's economy prior to 2000 experienced wide fluctuations in growth rate and exchange rate, high inflation, agriculture drought and other challenges of an economy in transition (en. wikipedia.org/wiki/Economy_of_Moldova). In the *Human Development Report* of 2003 (UNDP, 2003), the Republic of Moldova was ranked as a medium human development country with an inter-country rank of 108 and a Human Development Index value of 0.700, which is below the world average of 0.722. The Republic of Moldova has GDP per capita on the US$ Purchasing Power Parity Index of 2150, which is more than three times below the world average. Though Moldova has performed satisfactorily in terms of implementation of MDG goals related to education and gender equality, more effort is required in the area of poverty reduction, child health and the eradication of tuberculosis and HIV/AIDS (UNDP, 2003; 2005). Poverty needs to be tackled more strategically since poverty is growing rapidly across all segments of the population (UNDP, 2002).

China

As shown by recent statistics (United Nations, 2007), China is amongst the fastest growing countries with an average annual GDP growth rate of 9.4 per cent during the period 2000–2004. With population growth of 0.57 per cent, China has less than half India's population growth rate of 1.44 per cent. Similarly, China's literacy rate of 90.9 per cent is a major achievement (India's is 59.5 per cent). With regard to poverty, however, though China has been able to reduce poverty much faster than many other countries to 10 per cent of its population, about 50 per cent of its labour force still remains in agriculture with substantial unemployment and underemployment in the rural areas. One challenge is the marginalization of ethnic minorities and census data show that there are 55 ethnic minorities scattered mostly along the Chinese borders in the south, southwest, north and northwest. The macro picture on growth and poverty in China is indeed promising, but fails to reflect the fact that growth and poverty reduction have bypassed the marginalized and the disadvantaged groups, such as ethnic minorities.

The project

In West Bengal, the CVC tool was applied as part of a participatory poverty assessment for eliciting people's perspectives on poverty before negotiations with government for an external loan. The tool was applied to find out how people assessed decentralized governance, the quality of service delivery on the ground and related decisions and activities, the strengths and limitations and suggestions in this regard.

In Nepal, the original purpose of the CVC study was to develop an institutional participatory poverty monitoring mechanism to influence policies, strengthen broad-based national ownership of the PRSP, and develop public accountability and responsiveness of the PRSP to the needs of poor and disadvantaged people in Nepal (National Planning Commission, 2004). The tool was applied by the Nepal Planning Commission to elicit PRSP indicators from people's perspectives and how changes in poverty reduction could be captured, especially for those who were socially excluded.

In Moldova, the tool was piloted as a participatory monitoring exercise for a PRSP. The PRSP focused on the area of participation in the implementation, monitoring and evaluation of public policies, the main emphasis being implementation of the Economic Growth and Poverty Reduction Strategy Paper (EGPRSP) (Government of Moldova, 2004a; 2004b; SCERS, 2005).

In China, the CVC tool is currently being applied as part of a participatory monitoring exercise for a poverty reduction project situated in South West China (covering three provinces – Sichuan, Guangxi and Yunnan), the objective being to establish and support an approach for monitoring poverty impacts in the project.

Project formulation

In West Bengal, the research study using CVC was supported by the Government of West Bengal, Government of India and ADB, and undertaken by a field research agency called Development Tracks. In Nepal, the project was formulated and implemented by the Planning Commission of Nepal, while in Moldova is was planned and implemented by the Participation Council – a forum of NGOs, donors and government. Finally, in China, CVC was formulated and implemented by the provincial government and local government staff.

Project goals and objectives

In West Bengal, CVC was used in a field research study in a PPA for an in-depth and issue-based assessment of poverty from the perspectives of the poor (Development Tracks, 2005). In Nepal, one main objective was to develop tools people could use to monitor the PRSP and identify suitable indicators, as was the case in Moldova, while in China, the objective was to adopt participatory monitoring for a poverty reduction project.

Key elements of the project

Target beneficiaries

In India, the PPA study was done *in situ*, through participatory sessions with more than 4000 village participants, of which 55 per cent were women. The sampling frame was also representative of socially, culturally and ecologically vulnerable groups. Selection of districts took into account agro-ecological and social diversity and the incidence of income and human poverty. In Nepal, CVT was applied to poor communities and those socially excluded in two sampled districts. In Moldova, CVC was applied with villagers in two villages who had access to health and education services provided by the state. In China, the participants were the rural ethnic communities in sampled villages/townships in the provinces of Guangxi, Sichuan and Yunnan.

Project area

In West Bengal, the PPA study was undertaken in more than 100 locations, 95 per cent in rural areas and 5 per cent in urban/peri-urban localities, across 12 districts of West Bengal. The districts represented 12 different agro-ecological zones and different types of rural and urban poverty groups and areas. In Nepal, the study covered two districts: Saptari in the terai and Gorkha in the hills. The information was collected from both household surveys and focus group discussions. The samples included a total of 406 households and 24 focus groups with a gender balance. In addition to scoring the services, qualitative information was obtained mainly through the focus groups. In Moldova, the villages of Zubresti and Galesti of the Straseni region were selected for testing the CVT from the list of villages in which the National Bureau of Statistics conducts its Household Budget Survey, one of them being relatively poor and the other somewhat better off. The criteria for selection of the two villages included: (1) availability of the local public administration (LPA) units to host the event, and (2) available infrastructure (school and health care centres/policlinics). In China, 18 villages/townships were covered (6 villages/townships in each of the provinces of Sichuan, Yunnan and Guangxi). The villages were selected according to criteria such as remoteness of the village, presence of project-related services and those with large ethnic minorities. The target groups were the ethnic minorities for whom the poverty reduction project was intended.

Project activities

Key components were:

* exploring the CVC tool and needs assessment and setting objectives;
* preparing for workshops and field exercises;

- organizing facilitators' workshops;
- conducting field exercises;
- sharing findings;
- data collation, processing and report writing;
- presenting findings to policy makers and other stakeholders; and
- publishing reports and advocacy.

Key technical inputs

In a framework of good governance and effective institutions, CVT is based on a list of criteria for assessing attributes such as 'responsiveness', 'accountability', 'quality', 'cost', 'infrastructure', 'access' and other relevant criteria. These criteria may be clustered depending on the objectives, local conditions and the services to be evaluated. In the more detail the criteria are as follows:

- *Awareness* – the degree of information that local communities have about the availability of relevant services in the community, communities' understanding of the importance of services and ways of using the available benefits.
- *Access and inclusion* – the extent to which the services under assessment are accessible in time and space; whether every local community member is provided with equal opportunities to benefit from services.
- *Attitude and behaviour* – the way service providers behave with local community members; whether all the communities are treated equally and without discrimination.
- *Quality, timeliness and efficiency* – the quality of services; how timely they are; whether they are provided within a reasonable time; whether they have a positive impact on the communities; whether they are useful; and where providers are professional.
- *Infrastructure* – the status of infrastructure; quality of infrastructure; whether it is sufficient.
- *Responsiveness* – the extent to which the service providers respond to communities' needs and problems.
- *Cost (including hidden costs)* – the amount of cost involved in procuring such services; how affordable they are; how much one has to spend; whether one has to pay a bribe or not.
- *Sustainability* – whether the service under assessment will be available in the community after a certain period of time, regularly, and how do the local communities perceive the future of such services; and how predictable is the service under reference.
- *Suggestions for improvement* – the local communities forward suggestions to make the service more efficient, sustainable and beneficial.

CVC in more detail

CVC is different from the Citizen Report Card tool, which is mainly prepared through a structured questionnaire (see Adikeshavalu, 2004; Buhl et al, 2004a; 2004b; World Bank, 2001; 2004). CVC is a voice tool based on participatory group interactions rather than on any structured questionnaire.

The whole process of application of CVC can be divided into four parts:

1   Part one consists of focus group discussions (8–10 persons) on the basis of interview guidelines. Two or more services may be evaluated within the same group. Facilitators encourage participants to evaluate the service(s) according to predefined criteria, though scope for peoples' criteria is kept open in many exercises. Participants are requested to arrive at a common score as a group, which is preferably reached by the method of consensus. This then becomes the group score. If such a consensus cannot be reached, the facilitator notes the individual scores by participants. Finally, the group is requested to make suggestions and recommendations for the improvement of the services under discussion and their delivery.

2   In part two, semi-structured interviews are conducted with people working within the services or opinion leaders, mostly in order to avoid the influence of dominant participants during the process of small group discussions. Interviews are conducted on the basis of a semi-structured questionnaire where most questions are open. The semi-structured questionnaire also helps to: validate and verify by comparison, and engage opinion leaders and others, and ensures a higher quality of discussion and is useful for analysis and filling gaps.

3   In part three, field facilitators present the results of group discussions to service providers or local public authorities. This may happen shortly after the focus group discussions and interviews, or on a different day jointly agreed in advance. The community assessments of services provided are disseminated during meetings and discussions with the service providers based on the criteria for assessment. In such sessions, suggestions and recommendations for improvement are also raised.

4   In part four is analysis of data and preparation of reports for further dissemination. Since there is generally a number of villages and towns to be covered, there needs to be some time for organizing, collating data, processing and writing the report, and presenting it to different groups of stakeholders.

Depending on the size of the sample, the CVC process takes five to seven days including preparation and a field exercise per village/town that takes no more than two days. This is followed by report writing, which could take 2–15 days depending on the scale and size of application.

Timeframe

The CVC method was applied in West Bengal from 2004–2005, in Nepal from 2005–2006, in Moldova in 2006 and in China from 2007–2011.

Impacts and outcomes

Initial impacts include the follows:

- *West Bengal* – key methodology, results and lessons learnt were fed into a larger project for decentralization at district/ward level, which is still running.
- *Nepal* – while it is too early for impact assessment, field evidence shows that the tool is well tested and applicable. It has increased awareness of the community participants and has also empowered them to assess their own services and to pass feedback to official channels.
- *Moldova* – the participants from local communities enjoyed doing the assessments and the service delivery officials were ready to listen to the views of the participants, especially on service gaps and suggestions for improving education and health services. The officials also suggested actions on the spot to improve the quality of services. The local participants felt honoured to get an opportunity to provide their assessment and give their frank views and mark their service providers based on performance.
- *China* – the study is still in its initial phase but the group assessment shows that the local ethnic communities can easily distinguish between the criteria and provide their frank assessment and group score to assess performance of their service providers.

Total project cost

In India, the technical training inputs cost around US$15,000) (including workshop and field application for 100 villages in 10 districts) plus local travel costs of around US$5000/-). In Nepal and Moldova no costing data are available, while the project in China is still on-going.

Contributors

In West Bengal, government agencies contributed towards local travel and follow up workshops. In Nepal, the government provided links with local service providers and district officials. In Moldova, it linked with local service providers and helped in meetings and discussions, while in China, government agencies are contributing towards local travel and the required workshops. In none of the four cases was the private sector involved, though community groups play a central role in voluntarily giving their time to the CVC projects. External supporters of the projects are ADB and the Department for International Development (DFID) in

West Bengal, UNDP in Nepal and Moldova, and the World Bank and DFID in China.

Project management

In India, the implementing agency is the State Government of West Bengal and Indian research firm, Development Tracks. In Nepal, the Planning Commission of Nepal and national level NGOs are the implementers, while the Government of Moldova and Participation Council play this role in Moldova. The implementing agency in China is the Government of China, the provincial governments and ITAD Ltd, UK. Coordination of the projects is conducted by the relevant local, district and provincial authorities.

Monitoring and evaluation

Monitoring and evaluation in West Bengal is by state government and donors, by the government and UNDP in Nepal, by the NGO Participation Council, government and UNDP in Moldova, and in China by the government and ITAD Ltd, UK.

Challenges and how they were overcome

One common challenge faced with regard to participatory tools in general is that economists, hard core classical academics and technical experts lack flexibility in listening to the voices of the poor and also in appreciating and interpreting the qualitative data raised through such voices (Chambers, 1993, 1997; Mukherjee, N., 1995, 2002; Mukherjee, A., 2004). Lack of flexibility of project leaders' and staff with regard to participatory tools and listening to the voices of the poor were overcome to a considerable extent by means of running training workshops and experiential field learning sessions.

It was difficult to find good facilitators to conduct small group discussions for application of the tool. There was a dearth of good facilitators in many agencies and sometimes inexperienced facilitators were unable to handle tricky situations that arose and took more time than others in conducting sessions. To overcome this, field coordinators observed the field sessions and identified problems that inexperienced facilitators faced and sorted them out on the spot. Alternatively, experienced faciliators were paired with inexperienced facilitators to conduct focus group discussions.

Another challenge faced was that not all government bodies were prepared to hear the problems and suggestions raised by CVC. Some of the service delivery agencies and the top officials were willing to listen to people's assessment and undertake appropriate actions while others were somewhat reluctant and escapist.

It was realized that the best way was to start with the strengths of the agency as described by people before going into their weaknesses.

There is rising community expectations from their service providers. This is a general phenomenon wherein consumers have become better informed and expect better quality services from their service providers. The service providers often have many constraints and lack of technical expertise, funds and managerial skills to provide good-quality services. The high expectations of the consumers also influence their assessment of service delivery. Ways to overcome this included asking communities whether they were aware of the constraints faced by the service providers and enquiring about the possible contribution of the public towards better service delivery.

The service providers at the local level are not the decision makers. This was posed as a problem during the presentation of CVC findings to the service providers. It was decided that senior officials and decision makers should also be invited to such sessions so as to make them aware of public views and assessments, giving them the chance to respond immediately or over a period of time.

There were challenges in setting criteria for people's assessment of service providers. This issue was sorted out by keeping the list of criteria flexible so as to be able to add new criteria as required. Such new criteria could come from the participants themselves, from the facilitators or jointly.

Lessons learned

It is important to have country experiences and case studies ready for sharing and circulation among the decision-making and implementing agencies and also for the researchers and field facilitators. Such country experiences and case studies help them to appreciate the tool and also help them to visualize the processes involved and the outputs that could be derived from its application.

It is desirable to have data processors ready at CVT workshops and after field visits, preferably using a computer package such as SPSS. This helps to organize, collate and quickly process the data, and also helps to cross-check data and to identify gaps, if any.

It is prudent for the field team to discuss ways to manage people's expectations. Application of the tool makes many people think that their services will improve once they have made an assessment. However, it is important to explain to people that this is an exercise in people's assessment of service delivery, which will then be transmitted to the service delivery agencies and the outcomes will be decided by these agencies. It may or may not result in improvements as desired.

It is of utmost importance to demonstrate the significance of the tools to policy makers and service delivery organizations so that they do not feel threatened. It is important to explain to them the value of people's assessment of service delivery so that suitable improvements can be brought about. The whole exercise needs to be done in a positive manner.

A good team of facilitators should be selcted and then prepared through a workshop. This is perhaps the most important part of the whole story because a skilful set of facilitators can make the most of the opportunity, applying the tool in a positive way, managing people's expectations and diffusing delicate and explosive situations.

The team of facilitators should be ready to share immediate outcomes and also verify and cross-check field data. For any field application, the team of facilitators should be ready to summarize and present their field findings to different clientele groups as required and also to service delivery agencies and other officials and leaders as required.

Success factors

Success factors are as follows:

- The CVC tool is easy to use and can be adapted to different situations as required, as shown in the four countries.
- The tool is flexible in application and any type of service delivery can be assessed.
- It is adaptable in different countries irrespective of their level of development.
- With detailed guidelines, facilitators can apply it with ease. People as participants are able to understand its objectives and application.
- The tool is developing through its application in various countries.

Role of champions

It is essential to recommend and support CVC to policy makers and policy advisers, otherwise they may not appreciate the power of such a tool. Hence, the role of champions is important. In India, the field research firm served as its champion, applying it in a PPA. In Nepal and Moldova, UNDP Nepal and UNDP Moldova were the champions who supported use of the tool in practice. In China, it was ITAD who prepared the methodology and suggested ways to apply and adapt it.

Support

In the case of CVC, multi-stakeholder support is required since there are different stages of application of the tool. CVC involves not only public assessment but also sharing of information with service delivery agencies, senior officials responsible for decision making and implicit advocacy to influence decision making based on public perceptions. Hence, for CVT multi-stakeholder support should be solicited from local communities as consumers of services, local community leaders, service agencies, leaders, decision makers, government and donors.

Motivation

It is important to motivate both government and local communities for effective application of CVC. If the community feels that nothing much can be changed in the delivery of services, then the use of CVT will be constrained. And, similarly, the local service delivery agencies may feel that they face too many constraints to do justice to people's perceptions about their services. In both cases, the team of facilitators needs to look for opportunities to show how important public assessment can be and how small changes in the service delivery chain can improve quality of life for local communities.

Good practice

CVC represents good practice for the following reasons:

- It is a tool to capture 'voices', especially of the poor, to pass onto the service provider. It helps flag areas of concern and related issues in service delivery for future action. It helps empower the public to provide their opinions.
- It also helps to strengthen the role of local communities and establish a channel of communication between them and the local service providers. It helps providers to get connected with people to get public feedback and ideas on different aspects of service delivery.
- It is a tool for improving the quality of MDG-related services based on people's feedback. It also helps local communities to be involved in assessing the delivery of local services and suggests ways for improving of services and engaging local communities.
- At the policy and practice levels, it helps to make sense of what works and what does not work – the strengths and weaknesses of service delivery.
- It creates space for assessing the accountability of the service provider.
- It can be used as a strategic tool for the service provider who wants to provide quality services to local communities and who is looking for opportunities to improve performance.
- Regular use of the tool helps establish regular communication with people and creates a channel from the people to the service provider. In essence, it becomes a tool for participatory monitoring of public services. It could constitute a part of participatory poverty monitoring where poor people are involved in assessing public services through CVC on a regular basis.

Potential for scaling up and replication

In 1997–1999, CVC was first explored as a communication linkage matrix tool in Vietnam (Ha Giang and Quang Binh), as part of training under the Agriculture

Resource Conservation Project supported by UNDP/UNOPS/IFAD and the Government of Vietnam. It was noticed that the villagers were eager to assess delivery and quality of services by the local service providers and suggest ways to make improvements. CVC was later applied as part of a PPA in West Bengal (India) in 2004–2005 in 100 villages through participatory sessions with poor women and men, though with a limited set of criteria. The focus was more on the PPA than on CVC and outputs from application of the tool were merged with PPA as perspectives of the poor. Though the tool was applied there was no community score card prepared since that was not the prime objective. However, the application of CVC helped to provide a reasonable assessment by people on local governance and service delivery. It also PPA contributed in some measure towards steps taken by the state government to implement a participatory project on decentralized planning.

Later, when the Government of Nepal was in need of a participatory monitoring tool for monitoring MDGs, the CVC tool was offered. It was applied to two districts with socially excluded communities in Nepal to monitor government services in ten topical areas including schools, health, agriculture, livestock, drinking water, electricity, registration and land revenue collection. The sample size covered was a total of 406 households with 24 focus group discussions. Among many results, one important finding is that there is considerable variation in the number of service users of different services.

In Moldova, a tool was required for participatory monitoring of the EGPRSP for which CVC piloted in two villages where the use of questionnaires was mainly undertaken to validate outcomes from participatory interactions with different groups of clients of services. All criteria for CVC were applied to two MDG-related topics, education and health, and the results were shared with different stakeholders, including local governors. The criteria and the outcomes were assessed by a group of experts and facilitators and followed guidelines for participatory group discussions. Also, semi-structured questionnaires were finalized on that basis for application to larger areas for the purposes of monitoring.

In China, the CVC tool is being applied in three provinces for the purpose of monitoring a large project on poverty reduction. Monitoring is on-going and the results are yet to be collated. Experience from China shows that CVC is applicable and can produce a picture of people's assessment of service delivery at the local level. The data collated from different sample villages will provide a detailed assessment in the future.

Conclusions

The MDGs, though entrenched in the global development agenda, still need to be made practicable and feasible at the local level. Whatever the global agenda, the crux of the matter is that achieving the MDG lies with the primary stakeholders who have to be empowered to own the goals, assess them and feel satisfied with their progress at a local level. It is in the context of the primary stakeholders at the local level that much remains to be done and there exists a major vacuum. CVC is an empowering tool for local communities to assess their service delivery agencies and the pace of progress. It is a flexible tool and has been applied and adapted in four countries. It enables communities as consumers of services to articulate their voices in assessing local service providers. Field experience shows that the tool has wide applicability whether in terms of countries, regions or localities. The tool is easily applicable to a range of services, whether MDG-related or not. Based on a framework and criteria for good governance, the tool is equally applicable to government, non-government and private service delivery agencies. Experiential lessons in CVC are still emerging and developments to improve its strategic value continue.

Acknowledgements

Thanks are due to PRD, Government of West Bengal, Planning Commission, Nepal, UNDP-Nepal, UNDP-Moldova, Participation Council-Moldova, Mihail Peleah, Sujatha Viswanathan, Amitava Mukherjee, M. N. Roy, Dilip Ghosh, Dilip Pal, Subrata Chakravarty, Madhumita Parihari and the local communities engaged in CVT. Thanks are also due to Neil Fernando for his generous editing of the chapter.

References

Adikeshavalu, R. (2004) *An Assessment of the Impact of Bangalore Community Report Card on the Performance of Public Agencies*, ECD Working Paper Series 12, World Bank Evaluation Department, Washington DC, World Bank

Buhl, S., Wei, Q. and Xuixeong, W. (2004a) *Report Card – Satisfaction Survey, An initial Observation from China*, Technical Report 2, Sino–German Poverty Monitoring Project, Jiangxi Province, China

Buhl, S., Wei, W. and Xuixeong, W. (2004b) *Towards Comprehensive and Participatory Poverty Monitoring and Impact Evaluation in Jiangxi Province*, Sino–German Poverty Monitoring Project, Jiangxi Province, China

Chambers, R. (1993) *Challenging the Professions Frontiers for rural development*, Intermediate Technology Publications, London

Chambers, R. (1997) *Whose Reality Counts? Putting the first last*, IT Publications, London

Development Tracks (2005) *Participatory Poverty Assessment*, West Bengal, Interim Draft Report submitted to Asian Development Bank, Manila, Development Tracks

Drez, J. and Sen, A. (2002) *India: Development and Participation*, Oxford University Press, New Delhi

Government of the Republic of Moldova (2004a) *Economic Growth and Poverty Reduction Strategy Paper (2004–2006)*, Chisinau, Government of Moldova

Government of the Republic of Moldova (2004b) *Report on Public Participation in EGPRS Elaboration Process (December 2003 – June 2004)*, World Bank Grant TFP 50872 (GIU EGPRS), Chisinau, Government of Moldova

Mukherjee, A. (ed) (2004) *Participatory Monitoring*, Concept Publishing Company, Delhi

Mukherjee, N. (1995) *Participatory Rural Appraisal and Questionnaire Survey: Comparative field experience and methodological innovations*, Concept Publishing Company, Delhi

Mukherjee, N. (2002) *Participatory Learning and Action with 100 Field Methods*, Concept Publishing Company, Delhi

National Planning Commission (2004) *Poverty Monitoring and Analysis System*, Katmandu, National Planning Commission Secretariat

SCERS (2005) *Poverty and Policy Impact Report*, 2004, Chisinau, SCERS

UNDP (United Nations Development Programme) (2002) *National Human Development Report, 2002*, Chisinaum UNDP Moldova

UNDP (2003) *National Human Development Report, 2003* Chisinau, UNDP Moldova

UNDP (2004) *Nepal's Human Development Report*, Katmandu, UNDP Nepal

UNDP (2005) *National Human Development Report, 2005*, Chisinau, UNDP Moldova

United Nations (2007) World Economic Situation and Prospects, United Nations, New York

World Bank (2001) *Philippines Filipino Report Card on Pro-Poor Services*, Environment and Social Development Sector Unit, East Asia and Pacific Region, Washington DC, World Bank

World Bank (2004) *Community Report Card Surveys – A Note on the Concept and Methodology, Social Development Notes, Participation and Civic Engagement*, Note No. 91, Washington DC, World Bank

14

The P135 Programme for Socio-economic Development of Communes Facing Extreme Difficulties in Ethnic Minority and Mountainous Areas in Vietnam

Tran Van Thuat and Ha Viet Quan

Introduction

The Socio-economic Development Programme for Ethnic Minority Areas (SEDEMA), more commonly referred to as Programme 135 (P135) is a national poverty reduction programme that began in 1998 for a 7-year period and in 2006 was extended to 2010. Its target area is communes and villages in remote ethnic minority and mountainous areas facing extreme difficulties, with harsh natural conditions and few opportunities to participate in national and mainstream economic growth.

Villages and communes in these areas have high rates of household poverty, typically higher than the national average. While the poverty rate for the majority Kinh and Chinese is 14 per cent, that of ethnic minorities is 61 per cent (GSO, 2006). According to the Ministry of Labour, Invalids and Social Affairs (MOLISA), ethnic minorities that comprise 13.8 per cent of the population, are disproportionately affected by poverty, representing 36 per cent of the poor and this figure has been increasing (21 per cent in 1992, 29 per cent in 1998 and 36 per cent in 2005) (GoVN-MOLISA, 2007). The gap between regions and ethnic minorities and the majority is widening and this is observed between minority groups as well. For example, poverty rates for the Pa Co, Van Kieu and H'Mong ethnic minorities range from 30 to 60 per cent, while the rate for Tay, Nung and Muong rates are under 20 per cent.

Harsh natural conditions, weather, limited access to social services, lack of market access and poor access to electricity have negatively impacted ethnic minorities in the communes under P135.

Ethnic minority access to clean water and hygienic latrines is 12.8 per cent and 4.1 per cent respectively, while the rates for Kinh and Hoa are 52.6 per cent and 27.7 pe cent (GSO, 2004). The infant mortality rate for Gia Rai is 70 per 1000 live births, double the average and triple the rate for Kinh. The malnutrition rate for under-fives (weight for age) in 2005 for all ethnic groups was 25.7 per cent, while rates for ethnic minorities in the Northern Mountain and Central Highland regions were 34.3 per cent and 45.3 per cent respectively.

Communes have insufficient staff and the capacity of specialized staff and key officials is limited (most have not completed high school). It is difficult to attract skilled service providers such as doctors, nurses and teachers to these areas.

The project

P135 is a national programme established in 1998 to implement special government policies for extremely difficult communes. It promotes production and access to basic infrastructure, improves education, trains local officials and raises people's awareness for improved spiritual and physical life. The rationale for establishing P135 was to help people in ethnic minority and mountainous areas overcome poverty, narrow the income gap with other communes in other districts and provinces, and eliminate the risk of social instability. P135 was designed to address the different causes of poverty including those particular to ethnic minorities and remote areas such as low capacity, small landholdings, lack of knowledge, skills and market information, health problems, large family sizes, unemployment and vulnerability to risks (including social problems). Other typical causes contributing to poverty for ethnic minorities include: (1) low starting point, living in the poorest areas in the country with under-developed markets inappropriate to local potential and advantage; (2) dependence on mainly subsistence agriculture production applying traditional practices; (3) population sparsely distributed over large areas, and increasingly complex migration in some areas; (4) degraded environments; (5) weak and unsustainable infrastructure; (6) low literacy rates, education problems and unskilled human resources.

Programme formulation

P135 was designed in 1997 and approved in 1998 by the government for a period of 7 years. A second phase was formulated in April 2005 and approved in January 2006 to continue to 2010. MPI and the Committee for Ethnic Minority Affairs (CEMA) researched and designed both phases of P135 in coordination with relevant ministries and government agencies.

The development of both phases of P135 involved local needs assessments and widespread consultation with stakeholders, especially at the local level. Accordingly, a broad consensus was reached in the development, approval and implementation

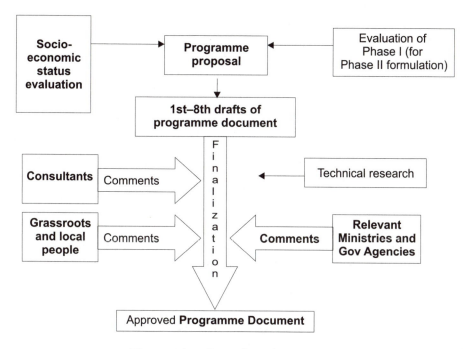

Figure 14.1 *P135 formulation process*

processes. To develop the second phase for example, CEMA, with technical assistance from UNDP, organized hundreds of consultations with local officials and people, consultants, specialists, relevant ministries and government agencies and donors. Eighteen national and international studies and in-depth technical consultancies were carried out to provide inputs for the phase II design, which also benefited considerably from the UNDP-government joint evaluation of P135's first phase.

P135's objectives

P135's overall objectives (in both phases I and II) are: (1) to radically accelerate production and promote market-oriented agricultural development; (2) to sustainably improve the socio-cultural life of ethnic minority people in extremely difficult communes and villages to narrow the gap in living standards among Vietnam's ethnic groups and regions; and (3) to eradicate hunger in the targeted areas and reduce the poverty rate to below 30 per cent.

P135 has a set of specific, measurable and outcome-oriented objectives and targets in line with the MDGs and Vietnam's own national development goals:

- *Production development*: to upgrade skills and develop new production practices among ethnic minorities so that by 2010 more than 70 per cent of households will have an average annual income per capita of over VND3.5 million (US$220).

- *Infrastructure development*: to ensure that all communes have essential infrastructure effectively serving the improvement of living conditions, production development and income, including roads, irrigation, schools, health clinics and electricity.
- *Improving socio-cultural living standards for people in extremely difficult communes*: to ensure access to basic social services including clean water and hygienic latrines, health services, improved primary and secondary enrolment, and universal free access to legal assistance to those in need.
- *Capacity strengthening*: to provide commune staff and village leaders with skills and knowledge to better administer and manage poverty reduction activities, including legal and investment management knowledge and skills; to strengthen capacity of communities and create conditions for them to more effectively participate in monitoring and supervision of investment and other activities implemented in the programme area.

Key elements of the programme

P135's first phase covered 2410 of the country's poorest communes, of which 1938 were in mountainous and 472 in lowland areas, with around 1.1 million households and over 6 million people. With a total government investment of more than VND9142 billion (US$ 571 million), from 1998–2005, P135 focused primarily on developing village, communal and inter-communal infrastructure. From 2006–2010, P135 goes beyond infrastructure to also cover agricultural production, capacity building and improved socio-cultural livelihoods.

Target beneficiaries and programme area

P135 is a national targeted area programme. Target beneficiaries are the poorest and extremely disadvantaged ethnic minorities and mountainous communes and villages defined through a simple set of specific criteria that include population size, remoteness, poverty rates, existence of essential infrastructure, and education and health indicators (enrolment rates, child and maternal mortality rates, etc.). Based on these criteria, local governments conducted assessments and selected extremely difficult communes and villages in a transparent, democratic and participatory manner.

In the first phase, 2410 of the poorest communes were selected as programme beneficiaries, representing nearly one-quarter of all communes and 15 per cent of the total population. Of these, 671 communes were assessed to have completed the programme's objectives, and, from 2006, the second phase targets 1920 extremely difficult communes, which includes communes from the first phase plus additional communes that have been re-zoned. From 2008, 2500 of the poorest villages in the surrounding zones will be added. The inclusion of targeted communes and villages is reviewed annually against the criteria, and from 2008, communes and villages that meet P135's targets will graduate from the programme.

Programme activities

Key components

P135 consists of four components:

- Market-oriented agricultural production providing agricultural extension and marketing services designed to increase household income.
- Community infrastructure development to improve access by the poor to social services and to increase their economic opportunities.
- Capacity building for local officials and communities to better plan, manage, implement and monitor investments.
- Improved socio-cultural livelihoods providing social services including clean water and sanitation, and assets such as housing and land.

Key activities by component

Activities to support market-oriented agricultural production and income generation include: agriculture, forestry and fishery extension; establishment of demonstration models; distribution of agricultural inputs; and equipment and extension services for post-harvest and processing activities.

Community infrastructure development includes: inter-village and village-to-commune roads; small irrigation schemes; construction or upgrading of schools and boarding facilities for students and teachers; construction or upgrading of commune clinics; market infrastructure; community halls; and clean water supply systems.

The capacity building component includes training activities targeting commune and village officials to strengthen their knowledge and skills for managing and implementing P135 and other socio-economic development programmes. Topics include: participatory planning; monitoring and reporting; financial management; grassroots democracy and local governance; gender; communications; and other topics specifically related to P135 activities. Training on the programme activities is also provided to communities. Under the component, funds are allocated for provinces to design their own training activities that meet specific needs including study and exchange visits.

The improved socio-cultural livelihoods component includes support to improve housing and clean water and sanitation facilities; communication on social programmes and services; school feeding; training for ethnic minority teachers; Vietnamese language teaching for ethnic minority pre-schoolers; financial support for ethnic minority boarding school students; and free legal services.

The second phase of P135 also includes a number of cross-cutting activities derived from lessons learned during the implementation of the first phase and other similar large-scale poverty reduction programmes in Vietnam. These include:

- a monitoring and evaluation system that includes an impact assessment methodology with baseline, mid-term and final impact surveys and an improved monitoring and reporting system;
- emphasis on decentralization with the goal of 100 per cent decentralization of programme management to communes by 2010;
- pro-poor budgeting with allocation of funds directed to communes based on poverty levels and other criteria determined by provinces;
- application of participatory planning, monitoring and evaluation at the commune level and strengthening of commune 'people's supervision committees';
- increased transparency of financial management, including quarterly financial reports, fund-flow maps and strengthened auditing; and
- a communication strategy focusing on behavioural change linked to programme objectives.

Key technical inputs

Technical inputs provided by P135 itself, UNDP (as the primary TA provider) and other donors include:

- evaluation of the first phase of P135 (CEMA, 2005b);
- research, studies and technical consultancies for the design and development of management and implementation guidelines for the second phase of P135;
- development and application of criteria for selecting target beneficiaries – the poorest communes and villages;
- design and operationalization of a results-based monitoring and evaluation system, including: impact evaluation, programme implementation monitoring and management information systems at both central and local levels including local participatory planning and monitoring;
- design and operationalization of an improved financial management system including financial reporting, expenditure reconciliation and pro-poor budget allocation (based on poverty-related criteria);
- development and operationalization of the capacity building component, including development of a capacity building framework, training materials, training of trainers and training;

- development and operationalization of a communication strategy and plan; and
- development and operationalization of coordination mechanisms, including a joint Government of Vietnam–Donor Partnership Committee for Budget Support to P135 for coordinating TA, reviewing P135 progress and making recommendations to the P135 National Steering Committee for improvements.

Timeframe

P135 was approved in 1998 for a period of 7 years up to 2005. In 2006, P135 was extended for a second phase up to 2010.

Impacts and outcomes

From 1999–2004, a total of VND8,434 billion (US$600 million) was disbursed from the central level and VND240 billion (US$15.1 million) from local levels under P135 for the construction of more than 20,000 small infrastructure projects at the inter-communal and commune levels, including roads (33 per cent), schools (24 per cent), small irrigation works (17 per cent), clean water supply (12 per cent) and electricity (8 per cent). As a result, the number of P135 communes with essential infrastructure increased significantly (see Table 14.1).

During the same period, P135 provided VND53.6 billion (US$3.3 million) for training to more than 155,000 commune officers and village leaders. This, together, with the P135 approach encouraging participation and decentralization, have contributed to enhancing people's participation and empowerment in commune-level government for managing and implementing P135. Sixteen per cent of P135 communes became 'investment owners', fully empowered and decentralized managers of P135 working in their own communities (CEMA 2005a; 2005b; 2005c).

P135 and the national targeted programme for hunger eradication and poverty reduction (HEPR) are among the key factors in the striking rate of poverty reduction in P135's main target areas, the Central Highlands and North West: 7 and 9 percentage points respectively per year from 2002–2004, helping explain why Vietnam is recognized as a world leader in poverty reduction (VASS, 2007).

Table 14.1 *Proportion of P135 communes with essential infrastructure*

Communes with roads	94%	Communes with small irrigation systems	81%
Communes with clinics	96%	Communes with solid primary schools	86%
Communes with solid secondary schools	73%	Communes with market place	44%
Communes with electricity	84%	Communes with clean water	58%

Source: CEMA (2005c)

Table 14.2 *State budget allocation*

Programme Content	GOV Budget (US$ million)	Percentage
Phase I Total	632	100
Production	24.74	4.0
Infrastructure	602	95.2
Capacity building	5.26	0.8
Phase II Total	780	100
Production development	132.8	17.18
Infrastructure	522.23	67.56
Operation and maintenance	52.17	6.75
Capacity building	34.79	4.05
Livelihood improvement	34.79	4.05
Monitoring and management	2.94	0.38
Total for Phases I and II	**1,412**	

Source: CEMA (2005a; 2007)

Total programme cost

Government budget for P135

The total state budget for P135 phase I was US$632 million and for phase II is US$780 million. A breakdown by component for each phase is shown in Table 14.2.

External assistance for P135

In 2005, DFID provided direct budget support of approximately US$17.2 million to P135. In 2007, a group of donors including the World Bank, Finland, Sweden, Australia, IFAD, DFID and Ireland committed US$330 million as targeted budget support to the second phase of P135. According to the progress made against the agreed budget support results framework, funds will be disbursed in tranches directly to the Government of Vietnam/P135. Donors' funding is then combined with the government budget allocated to P135 and both funding sources are disbursed and managed by the Government of Vietnam using its own state budget management systems and procedures.

An allocation plan for donors' funds to all programme components is being prepared using state budget proportions. However, according to donor requirements, there will be greater allocation for the production and capacity building components, and funding for the latter is proposed to boost the total allocation for capacity building to 7 per cent of the programme budget. In addition to budget support donors are contributing around US$7 million as parallel TA.

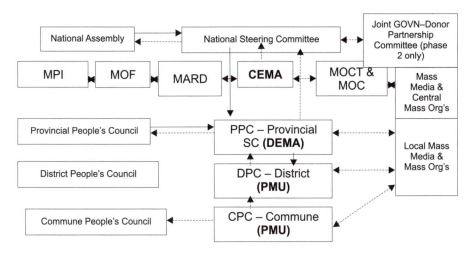

Figure 14.2 *P135 management and coordination structure*

Programme management

P135 is a government programme approved by the National Assembly. A National Steering Committee for poverty reduction programmes, chaired by a deputy prime minister with ministers from relevant ministries and government organizations as member participants is fully responsible for the programme's management function. Implementation, management and coordination of P135 rely on existing government structures and organizations, processes and procedures. Figure 14.2 shows the P135 management and coordination structure.

Each component under P135 has its own mechanism that not only adheres to common government mechanisms but also takes into account the programme's features, especially the fact that all activities are undertaken at and by grassroots levels. In the infrastructure component, for example, in principal all investments under P135 must strictly follow the law on construction and its relevant implementation guidelines promulgated by the government. However, as most construction works are of small scale and their scope of service is at village levels, the investment management mechanism is simplified to be appropriate with the programme's decentralization approach, so that communes manage the whole process within their capacity, aiming to achieve the programme target of decentralization to 100 per cent of communes. Similarly, in the production component, the decentralization approach is applied to strengthen grassroots democracy right at the village level. It requires standing units of provincial People's Councils and People's Committees to provide instruction down to beneficiary commune councils so that, in turn, these councils can effectively support communities in planning, setting targets and the scope of action, implementation, supervision and inspection.

Because P135's second phase is jointly funded by a group of donors through targeted budget support, the joint Government of Vietnam–Donor Partnership

Committee for P135 Budget Support has been established to facilitate dialogue between the government and international development partners on P135 management and implementation, coordinate TA, review P135 implementation progress and make recommendations to the P135 National Steering Committee for improvements.

Monitoring and evaluation

The first phase of P135 (together with the HEPR programme) was monitored mainly through local level progress reporting and central government monitoring visits and review missions. An evaluation of the first phase was conducted with UNDP technical support (GoVN-UNDP, 2004). A key area for improvement identified by the evaluation was the development and operationalization of a results-based monitoring and evaluation system that has been developed for the second phase, including a Roadmap and Results Framework[1] with expected impacts, outcomes and outputs and timeframe for P135's second phase. Based on these results, a monitoring, and evaluation system with clear targets and indicators at impact, outcome, output and process levels, and clearly assigned responsibilities for collecting and using data and information has been designed and is being operationalized. A baseline survey is being conducted for collecting baseline information and data for the second phase against the monitoring and evaluation indicators and a management information system is also being designed and operationalized. Mechanisms for identifying, documenting and disseminating lessons and best practices in P135 management and implementation, including 'horizontal learning and sharing' between P135 provinces and communes are being designed and operationalized.

In addition to the government's regular reviews and audits (by the State Audit of Viet Nam), the government and donors carry out semi-annual joint reviews of P135 implementation progress. A final evaluation is planned to assess the achievement of P135 results and impact on poverty reduction at the end of the programme in 2010.

Challenges and how they were overcome

P135 is a large and complex national programme with widespread coverage over various sectors and areas, implemented over a long period, and so faces a number of significant challenges. Through its own monitoring, a systematic evaluation supported by UNDP, the experience of DFID's budget support in 2005 and the collaboration of other donors, the government was able to identify key challenges in the implementation of P135's first phase and incorporate best practice to overcome these in the design of P135's second phase, which has completed 18 months of implementation.

Capacity and decentralization

Limited management and implementation capacity at grassroots levels is a major challenge for P135 implementation, especially for the objective of decentralizing programme management to all communes. Government staff at the commune level are inadequate both in terms of their numbers and qualifications (most key technical staff at the commune level have not completed higher secondary school) and most districts manage planning, implementing and monitoring of P135's activities. To address this challenge, P135's second phase has allocated more resources (7 per cent of the total budget in phase II compared to less than 1 per cent in phase I) to capacity building. The government has set clear targets for 100 per cent decentralization of programme implementation to communes as 'investment owners' by 2010, backed up by a specific policy to assess and stage communes towards this goal. A comprehensive capacity building programme with appropriate materials is being developed and operationalized to achieve those targets and support the ability of commune-level officials and people's supervision boards to facilitate meaningful participation of poor women and men in all stages of P135 management and implementation. This programme includes a flexible mechanism allowing provinces to design and implement their own capacity building at the local level combined with a comprehensive, nationally developed standardized training programme based on the wide breadth of existing experience in capacity building in similar projects in Vietnam.

Monitoring and evaluation

Another major challenge is designing and operationalizing a monitoring and evaluation system that can provide policy makers with reliable quantitative and qualitative information on P135 implementation, its impacts on the life of poor women and men as well as on the socio-economic situation in the poorest communes. A monitoring and evaluation system that includes impact evaluation and regular programme monitoring has been designed and is being piloted, and a baseline survey is being conducted. There have been and will be more regular monitoring missions and reviews organized as well as mechanisms for ensuring accountability and promoting greater transparency, including enhancement of people's participation in monitoring, review and supervision of P135 implementation, in line with the Ordinance on Grassroots Democracy in Vietnam.

Financial management

Although the allocation of funds for P135 is clear and transparent and funds pass directly to communes or projects, accounting, audit and review mechanisms in phase I were not sufficiently adequate to accurately assess or verify the use of funds. For example, implementation units and treasury offices filed separate financial reports that were not reconciled. In phase II of P135 the frequency of financial reporting is increased from annual to quarterly reporting and reports are reconciled with treasury figures to ensure money has been spent properly. In addition, regular financial and performance audits for P135 will be carried out and the capacity of the State Audit strengthened.

Public information and awareness

While P135 in Vietnam's remote areas has strong 'brand-name' recognition, there was no specific strategy in phase I for communicating programme information across and between implementation levels and to communities, and communication materials were rarely produced in local minority languages. In phase II, the government has developed a comprehensive and multi-directional communication strategy including objectives for both public information and behavioural change, utilizing a range of media channels and products developed in minority languages. Moreover, the government is working to allocate funds to support communication activities at both national and provincial levels.

Sustainability

The primary focus of P135's first phase was infrastructure development with only 4 per cent of the budget directed towards agriculture. The government realizes that basic infrastructure alone is insufficient to achieve P135's poverty reduction goals and more emphasis is needed to support income generation and market integration. Therefore, the second phase incorporates a self-help/self-development and market-oriented approach with significant funds (17 per cent of programme cost) and activities to support poor households' own economic development. The Ministry of Agriculture and Rural Development (responsible for the production component) has issued guidelines that promote improved agricultural production and marketing services to poor households, and encourages group approaches for extension services.

Regarding sustainability of infrastructure, the official policy is that costs for operations and maintenance be met by local authorities or communities that use infrastructure, however, these groups cannot raise the necessary funds for the typically greater operations and maintenance needs of upland areas. In phase II, the government has allocated 10 per cent of the infrastructure budget towards operations and maintenance.

Resource mobilization and coordination

One of the biggest remaining implementation challenges is mobilizing and allocating resources in an equitable and appropriate manner to province, district and commune levels. Different communes and villages under P135 have different population sizes and different levels of poverty and difficulty, and the second phase of P135 recognizes this by requiring specific, non-uniform allocations to communes based on their specific features and conditions, however, this makes suitable resource allocations difficult to formulate.

In addition, since P135 has several components and is one among a number of programmes and projects carried out concurrently in the same area, a challenge is integrating and coordinating the different activities under P135 and other programmes and projects to avoid overlap, therefore, an integrated management mechanism is needed.

The strong commitment of the Government of Vietnam and donors to implement the Hanoi Core Statement on aid effectiveness has laid a strong foundation for resource mobilization and coordination. As mentioned above, instead of supporting separate and parallel poverty reduction and rural development programmes and projects, donors have agreed to provide US$330 million as targeted budget support to P135. Together with the government's own efforts to mobilize additional resources and support from mass organizations and the private sector in Vietnam, donors' budget support not only provides additional resources needed to implement P135, but also helps to: (1) reduce the number of similar programmes and projects; (2) reduce transaction costs; and (3) increase synergy through coordinated efforts in strengthening the government's capacity, systems and mechanisms for managing and implementing its own programme.

Lessons learned and good practice

The Government of Vietnam's strong determination and commitment, together with special interest paid by the Communist Party, the state, all relevant bodies and the people in poverty alleviation and development processes is the most significant lesson for the success of P135. While making efforts to ensure mainstream economic growth is pro-poor, the government has recognized that additional efforts are needed to accelerate socio-economic development in the poorest ethnic minority areas so the poor in general and poor ethnic minorities, in particular, catch up with the majority and actively participate in and benefit from mainstream development. This is reflected in Vietnam's development goals, its own 'nationalized' version of the MDGs, which include the MDGs plus goals specifically targeting ethnic minorities. P135 is an additional effort to realize this dual pro-poor strategy and achieve Vietnam's development goals. Serving as a channel for additional state budget transfers to the poorest villages and communes, P135 resources are allocated within the framework of national socio-economic development planning and budget allocation, making that framework even more pro-poor.

P135 is recognized popularly and by the Government and donors as having an effective and clear targeting strategy with simple and clear development targets in line with the MDGs. P135 has applied a set of simple, transparent and participatory criteria for defining targeted villages, communes and households, and its simple and clear targets have been publicly and widely communicated to all stakeholders.

P135's effectiveness in terms of achieving expected results is due to simple, transparent, results-based and pro-poor resource allocation. During the first phase, a fixed sum of VND500 million (US$33,000) per poor commune was allocated and this formula of equitable distribution of limited resources has the benefit of simplicity, clarity and transparency. In the second phase, as P135 gets more complex in terms of programme content, the central government and provinces need to develop clear and equitable mechanisms for non-uniform budget allocations to communes and villages based on specific poverty and socio-economic criteria and performance results to ensure allocations are results-based, pro-poor and meet the different needs of villages and communes.

Decentralization and participation with adequate matching support in capacity development at local levels are key for effective management and implementation of P135. P135 management and implementation is decentralized to commune and village levels with clear criteria for communes to be the real programme 'owners'. The improvement in local people's participation in making all decisions regarding implementation of P135 in their communes and villages is attributed both to the Ordinance on Grassroots Democracy Decree and P135's strong support to strengthening the capacity of local governments and people.

As a large national programme added to the national Socio-Economic Development Plan, P135 has created very little additional administrative burden as it relies on existing government systems for management and implementation, including for financial management and monitoring. This arrangement also helps avoid both the need for creating extra mechanisms to implement and manage P135 and provides better opportunities for coordinating implementation of P135 activities with the implementation of mainstream socio-economic development plans.

The government's and donors' strong commitment towards moving forward the agenda of aid effectiveness in Vietnam, plus P135's impressive past achievements and ambitious but feasible design for the second phase have offered a unique chance for harmonizing donor support in rural development and poverty reduction programmes at local levels along the national programme. Donors' targeted budget support of US$330 million to P135 not only helps the government to mobilize necessary resources for an important national programme, but also helps reduce transaction costs and improve the synergy of government and donor efforts for national ownership and leadership, and enhancing national systems and capacity for the government to effectively manage its own national programmes and plans to achieve the MDGs.

Effective utilization of neutral and objective technical support from UNDP has played a key role in P135's success. UNDP supported an independent evaluation of P135 phase I and has helped build donors' confidence in P135. UNDP's timely and effective support in preparation and negotiations for support agreements with donors has helped make targeted budget support to P135 possible. UNDP support in the feasible and sound design of P135 phase II, based on situation analyses and needs assessments, improving the P135 monitoring and evaluation system, enhancing transparency in P135 financial management and mobilizing maximum participation, has helped phase II achieve greater effectiveness as well as to attract donors' interest.

Potential for scaling up and conclusions

P135 began in 1998 as a national targeted programme to reduce poverty and improve the livelihoods of ethnic minorities and communities in remote, mountainous areas. After seven years of implementation, P135 has made a major contribution to poverty reduction in Vietnam's ethnic minority and mountainous areas and demonstrated the value of targeted programming. Nonetheless, although there has been a net reduction in overall poverty, ethnic minorities represent an increasingly greater proportion of the poor and are benefiting less from overall economic development than the majority. The government is committed to ensuring equitable and accessible socio-economic development for all and bringing ethnic minority and mountainous areas into the national mainstream development, and has extended P135 for a second phase of five years to 2010. In doing so, the government objectively reviewed both the successes and failures of P135's first phase, and has designed a second phase that maintains and builds on the programme's strengths while ambitiously incorporating best practice drawn from national and internationally funded rural development programmes in Vietnam. In this respect, phase II of P135 already represents a scaling up of the programme, and the adoption of innovative and cutting-edge approaches for socio-economic development and poverty reduction makes P135 a flagship project for the government in terms of national poverty reduction programming. P135's second phase has already completed 18 months of implementation, and, though still early, it is already showing results that can be a model for other programmes in Vietnam and possibly the region in terms of specific practices and mechanisms for mainstreaming and operationalizing MDGs into national and local development programmes, as well as a success story for targeted budget support. In terms of donor coordination and collaboration, P135 can be a model for how aid can be better harmonized and incorporated to support and strengthen government programming, as the programme support modality – including budget support – is increasingly adopted by donors.

Note

1   The Results Framework contains key P135 expected results and is used for monitoring progress towards results agreed between the government and donors. These results act as 'triggers' for periodic transfers of donors' budget support to P135.

References

CEMA (Committee for Ethnic Minority Affairs) (2005a) *SEDEMA Programme Document 2006–2010*, CEMA, Hanoi

CEMA (2005b) *Report on Capacity Building for Local Cadres in P135*, CEMA, Hanoi

CEMA (2005c) *Report on Infrastructure Component of P135*, CEMA, Hanoi

CEMA (2007) *Plan for Use of Additional ODA Allocation to P135*, CEMA, Hanoi

GoVN-MOLISA (Government of Vietnam-Ministry of Labour, Invalids and Social Affairs) (2007) *Programme Document of the National Targeted Programmes for Poverty Reduction 2006–2010*, MOLISA, Hanoi

GoVN-UNDP (Government of Vietnam-United Nations Development Programme) (2004) *Taking Stock, Planning Ahead: Evaluation of the National Targeted Programme on Hunger Eradication and Poverty Reduction 135*, MOLISA, Hanoi

GSO (2004) *Vietnam Living Standards Survey 2002: Statistical Abstract*, Statistical Publishing House, Hanoi

GSO (2006) *Vietnam Living Standards Survey 2004: Statistical Abstract*, Statistical Publishing House, Hanoi

15

Empowering Women through Home-based Income-Earning Opportunities in Malaysia

Sheau Ching Chong and Audrey Desiderato

Introduction

The generation of income-earning opportunities for poor women is an important indicator of improved gender equality and empowerment. A woman's ability to earn an income translates to improved nutrition and medical care for her family and more gender-equal education opportunities for her children. Moreover, a woman's earning power leads to greater self-confidence, which, in turn, moves her to pro-actively improve her life through self-governance.

For those women fortunate enough to find jobs, a 2002 survey conducted by eHomemakers on low- to middle-income female office and factory workers revealed that the lower income urban worker sacrifices almost 40 per cent of her monthly salary on fixed working expenses such as commuting, childcare and personal expenses for her work image. Thus, the real take home pay is not commensurate with the wage needed to cover household expenses. The research also showed that ICT is vital for the creation of a work option that would allow women to earn a higher real income by working from their homes (eHomemakers, 2002).

An increasingly popular means for poverty alleviation is to train the poor in ICT for income-earning purposes. Following the global effort to bridge the digital divide, poor rural women have successfully gained income-earning opportunities in non-agricultural sectors through employment in telecentres.

While ICT in development movements continues to grow, it is unfortunate that many poor urban women are still left behind. Although slums and low-income housing are surrounded by modern infrastructures, the urban poor women face many barriers to accessing ICT resources and training. The barriers range from high financial costs, their triple work burden and training schedules that clash with their daily priority tasks. They are thus unable to improve their lives in an increasingly competitive urban setting (Loh-Ludher et al, 2006, pp27–31).

Urban poor women such as the disabled, chronically ill, mothers of disabled or chronically ill children and single mothers who must support their households as both caretakers and income earners face extremely high barriers due to the immobility they face. In addition, these women also face cultural barriers in the form of gender role expectation. Disadvantaged women of the above profile are still expected to fulfil their roles at home as wives, mothers, daughters and sisters instead of giving themselves time and the mental energy to acquire new skills and knowledge (Loh-Ludher et al, 2006, pp25–31). Self-improvement efforts are a low priority or non-existent in their lives.

Additional research conducted by eHomemakers in 2005–2006 on Southeast Asian homeworkers (Czarina et al, 2005) explored their situations. While home-working is a growing sector, allowing those facing issues of immobility to contribute to the economy by earning income from home, it is not officially recognized as a part of the Malaysian formal economy (Loh-Ludher et al, 2006, pp24–36). Thus, there is an absence of regulating policies for the sector. Homeworkers are left facing multiple forms of discrimination and exploitation. They possess little or no bargaining power to secure fair prices and wages, and are often exposed to health and safety problems.

The project

Due to their inability to work outside of the home, these women would especially benefit from home-based ICT-focused employment opportunities. Working at home options effectively increase women's participation in the economic sphere as they allow women an opportunity to balance traditional roles with income-earning opportunities without giving them a triple burden (work, household and children). To this end, eHomemakers provides a grassroots e-network aimed at overcoming the extreme lack of information on working at home, connecting thousands of women facing similar barriers and reversing the social prejudice homeworkers face in an informal economic sector. eHomemakers promotes the use of ICT such as mobile phones, computers, the internet and an integrated plat-form called the Distributed Work Management Application (DWMA) (web-to-handphone) for both income-generating opportunities and grassroot-to-grassroot self-help for women who aspire to become homeworkers, teleworkers or home-business owners. The web portal and integrated platform allow easy interconnec-tivity between women for discussion and mutual support.

In order to help disadvantaged homemakers such as single mothers and the disabled, eHomemakers established a project titled 'Salaam Wanita' (Recognizing Women). eHomemakers has researched the needs and barriers that urban poor women face in order to formulate a multi-faceted, end-to-end approach to steer these women towards self-reliance. Specifically guided by the research, eHomemakers ensures that once it provides training for disadvantaged women it does not abandon them; instead, eHomemakers' e-members (over 15,000) and core team are dedicated to providing critical assistance, mentorship and counselling, besides marketing and work sourcing support throughout their transition to self-sufficiency. DWMA allows low-income disadvantaged women to generate an income from home, overcoming their physical and social circumstances, by connecting them to the eHomemakers network and facilitating the earning of more income through ICT enablement. For example, a woman can market her catering service via the eHomemakers network, process orders through her mobile phone and cook from her very own kitchen without having to pay travel outside of the home (Krishna and Puvaneswary, 2005).

Project formulation

The eHomemakers network was formed via grassroots initiatives by middle-income homeworkers and homemakers who wanted to create a resource and support network to connect to other homeworkers. The network (first known as Mothers for Mothers) was formed in 1998 by a single mother along with a group of multi-ethnic homemaker volunteers.

In 1999, a static website was built by volunteers to meet the information-hungry homemakers and provide a woman-to-woman networking platform at no financial cost to members. As they encountered public prejudices labelling them as useless 'housewives' who did not contribute to society, the initial members soon saw that static information provision would not suffice to help women break through gender discrimination and ICT barriers.

In the first few years, the Mothers for Mothers network organized a number of 'Working @ Home' conferences without any funding. The volunteers creatively found solutions to offset costs by bartering with companies. As the network successfully grew, its empowerment activities expanded to reach socially and financially disadvantaged members. To increase its capacity and accommodate increasingly diverse groups of women, the Mothers for Mothers network was replaced in 2002 by eHomemakers. A trilingual, interactive community portal was built under a one-year community grant (Demonstrator Application Grant) from the Malaysian government.

Project goals and objectives

The core objectives of eHomemakers are:

- to develop a self-sustaining social enterprise by leveraging on the resources cultivated from the 15,000 strong e-community to maintain gender empowerment activities;

- to build an e-community of ICT savvy homemakers, homeworkers and home-preneurs and provide them with a platform for self-help and people-to-people activities in business and work;
- to encourage homemakers, especially the disadvantaged, to generate income through home-based activities and ICT usage;
- to disseminate family-orientated information at a one-stop e-centre to enable members to be smart and efficient in balancing home and work life; and
- to integrate the principles of sustainable development into our programmes so as to be part of the MDGs in Malaysia.

Project goals are:

- to sustain a grassroots e-network for mutual assistance and gender empower-ment through information provision, interactive activities, networking and teletrading in addition to ground-based training, work sourcing and business activities;
- to raise the profile of unpaid work, telework and homebased work in Malaysia through research, especially gender-based analysis, information dissemination and advocacy;
- to educate women to enhance their skills and talents through the use of ICT by educating them on ICT usage and importance;
- to provide disadvantaged women with training, long-term support and an e-platform for self-help and cluster-to-cluster assistance;
- to facilitate strategic partnerships with the small office, home office and ICT community;
- to develop a replicable model for an efficient grassroots e-social enterprise; and
- to promote the concept of corporate social responsibility (CSR) in the Malaysian corporate sector.

Key elements of the project

Target beneficiaries

Even though eHomemakers' members were initially comprised of Malaysian mothers in the middle to lower income groups in 1998, it has grown to include unmarried women and grandmothers, and even some househusbands who support their wives. Today, the ratio of women to men in e-membership is 3:1. Most members are from the urban/peri-urban areas, married and in the 30–50 age group. About 10 per cent of the over 15,000 e-members, comprising both genders, come from the Association of South-East Asian Nations (ASEAN) region. Beneficiaries also include over 300 Salaam Wanita members who are unemployed and residing in slums and low-cost housing areas.

Project area

The e-members are located in the urban and peri-urban areas all over Malaysia where ICT resources are accessible. Salaam Wanita members are located in and around Kuala Lumpur and Ipoh.

Project activities

Key components

Key project components include:

- grassroots management as opposed to a top-down approach that ensures that the needs of target groups are clearly understood;
- the promotion of ICT for income-generating opportunities allows diverse groups of women to work from home, empowering them to set up e-businesses, market online and through phones, do freelance work and telework;
- the eHomemakers' virtual office that allows for cost savings while providing a successful, replicable organizational model for members;
- eHomemakers is self-sustaining via revenue generation through web banner ads, newsletter ads, corporate sponsorships, consultancy fees and research grants;
- the Salaam Wanita project is designed to alleviate urban poverty among homebound disadvantaged women;
- eHomemakers undertakes gender-based action research and is actively involved in promoting healthy policy changes concerning ICTs for urban poor women and the homeworking sector. eHomemakers also works hard to encourage the public to refer to its members as 'homemakers', 'teleworkers' or 'homepreneurs' rather than the negatively charged term 'housewives' in order to pave public acceptance of homemakers into the formal sector.

Key activities

Key project activities include the following:

- *Teletrading* – eHomemakers provides this free service to allow small home businesses with little capital and no advertising budget to get a wide exposure through the network.
- *Newsletters* – eHomemakers members can receive both cyber and printed newsletters, for example, *Home + Work* highlights achievements of homepreneurs to inspire potential home workers and homepreneurs.
- *Portal section resources* – various sections of the portal such as *Homebiz Management, Homebased Profiles* and *IT Tips & Issues* provide resources developed by members and experts that enable women to work from home, embark on entrepreneurship and sustain their home businesses.

- *Forum maintenance* – the forum board is an avenue for members to network and exchange ideas and experiences. Typical day-to-day postings discuss the difficult process of decision making, the authenticity of home-based jobs available on the internet and various e-books/resources for life-long learning.
- *Research* – eHomemakers has published research on ICT and gender dynamics to advocate for the development of innovative strategies geared towards benefiting the urban poor.
- *Events* – eHomemakers hosts annual Mother's Day competitions, celebrating mothers that are exceptional change agents in their community. In addition, eHomemakers hosts a series of seminars geared towards working at home.
- *Salaam Wanita training, product marketing and securing of homebased work* – eHomemakers provides basic eco-basket weaving skills and markets the finished products for the women. Women who have gone through training in computer skills, customer service skills and speaking skills are in an on-going project called 'Unlimited Potential' to secure them freelance homebased ICT work.
- *Justmarketing.info website* – eHomemakers maintains a website to market the services and products for Salaam Wanita members including the innovative hand-woven eco-baskets made out of used magazines and flyers.
- *Donations appeal* – eHomemakers coordinates appeals to its over 15,000 members and other donors to secure donations in the form of cash, food, medicines, used computers, used mobile phones, fax machines, printers and scanners to benefit its 300 plus Salaam Wanita members, thus facilitating assistance from those who have the most resources to those with the least.

Key technical inputs

Key technical inputs include the following:

- www.ehomemakers.net is built with open-source software with a 'cut-and-paste' CMS (content management system) enabling the team to manage and update the portal. It is hosted by Lunar Pages (www.lunarpages.com).
- DWMA uses ADSL, internet access and cellular communications short message service to connect women with mobile phones to eHomemakers' larger network. The DWMA web application server is hosted on an APACHE web server running over the Fedora Core Linux Operating System platform. The DWMA application manages and tracks all recorded users/administrators within a local database system. Users and administrators log into the DWMA application using any available web browser to view, set, create or delete new job schedules, users and administrators. A fixed internet protocol address is assigned to the server with a fixed domain name.

Timeframe

Table 15.1 shows the development of the eHomemakers initiative over time.

Table 15.1 *The development of eHomemakers*

1998	Mothers for Mothers network formed by volunteers
	Organization of series of 'Working @ Home' conferences began and working at home movement grew
1999	Static website www.mom4mom.com was built
2000	Publication of *Working @ Home: A Guidebook for Working Women and Homemakers*, in English
2001	Demonstrator Application Grant proposal to build www.ehomemakers.net was submitted to the government
	Publication of *Working @ Home: A Guidebook for Working Women and Homemakers*, in Bahasa, Chinese and Tamil
2002	One-year Demonstrator Application Grant awarded to build a trilingual portal
	Won the 2002 Pan Asia Networking Small Grant to research disadvantaged women's entrepreneurial and ICT barriers
	Completed small research project on the costs of working
	Quarterly printed newsletter, *Home + Work*, launched
	Annual Mother's Day contest and award inaugurated
2003	www.eHomemakers.net replaced www.mom4mom.com
	200 Salaam Wanita members completed basic ICT training
	Monthly e-news to e-members started
	eHomemakers won the Pan Asia R&D Small Grant to research and develop a web-short message service/fax integrated application (DWMA)
	Donations to help women in dire needs (medical, housing, food) begin to be generated from eHomemakers' members
	Founder was the sole winner of the Women's Electronic Network Training (WENT) award given at the World Summit on the Information Society (WSIS) I by the Association for Progressive Communication (APC) and Sookmyung Women's University, South Korea
	Completed a gender dynamics study on women teleworkers
2004	eHomemakers won the International Development Resource Center (IDRC) competitive grant for research entitled 'Research on Homeworkers and ICT in Southeast Asia'
	www.justmarketing.info built to market disadvantaged women's products and services
	Most of the disadvantaged women trained in basic computers found work in offices and thus graduated from the Salaam Wanita project. The rest continued to be given empowerment training. A group of 120 women was trained in eco-basket weaving
2005	Malaysian government announced its support for the home-office concept after nearly eight years of advocacy by eHomemakers
	eHomemakers research papers incorporated into the University of Pennsylvania's Gender/ICT Encyclopedia

Table 15.1 *(continued)*

	eHomemakers was the runner-up in the Global Knowledge Partnership (GKP) Gender and ICT Awards at WSIS II
	Eco-basket group continued to self-train and improve in quality
2006	Salaam Wanita eco-basket project began to secure corporate orders through more design innovations
	Research on 'Homeworkers and ICT in Southeast Asia' completed
	US-based advocacy project partnered with eHomemakers by sending summer interns to prepare the basket project to enter Fair Trade
	Formed strategic partnership with local corporate sector business, Malaysian Internet Resource Center to incubate micro-businesses and with British Telecom's Global Internet Research Center for innovation and seed funds, and with the Lordman Alliance for business referrals
	Seventy disadvantaged women were trained in basic computer skills to enable them to serve as home-based administrative assistants
2007	Rebuilding of justmarketing.info website under way to market Salaam Wanita products and services overseas under Fair Trade. Stabilizing of eco-basket project through product range consolidation and rebranding
	Became an actively participating member of GKP
	Stabilization of the virtual office and resolution of technical problems of www.ehomemakers.net
	Beginning of a process to construct a platform for a more sustainable revenue model to enable eHomemakers to continue to help the poor
	Developed and published the Malaysian government's working from home guidelines
	eHomemakers founder invited to chair session in Global Knowledge III Conference in December

Impact and outcomes

Impacts and outcomes include:

- official recognition of *Working @ Home* guidebook in 2005 by the Ministry of Women and enhanced coverage by the press to pave the way for an increase in government-sponsored working from home activities as a tool for poverty alleviation;
- increase in home-based ventures among members;
- transformation of vulnerable women into empowered individuals (Salaam Wanita);
- promotion of social entrepreneurship within eHomemakers network;
- generation of ad revenue for network's sustainability by transforming business opinions of homeworkers;
- encouragement of gender equality in the ICT sector and promotion of ICT-based micro-businesses and SMEs;

Table 15.2 *Growth in eHomemakers' membership*

Year	New members
2002	1651
2003	1776
2004	1600
2005	1044*
2006	1667*
July 2007	1225**

Note: *eHomemakers portal encountered technical bugs and errors; **This is only for the first six months of 2007.

Table 15.3 *Comparison of portal activities between 2005 and 2007*

Portal Activities	2005	July 2007
Number of exchange ad posts	407	598
Total forum board posts	550	2045*
New topics added to forum board	120	444

Note: *Most active topic is on 'work @ home decision making'.

- mentoring of women entrepreneurs through grassroots ICT platforms;
- development of a sustainable social e-enterprise model;
- publication of *Working @ Home: A Guidebook for Working Women and Homemakers*, distributed to 20,000 readers;
- publication of monthly e-newsletter (7000 subscribers) and quarterly printed newsletter (10,000 subscribers);
- sustained growth in membership registration (see Table 15.2); and
- an increase in discussion topics and member participation (see Table 15.3).

Total project cost

Table 15.4 illustrates the project's revenue streams.

Project management

The core eHomemakers team is headed by an executive director with overall accountability to sponsors, funders, partners and advertisers. The executive director supervises the sub-teams, each of which has a team leader who is responsible for making joint decisions with team members on implementation of various projects. When critical decisions are needed, the team leader or the executive director compile the team's feedback and send a document outlining advantages and disadvantages. A decision is taken on the options most favoured by the team to ensure a more egalitarian form of decision making.

Table 15.4 *Source of eHomemakers' revenue*

Source	Revenue type
Government	One-year Demonstrator Applicant Grant
Revenue-generating activities	Commissioned research and grant awards
	Ad revenue (website and newsletters)
	Strategic partnerships on a project basis
	Bartering with private sector
	Consultancy fees (outsourcing, teleworking)
Private contributions	Corporate sponsorship of ground and cyber activities
	Member donations to assist disadvantaged women
	Founder's personal commitment when funds are low

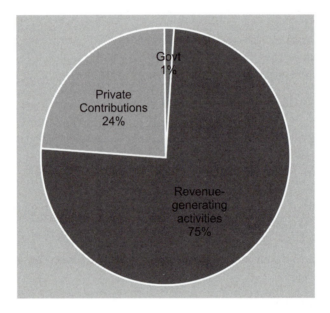

Figure 15.1 *eHomemakers cost breakdown according to revenue source*

Source: www.ehomemakers.net

All financial transactions are audited by eHomemakers' finance manager and by an external auditor. The information is made available to sponsors and funders upon request. All eHomemakers members can read updated information on activities in the portal and are free to call, email, SMS or send letters to the core team. Prompt replies are given and timely actions are taken.

Monitoring and evaluation of project activities

Monitoring and evaluation activities include:

- use of gender evaluation methodology standards and other international standards on research projects to ensure a high level of impact and statistics for advocacy purposes;
- internal management reports for the core team, a virtual office team, to evaluate output achievements on a monthly and weekly basis that are available to the whole team online;
- a gender governance framework derived by eHomemakers for gender impact evaluation of eHomemakers' project activities;
- portal membership can be recorded, as well as the website's unique visitors, hits, page views and downloads to ensure a steady increase in membership acquisition and website activities; and
- user feedback to the portal and DWMA are taken into consideration in all activity planning and implementation.

Challenges and how they were overcome

Project design

eHomemakers is the only e-social enterprise with a large e-community in Malaysia, and the only one managed solely by women. The name 'eHomemakers' initially prevented the group from gaining professional respect due to its association with negatively perceived 'housewives'. To help overcome this challenge, eHomemakers is continuously advocating for the term 'housewives' to be replaced by 'homemakers'. In addition, eHomemakers makes clear that this is a social enterprise that uses business principles to help women telework and form micro-businesses to balance work and family needs. While others measure success in terms of financial profit, eHomemakers measures its success in terms of social profit – women empowering themselves at various stages of their lives under different situations. A communication gap with the male-dominated ICT sector and extremely profit-oriented private sector still exists, however, eHomemakers is confident that with increasing exposure and time the e-social enterprise will be one that will garner respect and support.

Management

During the Demonstrator Application Grant (2002–2003), eHomemakers had over 60 full-time and part-time workers forming a virtual office, working mostly on portal building. However, many left for more lucrative jobs after they gained valuable experience with the team. Luckily, a small group of dedicated teleworkers has stayed on to become knowledge workers. A virtual office work culture has thus emerged characterized by documentation, achievement, problem tracking, lateral decision making and teamwork.

The other challenges of the virtual office have to do with the fact that it is a relatively new way of running an office. The eHomemakers team must rely on communicating via email, a high degree of organization and documentation, and a fast-pace working environment. This can be challenging when new team members come on board, uncomfortable with self-directed work, or unfamiliar with using ICT to achieve a faster-paced, organized environment. Challenges occur when the staff members are unable to supervise themselves, especially because the eHomemakers power relations are more horizontal than hierarchical. Since most Malaysians are used to face-to-face meetings and top-down instructions, it is difficult to accustom them to the practices of a virtual office where interactions are mostly done online. The means to overcome these challenges is to facilitate an easier and increasing means of communication and accountability. For instance, each team member must submit both weekly and monthly progress reports for the whole team to see online, all members are signed onto Skype during working hours.

Implementation

eHomemakers' e-community building requires strong technical capacity and community building knowledge. Unfortunately, Malaysia lacks support for ICT for development, technical/management assistance networks and pro-bono advice for social enterprises. In addition, the nascent ICT sector lacked corporate ethics; seven of eHomemakers' technical partners closed down in the middle of ICT development activities or did not follow-up with warranties. Without funds to pursue legal actions, eHomemakers faces great challenges in deciphering if technical partners are taking advantage of the organization's lack of advanced IT and legal resources. To overcome these, the eHomemakers team works hard towards self-learning, building IT knowledge through technology news publications and advocating corporate ethics to the ICT sector.

The ICT sector in Malaysia is geared towards hardware selling and software development. So far, eHomemakers has not found any company that is interested in assisting social enterprises in technological development for social purposes. Most companies are into securing large, one-time contracts rather than several small contracts. Those that were willing to take on small, non-profit contracts have not served eHomemakers' needs well as they left technical problems unattended to for weeks, leading to frustrating downtime. eHomemakers is still working to overcome this challenge.

Financing

eHomemakers' status as a social enterprise prevented it from receiving government or external funding. eHomemakers' income generating activities distinguish it from non-profits, but are not substantial enough to be considered equal to profits earned through traditional business practices. This puts eHomemakers in a very difficult position in Malaysia because there is no provision for social enterprises. The government focuses its assistance on government agencies and traditional NGOs that rely on government largess to sustain themselves. Therefore, limited funds have been a constant constraint to innovations and extending activities to reach more disadvantaged, low-income women requiring special assistance. eHomemakers has been able to overcome the obstacle of limited financing by drastically lowering administrative and operational costs, pursuing revenue-generation activities and continuously providing a valuable resource for loyal members.

Barriers to women

The single most problematic barrier preventing the disadvantaged women from taking up ICT-enabled and entrepreneurial opportunities is a product of culture and experiences. Most eHomemakers' beneficiaries have been bound to the home and family responsibilities for years to care for their families. Isolation, combined with low self-confidence and their status as low-income women prevent them from venturing outside the home to seek an income. The cycle of low self-confidence, high risk aversion and passivity is difficult to break through and prevents disadvantaged women from taking steps to improve their lives and from persisting in self-improvement activities when challenges present themselves. eHomemakers has helped women overcome this by guiding women through the 5As Process of Change (outlined below). eHomemakers also provides the social support that is lacking to help a woman lift herself out of complex circumstances – constantly providing suggestions and in-person mentorship, as well as support through the e-community.

Budget constraints prevent the acquisition and maintenance of equipment and the internet. An aspiring homeworker's small capital costs can become a financial burden when there are additional business expenses required to set up a home-based income-generation work station and start the business rolling. eHomemakers has been able to partially overcome this by helping women acquire used ICT equipment through the eHomemakers network (via donations) and by appealing to some companies' CSR initiatives. Tips on maintenance and operations are available on the eHomemakers network, where members can access resources and post on the forum board. Another solution is to use lower-cost ICT solutions such as mobile phones.

Lessons learned

Success factors

Based on research findings, eHomemakers chooses a holistic approach to economic and social empowerment to ensure sustainability of activities. Continuous capacity building is required; skills training and information provision are combined with mentorship, support, counselling, regular seminars, workshops, web-enabled marketing opportunities and practical tips to provide a multi-faceted approach to women's economic empowerment.

In addition, eHomemakers learned that the faster a disadvantaged woman can gain returns for her activities and investment, the more confidence she has in her skills, thus facilitating the ease of entry into entrepreneurship. Finally, it is important to remember that the simplest form of technology such as a mobile phone linked to an integrated platform is the best ICT solution for low-income women.

eHomemakers is self-sustaining and not reliant on donor or government funding. eHomemakers generates revenue by selling advertising space on the website/newsletters; its research projects are conducted through award grants. eHomemakers operates like a business, centred on efficiency, and balances revenue and costs at a sustainable level. The difference between a regular enterprise and a social enterprise is that eHomemakers measures its profit in terms of social profit or impact. In order to maximize social profit, eHomemakers has formed a virtual

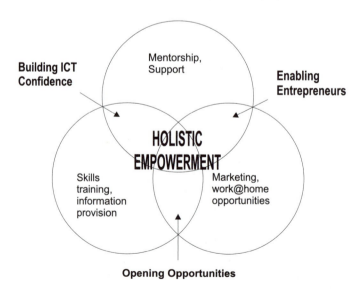

Figure 15.2 *eHomemakers' holistic approach to empowering disadvantaged women*

Source: www.ehomemakers.net

team allowing it to run on a very small operational and administrative budget to ensure that the bulk of the revenue generated is used for project activities. Furthermore, eHomemakers' 15,000 members provide a reliable pool of volunteers and donated goods or services for the poor. Until eHomemakers can earn more revenue through its social business model, however, the financial constraints limit the number of poor women it can reach and help. Thus, although considered a success, eHomemakers is currently working to improve its financial sustainability.

ICT combined with entrepreneurship is key to women's self-sufficiency, and importantly, barriers to entry need to be identified by monitoring and tracking changes through the use of indicators. The 5As Process of Change within the gender governance framework, as proposed by eHomemakers, assists women to take ownership of the management of networks, information sharing and activities to enable and empower them to work from home. Each stage of the 5As Process of Change reflects different levels of economic empowerment. Disadvantaged women must go through the first three levels to break through barriers (awareness, acceptance and action) before entering the e-entrepreneurship building levels (assimilation and assessment). The assimilation stage is the beginning of the process of change where a woman is able to use ICT for business by networking and managing information resources on her own.

When a woman reaches the assessment stage, she completes the process of change to reach gender governance by evaluating her own efforts to overcome barriers and take action. Once a woman has completed the 5As Process of Change, she has acquired the ability to grow her business through the use of ICT and becomes an active member in business and cyber support networks. Her feedback,

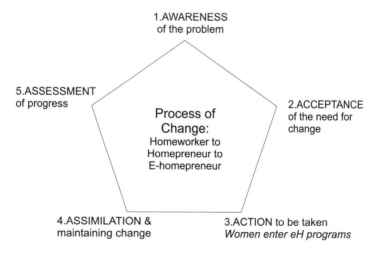

Figure 15.3 *eHomemakers' 5As Process of Change*

Source: www.ehomemakers.net

inputs and active responses towards the networks' needs form part of the governance of information networks that she belongs to.

Support

Through its tightly-knit cyber-community, eHomemakers ensures that members are loyal to the network and that eHomemakers' activities remain loyal to members' needs. eHomemakers promotes partnerships between women of different interests and talents, the skilled and the unskilled, those who are mobile and those who are less mobile. It also caters to Malaysia's multi-ethnic society by ensuring that the portal is trilingual and that the *Working @ Home* guidebook is available in four languages. Furthermore, middle-income members often volunteer their time and services, besides donating used resources and small cash to aid disadvantaged women.

In addition to its strategic partnerships with corporations such as MIRC, GIRC and the Lordman Alliance, eHomemakers has secured support from higher-income women's groups such as The Association of British Women in Malaysia. These groups of women empathize with eHomemakers' mission and support the organization by volunteering, making donations, purchasing Salaam Wanita's eco-baskets and helping to establish strategic connections through their social circles.

Role of champions

Salaam Wanita members who have successfully overcome their disadvantages by taking control of their lives provide the motivation and drive for eHomemakers' dedication to its mission, project activities and methods. These women's experiences, feedback, challenges and triumphs allow eHomemakers to be continuously finding new ways to improve its activities. Champions are women who prove that disadvantaged women, with the right kind of help, can become excellent role models to attaining empowerment through the 5As Process of Change.

For example, Norarita, a Salaam Wanita member from Ipoh, joined the group in 2002 as a basket weaver and has now evolved to coordinate basket orders for up to ten other Salaam Wanita members. Working outside the home was not an alternative for Norarita as she could not afford the childcare facilities for her sons, who suffer from paralysis and speech difficulties. When she was approached by a Salaam Wanita coordinator, she jumped at the opportunity, regularly attending the various seminars and skills training workshops hosted by eHomemakers and practising weaving techniques after her family had gone to bed. It is no surprise that Norarita has become an enthusiastic networker, taking advantage of her circle of contacts to market her products and obtain other home-based job opportunities. Nowadays, Norarita is more secure about her family's future, knowing that she has what it takes to face her children's increasing medical costs. She is a champion because she took it upon herself to contribute to Salaam Wanita by organizing and coordinating the other weavers in Ipoh, becoming a self-motivated micro-entrepreneur and inspiring other disadvantaged women to stand on their own two feet.

Good practice

eHomemakers' low cost ICT, person-to person empowerment concept is unique. It is the only local e-community that promotes working from home by providing free resources and a platform for homemakers and homeworkers to teletrade. As a grassroots initiative, it best serves the individual beneficiaries as much as the beneficiaries' local communities because its information and activities are generated by the beneficiaries themselves. In addition, the activities not only provide resources, tips and income-earning opportunities; but also a close-knit support group for women whose voices and concerns are not usually heard or addressed. Furthermore, the e-community becomes self-propagating with members helping disadvantaged members through donations of resources and volunteering. Thus, eHomemakers allows all women to participate in empowerment and to manage the information network together, driving self-governance, corporate governance and, perhaps one day, e-governance for the government.

eHomemakers is able to sustain itself through a social enterprise model; it exists neither as a non-profit organization nor a profitable business. Rather, it is an e-enterprise driven by a social mission, sustaining itself by trading goods and services for a social purpose. eHomemakers' operations accomplish its social aim and they are sustained by revenue generated through its various activities. The social enterprise model should be promoted because it yields a high level of productivity and autonomy, calculated risk-taking, community benefit as a main mission to all activities, citizens' initiatives, egalitarian decision-making, accountability, a participatory process and impact maximization.

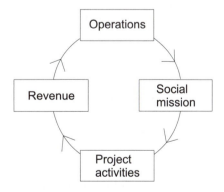

Figure 15.4 *eHomemakers: A social enterprise model*

Source: www.ehomemakers.net

eHomemakers' mission and community affiliation with a group long-deprived of recognition and assistance, creates a remarkable bond between its members who would otherwise not have access to important resources, support and a place to openly discuss gender and work issues. In the ICT world created by eHomemakers, ethnicity, class and religious differences are eliminated, and people are encouraged to help themselves and each other through the e-community. The promotion of collaboration among a diverse group of women (middle- and low-income women, Malay, Chinese and Indian women and skilled and unskilled women) creates a community devoid of discrimination and a comfortable place for women to access the things they need to become empowered. Moreover, the valuable exchanges between this diverse group of women, including donations from middle-income to lower-income women regardless of race and religion, elicits a momentum that adds to the organization's long-term sustainability, growth and capacity.

Potential for scaling up and replication

Scaling up and replication have potential for the following reasons:

- The CMS of the portal is enabled with open source software; it is simple and user-friendly. Thus, homemakers can be trained to be IT managers of such an information network.
- eHomemakers has prepared a series of easily understandable working manuals from managing a cyber office to how disadvantaged women can work at home.
- The DWMA can be used to transmit quick information and organize production lines that are located in diverse sites. If this application and the social enterprise model are replicated, they could be used to help a network of rural villages or a network of urban-based individuals to work at home or group market their home-based products or services.
- The *Working @ Home* book is available for translation and modification by other organizations into other languages to promote working at home in different countries.

Conclusions

To localize gender equality and empowerment in Malaysia's urban and peri-urban areas, eHomemakers has created a low-cost ICT-assisted economic empowerment project that is research-based, grassroots-managed and self-sustaining. This means that the project directly addresses core problems faced by the beneficiaries because the network's training and empowerment resources are themselves generated by the beneficiaries. Furthermore, its social enterprise model ensures that it is cost effective, impact oriented and sustainability focused so that no activity is planned without building a workable revenue model for implementation and sustaina-bility.

As eHomemakers' activities continue to increase homemakers' confidence and productivity, eHomemakers will continue to establish strategic partner-ships, thereby advancing CSR among the Malaysian corporate sector to help the poor through self-reliant activities. In all, eHomemakers is making large steps to improve its community capacity and credibility, advocate for inclusion of the homeworking sector into the formal sector, and strengthen the homeworking sector through ICT for development, especially for the long-neglected urban poor with no political power.

References

Czarina, S. A., Chong, S. C. and Tan, A. (2005) *Homeworkers and ICTs in Southeast Asia*, International Development Research Center, Ottawa, Canada

eHomemakers (2002) 'Survey on the quality of life', 16 May, www.ehomemakers.net

International Development Research Center, Ottawa, Canada, www.ehomemakers.net/en/gallery/Malaysia-I-Fin_Report_1_.pdf

Krishna, U. and Puvaneswary, S. (2005) 'eHomemakers Network – Teleworking moms unite!', *I4d online*, www.i4donline.net

Loh-Ludher, L. L., Sandrakasan, S., Dilling, S., Kheng, S. M. L., Fong, F., Abu Hassan, S. A., Pei Yen, A. L. and Ravichandran, R. (2006) *Homeworkers and ICTs in Malaysia*,

PART V

Social Safety Nets and Microfinance

Poverty Reduction and Millennium Development Goal Localization: A Case Study of the Income Generation for Vulnerable Group Development Programme in Bangladesh[1]

Nahleen Zahra and Naomi Hossain

Introduction

The Income Generation for Vulnerable Group Development (IGVGD) programme supplements the government's Vulnerable Group Development (VGD) programme, which, in turn, emerged out of a government feeding programme, the Vulnerable Group Feeding (VGF) programme, established in 1975.[2] The social context at that time included wide public sympathy for the post-conflict condition of poor and vulnerable women, many thousands of whom had lost traditional sources of male protection during the 1971 war of independence (Kabeer, 2002). Economic crisis led to famine and mass popular disillusionment led to political crisis, culminating in a series of coups and military rule that lasted until 1990. Food aid had been used to protect the urban middle classes, so by targeting the rural poor the VGF programme represented a shift towards more pro-poor food security policy. After further coups and a change in government from 1982, the VGF programme began a reorientation from relief to a focus on development leading the VGD programme (see Attwood et al, 2000). Influences behind this reorientation included that by the 1980s, donors were discouraged by the slow pace of progress on poverty and were pushing for a stronger poverty focus and greater development orientation in food security policies. At the same time, NGOs had demonstrated success with microcredit, linking relief and development and working directly with poor rural women. Donors were also pushing for more space for NGOs. It was in this context that BRAC (Building Resources Across Communities) was approached in 1985 to help orient the VGD programme towards sustainable development.

The project

The original rationale behind the VGF programme was to reorient food security policy towards the poor, away from the traditional focus on protecting the politically powerful urban population. In 1975, factors supporting change included that the new military ruler was comparatively insulated against pressures from organized middle-class groups. Lessons from the famine were also influential: officials and politicians recognized that mass food insecurity seriously damaged regime legitimacy, while donors learned that public food stocks were precarious and in need of further donor support, and that food aid needed to be targeted to the rural poor (see Attwood et al, 2000; Chowdhury and Haggblade, 2000).

The change in title and reorientation in the early 1980s were nominal until BRAC was approached by the UN-funded World Food Programme (WFP) in 1985 to develop an intervention with a stronger development focus. The rationale behind BRAC's pilot project was that it was necessary and possible to work directly with women, as traditional sources of male protection had been significantly eroded; such an approach was still uncommon in the 1980s. BRAC had also learned to link relief and development activities through its experience of linking feeding programmes to functional education for women in Jamalpur and Rangpur during the floods and famine of 1974–1975, with support from UNICEF and Oxfam.[3]

Project formulation

The IGVGD programme evolved on the basis of learning and adaptation, including through close monitoring, research and evaluation. This emphasis on learning and evolution in programme design is characteristic of BRAC programmes and is recognized as key to its successes. Research into poor people's constraints was, from the outset, important to programme design. In the 1970s, BRAC staff spent weeks at a time observing how poor women managed their livelihoods.[4] By the mid-1980s, BRAC research was showing that the poorest women were not participating in microfinance programmes, partly because of chronic food insecurity. VGD food aid was identified as a starting point for addressing the needs of the ultra poor, as it could provide support during the period of training and microenterprise development (Halder and Mosley, 2004).

The most important feature of the project formulation process was the initial pilot project, through which 1000 women were trained for 2 years in different income-generating skills. At the end of this period, most were able to use these new skills to earn close to what they had received through the food grain subsidy. BRAC worked with the Ministry of Relief and Rehabilitation to replicate this strategy and an agreement was reached between the Government of Bangladesh, WFP and BRAC to implement the IGVGD programme from 1987 (Sattar et al,

1999). The programme continued to evolve, with micro-credit being added as a component in 1989 (Matin and Yasmin, 2004).

Key elements of the project

Target beneficiaries

The IGVGD programme targets destitute rural women who have little or no income earning opportunities. Eligibility criteria include:

- being widowed, separated, deserted, divorced or having a disabled husband;
- owning less than 50 decimals of land;
- lacking a regular or adequate income (set at Tk300 (US$4.4) per capita per month, or about a quarter of the World Bank's 'dollar-a-day' poverty line);
- household depending on wage labour for at least 100 days per year;
- lacking productive assets;
- not being a member or beneficiary of other development programmes or NGOs.

In addition to the above criteria, preference is given to participants who are able to participate in training, income-generating activities and social development activities. The programme has further focused on women of child-bearing age since 2000 (Halder and Mosley, 2004, as the Government of Bangladesh established old age and widows' allowances during the 1990s. To date, the programme has reached more than 2 million women throughout the country.

Areas from which beneficiaries are to be selected are determined on the basis of food insecurity and vulnerability maps prepared by WFP with the Planning Commission. To make the development package feasible, priority is given to very poor communities and with at least five women in each village. To prevent against bias or leakage, committees at different levels of the system participate in beneficiary selection, with women representatives playing a more important role since the 2000s. Beneficiaries are expected to satisfy at least the first three of the six eligibility criteria. While there are concerns about the extent of bias in beneficiary selection, most evaluations suggest that beneficiaries usually meet eligibility criteria. However, concerns arise because even eligible beneficiaries are not always the very poorest and many acquire membership cards through personal connections with local government representatives, while women who lack such connections may be excluded. This helps to explain why there is so much local discontent about who gets excluded, even while most local people recognize that a majority of beneficiaries are genuinely needy. This also reflects the serious challenges faced by a social protection programme having to select poor beneficiaries in a context in which there are many more eligible poor women than the programme can provide for (Hossain, 2006).

BRAC then selects between 80 and 90 per cent of the VGD participants for the IGVGD programme. The physical and training demands of IGVGD programme membership mean that it is usually the oldest and least fit women who are excluded. The process of selection is also closely but informally scrutinized by the community and formally by the relevant committees, NGO partners and monitors from WFP and the ministries.

Project area

IGVGD is a national programme, spread across 296 *upazilas* (sub-districts; there are 464 in total) designated as among the most food insecure regions, according to the Vulnerability Analysis and Mapping system. WFP and other donors target their resources at areas designated as 'very highly' or 'highly' food-insecure, while some of the resources contributed by government go to areas that are less food-insecure, but within these are targeted at women vulnerable to food insecurity. A minimum of five women must be selected from each village to facilitate delivery. If all villages cannot be covered in any given cycle, those left out are included in the following cycle (Del Ninno, 2000).

Project activities

Once selection has taken place, a series of bureaucratic directives is delivered from the coordinating Ministry of Women and Children's Affairs to the Directorate of Relief and Rehabilitation, down through to the sub-district implementing officials, and further down to the local councils, where actual distribution takes place. Grain is typically delivered on the same day each month.

Officially, all VGD members, including IGVGD participants, are supposed to receive 30 kilograms of wheat grain (or rice and wheat) each, for an 18-month period. This food ration is considered vital to the success of the IGVGD programme because it gives recipients the 'breathing space' or 'window of opportunity' afforded by a minimum level of food security, which then enables them to deposit weekly savings, participate in training activities and begin to plan their livelihoods (Halder and Mosley, 2004; Matin, 2004).

Training is then provided on income-generating activities that require low initial capital outlays. After an initial experiment with sericulture, for which marketing proved difficult, the main focus has been on poultry-rearing. An important area of success here has been the strong partnership between BRAC and the Livestock Department of the Government of Bangladesh, which supports participants with training, vaccination and other veterinary services free of charge.

Social development is channelled through members' participation in weekly village meetings organized by BRAC staff, consisting of between 25 and 30 members of BRAC's microfinance programmes. These group meetings play two roles: they facilitate savings collection, with each participant expected to save at least Tk25 (US$0.37) per month; and they provide the group with a space in which to discuss social issues, domestic and enterprise problems. Other training in social and legal awareness also takes place, and members have access to the benefits of BRAC's healthcare programme, including preventive, promotive and basic curative care services.

After six months of training, participants receive the first of two loans. They are expected to supplement these loans with their accumulated savings in order to start enterprises. Loans are repaid over 45 instalments, so that by the end of the cycle of free food grain transfer, most participants will have taken the important step of having paid off their first loan and received their second. By the end of their programme cycle, IGVGD participants should be in a position to access and use mainstream microfinance services.

Impact and outcomes

Impact assessment studies in the early 1990s uncovered modest positive impacts on income and a significant degree of income diversification, suggesting reduced vulnerability. The women had also acquired assets and goods, some awareness of rights and social issues, and a greater capacity to participate in NGO programmes, particularly among married women (see Halder and Mosley, 2004). Qualitative studies found that social indicators had improved, including a notably greater tendency to invest in children's education (Sattar et al, 1999).

In the 2000s, impact assessment of the VGD programme (between 80 and 90 per cent of these are also members of the IGVGD) analysed panel data (surveys of 400 VGD participants at the beginning of a cycle, in the middle and three years after – 1994, 1996 and 1999). The analysis found the following positive changes in beneficiaries' lives and livelihoods:

- less landlessness;
- increase in homestead land ownership;
- decline in begging;
- rise in dignity and social status within the community;
- some savings had been made;
- increased ownership of basic household goods;
- slight rise in income (the highest point was immediately after the programme ended in 1996); and
- two-thirds of IGVGD graduates (a subset of around 90 per cent of all VGD beneficiaries) had joined microfinance programmes.

Less positive findings included that around one-quarter of VGD participants could not cope once the food aid part of the programme was over and reaped no gains from the development part of the programme. They were hoping to re-enter the programme to receive food aid again. And some one-third of IGVGD graduates had not joined microfinance programmes. Reasons for not wanting and taking microfinance loans included fear of debt, repayment constraints and lack of confidence (Webb et al, 2002).

In a survey that is not nationally representative or representative of later cycles, but which reflects actual conditions in survey areas, Webb et al (2002) found that a majority of IGVGD participants neither take up all parts of the package nor intend to participate in all parts of the programme when they join. Only about 9 per cent of beneficiaries participate in all components of the programme, while 34 per cent continued to be members of BRAC microfinance programmes. The researchers found a significant gap between the hopes and constraints of participants and the expectations of programme planners (Webb et al, 2002). This gap suggests important differences in attitudes towards the programme by local government officials and some programme beneficiaries on one side, and NGO and donor agency staff on the other (Hossain, 2006).

An additional important impact of IGVGD is that it has demonstrated how it is possible to enable access to microfinance services by very poor women who would probably not otherwise have done so (see Hashemi, 2001). An estimated 1.5 million women have, to date, accessed microfinance services, who were otherwise unlikely to have done so.

A sense of the scale of the programme can be gauged from the following: in 2006, 518,000 VGD beneficiaries were selected, of whom 466,000 were later selected for the IGVGD programme. Of these women, 99 per cent received training and 67 per cent went on to take loans under the microfinance programme. A total of over Tk2 billion (almost US$32 million) was disbursed in loans during that year.[5] Table 16.1 shows

Table 16.1 *Self-reported change in women's lives due to the IGVGD programme*

	Food Aid + Savings (per cent)	Food Aid + Savings + Training (per cent)	Full Participant (per cent)
Is life better now?			
Better	24	32	54
Same	57	51	33
Worse	19	17	13
If better, why?			
Able to feed family	74	70	90
Meet other basic needs	16	17	0
Run a business	3	9	7
More confidence	5	4	0
More skills	0	0	0
More income control	0	0	3
Other	3	0	0

Source: Webb et al (2002)

Table 16.2 *Proportion of financial allocation by component of IGVGD programme*

Transfer A	Training B	Operating Costs C	Total Allocation D
US$8.48 per person	US$10.32 per person	US$1.68 per person	US$20.48 per person
41.41%	50.39%	8.20%	100.00%

Note: Column A shows the value of the food aid, Column B shows the cost of training and Column C shows the operating cost (found by deducting the values in Columns A and B from the total in Column D).

Source: data from Management Information System, IGVGD Programme, BRAC, Dhaka

the self-reported change in women's lives due to participation in the IGVGD programme.

Total project cost

The cost of service to IGVGD clients includes all contributions in cash and kind from donors and the Government of Bangladesh. Funding for the programme is received from the Donor Consortium,[6] WFP, BRAC and the Government of Bangladesh. Table 16.2 shows the proportion of financial allocation that reaches each beneficiary.

A review study conducted in 2004 showed that the mean increase in the net income of IGVGD women was nearly Tk12,000 (US$200 at the exchange rate at the time of study). It also found the returns on investment (RoI)[7] to be around 88 per cent (Posgate et al, 2004).

Project management

Implementing agency

As already mentioned, the IGVGD programme is a joint collaboration between the Government of Bangladesh, WFP and BRAC, the largest NGO in Bangladesh. The Ministry of Women and Children Affairs (MOWCA) is in charge of the central planning and for preparing the Government Order (GO). The GO, in turn, is issued to the Relief and Rehabilitation Directorate (RRD). The District Relief and Rehabilitation Officer (DRRO) is in charge of district level coordination for the implementation of the VGD programme. An outline of roles and responsibilities is in Table 16.3.

Table 16.3 *Major actors and their role in the IGVGD programme*

Partners	Roles and responsibilities
MOWCA	IGVGD beneficiary selection Arrange funds for training Extend administrative support Monitor programme progress
DRR	Allocate and distribute food aid Extend administrative support
WFP	Provide food aid Arrange funds for training Monitor programme progress Coordinate between Government of Bangladesh and BRAC
PKSF and other banking institutions	Provide credit funds
BRAC	Development and implementation, including arranging income generating activities and social awareness training, providing credit and sector support, savings management and follow-up, supervision and monitoring Mobilize donor funds for training Research and evaluation

Source: Matin and Yasmin (2004)

Monitoring and evaluation

The government and WFP assume responsibility for programme monitoring through reviews of BRAC's monthly and quarterly reports. BRAC supplies these on the basis of its internal management information and reporting systems. BRAC documents and accounts are open, and training and credit funds are disbursed to BRAC under annual external audits by chartered accountants appointed by WFP on behalf of donors. There are also regular internal audit procedures. WFP staff also conduct field visits to spot-check programme progress. External reviews and evaluations take place regularly, while BRAC's independent and internal Research and Evaluation Division undertakes periodic research on various aspects of IGVGD. Evaluation of the IGVGD programme has been an important element of the learning around what has worked and what has not.

Challenges and how they were overcome

A significant challenge faced by the IGVGD programme is that despite its impressive achievements in reducing vulnerability and poverty, a significant proportion of beneficiaries make less progress, and around one-third do not succeed in engaging in mainstream microfinance programmes. The key lesson from this is that some of the very poorest need additional and more intensive forms of support if they are to move out of extreme poverty. This includes careful selection as well as more intensive mentoring and support for developing enterprises and stronger social and health support. The central new project in BRAC's Challenging the Frontiers of Poverty Reduction/Targeting the Ultra-Poor (CFPR/TUP, from 2002) programme takes these lessons and translates them into a carefully sequenced set of interventions. After a successful pilot phase, the CFPR/TUP programme is now expanding to 40 districts to cover 800,000 ultra poor households.

In the process of scaling up during the 1990s, BRAC had to rapidly expand its network of offices and staff in order to implement the programme in new areas. When the MOWCA took over programme management from the Ministry of Relief, the programme also faltered as the new ministry lacked a substantial presence in many sub-districts. Eventually, this challenge was overcome as the RRD continued its role in these areas, involving a considerable amount of inter-ministerial and inter-agency coordination (Matin and Yasmin, 2004).

More recently, a significant risk has emerged in the form of avian influenza. As a member of the National Bird Flu Prevention Committee, BRAC has developed a full-blown avian flu prevention strategy. This includes collection and dissemination of information about prevention strategies used elsewhere, deployment of 'disease surveillance teams' comprised of 40 staff members who collect samples of bird droppings to be tested in government laboratories, training of wet market chicken traders in Dhaka city and other awareness-building activities for farmers and hatchery owners. So far, BRAC staff have collected 14,000 samples of bird droppings, provided awareness training to 15,000 farmers in 'hot spot' areas and printed and distributed 100,000 leaflets and 30,000 posters to raise awareness of the disease.

Differences between the key partners have also occasionally challenged the programme. These differences include beliefs about the proper objectives of the programme: while WFP and BRAC emphasize the developmental aspects of the VGD/IGVGD partnership, local government representatives tend to empha-size the food aid aspects, as distribution of government food aid is an important feature of the role of local politicians; a similar difference exists around the purpose and management of savings (Matin and Yasmin, 2004). These differences create different imperatives for beneficiary selection (see Hossain, 2006). Differences also arise around different timetables, which are important because of the careful, time-sensitive sequencing of the programme elements.

Partnership challenges have been addressed in different ways. During the pilot phase of the IGVGD programme, a newspaper broke a story about BRAC taking money from poor women and making them work for their food aid. While initially at least a public relations disaster for BRAC, this finally forced them to interact more closely with the relevant ministries and resulted in a stronger rela-tionship with the Ministry of Relief (then in charge of VGD). Collaboration with government remains challenging, however, and BRAC's CFPR-TUP programme was partly developed to design a programme with ultra poor women over which

BRAC has more control. At the same time, however, some parts of the government–BRAC partnership, notably with the Livestock Ministry, have been mutually beneficial and resulted in improved services on both sides (Matin and Yasmin, 2004).

Leakage and corruption have been concerns, and management of VGD beneficiaries' savings shifted to BRAC from local government representatives in 1998, leading to initial obstruction by some councils. While the extent of food grain leakage has been a subject of some debate (see Hossain, 2006 for a discussion), there have been recent efforts to tighten up on grain distribution processes in the VGD programme. This includes the use of standardized containers with amounts clearly marked, following the recommendations of a study that documented processes of leakage (Akhter et al, 2004).[8]

Lessons learned

Success factors

A key success has arisen from BRAC's emphasis on evolving programme design on the basis of learning and evaluation about what works. Learning from doing and close regular monitoring and evaluation are key principles of BRAC's approach. As noted above, BRAC learned about the need for a stronger relationship with key ministries after an initial public relations disaster. Adaptations in programme activities and process, including the introduction of microcredit, also resulted from close attention to the implementation process and its results.

The role of champions and support

The Government of Bangladesh has been a vital supporter through its continued support for the food aid and the space it has made for BRAC to strategically link up with the VGD programme. As is appropriate, BRAC has constantly sought to emphasize that the VGD programme is a government programme, and that local government representatives are crucial to the programme. This has helped to establish the norm that the government is responsible for trying to support the poorest and most vulnerable with food aid. The Government of Bangladesh has demonstrated that it can manage this important task.

The role of WFP in supporting the Government's VGD programme, and then in supporting the innovation of the IGVGD programme, has also been crucial. A feature of this support has been WFP's consistent stress on the development and gender equity dimensions of the programme, pushing to align the programme towards these goals.

Good practice

There are three key reasons for viewing the IGVGD programme as an example of good practice. First, IGVGD represents a case of successful government–NGO partnership, which demonstrates how the advantages of both sides can be harnessed. In particular, it brings together the advantages of targeting undertaken by local government representatives with the additional monitoring and community knowledge afforded by BRAC, which ensure the targeting and distribution of benefits remain reasonably fair and closely monitored (Hulme and Matin, 2004).[9] Partnerships of this kind are frequently challenging, particularly when delays result from differences in administrative timetables and capacities between the partners. In the case of IGVGD, these have usually been overcome, and there have been some valuable and mutually productive lessons for both partners.

The second reason IGVGD is good practice is that it shows the possibilities of bridging the gap between welfare and development programmes to reach the ultra poor. Relief in the form of food aid has been vital in giving the ultra poor that 'critical push' – the skills and the support – to build more sustainable livelihoods. For a majority of this group, this has also meant the chance to access resources such as microfinance more effectively. In the view of one expert writing in 2001, the creative linking of microfinance to a safety net had meant that more than 600,000 destitute women accessed microfinance services who would probably not otherwise have done so (Hashemi, 2001). The numbers of those who accessed microcredit have risen considerably, with over 300,000 women taking loans in 2006 compared to fewer than 40,000 in the early 1990s.

The third reason IGVGD represents good practice is that there was strong commitment to learning and evaluation throughout. The lessons from IGVGD have supported improvements and extensions to the original model, and have also fed into the design of other programmes for the ultra poor, in particular, BRAC's CFPR/TUP programme, which is a multi-dimensional programme to tackle concentrations of extreme poverty in Bangladesh.

Potential for scaling up and replication

The IGVGD programme experienced a successful rapid process of scaling up during the 1990s, demonstrating its great potential. Since 2001, BRAC has incorporated lessons from the IGVGD programme to develop new programmes targeted at the ultra poor. An important lesson was that there were distinct groups among the highly differentiated rural poor, usually the poorest of the poor, who were unlikely to be selected as VGD beneficiaries or to become mainstream BRAC microfinance programme members. BRAC had also learned from the IGVGD experience that a carefully sequenced programme of interventions designed both to support and to build capabilities to earn and save, could work for the ultra poor. The key

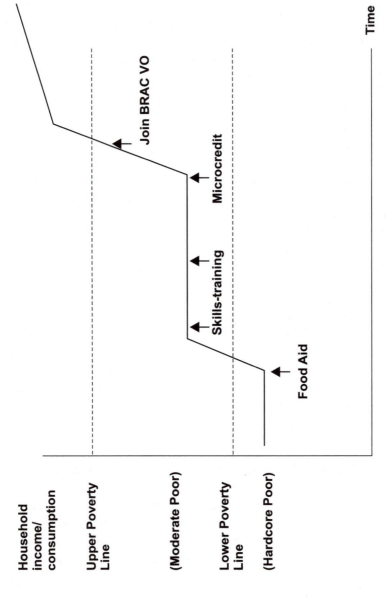

Figure 16.1 *Summary of the IGVGD programme*

Table 16.4 *The IGVGD programme at a glance*

Sl no.	VGD session	Total no. of VGD cardholders brought under development package	Total no. of trained cardholders	Total no. of borrowers	Total loan disbursement (US$)
1	1988–1990	41,792	40,744	15,319	202,963
2	1990–1992	60,391	57,929	37,151	679,496
3	1992–1994	107,594	105,504	79,834	2,302,590
4	1994–1996	192,596	185,096	178,933	7,497,957
5	1997	248,469	248,129	169,206	3,223,634
6	1998–1999	304,084	284,689	164,533	3,375,693
7	1999–2000	285,817	284,072	190,256	10,905,724
8	2001–2002	264,510	258,500	184,796	10,340,829
9	2003–2004	292,200	291,149	197,563	14,338,836
10	2005–2006	466,200	463,557	313,096	31,748,886
	Total	**2,263,653**	**2,219,369**	**1,530,687**	**84,616,610**

Source: BRAC (2007)

elements of the programme are asset transfer, a stipend, close training and support, health care and a social support network over an 18-month period, followed by less intensive support. The CFPR/TUP programme is now in its second phase after a successful pilot programme that is currently being considered for replication in Haiti, Pakistan and India. Table 16.4 and Figure 16.1 summarize IGVGD programme activities.

Notes

1 Note on sources: this paper draws heavily on earlier studies of the IGVGD programme by Imran Matin (2003 with David Hulme, 2004 and 2004 with Rabeya Yasmin) and by Naomi Hossain (2006).
2 A programme bearing the VGF title still exists, supplying food grains to selected poor households during crises and the lean season.
3 The details of the origins of the IGVGD pilot are from an interview with the founder and current chairman of BRAC, F. H. Abed, conducted in 2005.
4 Personal communication with F. H. Abed.
5 Data from BRAC's IGVGD records.
6 The donor consortium includes DFID, EC, CIDA and NOVIB.
7 RoI is found by dividing the mean increased net income over a cycle by the financial allocation per beneficiary (unit cost).
8 Information on actions taken to reduce leakage is taken from an interview with Aldo Spaini of the WFP in Dhaka in 2006.
9 These issues, including debates about leakage and corruption in the programme, are discussed in Hossain (2006).

References

Atwood, D., Jahangir, A. S. M., Smith, H. and Kabir, G. (2000) 'Food aid in Bangladesh: From relief to development' in Ahmed et al (eds) *Out of the Shadow of Famine: Evolving Food Markets and Food Policy in Bangladesh*, Johns Hopkins University Press/IFPRI, Baltimore, MD

Akhter, A. U., Rashid, S., Sharma, M. and Zohir, S. (2004) 'Food aid distribution in Bangladesh: leakage and operational performance', *IFPRI Food Consumption and Nutrition Division Discussion Paper no. 173*, Washington DC, International Food Policy Research Institute

BRAC (2007) *Income Generation For Vulnerable Groups Development Program (IGVGD). Proposal For 2007–2008 Cycle*, Dhaka, BRAC

Chowdhury, T. and Haggblade, S. (2000) 'Dynamics and politics of policy change' in Ahmed et al (eds) *Out of the Shadow of Famine: Evolving Food Markets and Food Policy in Bangladesh*, Johns Hopkins University Press/IFPRI, Baltimore, MD

Del Ninno, C. (2000) *Efficiency of Targeted Food Programs: An Investigation of the VGD and RD Programs,* Working Paper No. 3, Food Management and Research Support Project (FMRSP), Ministry of Food, Dhaka, Government of Bangladesh

Halder, S. and Mosley, P. (2004) 'Working with the ultra-poor: Learning from BRAC experiences', *Journal of International Development*, vol 16, pp387–406

Hashemi, S. (2001) *Linking Microfinance and Safety Net Programs to Include the Poorest: The Case of IGVGD in Bangladesh*, Focus Note 21, CGAP, Washington, DC

Hossain, N. (2006) *The Politics of What Works: The Case of The Vulnerable Group Development Programme in Bangladesh*, background paper for the Chronic Poverty Report 2007/8, Manchester, University of Manchester/Chronic Poverty Research Centre

Kabeer, N. (2002) 'Safety nets and opportunity ladders: Addressing vulnerability and enhancing productivity in South Asia', Working Paper 159, Overseas Development Institute, London

Matin, I. (2004) 'Delivering inclusive microfinance with a poverty focus: experiences of BRAC', *BRAC RED working paper*, Dhaka, BRAC Research and Evaluation Division, http://www.bracresearch.org/reports_details.php?scat=23&v=0&tid=32

Matin, I. and Hulme, D. (2003) 'Programs for the poorest: Learning from the IGVGD program in Bangladesh', *World Development*, vol 31, no 3, pp647–665

Matin, I. and Yasmin, R. (2004) 'Managing scaling up: Challenges of a program for the poorest: Case study of BRAC's IGVGD program', in CGAP (ed) *Scaling up Poverty Reduction: Case Studies in Microfinance*, Washington DC, CGAP/World Bank

Posgate, D., Craviolatti, P., Hossain, N., Osinski, P., Parker, T. and Sultana, P. (2004) 'Review of the BRAC/CFPR Specially Targeted Ultra-Poor (STUP) Programme: Mission report', unpublished report, BRAC Donor Liaison Office, Dhaka

Sattar, G., Chowdhury, N. S. and Hossain, M. A. (1999) *Food Aid and Sustainable Livelihoods: BRAC's 'Innovations Against Hunger' Research and Evaluation Division*, BRAC, Dhaka

Webb, P., Coates, J., Houser R. (2002) 'Does microcredit meet the needs of all poor women? Constraints to participation among destitute women in Bangladesh', Discussion Paper No 3, Food Policy and Applied Nutrition Program, Tufts Nutrition, The Gerald J. and Dorothy R. Friedman School of Nutrition Science and Policy, Massachusetts

17

Beating the Odds: How Progresa/ Oportunidades Became Mexico's Major Poverty Alleviation Programme

Evelyne Rodriguez

Introduction

In early 1995, poverty in Mexico was a critical problem (and it still is). Almost a third of the population lived in extreme poverty – 4.8 million families, of which 2.8 million were rural. As these families are larger, four out of ten children were poor. In addition, indicators of health, education and nutrition were significantly different between the poor and the non-poor. However, even among the poor, there were large differences in the severity and depth of poverty as well as in their human capital; the marginalization of the rural poor exceeded that of the urban poor (a full description of poverty indicators can be found in Progresa (1997) and Levy and Rodriguez (2004)).

Poverty alleviation was conventionally based both on the provision of health and education services and on a large number of targeted and generalized food and education programmes, mostly unconditional. However, universal actions although indispensable, were not enough to increase the health and education status of the poor as these families did not benefit fully from them. For example, poor families may not send their children to school (even if it's free) because of the costs of school supplies and transportation and of the forgone contributions of children to household tasks or monetary income. And even if children go, their school performance might be hindered because of malnutrition or bad health. This has medium-term implications because those children enter the labour market at a disadvantage.

Also, food subsidies were basically income transfers, only partially reaching the poor and ineffective nutritionally. Despite the growing resources, infant malnutrition for rural children under five remained at 50 per cent from 1974 to 1996.[1] Additionally, food subsidies were dispersed in many programmes and operating agencies: 17 food programmes were managed by 7 agencies. They were characterized by:

1   a large percentage of resources channelled to generalized subsidies;
2   urban/rural imbalance and large inclusion and exclusion errors – 60 per cent of poor rural families did not receive any support from the government;
3   uncoordinated operations and little transparency;
4   duplication of efforts and excessive bureaucracy; and
5   lack of evaluation.

The conceptual motivation for a different approach was based on the vicious circle poor families are immersed in, which, if nothing is done, is transmitted from one generation to the next: illiteracy, high morbidity, high levels of fertility and infant mortality, inability to take risks, inability to demand educational services, low income and few resources distributed among numerous families. Deficiencies in education, health and nutrition are both causes and effects of persistent poverty and are closely interrelated.[2] Additionally, incomes of poor families would not grow rapidly even with high economic growth. Therefore, these families needed both to increase their income today and tomorrow. Until 1995, policy efforts attacked these objectives with different instruments.

The 1994–1995 economic crisis aggravated the situation of the poor. In March 1995, the economic crisis opened a window of opportunity[3] for the Ministry of Finance to propose a new poverty alleviation strategy that included the substitution of food programmes, both targeted and generalized, for a conditional cash transfer programme targeted at the poor and linked to the attendance of vulnerable family members at health centres. This proposal was received with great scepticism and opposition by some Mexican policy makers as well as by international agencies. In Mexico, some policy makers saw the proposal as 'a neo-liberal attempt to eliminate subsidies for the poor' and as 'an imposition by international agencies'.[4] Political parties were concerned about a federal programme that would 'give out money', presumably with electoral and political motives.[5] International agencies thought it was operationally and politically unfeasible. At that time, the Mexican and international conditional cash transfer programmes were mainly focused on the educational sector, for example, scholarships linked to attendance or performance. Conditionality for in-kind transfers was focused in the health sector. There was no known experience of conditional cash programmes linked to health.[6] Additionally, most efforts to eliminate generalized food subsidies of basic staples around the world had failed.

In this context, a pilot programme was started in October 1995 to test two main concerns: the substitution of in-kind for cash supports because of the potential use of this income for harmful consumption (for example, alcohol) and conditioning these transfers to the regular attendance at health centres. Based on its results, the decision to launch Progresa was taken in June 1996, however, the programme was not started until August 1997, mainly due to very intense discussions and analysis, not only of the programme but of the changes it implied to food subsidies.[7] The conceptual and strategic shift in poverty alleviation policy that gave rise to Progresa and to changes to other programmes was the subject of a wide-ranging and intense debate, mainly within the executive branch of government but also within Congress, political parties, local authorities and interest groups. Two years elapsed from the original proposal to programme start-up, although discussions and the implementation of further changes to remaining food programmes continued throughout President Zedillo's administration (1994–2000).

The project

Objectives

Progresa/Oportunidades seeks to break the vicious circle of poverty of extremely poor households. In particular, the objectives are:

- to improve the health and nutritional status of poor families, especially of pregnant and nursing women and children under five years of age;
- contribute to poor children's completion of primary, secondary and high school education;
- integrate education, health and nutritional interventions;
- encourage responsibility and active participation by all family members; and
- redistribute national income towards poor families.

Key components

Progresa consists of three complementary components that are given as a package to beneficiary families:

1 *Nutrition and food consumption.* A basic cash transfer per family (regardless of its demographic structure) is granted conditional on both the attendance of all family members at health clinics according to their risk profile, and the attendance of the mother to monthly lectures on hygiene and health. Additionally, to overcome micronutrient deficiencies and intra-household inequality in food distribution, all pregnant and breastfeeding women, all children under two and all undernourished children between three and five years old receive food supplements that provide an average of 20 per cent of calories and 100 per cent of micronutrients required.

2 *Healthcare.* A free basic healthcare package is given to all family members, promoting predominantly a preventive approach. Additionally, education and training in health, nutrition and hygiene through regular lectures seek to

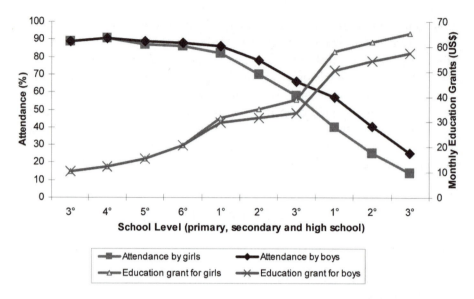

Figure 17.1 *School attendance and education grants (2005)*

Source: Levy (2006)

provide them with information to make better decisions regarding their cash transfers and health.

3   *Education.* Children and young people under 22 enrolled between third grade of primary and third grade of high school receive scholarships conditioned on regular school attendance and transfers for school supplies. Scholarships have two characteristics:

- they increase with grade levels to cover the rising opportunity costs of sending children to school; and
- are higher for girls than for boys at secondary level in recognition of the gender gap in enrolment.

Figure 17.1 shows the relationship between school attendance at the beginning of the programme and the amount of educational grants by grade.[8]

Programme operation

Beneficiary households are selected through a non-discretionary and transparent targeting procedure that is made in three stages:

1   geographical targeting to identify the poorest localities and areas within urban areas and their access to education and health services;[9]
2   individual targeting by proxy means testing using discriminant analysis (to avoid exclusion errors, in the poorest communities and areas surveys are applied as a census); and

3   in the case of rural areas, verification of the list of beneficiaries in a community assembly.

When inclusion or exclusion errors are reported, cases are reviewed on the basis of the survey. Once beneficiaries are selected, they have the right to stay in the programme for three years as long as they comply with the conditions. At the end of that period families need to be recertified.

The recipients of all transfers to the household are the mothers, in recognition that they are closer to family needs than men.[10] All cash transfers are adjusted twice a year to the consumer price index and individually paid to the mother every two months. Payment is conditional on the monthly validation of attendance at health and educational services; and nutritional supplements are given monthly at health clinics.

Total amount per household varies depending on the number of children enrolled in school, their grade level and their attendance. In 2005, on average, transfers in kind and cash added up to US$44 per month, approximately 25 per cent of the income of the rural poor households and between 15 and 20 per cent of income of the poor urban households. The average monthly cash transfer was US$38.

Project area and total project cost

In 2005, with a budget of US$2.8 billion, Progresa/Oportunidades covered 5 million families – basically all of its target population, of which 68 per cent were rural. This coverage implied grants for 5.3 million children and youngsters; nutritional assistance to 2.1 million children and close to 1 million women; and 42.5 million medical consultations in that year. Accreditation of conditionality involved 80,275 primary schools, 24,599 secondary schools, 7629 high schools and 15,724 health clinics in 86,901 localities, of which 97 per cent have less than 2500 inhabitants. These figures show the size of the operation of the programme.

Progresa/Oportunidades reached its target size in eight years; with a gradual growth in beneficiaries and budget as shown in Table 17.1. Faster growth could not have been achieved because of lack of both financial resources and operational capacity and experience. It must be noted that out of the total budget, less than 6 per cent is devoted to operational expenses.

Management

The programme is operated by three ministries (Health, Education and Social Development) and the Social Security Institute (IMSS).[11] A coordinating agency was created (Conprogresa[12]) that is responsible for programme operations, in particular for conducting surveys, applying the scoring systems, overseeing benefits payments and generating data for evaluation. It has a board of directors and a

Table 17.1 Progresa/Oportunidades: Coverage of families and students with grants and budget (2005)

	1997	1998	1999	2000	2001	2002	2003	2004	2005	2005*
Beneficiary families	300.7	1,595.6	2,306.3	2,476.4	3,116.0	4,240.0	4,184.4	5,000.0	5,000.0	
Students with grants	101.1	1,299.0	2,192.6	2,485.3	3,325.5	4,361.2	4,603.1	5,100.3	5,298.8	
Total Budget	**876.4**	**5,516.3**	**9,592.2**	**12,190.0**	**15,204.0**	**21,179.1**	**24,503.3**	**26,675.3**	**30,151.2**	**2,817.9**
Total Transfers	**428.2**	**4,742.1**	**8,963.1**	**11,683.4**	**14,308.8**	**19,959.8**	**22,998.9**	**25,044.1**	**28,445.5**	**2,658.5**
Cash Transfers	286.7	2,425.6	7,312.2	9,800.5	11,961.0	16,347.9	20,055.6	21,667.8	24,617.1	2,300.7
Food transfer	121.9	1,283.4	3,774.9	4,710.6	5,208.1	6,823.8	8,081.2	8,715.7	9,479.2	885.9
Education (grants/school supplies)	164.8	1,142.2	3,537.3	5,089.9	6,752.9	9,524.1	11,974.4	12,952.1	15,137.9	1,414.8
In Kind	141.5	2,316.5	1,650.9	1,882.9	2,347.8	3,611.9	2,943.3	3,376.3	3,828.4	357.8
Nutritional supplements	46.3	1,203.9	940.9	1,073.2	1,123.9	1,763.6	933.2	642.0	665.7	62.2
Health	95.2	1,112.6	710.0	809.7	1,223.9	1,848.3	2,010.1	2,734.3	3,162.7	295.6
Operating expenses (OE)	448.2	774.2	629.1	506.6	895.2	1,219.3	1,504.4	1,631.2	1,706.1	159.4
OE as % of total spending	51.1%	14.0%	6.6%	4.2%	5.9%	5.8%	6.1%	6.1%	5.7%	5.7%

Source: Levy and Rodriguez (2004) and Levy (2006)

* Figures are in millions of pesos except last column, which is in US dollars.

technical committee that acts as the decision making body, with representatives of the above mentioned ministries and agency, and the Ministry of Finance.

The programme is ruled by two sets of regulations. First, specific regulations in the Budget Decree approved by Congress setting general operating criteria, provisions on transparency and access to information and the budget of the programme. Second, detailed operating regulations issued by the executive based on the Budget Decree. The latter play a critical role in proper programme performance, since they set forth all operating criteria, benefits and obligations of beneficiaries, as well as the responsibilities of the various government ministries and agencies involved. They also reduce discretionality, provide transparency of information and establish monitoring indicators and the criteria for evaluation.

Impacts and outcomes

Due to the novelty of Progresa's approach and to the controversy about many of its design aspects, evaluation was designed simultaneously with the implementation of the programme. The evaluation was necessary to test whether the design hypothesis was correct, especially on the issues that had raised greatest concern, and to quantify the impacts of the programme, but also to determine whether design guidelines were being followed and identify if observed outcomes were attributable to implementation or design aspects. Additionally, monitoring was implemented, although not very effectively at the beginning, to detect and correct operational problems.

At the outset of the Programme, the International Food Policy Research Institute (IFPRI) was hired to evaluate the programme; officials of the highest levels set the terms of reference and selected the specific consultants. A sample scheme and a baseline survey were designed to allow statistical evaluation of the results, through the continuous monitoring of 24,000 families. As Progresa's coverage expanded gradually, evaluation was based on a double difference estimator between beneficiary families and a control group. The first results were delivered in October 2000 and covered the programme's first three years of operation. IFPRI indicated that 'the research results show that after just three years, the poor children of the rural communities of Mexico where Progresa operated are attending school longer, eating more diversified diets, getting more frequent health care and are learning that the future may look quite different from the past' (IFPRI, 2000). Since then, there has been a systematic and sustained effort to evaluate the programme.[13] Additionally, based on Progresa's evaluation database, there has been a proliferation of empirical research in major universities around the world.

The results of the different impact evaluations show positive and significant results. The findings in rural areas show that the programme is cost effective, it selects its target population appropriately and it has had a positive impact on education, health, nutrition and diet. It has reduced poverty and inequality in participating communities. It has raised the transition rate from primary to secondary education and has increased attendance at secondary and high school level. It has improved the health of children and adult beneficiaries and it has expanded the use of family planning methods. In parallel, it has increased the quantity and quality of food consumption, helped improve nutritional indicators and reduced child labour. There is no evidence of increased alcohol consumption or domestic violence. Progresa's benefits extended to non-beneficiary families who live in participating communities. Additionally, the programme may be triggering permanent changes in income-earning capabilities and encouraging a gradual shift in intra-household relationships, reducing gender inequality. Evaluations in semi-urban and urban areas point in the same direction.

Results on operations[14] are less positive. They indicate that although the quality of the programme's coverage and operation has improved, there's ample room for improvement as there are significant variations in operational performance during the year, across states and across the various health institutions. Problems have also been reported in the supply of medicines and nutritional supplements and on the timely delivery and accuracy of evidence of compliance of beneficiaries with required conditionality. Results point to the need for greater supervision to verify qualification for and delivery of programme benefits. Regarding health and educational services, evaluations have also identified insufficient quality as one of the programme's greatest potential problems; the objectives of human capital investment can only be obtained if greater attendance of beneficiaries at schools and health centres translates into improved education and health indicators.

Regarding impact and operational evaluations, three issues are worth noting: (1) results have not been unambiguously positive and there have been (and still are) significant problems and challenges; (2) the programme has been improved both in its conceptual design and its operation based on these results;[15] in this way, monitoring and evaluation have played an important role through continuous feedback; and (3) some of the problems and mistakes have taken too long to correct and some are yet to be fully corrected. In the absence of these, impact would have been larger by now.

Changes in other programmes

Food subsidies, generalized and targeted, were to be phased out as part of the strategy associated with Progresa/Oportunidades; this was largely achieved (but not fully). From 1994 to 2005, there was an increase of 30 per cent in total resources directed to food subsidies and to Progresa/Oportunidades. However, as Table 17.2 shows, there was a significant change between generalized and targeted subsidies as the former passed from 72 per cent to 2 per cent of total resources, and in the distribution of resources between urban and rural areas,[16] translating

Table 17.2 *Budget for food subsidies and Progresa/Oportunidades (1994–2005) (millions of pesos)*

	1994	1995	1996	1997	1998	1999	2000	2001	2002	2003	2004	2005
Generalized food subsidies	1,846	1,690	1,587	750	289	62	48	58	21	35	121	52
1. Subsidy for the wheat flour-bread chain	744	446	0	0	0	0	0	0	0	0	0	0
2. Generalized tortilla subsidy	739	852	1,287	569	186	0	0	0	0	0	0	0
3. Diconsa	362	393	300	181	103	62	48	58	21	35	121	52
Generalized food subsidies as % of total	72%	68%	63%	45%	19%	4%	3%	3%	1%	1%	4%	2%
Targeted subsidies	702	801	922	929	1,264	1,478	1,672	1,962	2,522	2,751	2,948	3,253
4. FIDELIST tortilla subsidy	186	193	239	210	227	180	157	140	106	21	0	0
5. LICONSA milk subsidy	218	296	297	239	171	42	0	0	16	21	38	58
6. Children in Solidarity food packages	64	78	44	55	39	31	27	26	24	24	22	21
7. INI food packages	17	21	24	26	26	26	26	27	25	24	24	28
8. DIF	214	204	306	303	273	290	300	334	358	359	360	317
9. Others	3	9	12	14	13	13	13	14	14	13	11	10
10. Progresa	0	0	0	82	516	896	1,139	1,421	1,979	2,290	2,493	2,818
Targeted subsidies as % of total	28%	32%	37%	55%	81%	96%	97%	97%	99%	99%	96%	98%
Total	**2,549**	**2,491**	**2,509**	**1,679**	**1,553**	**1,540**	**1,720**	**2,020**	**2,544**	**2,786**	**3,069**	**3,305**

Source: Levy and Rodriguez (2004) and Levy (2006)

into a redistribution of income in favour of the poor and the virtual elimination of food subsidies to the non-poor.[17]

Critical elements for policy change and continuity

Progresa/Oportunidades has faced opposition and challenges to its continuity and consistency throughout its lifetime, but there have been three critical moments. First, from 1995–1997, the challenge was convincing policy makers that it was not only a good idea but also politically, operationally and financially feasible. Second, during the transition from President Zedillo to President Fox in 2000. Third, in late 2001 and 2002, when the programme's coverage and budget were so big that it was a 'temptation' to use the programme and/or its budget for other objectives or programmes.

When Progresa was first proposed, its most controversial aspect was the granting of direct monetary transfers rather than in-kind transfers, however, at that time and throughout the process, there were concerns about many other design issues such as the targeting mechanisms and giving the money to women, and about the effectiveness of allocating funds to subsidize demand rather than to strengthen the supply of services. In addition, there were doubts about operating capacity, particularly in the health care sector, to implement a large-scale programme conditioned on regular attendance to services, and differences of opinion about which institutions should do what.

Discussions were conducted at the highest levels of each ministry and institution involved. Not only was a new programme being established, a new strategy was being implemented that entailed: (1) a new conceptualization of the human capital dimension of poverty alleviation policy; (2) a less paternalistic and corporativist role for the federal government together with greater responsibility of beneficiaries; (3) a restructuring and, in some cases, elimination of existing programmes and institutions; and (4) a reallocation of budgets and programmes among ministries with, in some cases, a negative impact on private interests. Furthermore, the strategy implied loss of income for some groups and changes in the power structure. Party politics added another layer of complexity. Clearly, launching Progresa without changing existing programmes would have been faster and easier, but it was not desirable in terms of achieving an efficient, effective and consistent poverty alleviation policy, nor was it possible for budgetary reasons.

What were the critical elements for policy change and continuity of Progresa/Oportunidades? First, President Zedillo's political will and his support to the Ministry of Finance, specifically to the Deputy Minister for Budget, Mr Santiago Levy, who was one of the main architects and the champion of the programme since its very initial phase.[18] Second, the fact that the Ministry of Finance proposed and conducted the design and implementation of the programme and the change in the poverty alleviation strategy. This ministry had both legal authority and access to information to monitor all ministries and agencies of the federal government. This allowed for a horizontal approach both in the analysis and in the design and implementation. The economic crisis and the need for budgetary austerity increased during 1995–2000. It also facilitated access to funds to expand the programme and strengthen the supply of healthcare and education services – a rare case, as usually new programmes' first challenge is funding. Third, the pilot project that helped overcome the most controversial issue – cash transfers. Fourth, focusing discussions as much as possible on objective and technical elements. During the design phase, technical briefings were prepared for the discussion of each issue of the programme, analysing available statistical information and Mexican and international experiences. Additionally, extensive public documents and presentations were prepared explaining the motivation for change, the programme itself and its relationship with the poverty alleviation strategy and other subsidy programmes. From the outset, an analysis of Progresa was included in the Federal Budget every year and Congress approves the budget and approved a specific article establishing the general criteria for the programme's operation. These documents contain a clear and much more extensive and technical explanation of the programme than had been done for most social programmes in the past (see PROGRESA, 1997; SHCP, 1997; 1998; 1999; 2000). Fifth, the issuance of very detailed public operating regulations for the programme, outlining each institution's responsibilities to minimize interagency coordination conflict. Sixth, external evaluation of Progresa's operation and impact with the participation of well-known national and international experts that included those aspects of Progresa where there had been differences of opinion. Finally, no association of the programme with any political or partisan activities, which was done by: (1) no political appropriation of the programme by President Zedillo; (2) establishing in the Budget Decree that all public forms and documents of the programme should include an explicit notation about this; (3) postponing the launch of the programme after the federal 1997 elections and suspending incorporation of new beneficiaries during the political campaigns of 2000; and (4) delivering benefits directly to women without intermediation of local leaders or organizations.

It must be noted that many of the above elements were actually a result of the intense discussions and debate. Paradoxically, although these delayed the start of Progresa, the discussion of each conceptual and operational element helped improve the design and also devoted greater attention to the transparency of programme operation and to the evaluation of its impact. These elements enhanced the programme's legitimacy and increased the likelihood of its continuity. They also helped to make Progresa a much more complete and better articulated programme than that proposed in March 1996.

Continuity during the transition from President Zedillo to President Fox and the first years of the new administration can be attributed in addition to the elements described above to the following: (1) results of IFPRI's evaluation were ready before President Fox took office and were presented personally to him by Mr Levy; (2) the increasing international recognition of the programme provided an unbiased opinion about the programme to the incoming administration; (3) two of the architects of the programme remained in high positions during part of President Fox administration, one in IMSS and another in the Ministry of Finance and both as members of the decision-making body of Progresa; (4) for fiscal year 2002 the Budget Decree established that all decisions regarding the programme were to be taken by consensus by the different participating institutions; and (5) the loan signed with the InterAmerican Development Bank in 2001 introduced a new interested party that has contributed greatly to the technical analysis and discussion of the main aspects of the programme.

Finally, it must be noted that since the design phase of Progresa it was recognized that Mexico needed a sustained and long-term effort in human capital investment. Most of the elements described here were introduced with the explicit objective, among others, to increase the probability of continuity of the programme.

Lessons learned

After ten years in operation, Progresa/Oportunidades has surpassed the expectations of many and overcome the two main limitations of poverty alleviation efforts: too small in scale or too short lived. This has been the result of very careful design and implementation. What can be learned of Mexico's experience? From a public policy design perspective, what stands out is the importance of good diagnosis to first model a poverty alleviation strategy; then the need to decide on the intended objectives and behaviour changes; and finally, it is important to decide if a conditional cash transfer (CCT) would be a pertinent programme rather than a universal intervention, and if and how it would substitute or complement other programmes in this strategy. From a micro-economic perspective, a first lesson is how the substitution of isolated income transfers to the poor through various means for a cash transfer can be more efficient and the importance of conditions to make it politically and operationally feasible. It must be noted this is applicable to most subsidies, not only those related to food. Second, linking the cash transfer (or even any transfer) to appropriate incentives can increase impact, help break the vicious circle of poverty and increase the responsibility of beneficiaries. Without these incentives, the change in poor households' behaviour in a socially desirable way might take too long or even not occur (when the price effects of pure monetary transfers are not enough). Third, the possibility of increasing impact by focusing on the household instead of only on individuals is important, as are exploiting complementarities and concentrating on the interventions of highest impact through the life cycle of families and individuals. A fourth lesson is the need to design simultaneously the programme and its monitoring, impact and operational evaluation; as well as to link them through appropriate feedback. Finally, from a political economy perspective, the institutional setting and decision making process are vital in order to phase out, transform and/or coordinate various agencies or programmes. Design and implementation must consider the political sustainability and the consistency and coherence of the overall effort.

Conclusions

What is next for Progresa/Oportunidades after ten years? The programme still faces critical challenges, some of which pertain to the realm of the programme, others to policy making in general. Regarding the programme itself, although differences in health and education between the poor and non-poor have been narrowed, they have not been eliminated yet. The programme must be sustained for at least another decade. However, positive impacts in the future will be the result of two circumstances. First, the enforcement of conditionality that requires continuous monitoring and external auditing. In its absence, the programme runs the risk of becoming a pure income transfer with just income effects on human capital. Second, the adequate supply and quality of services. Individuals that attend health clinics and schools must receive services that increase their human capital; conditionality must add value not just impose costs on beneficiaries. Maintaining the conceptual consistency of the programme by sticking to its objectives is central. The current scale of coverage and budget are a continuous temptation to add objectives and/or components not relevant to the programme.

Regarding public policy, the challenge is consistency and coherence of the different actions in the poverty strategy and with the general structure of incentives created in social policy. In particular, two issues must be addressed. In the short run there is a need for other programmes and policies to improve education and income, aside from Progresa. Although Progresa covers practically all poor families in Mexico, some of its members, the adults and the young people who had already left school before joining the programme, will not benefit from the educational component of the programme. In the medium term, Progresa's impact in effective poverty reduction will be observed once the children of current beneficiary families become adults and enter the labour market. It will be then that the increased human capital can be expected to translate into higher incomes, smaller families, healthier members and so on; only then it can be assessed if the intergenerational circle of poverty has been broken. This requires good job opportunities for the newly educated.

Notes

1 By design, food programmes had a limited nutritional impact since they were not linked to primary health care and nutritional education; nor were they adequately focused on the most vulnerable members of the household. In particular, there was no coverage of children under two years of age and of pregnant women and nursing mothers.

2 An abundant literature exists on this subject; an excellent review can be consulted in Lipton and Ravallion (1995). Levy (1994) presents the empirical evidence for Mexico.

3 In December of 1994, a major macro-economic crisis developed, resulting in a drop in GDP of approximately 6 per cent in 1995; the largest reduction in economic activity in more than five decades. During the discussions on how to protect the poor from the effects of the crisis some members of the Cabinet proposed strengthening existing food programmes.

4 In 1995 and 1996, Mexico negotiated with international organizations for financial support. Those that opposed the programme argued the changes were being imposed by these organizations, even though the proposal and its implementation was a decision of the federal government. To avoid any doubts, no international lending was linked to Progresa until 2002.

5 Federal elections were held in July 1997 and presidential elections in July 2000. Procampo, the only other programme that granted monetary transfers in rural areas at the time was launched in 1994 just before presidential elections in that year; the opposition argued that it had been used for political motives.

6 There were many programmes linking in-kind food supports to attendance to health centres, but not cash transfers linked to the same behaviour. Major educational CCTs were Bolsa Escola in Brazil and Niños in Solidaridad in Mexico.

7 From 1995 to 1997, all aspects of Progresa were discussed extensively in the Social Cabinet of the President's Office and in a special group at the level of deputy ministers; informal consultations were held with the governors of several states. In parallel, in 1995, another inter-ministerial group working separately from Progresa was set up to assess the distortions affecting the maize flour–tortilla chain and to discuss and negotiate adjustments to targeted and generalized food subsidies.

8 In 2001, the education component was expanded to include education grants for high school. Additionally, mandatory lectures on addictions, violence and family planning were introduced for this age group. Subsequently, in 2003, a system of additional deferred payments was added.

9 Communities are ranked based on a marginality index created in 1996 as part of the preparatory works for Progresa. Progresa started in the poorest rural areas with access to health and education services.

10 Household income allocation is determined not only by the amount of income but also by who receives it. In general, women have a different marginal propensity of consumption than men as they spend more on food and health care for children as well as on other household goods. See the evidence in IFPRI (1995) and Grosh (1995).

11 Accordingly, the programme's budget is divided in the three ministries: Health (nutritional supplements and resources to cover costs for additional demand in health clinics); Education (educational grants and school supplies); and Social Development (basic cash transfer and operating costs). The programme is totally funded by the federal government.

12 When the programme was renamed in 2002, Conprogresa changed its name to Coordinacion General de Oportunidades.

13 A summary of all these evaluations can be found in Levy (2006) and Levy and Rodriguez (2004).

14 Monitoring is done on the basis of two systematic data sources: (1) 64 indicators reported by the various programme operators; and (2) sentinel points that track operation indicators in a panel sample of 1000 beneficiary communities. Operation has also been evaluated by external consultants.

15 Evaluation led to substantive corrections to: the targeting system; the extension of school scholarships for three additional years; and the modifications in the formula for nutritional supplements. The last of these is an example of the mistakes of the programme; although an evaluation made the recommendation in 2001 and all the participant institutions agreed with it, it took more than four years to correct.

16 In 2005, 88.6 per cent went to rural areas in contrast to 31.4 per cent in 1994, matching more closely the geographical distribution of poverty in Mexico and the observed differences in its depth and severity.

17 In 2005, two programmes Progresa/Oportunidades and the school breakfast programme accounted for 93.2 per cent of total resources, however, there are still resources devoted to other food programmes difficult to justify on poverty alleviation grounds. These are a result of lack of consistency in the general poverty alleviation strategy, institutional inertia and the pressure of producers who see these programmes as marketing channels.

18 Mr Levy was Deputy Minister for Budget in the Ministry of Finance and Public Credit from December 1994 to November 2000, and General Director of the Mexican Social Security Institute from December 2000 to October 2005. During 1995–2000 he led the work and negotiations that culminated with the start of Progresa, from 1995–2000 the transition from generalized to targeted subsidies and the growth of Progresa and the complementary investment in the supply in health and education services. During 1997–2005 additionally he was a member of the decision-making body of Progresa/Oportunidades.

References

Grosh, M. (1995) 'Towards qualifying the Trade-off: Administrative costs and incidence in targeted programmes in Latin America', in Van de Walle and D. and Nead, K. (eds) *Public Spending and the Poor: Theory and Evidence*, Baltimore, Johns Hopkins University Press

IFPRI (International Food Policy Research Institute) (1995) *Women: The Key to Food Security*, Food Policy Report, Washington DC, International Food Policy Research Institute

IFPRI (2000) *Is PROGRESA Working? Summary of the Results of an Evaluation by IFPRI*, PROGRESA Report: 2000, Washington DC, IFPRI

Levy, S. (1994) 'La pobreza en México' in *Félix Vélez* (ed) *La Pobreza en México: Causas y Políticas para Combatirla*, Mexico DF, Fondo de Cultura de Económica

Levy, S. (2006) *Progress Against Poverty: Sustaining Mexico's Progresa-Oportunidades Programme*, Washington DC, Brookings Institution Press

Levy, S. and Rodriguez, E. (2004) *Economic Crisis, Political Transition and Poverty Policy Reform: Mexico's Progresa-Oportunidades Programme*, Policy Dialogue Series, Washington DC, InterAmerican Development Bank

Lipton, M. and Ravallion, M. (1995) 'Poverty and policy', in J. Behrman and T. N. Srinivasan (eds) *Handbook of Development Economics, Vol III*, pp2553–2675, North-Holland

Progresa (1997) *Programa de Educación, Salud y Alimentación*, Mexico DF, Poder Ejecutivo Federal

Rodríguez, E. (2006) *Progresa/Oportunidades y la Política de Gasto Público en el Desarrollo Productivo Rural, 1995–2005 Estrategias Complementarias en el Combate a la Pobreza?*, manuscript prepared for the IDB, Washington DC, InterAmerican Development Bank

SHCP (Secretaría de Hacienda y Crédito Público) (1997) *Exposición de Motivos del Proyecto de Presupuesto de Egresos de la Federación 1998*, Mexico DF, SHCP

SHCP (1998) *Exposición de Motivos del Proyecto de Presupuesto de Egresos de la Federación 1999*, Mexico DF, SHCP

SHCP (1999) *Exposición de Motivos del Proyecto de Presupuesto de Egresos de la Federación 2000*, Mexico DF, SHCP

SHCP (2000) *Exposición de Motivos del Proyecto de Presupuesto de Egresos de la Federación 2001*, Mexico, SHCP

18

The Phil-Health Indigent Program: A Locality-Based Health Insurance Programme for the Poor in the Philippines

Ed Aurelio C. Reyes

Introduction

The Phil-Health Indigent Program was established in the context of the country's worsening poverty situation, decentralization and the establishment of the Philippine Health Insurance Corporation (Phil-Health) to take the lead in implementing the country's National Health Insurance Program.

According to figures compiled by the World Bank, the Philippines is the only country in East Asia in which the absolute number of people living on less than US$1 a day remained constant over the 1981–1995 period (UNDP, 2000). Exacerbating the situation is the country's debt problem and growing income inequality. The level of the country's public debt has ballooned to such magnitude that substantial portions of its budgetary resources are allocated to service that debt, at the expense of vital infrastructure and social programmes.

The mid-1990s witnessed a significant increase in income inequality, a pattern that appears to persist. During that period, only the top 10 per cent of the population increased its share of total income, while the remaining 90 per cent lost its income share. In 1999, the National Statistics Office estimated that, of the 14.7 million families in the Philippines, the top 20 per cent earned 14 times more than the lowest 20 per cent. A study prepared in 2000 estimated the Philippines' gini-coefficient to be 0.45. Most of the poor are lowland landless agricultural workers, lowland small farm owners and cultivators, industrial wage labourers, hawkers, microentrepreneurs and scavengers. In contrast, those belonging to the higher income strata obtain a bigger share of their incomes from wages and salaries. Poor households are the most vulnerable to changes in economic conditions and access to health is the most adversely affected as revealed in a July 2007 survey conducted by the Ibon Foundation (2007). This situation, in turn, impacts on population growth as well as susceptibility to contagious diseases including HIV/AIDS, dengue and avian flu.

With democratization under the Aquino administration (1986–1992), Congress enacted the Local Government Code of 1991. That law devolved to local governments key functions hitherto held by national government agencies. These included functions relating to health, environment, agriculture, social welfare, infrastructure, economic development, some aspects of education and local public finance. Premised on the principle of subsidiarity, the law took cognizance of local government's key role in fostering the welfare of its communities, particularly those of its poorer members.

The Social Reform Agenda (SRA) of 1993, formulated during the Ramos administration, is one of the government's most comprehensive development frameworks for fighting poverty. Its strategies aimed at improving access to basic social services, income generation and self-reliance by promoting local autonomy. The SRA entrenched the decentralized governance system as a pillar of the government's development effort.

In 1969, the Philippine Medical Care Act (Republic Act No. 6111), known more widely by its acronym, Medicare, provided for increased medical care benefits mostly to the regularly employed, particularly those also covered by the Government Service Insurance System for public employees and the Social Security System for private sector employees. It failed to cover the larger sections of the population who were unemployed, underemployed or employed by the so-called informal sector: essentially the poor. The Medicare law was replaced by the National Health Insurance Act (NHIA) of 1995, which modified the Medicare system with the creation of the Philippine Health Insurance Corporation (Phil-Health) to administer a new setup designed to expand coverage to previously unserved sectors. The NHIA also established the National Health Insurance Program, to be implemented by Phil-Health, with the mandate to 'provide all citizens with the mechanism to gain access to health services in combination with other government health programs' (Department of Health, 2007).

The project

Access to health is the most pressing concern of most households. During adverse changes in economic conditions, it is not the lack of food but access to health services and medicines that figures prominently among households' concerns, especially among the poor (Ibon Foundation, 2007). Faced with a serious debt problem, the government can provide for only 38 per cent of expenditure on health services. Most health expenses are shouldered by private households (55 per cent). Private and state health insurance cover only 2 per cent and 5 per cent of their clients, respectively (National Confederation of Cooperatives of the Philippines, undated). With the poor, especially the unemployed and under-employed among the most vulnerable to adverse situations, better ways of making health services accessible to them became, and even now remain, a major challenge. With public health service delivery functions now devolved, that challenge falls squarely on local government units. Unfortunately many are as financially stretched as the national government, with devolved funds not quite matching the cost of devolved (especially health) functions. It is this situation that the Phil-Health's Indigent Program, with its component capitation scheme, was designed to address. The government saw the health insurance system, particularly the public health insurance system, as its main tool for ensuring the poor's access to quality health services. However, fully cognizant of local government's financial and health service delivery limitations, a scheme had to be devised to encourage them to use the health insurance system for its poorest constituencies.

At the time the Phil-Health's Indigent Program was conceptualized in 1997, less than 26 per cent of the population (about 22 million) were covered by health insurance, of which the Phil-Health accounted for 90–95 per cent. The overwhelming majority of those covered, estimated at more than 95 per cent were regularly employed personnel from the government and private sectors, plus their beneficiaries. Some 34,000 cooperative societies also provide insurance services to the poor. A study conducted by the International Labour Organization estimated that only 1.25 million were beneficiaries of some 935,600 documented microinsurance schemes in the Philippines (ILO, 2005). Of these schemes, only a handful involve the provision of health insurance services. Considering that members of poor families number close to 20 million, much needed to be done in terms of health insurance coverage.

Project formulation

The NHIA was conceived in the light of frustration over the earlier Medicare system and the need to expand the health care insurance system to cover those who are not regularly employed. An expanded system, coupled with decentralized government, was thought to be an effective way of delivering health services to those who needed the services the most. This was the germ of the idea communicated to members of Congress who eventually enacted the NHIA law.

The support of local government units through their leagues had to be mobilized, to make the intent of the law a reality. Local governments had to invest in improvements in local health facilities and services. For lack of funds, devolved facilities had not been properly maintained and managed.

In its initial stages, Phil-Health's Indigent Program had to 'ride on' the implementation of President Ramos' Social Reform Agenda that listed the 20 poorest provinces, dubbed as 'Club 20' as priority sites for implementation. In this manner, the Indigent Program gained the support of the highest office of the country. At the start, only two provincial local governments actively patronized the programme although all 20 had entered into a Memoranda of Agreement with Phil-Health. Initial successes, however, led to more buy-ins, especially as the Capitation Scheme went into full implementation.

The programme had (and continues to have) the support of various levels of government as well as of a growing number of private entities. Support from the legislative branch eventually translated into the passage of the NHIA of 1995, including provision for a Capitation Scheme that comprises an important component of the incentives package to entice local governments to invest in health. The Congress and Senate have continuously supported the programme as evidenced by growing appropriations from an initial P500 million (US$10 million) to the current P3.5 billion (US$70 million).[1] In addition, legislators from both the Senate and Congress set aside amounts from their Countrywide Development Funds to support the Indigent Program.

The Department of Health has been at the forefront of advocacy work for the Phil-Health Indigent Program, especially among local government units. Its regional offices provide various kinds of training in the field of effective health care and public health management.

The strongest support, however, has been from the local government units: the provincial governments with their provincial and district hospitals; the city and municipal governments with their rural health units (RHU) and city health centres (CHC); and the *barangay* (village) officials, who actively assist in seeking out indigent families. Local governments provide the funds to pay for the insurance premiums of indigent families. From the original two provinces that joined the programme, today there are close to 200 provinces, municipalities and cities participating. Besides the premiums, local governments have taken advantage of the Capitation Scheme to improve their health facilities, many bringing these on par with accredited private health service providers much to the advantage of the poor who can often fully afford only the services of public facilities even with their insurance coverage. Local governments have adopted central administrative and operating systems in which funds are managed in such a way that revenues from health operations are earmarked for more health service delivery for the poor.

Within the private sector, hospitals have supported the programme by ensuring high quality service for indigents, upgrading their overall capabilities, systems and equipment, and enrolling and properly participating in the system. Certain civic organizations and foundations, especially corporate foundations, have been mobilizing funds to augment the counterparts either of Phil-Health or of the local government units. Some of these private sector sponsoring entities assume the role of local government in sponsoring indigent families to enable their enrolment in the system.

Project goals and objectives

The NHIA that created Phil-Health states among its guiding principles, that 'the government shall be responsible for providing a basic package of needed personal health services to indigents through premium subsidy, or through direct service provision until such time as the program is fully implemented'. Created to operationalize this mandate, the Phil-Health Indigent Program seeks to cover more indigents of the country to ensure access to quality health care services, and to eventually wean them from dependence on the programme by helping them raise themselves from their very status of indigence.[2]

The Phil-Health Indigent Program's goals are:[3]

- to sustainably provide increasing access to health care systems, both preventive and curative, through health care financing for all indigents, specifically for the most vulnerable sectors such as women, children, senior citizens and the physically infirm;
- to enable indigents to save what they would otherwise be spending on health care and use these savings as new capital for small-scale entrepreneurship to create opportunities for upward social mobility; and
- to provide necessary assistance to local government units to provide effective access for their indigent constituents' to basic services until it is fully self-reliant in operating the upgraded health care services. Helping local government perform well on the devolved mandate for health care service provision has been this programme's distinct service and contribution to the historic decentralization and localization process spearheaded by the enactment of the Local Government Code.

The timeframe for the full implementation of the Indigent Program is 15 years, after which the country should have achieved universal health coverage of its indigent population.

Key elements of the project

Certain attributes make up the key components of the Phil-Health Indigent Program. First and foremost, the programme is sharply focused on serving and uplifting the poorest of the poor through the provision of quality health services. Second, it seeks to achieve this through a strong partnership with local government. Third, the programme provides an effective incentive scheme to encourage local government to invest in health facilities and service delivery. Finally, as mentioned earlier, the programme endeavours to eventually wean the indigent enrolees from dependence on the system by enabling them to attain upward social mobility. In this connection, the programme has started building partnerships with cooperatives and other enterprise-oriented organized groups to take over assisting their members to move from indigence to stable income status within the informal sector.

Target beneficiaries

Households whose members have a per capita income of P11,500 (US$250) per annum or lower are eligible for coverage. These households are identified by the local government units through their social welfare officers and *barangay* officials. Phil-Health assists in the selection process. The programme is open to all provinces, cities and municipalities willing to shoulder the premiums and improve the level of health service delivery to their poor constituents.

Two modes of paying for health services

The Capitation Scheme

Briefly, the Indigent Program keeps a list of enrolled indigents per locality per year, and serves these people in two ways. One way is through free out-patient treatment of indigents at the municipal RHU or the CHC. The RHUs and CHCs, however, need to be accredited as a Phil-Health facility to ensure that the service and supplies delivered are of acceptable quality. The Indigent Program uses the Capitation Scheme to fund the out-patient services of RHU/CHC facilities and for other purposes as the recipient local government unit may decide. Under this scheme, Phil-Health pays the sponsoring government unit P300 (US$6.50) per year of indigent enrolment. The amount is released by the government unit to the RHU/CHC where the enrolled families are listed. The RHU/CHC may use the fund to buy essential drugs, acquire supplies and materials critical to effect delivery of primary health care services and pay for referral fees. This results in improved capabilities and quality of service of the health care facilities. Some local governments have been able to purchase critical medical equipment or completely refurbished medical facilities using capitation funds. The key to this scheme, however, is that the government unit is enticed to improve its facility and service delivery system to a level where it becomes eligible for accreditation by Phil-Health. As an accredited health service provider, the RHU/CHC may then serve individuals (including non-indigents) who have Phil-Health coverage.[4] Otherwise, the indigent family has to be served by an accredited private health service provider.

Reimbursement of hospital expenses

The second way is through reimbursement by Phil-Health of hospitalization expenses of the enrolled indigents. As in the case of the RHUs and CHCs, the hospital used must be an accredited facility. Indigents needing tertiary level care are referred to an accredited hospital by the RHU or CHC as the case may be.

Phil-Health reimburses a substantial portion of enrolled indigents' hospital bills, professional fees and medicine expenses. This usually ranges from 50–80 per cent of ward rates.

Inter-government cooperation in the Phil-Health Indigent Program

Local government units have the primary responsibility of providing health care services for their constituents. The municipal and city governments, with their RHUs and CHCs are officially responsible only for primary health care, but enrolment in the National Health Care Insurance System allows them to send their constituents to hospitals that are primarily the responsibility of provincial/district/ city hospitals. The referral system has improved coordination in the delivery of health services, especially between provinces, municipalities and cities.

Project activities

Advocacy

The programme conducts regular orientation visits to local government units. For non-participants in the Indigent Program, the orientation serves as a tool to entice them to join. For existing programme participants, the orientation serves as a venue for updating new 'products and services' of the Indigent Program. Updates include new items in the list eligible for reimbursement or systems and procedures governing the programme. An orientation to new local government units includes discussions on the moral/ethical and legal responsibilities of local government and its officials as well as incentives for meritorious performance. Added to this are full explanations on the workings and benefits that may be derived from the Capitation Scheme. Samples of documents to be signed by the local government officials are presented. Generally, the Capitation Scheme generates the most interest among local governments.

Prior to the introduction of the Capitation Scheme, Phil-Health focused on the reimbursement of hospital bills of policy holders, an arrangement that benefited principally the provincial and city governments.[5] There was no provision for covering outpatient services, which involved mainly the municipal RHUs as well as the CHCs. Furthermore, at the time the Indigent Program was introduced, local governments were faced with financial problems spawned by inadequate funding to maintain and operate local health facilities. It was no surprise then that government units, especially the municipalities whose support the provincial leadership needed, were tepid to the offers of partnership (via a Memorandum of Agreement) to address the health problems of the poor.

Process of local government enlistment to the programme

The process of enlistment to the Indigent Program is as follows: first, the local legislature passes a resolution adopting the programme and authorizing the authority to enter into an agreement with Phil-Health; and second, the same body enacts an ordinance adopting the capitation fund on the Indigent Programme's outpatient benefit package.

Enrolment of eligible beneficiaries

The process of enrolment of eligible beneficiaries to the Indigent Program involves the following steps:

- The local social welfare officer, in cooperation with the *barangay* chairperson, draws up a list of enrolees, using Phil-Health guidelines for proving indigence. At present, the guidelines are income-based, but this is being phased out in favour of minimum basis needs (MBN) and community-based monitoring information system (CBMIS).
- The list is submitted to the Provincial Health Board for approval.
- The approved list is then submitted to the Phil-Health Indigent Program, which proceeds to enlist the local government unit's enrolees into its master database, computes the requisite amount of premiums that need to be paid and computes the capitation fund due the government unit.
- Phil-Health issues the enrolees' service availment cards.

The LGU's share to the premium payments of indigents (amounting to P1188 or US$26.40 per family) depends on its classification: first to third class municipalities have to shoulder bigger amounts per beneficiary than fourth to sixth class municipalities. Specifically, first to third class cities and municipalities are given counterpart funds equivalent to 50 per cent of the total premium payments they have to make. Fourth to sixth class municipalities receive Phil-Health counterparts of up to 90 per cent of the premium until such time that they can be upgraded to third class (Torres, no date).

Release of capitation fund

The capitation fund, computed by multiplying the number of indigent enrolees by the current fixed per capita amount of P300, is released in quarterly tranches. This fund is used in the operation and upgrading of RHUs or CHCs or for other healthcare related uses. It has been used to purchase medicines (62 per cent) and equipment/supplies (average of about 20 per cent). The use of the capitation fund for administrative expenses is limited to not more than 12 per cent of the capitation amount. Of the amount used for administrative expenses, half must be paid to the RHU/CHC physician and the other half to be shared by the centre's staff members. This guideline has encouraged many health personnel to stay on, a welcome respite from the current exodus of health personnel to Europe and the Americas. Local governments have also used the capitation fund to purchase direly needed equipment including ambulances, x-ray machines and laboratory materials.

Use of health services

The programme features an outpatient benefit package that covers primary consultations with a physician, diagnostic and laboratory tests and chest x-rays. This package is provided through RHUs and CHCs. These facilities are paid a fixed fee of P300 per indigent household per year. As administrators over these RHUs, local government units receive this amount that is specifically designated to be used to complement health centre funds, under well-defined guidelines for fund spending. Members are also entitled to a basic inpatient package similar to the package offered for employed and individually paying members. Members needing hospitalization can avail themselves of the services of 1,512 Phil-Health accredited facilities, both public and private, found all over the country. Providers are reimbursed for services rendered subject to maximum caps or ceilings for specific items (for example, room and board and diagnostics). Professional fees are paid subject to a relative unit value system based on a classification for procedures made (Management Sciences for Health, 2002).

Using the cards issued to them, policyholders go to RHUs and CHCs either for routine or symptom-induced check-ups. Depending on the results of these check-ups, the RHU/CHC decides on the kind of treatment: an outpatient treatment or hospitalization. For outpatient treatments, the card entitles the policy holder to free services and medicines. If hospitalization is needed, the RHU/CHC officer-in-charge writes a referral letter that the indigent presents to the accredited hospital.

The local government unit handles all the administrative requirements needed to reimburse the services, facilities and supplies it advanced to meet the needs of policyholders, including the collection of capitation funds due to the RHUs and CHCs. The government units issue local guidelines to translate Phil-Health policies and rules. These include guidelines for the use and allocation of capitation funds as well as reimbursement of advances made by government hospitals to policyholders.

Accreditation of health facilities

Phil-Health regularly inspects and accredits health care facilities operated by both public and private health service providers who apply for accreditation. The Department of Health and Phil-Health are guided by rules and regulations setting the standards for accreditation. Many government units have used accumulated capitation funds to refurbish, re-equip or modernize their health facilities to ensure that they obtain Phil-Health accreditation.

Training in health service delivery

Technical inputs and training services for local government health units are facilitated by the regional offices of the Department of Health. These services are provided on a case-by-case basis, mostly through customized courses. Support from external donors has helped expand the capacity of the regional Department of Health offices to respond to the local government units' training needs.

Implementing agency

The National Health Insurance Act mandates the Phil-Health to implement and manage the National Health Insurance Program, including its component Indigent Program. More specifically, the Phil-Health Indigent Program is implemented and managed by the Phil-Health's Program Management Group for Membership and Marketing. This group coordinates all partner organizations, especially the local government units and their health care facilities. It also works closely with the relevant national government bodies, including the Congress and the Senate. Phil-Health is also responsible for monitoring the programme.

Total project cost

The programme's costs consist essentially of premiums paid for jointly by Phil-Health and local government units. Each enrolment incurs a cost of P1188 (US$26.40). As of April 2007, the programme had cost the government about P4.7 billion a year (US$104 million). This cost is shared between the national government's National Health Insurance Program and local government. Local government's share, however, depends upon its classification, as discussed earlier. It must be noted that of the total amount, P1.18 billion (US$26 million) or roughly 25 per cent goes back to local governments in the form of capitation funds to help them improve their health facilities and maintain appropriate stocks of medical supplies.

Impacts and outcomes

In addition to increased revenues to Phil-Health (growth rates as high as 166 per cent in high enrolment sites), undoubtedly the Indigent Program, particularly through the Capitation Scheme, has led to the upgrading of the capability of many local government units to deliver high quality healthcare services to their constituents. A fine example is the province of Bukidnon in Mindanao, where the provincial government financed the establishment of well-manned and well-supplied health stations in all towns to augment the capabilities of the RHUs in providing primary health care. With the flexibility offered by insurance financing,

---

Box 18.1 BINDOY: A LOCAL GOVERNMENT UNIT'S SUCCESS
WITH THE CAPITATION FUND

Bindoy is a fourth class municipality in Negros Oriental in Central Visayas, with indigent households estimated at 70 per cent of the total. It had earlier been wholly-dependent on its internal revenue allotment from the national government. With widespread poverty and high incidence of preventable diseases in all its 22 *barangay* and with a high birth rate (18 per cent) threatening to worsen its health-related problems, Bindoy partnered with the Phil-Health Indigent Program and launched its own Bindoy Social Health Insurance Indigence Program (BSHIIP) and started health care reforms.

In just three years, from 2002 to 2005, using the programme's Capitation Scheme, Bindoy increased the number of indigent constituents served by its RHU from 562 to 5072! Over the same period, the municipal health budget rose from P3.74 million (US$74,800) to P4.38 million (US$876,000). Led by Mayor Valente D. Yap, the local government of Bindoy decided to have a steadily increasing figure for its premium contribution from P398,893 (US$7978) in 2002 to P4,485,292 (US$89,706) in 2005, with capitation funds tracing an almost identical graph line, from P482,004 (US$9640) in 2002 to P4,741,394 (US$94,828) in 2005. Premium contributions also rose steadily but on a less steep graph line, from P261,360 (US$5227) in 2002, to 2,162,010 (US$43,240) by 2005.

In line with the Local Government Code, health care service provision is now in the hands of local government units such as Bindoy, with them developing programmes, sourcing funds from many possible sources prominently including the Phil-Health Indigent Program, and taking care of expenses even of healthcare personnel.

---

the Indigent Program has inspired local officials to develop and employ creative solutions to their health problems. The case of another municipality is presented in Box 18.1.

In some places, local public health facilities have improved so much as to pose serious competition to private health service providers. Whether this is good or bad news remains to be seen. Whatever the case, some observers have noted that in some places, the competition has resulted in lower hospital rates.

The Indigent Program has expanded the coverage of local health service delivery to unprecedented levels. Previously, hospital services were provided directly by local government units. Under this old mode a provision of P500,000 (US$9000) for hospitalization expenses could cover only 75 patients, based on an average value of P6600 (US$128) per claim. Under the insurance system, that same amount can cover 4000 families or up to about 20,000 beneficiaries. The incentives provided by the Capitation Scheme have encouraged governments to enrol poorer constituents, effectively increasing the poor's access to quality primary health services and facilities.

Participation in the programme has increased the use of primary health care facilities. There is anecdotal evidence to support the observation that such an increase is significantly attributable to the renewed interest of women in pre- and

Table 18.1 *Indigent enrolment figures by region (April 2007)*

NCR/Rizal	327,026
CAR	89,999
ILOCOS	286,532
CAGAYAN VALLEY	196,131
CENTRAL LUZON	414,739
CALAZON	242,688
BAMIMAROPA	147,719
BICOL	197,722
WESTERN VISAYAS	292,223
CENTRAL VISAYAS	304,190
EASTERN VISAYAS	172,654
WEST. MINDANAO	129,515
NORTH. MINDANAO	612,353
DAVAO PROVINCES	102,747
SOUTH. MINDANAO	307,251
CARAGA	100,658

Source: Phil-Health Corporate Planning

post-natal care and even childbirth, these services being accessible to indigent policyholders. One indication of success in this regard is the number of days drug stocks were recorded as insufficient in RHUs and CHCs. In high (Phil-Health) enrolment areas, the average was 35 days compared to 180 days in areas with low enrolment rates. Studies conducted by the Department of Health also show that local health facilities in high enrolment areas were 'well stocked and well equipped' compared to those in low enrolment sites. Likewise utilization rates, measured in terms of per capita visit rates per year, of RHUs and CHCs were higher (equivalent to 4.9 per 100 person days of listed members) in high enrolment sites compared to those in low enrolment sites (2.5 per 100 person days of listed members).

Health insurance has changed the way local public health provision is financed (albeit partially). One way is through the capitation fund and another through direct reimbursement of advanced services, supplies and facilities. This has created a strong motivation for local government units to provide services to the poor at levels unheard of even in the recent past.

There is at least one anecdote indicating that the programme has positively impacted on local politics by reducing patronage. A mayor explained that he expected to reduce the number of people approaching him for assistance once the health insurance programme is implemented in his municipality. He has so far been unsatisfied with the result but is hopeful that it will change for the better.

Challenges and how they were overcome

Initially, local government units did not respond positively to invitations to participate in the programme for a number of reasons:

1   the initial design benefited principally provinces and cities that were responsible for the operation of hospitals;
2   the programme was viewed as a 'cost centre' requiring the usual counterpart funds; and
3   there was general discontent among local governments over the inadequacy of funding for health operations vis-à-vis the magnitude of the responsibility.

The introduction of the capitation funding scheme and the cost sharing scheme between national and local governments to cover premium payments changed the minds of local government officials. Further, many officials also saw participation as a concrete way of gaining electoral advantage.

A second major challenge was the selection of enrolees. Political patronage figured prominently in their selection and this had to be overcome by ensuring that official guidelines were followed. In some instances, non-governmental groups were asked to assist in the selection. This challenge continues to be an on-going concern and only the vigilance and dedication of the concerned local officers, specifically the social workers and the village leaders, Phil-Health officials and civil society groups, can minimize the influence of political patronage in the selection process.

A third challenge is changing the way local officials view the capitation fund. Phil-Health officials are wary of the view that the capitation fund is a 'return on investment'. This was and still is being overcome by painstaking education work among local government units to make them realize that the fund is provided as a means to improve health service delivery and reduce health service delivery costs.

Information on the entitlements that come with being insured has been confusing and, in certain cases, conflicting. This includes poor information on the obligations of the insured, particularly on the matter of what is and is not covered by the insurance. Often this has led to confusion over what the insured needs to pay for. This has inconvenienced both the indigents and the local private and public service providers. Information dissemination on such entitlements was and continues to be inadequate. Phil-Health, together with the Department of Health and the local government units, has agreed to address this information need.

Inequality of coverage among regions is conspicuous (see Table 18.1). The programme's management believes, however, that government units now lagging behind the others in terms of enrolment will catch up as soon as they realize the advantages of increasing their indigent enrolees.

Finally, there is the challenge of weaning beneficiaries off the programme. To address this, the management is developing a weaning process, involving cooperatives and other enterprise-oriented organized groups. In the meantime, beneficiaries are given the opportunity to cross over into the informal sector, that is, becoming members of organized groups such as cooperatives and microfinance (including microinsurance) institutions who can provide livelihood opportunities in addition to insurance. This scheme is in its initial stage. At the time of writing, there were about a dozen organizations that had formed themselves into KASAPI, an informal sector group that is fully paying for indigent enrolment outside the Indigent Program. Indigents currently enrolled by the local government units may transfer to KASAPI, which has its own package of support to indigents. Transferees will then be registered under a new health insurance programme. By way of incentive, Phil-Health provides a 10 per cent discount to these organizations when they reimburse the hospitalization expenses of their members. A disadvantage is that transferees lose their eligibility for outpatient benefits, a service exclusively for indigents enrolled by the local government units.

Lessons learned

The following lessons stem from the project:

*   A well-designed incentive system can entice local governments to invest in services critical to the poor.
*   Cooperation between national and local authorities can greatly improve the chances of services being delivered to the poor.
*   Challenges classified as political, such as political patronage or the absence or lack of political will, are concerns that can be overcome through dedicated abidance to official rules and regulations.

Potential for scaling up and replication

The programme has been scaled up from the original 20 provinces to all local government units in the Philippines.

Conclusions

The Indigent Program continues to evolve, even after 12 years of implementation. Its weaknesses and defects were addressed while providing a platform for effectively delivering health services to the poor through the local governments. The operation and development of this system, which has led to the reduction of the healthcare burden of indigent families, offers a rich experience from which to draw lessons in designing social service delivery systems for the poor. The concepts and operating systems used deserve to be sustained, studied and replicated.

Notes

1 Interview with Ms Arsenia Torres, Manager, Program Management Group for Membership and Marketing.
2 Indigents are given the opportunity of crossing into the informal sector owing to partnerships with organized groups such as cooperatives and microfinance insurance providers. This is only at its starting phase.
3 Interview with Ms Arsenia Torres, Manager, Program Management Group for Membership and Marketing.
4 The accreditation may be partial or full, depending upon Phil-Health's stringent evaluation of the facility.
5 Hospital operations were devolved to the provinces and cities while municipalities were responsible for primary health care and the operation of RHU (basic health facilities that resemble clinics).

References

Department of Health (2007) 'Best Practices: Health Financing', Metro Manila, Department of Health

IBON Foundation (2007)

ILO (International Labour Organization) (2005) *Inventory of Micro Insurance Schemes in the Philippines*, Geneva, International Labour Organization

Management Sciences for Health (2002) *In-Patient Capitation for Indigent Members of the National Health Insurance Program*, Management Sciences for Health

National Confederation of Cooperatives of the Philippines (undated) 'Health Micro Insurance in the Philippines: The NatCCO-SEDCOP Experience', prepared for the Institute of Public Health Management Center for Health Micro Insurance, Metro Manila

Torres, A. B. (no date) 'The National Health Insurance System (R.A. 7875 as Amended by R.A. 9241)'

UNDP (United Nations Development Programme) (2000) *Human Development Report 2000*, New York, UNDP

The VimoSEWA Self Employed Women's Association Microinsurance Programme, India

Tara Sinha and Lionel Siriwardena

Introduction

Microfinance services for low-income groups and communities have been expanding in the last two decades, with active participation by NGOs, development finance institutions and down-scaled commercial banks. Although the focus has been on providing microcredit and savings to a large number of small clients with deeper outreach, the challenge of reaching the poorest remains unmet due to high risks and costs. In the 1990s, various attempts on diversification and innovations of financial services shifted towards developing microinsurance products to reduce the vulnerability of the poor to income and expenditure shocks. Most microfinance institutions (MFIs) have focused attention on integrating microinsurance as a risk protection devise for themselves and their clients. From the beginning of this century, MFIs have moved beyond 'minimalist lending' to the poor to microfinance quality enhancement and risk diversification through the development of microinsurance schemes to protect clients against the risks that can lead them further into poverty.

CGAP (2003) has defined microinsurance as 'the protection of low-income people against specific perils in exchange for regular premium payments proportionate to the likelihood and cost of the risk involved'. The term 'insurance' is defined as financial services that utilize risk pooling to provide compensation to individuals or groups that are adversely affected by a specific risk or event.

Most MFIs in the world have undergone numerous difficulties in their attempts to expand the outreach of financial services to the rural poor on a viable basis. The situation with regard to microinsurance is even more challenging as formal insurance companies have failed to reach the poor with insurance products that meet the preferences and expectations of poor clients. Some progressive

NGOs have developed microinsurance programmes to provide risk protection to the poor. SEWA Insurance, the insurance programme of the Self-employed Women's Association (SEWA), is one such programme.

The project

SEWA was founded by Ela Bhatt in 1972 as an organization of poor, self-employed women workers. They are women workers who earn a living through their own labour or small businesses; they are unprotected, vulnerable to various risks and remain invisible and uncounted. SEWA's main goal is to organize poor women workers to obtain work security, income security, food security and social security at least in terms of health care, childcare, insurance and shelter. SEWA organizes poor women workers in the informal economy against the many constraints and limitations that are imposed on them by society and the economy, and takes joint action through their labour union and cooperatives. Its development activities are aimed at strengthening their bargaining power and offering them alternatives for secure and healthy lives.

According to the law, a union can only be formed by people working for an employer; hence the Labour Department of Gujarat raised an objection, saying that the women in the informal sector, having no employer, could not form a union. SEWA was successful in breaking this major structural barrier through strong negotiation with the government, arguing that a union must exist for the protection of poor informal sector women workers against exploitation by employers or business owners and also for obtaining minimum social and health security. Thus in April 1972, SEWA was registered under the Trade Union Act of 1926, as a part of the Women's Wing of the Textile Labour Association. SEWA was the first registered union for unorganized women workers. Since its inception in the early 1970s, SEWA has been working towards organizing and empowering poor and self-employed women workers in rural and urban areas in India. SEWA has organized self-employed women from different trades and helped them get regular employment, easy access to credit, childcare, healthcare facilities, microinsurance and so on. SEWA is more than an organization, it is a movement.

Project formulation

SEWA adopts an integrated and needs-based approach to organizing the member-based movement of about 1 million poor, informal sector women workers of India. SEWA works in 7 states of India and 14 districts of Gujarat. SEWA's membership in Gujarat is currently around 500,000, with two-thirds of its members living in rural areas. Members represent more than 125 different kinds of trades. There are about 3500 local producers' groups and 9 economic federations. Its members work in markets, in their own homes, in fields (their own and belonging to

FULL EMPLOYMENT	SELF RELIANCE

✓ WORK SECURITY
 	
✓ INCOME SECURITY
 	
✓ FOOD SECURITY
 	
✓ SOCIAL SECURITY
 	
   • Health care
   • Childcare
   • Insurance
   • Housing
	✓ ECONOMIC
	   (Of woman worker and her
	   collective)
	
	✓ DECISION MAKING

Figure 19.1 *SEWA's twin objectives*

others), in forests, on riverbanks and in the desert. The members are divided in four categories: home-based workers, vendors or hawkers, manual labourers and service providers, and producers. A wide range of activities organized by SEWA include organizing the informal sector women into their own organizations, capacity building, livelihood security activities, marketing services, microfinance services, social security activities including microinsurance and policy level action.

SEWA's vision is that all poor women workers in the informal economy should have full employment and be self-reliant. The various programmes that have been initiated by SEWA aim at the realization of this vision. Figure 19.1 lists the elements of 'full employment' and 'self-reliance' as envisioned by SEWA.

The range of crises that the poor are vulnerable to is large. It includes accidents, sudden hospitalization, death of a breadwinner and loss of crops or assets due to natural calamities such as floods, cyclones and droughts. Expenses incurred during such crises are met either by borrowing from moneylenders, sale or mortgage of assets or by drawing on scarce savings. The affected household suffers a simultaneous reduction in income and savings and an increase in debt and expenditure. Each such crisis leaves a poor family weaker and more vulnerable, and women are invariably responsible for managing the household, and coping with such crises.

Poor self-employed women and their households are not protected from such risks through any social security programmes. Unlike formal sector workers, who get health and death benefits from their employers, these workers have no recognition as workers and therefore do not get any benefits that workers are entitled to. The few government social security schemes that exist for poor households are barely known to the people and are made more inaccessible by complicated procedures.

Insurance is a mechanism that can help the poor combat the vulnerability caused by exposure to such risks. The objective of setting up SEWA Insurance was thus to set up such a risk fund to protect poor households from the most commonly faced crises. By pooling into a risk fund to cover stipulated risks – such as illness, loss of assets, death and widowhood – members would be able to protect themselves from unexpected losses. Such risk pooling in large numbers would allow the few affected SEWA families to be compensated for their losses by distributing the cost among a larger group. The purpose was to give members a sense of security that would help them plan for the future. It would prevent decapitalization and support people's efforts towards self-reliance.

It was with these objectives that SEWA started VimoSEWA (*vimo* means insurance in Gujarati) in 1992 for its members. VimoSEWA or SEWA Insurance provides life, accident, hospitalization (minimum stay of 24 hours) and asset insurance as an integrated package. Membership is voluntary. Women are the principal members and can also buy insurance for husbands and children. Most members pay an annual premium and this amount is passed on to insurance companies, which shoulder most of the financial risk. Members also have an option of making a one-time fixed deposit in SEWA Bank – the interest from this deposit is used to pay the annual premium.

Key elements of the project

Target beneficiaries and project area

SEWA started in Ahmadabad City in 1972 and gradually expanded to rural areas in Gujarat. SEWA now has sister SEWAs in seven other states of the country. In all its areas of functioning, SEWA's first strategy is to organize poor self-employed women, who are its target group. Once the union or collective is started, the other programmes to promote full employment and self-reliance are initiated.

Project activities

When SEWA Insurance started in 1992, the primary thrust was on enrolling members in Ahmadabad City. This was because the insurance team and SEWA Bank (a cooperative bank for SEWA members) were located in the city. As the insurance programme stabilized, it expanded to the rural members in the eleven districts. Membership grew steadily from 7000 in 1992 to over 30,000 in 2000. In 2001, membership jumped to over 90,000 – an increase attributed largely to a greater appreciation for insurance following a devastating earthquake in January 2001. By 2007, SEWA Insurance had over 170,000 members. Two-thirds of the scheme members were in rural areas and one-third in Ahmadabad City. SEWA's

Table 19.1 *SEWA insurance schemes (2007) (US$)*

Scheme 1				
	Member	Spouse	Children	Total
Annual Premium	2.98	2.38	2.38	7.70
Fixed Deposit	50.00	35.71	–	85.710
Natural Death	178.57	178.57	–	–
Mediclaim	47.62	47.62	59.52	–
Asset Loss	238.10	–	–	–
Accidental Death	952.38	595.24	–	–
Accidental Death (Spouse)	357.14	–	–	–
Scheme 2				
	Member	Spouse	Children	Total
Annual Premium	6.55	5.36	2.38	14.29
Fixed Deposit	119.05	95.24	–	214.29
Natural Death	476.19	476.19	–	–
Mediclaim	142.86	142.86	59.52	–
Asset Loss	476.19	–	–	–
Accidental Death	1547.62	1190.48	–	–
Accidental Death (Spouse)	357.14	–	–	–

Note: Additional benefits for fixed deposit members are: maternity benefits of Rs300 (US$7.14), dentistry at Rs600 (US$14.29) and hearing problems at Rs1000 (US$23.81). A Rs20 (US$0.48) discount is given to members who purchase a family insurance package (member, spouse and children).

current insurance schemes are shown in Table 19.1. Scheme members are spread over seven states in India, with a concentration in Gujarat.

Impacts and outcomes

The objective of SEWA Insurance is to provide financial protection to its members at times of unexpected loss. The most direct achievement has been the amount received by members as reimbursements since the inception of the programme. Over the last 14 years, SEWA Insurance has paid out about Rs85,795,244 (approximately US$2 million) in claims to 48,524 members.

The programme has succeeded in building the understanding and acceptance of insurance as a risk protection tool among poor women. Self-employed women have begun to see insurance as a mechanism for financial planning. The steadily increasing membership of SEWA Insurance testifies to its acceptance among poor families.

The programme has created a cadre of grassroots workers who sell and service insurance. Insurance as a concept is difficult to understand and even more complex to explain. This is especially so when it has to be explained to persons who have no knowledge of insurance and almost negligible experience of formal systems. SEWA Insurance *aagewans* (grassroots sales and administrative workers) have not only successfully marketed insurance but are also able to respond to the questions and doubts raised by members.

As a result of SEWA Insurance's successes, there is recognition of the insurability of the poor among policy makers. Insurance companies tend to see the poor as bad risks and therefore uninsurable. However, it is now seen that the poor are insurable and willing to contribute towards their risk protection. Senior leaders of SEWA are members of the Board of the Insurance Regulatory and Development Authority (IRDA) of India and its Advisory Council for Health Insurance. SEWA's experience contributed to the formulation of the Microinsurance Guidelines issued by the IRDA in 2005. SEWA is also being consulted by the Labour Ministry of the Government of India for scaling up microinsurance in four states of India.

Project management

SEWA Insurance is run by a team of full time staff and local women leaders called 'aagewans'. As shown by Figure 19.2, the *aagewan* is a grassroots level worker who is the primary contact person for the SEWA Insurance member and the critical link between the member and the scheme administrators.

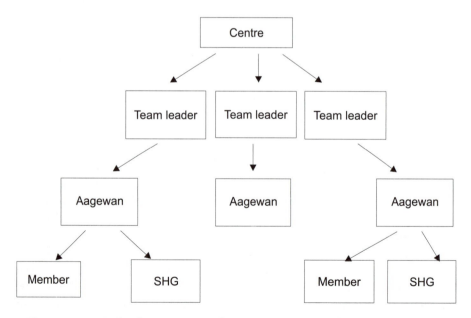

Figure 19.2 *Stylized presentation of SEWA Insurance implementation structure*

Source: chapter authors

All insurance claims are reviewed by a claims committee and 80 per cent of the committee members are representatives of various trades from whom SEWA draws its membership (20 per cent are staff). All medical claims are reviewed by a doctor.

Monitoring

The product has been continuously revised in response to the needs of the members. Initially, the insurance cover was available only to SEWA's women members. In response to member's needs, insurance cover was extended to husbands in 2000 and to children in 2003. This responsiveness to members' needs has increased its value to members.

SEWA members are involved in all stages of the scheme's administration. Their input is sought in product design, claims servicing and implementation systems. The involvement of the members enables the programme to evolve in accordance with the members' needs and increases their sense of ownership in the programme. It also adds to the transparency of the programme, as the rationale for all decisions are known to all stakeholders.

Challenges and how they were overcome

One of the early challenges faced by SEWA Insurance was negotiating the claims processing systems of the insurance companies. SEWA Insurance wanted to settle the claims as speedily as possible, but the insurance company procedures took a lot of time. Also the level of documentation required by insurance companies was sometimes difficult for SEWA members. For instance, United India Insurance Company had no previous experience with below poverty line markets. The hospitalization policy stated that claims would only be paid if the hospital had ten or more beds. SEWA Insurance found that members sometimes used quality facilities with fewer beds because of their convenient location, yet these claims were rejected. To reach qualifying facilities meant members had to travel, adding transportation costs and inconvenience. The minimum coverage available in the policy was unaffordable for the majority of SEWA members. The ratio of claims rejections was high and reimbursements took two to six months – a problem for BPL households with severe cash flow constraints. Any delay in claims reimbursement could result in members borrowing from moneylenders, adding to their burdens. Consequently, SEWA Insurance began offering inhouse health insurance in 1994 and then added asset insurance in 1996. For a period of time, therefore, between 1994 and 2000, SEWA delinked part of its operations from the insurance company, purely to be able to respond faster to its members. Over time, SEWA Insurance has been able to negotiate with the insurance companies to overcome these hurdles.

Another challenge is balancing the affordability of the insurance product and the protection that it offers. For instance, SEWA Insurance would like to offer greater financial protection under its hospitalization cover, but the cost of that insurance becomes unaffordable for SEWA Insurance members.

It is important to stay in touch with the members, both for them to remember that they have insurance and for their trust in the programme. A large proportion of SEWA members have limited literacy skills – written communication is thus not very meaningful to them – personal contact, however, is highly valued. As the membership increases and becomes more diversified geographically, ensuring regular contact with members becomes a challenge.

Educating members about the concept of insurance and about the terms of the membership is critical for members to be able to utilize the protection in times of loss. However, both the concept of insurance and the terms of the policy are not easy to explain or understand. It is time-consuming to explain insurance to members, but our experience has shown that the time spent on this is necessary and worthwhile.

Retaining members in programme is another challenge. Members tend to feel that if they have not received a claim benefit after being in the programme for one or two years, the insurance has no value and should be discontinued. However, once the members understand the concept of solidarity that underlies insurance, and the fact that it is the small contributions of many that goes to provide protection to the few who unfortunately suffer a loss, they are convinced.

Financial viable SEWA Insurance is the goal but it is a challenge. The costs of administering a microinsurance programme are high due to the large number of transactions of small value. At the same time, premiums have to be kept affordable. SEWA Insurance is constantly reviewing its systems and procedures to lower administrative costs and streamline its operations. One such new, efficient and cost-cutting system is its cashless tie-ups with hospitals. Now members get their claim reimbursement while still in hospital – but in facilities with whom they have negotiated fees and some quality standards. These tie-ups are popular with SEWA members and have reduced claim costs.

Lessons learned

SEWA's approach is one of struggle and development. SEWA recognizes that to cross new frontiers, struggle is inevitable, and this was the case with insurance. It took several rounds, over many years, of approaching the insurance companies to provide health insurance to self-employed women before it was accepted by them. SEWA does not think in terms of success or failure but in terms of a long struggle and periodic realignments of strategy so as to achieve the larger goals.

It is very important to have a learning attitude and to be open to change. The insurance programme, as with all SEWA activities, was developed in response to the demand from the members. Over the years, the microinsurance product, its delivery mechanisms and administrative systems are constantly evolving to respond better to members' needs. A key strength of the programme is its readiness to adapt and innovate.

The poor are willing to pay for insurance. Even though their incomes are meager, once the poor understand how insurance works, they are willing to pay towards the premium. SEWA members have demonstrated that if microinsurance services are effective in protecting against health and survival risks, they willingly contribute towards a microinsurance package for the protection and continuity of life without falling again into a poverty trap.

Member-based organizations are best suited to implement microinsurance. The participation of members in enrolment and claims servicing eliminates any information asymmetry that can exist between programme managers and insurance members. Representatives of members in decision making structures also increase the credibility and transparency of the programme in the members' perception.

Member education about the insurance scheme is crucial to its success. Insurance as a concept takes time and experience to understand. Further, insurance as a product is bound by specific rules and conditions, which are not always easy to understand. Educating members about the concept of insurance and about the scheme's rules is critical to its successful utilization by members. This is also necessary to prevent member dissatisfaction with insurance. The majority of SEWA's membership has limited literacy abilities and member education focuses more on visual techniques rather than written materials. SEWA Insurance uses a variety of education methodologies, including films, street plays and group meetings. The short films have been particularly effective in explaining the concept of insurance to members.

Given the multiplicity of risks faced by the poor, they need an integrated insurance package that covers multiple risks. By bundling the various risk covers, the poor family gets protection through a single policy.

Voluntary insurance programmes can face risks of adverse selection. Adverse selection refers to the phenomenon of a high percentage of high-risk individuals enrolling in the scheme, making it financially unsustainable. To counter the threat of adverse selection, group enrolment is preferable to individual enrolment. SEWA Insurance is encouraging members to buy the family package that provides protection to the member, her husband and children. This not only provides more comprehensive protection to the family, it also reduces adverse selection to some extent.

Convergence between programmes that have synergy increases programme effectiveness and efficiency. SEWA also has a health programme that coordinates primary healthcare for SEWA members. The health services are provided by a trained cadre of community health workers who provide health education and curative and referral services. These *aagewans* are extremely effective as insurance sales persons because of their rapport with women in the communities. They are also able to provide referrals to members for hospitalization, a risk covered by SEWA Insurance.

An appropriate regulatory framework is needed to make different institutional options and partnerships work efficiently. It may need to accommodate new players or facilitate the existing ones to integrate with the formal market. This does not necessarily mean a separate law specific to microinsurance; it could also comprise of amendments to the insurance legislation.

The *aagewans* in SEWA Insurance are the true champions of the programme. For the members, they are the face of SEWA Insurance, and the credibility of the insurance progamme rests on the *aagewans*. All *aagewans* come from low-income families and have little formal education. Yet, they are able to learn and communicate effectively to members the complex concept of insurance and learn the system for processing insurance claims.

Good practice

An important reason for the programme's success has been the fact that it is nested within SEWA Union. The strong grassroots network built up by the union and its credibility in the member communities provided a firm foundation for the insurance programme. Several features of the product, servicing and scheme management have contributed to its success. The product bundles critical risk covers needed by the poor: insurance for loss of life through natural and accidental causes, hospitalization and damage to house and loss of household assets. This integrated insurance product provides comprehensive protection to the members.

SEWA has been a pioneer in the field of microinsurance, making insurance available to the poor at a time when insurance penetration even among the middle class was extremely low. Further, its special contribution has been to recognize the multiple risks faced by the poor and in designing a product that aims to cover, through a single package, the most common of these risks. In recent years, several microfinance organizations have begun to offer life insurance and there has been some increase in community-based health insurance schemes for the poor. However, the bundling of life, accident, asset loss and health insurance continues to be perhaps the most comprehensive insurance product for the poor.

The potential for scaling up and replication

SEWA Insurance started with a membership of 1700 in 1992. This membership has steadily grown and stands at 180,000 members in 2007, as shown in Figure 19.3.

The sharp rise in membership in 2001 was after the devastating earthquake that shook Gujarat in January 2001. Insured members whose homes were damaged

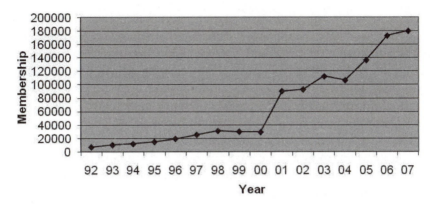

Figure 19.3 *SEWA Insurance's membership growth*

Note: insurance policies typically run for a calendar year. When the programme started in July 1992, SEWA Insurance's insurance policy year was July to June. July to December was a six-month bridge period. In January 2003, the insurance policy year was changed to a calendar year. Members requested this change as they felt it was easier for them to arrange for the insurance money during the months preceding January than in the months preceding July, often the wedding season in Gujarat.

Source: Chapter authors.

or destroyed during the earthquake were paid compensation through their insurance policies. This had a demonstration effect and a large number of members joined in July 2001. There has been a steady increase in the membership since then, except for a drop in 2004.

Scaling up over the years has led to several changes in the organization's structure and functioning. As the membership and geographic spread of the programme has increased, the SEWA Insurance administrative team has increased in size.

In its earlier years, the programme team comprised primarily of trained grassroots workers. Over the years, professionally trained team members have been brought on board, but the functioning style continues to be member-focused and member-driven.

From an early system of manual records, SEWA Insurance has now moved to computerized systems for all its operations and data management. SEWA Insurance has developed customized software to suit its data management needs.

Conclusions

Today, there is much discussion about the need for insurance for the poor among governments and the donor community. There is increasing recognition that to prevent those near the poverty line from falling into poverty, and for keeping the poor from sinking deeper into poverty, risk protection mechanisms are critical. Microinsurance is firmly an element of the development agenda.

To increase its reach, there are some important challenges on both the supply side and demand side. On the supply side, important questions are, 'what are the suitable products for the poor?' and 'how can this service reach the poor?'. On the demand side, the challenge is, how does one create the demand for a service that may or may not yield visible benefits to those who pay for it? Insurance, unlike savings and credit, implies the outgoing of funds (premium) for an uncertain inflow (compensation only in the event of the insurable loss).

There is no longer the need to demonstrate that the poor benefit from insurance and are willing to contribute a share of the cost of insurance. SEWA Insurance and others have shown the benefits of such a programme. An in-depth impact study is still required to assess the extent to which workers have been prevented from slipping into indebtedness and further poverty. But the fact remains that substantial economic support – about US$2 million – has reached poor families. The discussion has now moved to the next level, to find out how best insurance services for the poor can be designed and implemented. We believe that in the coming years the collective inputs from various stakeholders will greatly strengthen microinsurance services for poor families.

References

CGAP (2003) Occasional Paper No 7, Working Group on Microinsurance, CGAP, World Bank, Washington, DC

PART VI

Community Mobilization and Advocacy for the Millennium Development Goals

Sailing the Nile for the Millennium Development Goals: A Yearly Festival of Development, Human Rights and Volunteerism in Egypt

Layla Saad and Yasmine Mahmoud

Introduction

Egypt is located in the northeast of Africa and is bordered by the Mediterranean Sea, the Gaza Strip, Sudan and Libya. It is mainly a desert nation with productive arable land accounting for only 4 per cent of its total area found along the Nile River and Delta, Egypt's most notable geographical feature.

The current population stands at approximately 80 million (increasing at 1.7 per cent per annum) and is concentrated on the aforementioned 4 per cent of the land, which includes Cairo, the capital, home to almost 18 million people. Youth between the ages of 15 and 24 account for 20 per cent of the total population (Common Country Assessment, 2005). Despite this young people are not viewed as key participants in development processes. According to the 2004 Youth Aspirations Survey, the overwhelming majority of youth (67–84 per cent) have never taken part in any form of activism, clubs, unions and/or protests. Gender imbalance is significant in this deeply patriarchal and male-dominated society that limits opportunities for women to participate in political and economic life. Women's representation is far more pronounced within non-governmental and civil society organizations (Common Country Assessment, 2005).

In the early 1990s, Egypt embarked on a rigorous Economic Reform and Structural Adjustment Program (ERSAP) that utilized market liberalization and privatization as central strategies for overcoming and transforming a lagging state-dominated economy (UNDAF, 2002). Recently, Egypt has experienced substantial economic growth reaching 6.9 per cent in 2006, a rate expected to increase

Figure 20.1 *The Sailing the Nile logo, revamped in the 2007 campaign*

Figure 20.2 *Feluccas in Aswan during the 2006 campaign*

throughout 2007–2011. This has led to significant advancements in human development on a national level, pulling Egypt out of the low and into the medium category of human development (HDR, 2005). Noteworthy improvements have been made in the areas of health, with substantial declines in child, infant and maternal mortality rates and in education, which saw an increase in school enrolment and a reduction in adult illiteracy.

Despite this, a recent study has shown that 40 per cent of Egypt's population is still affected by poverty (World Bank, 2007). General economic trends tend to blur serious rural/urban and regional disparities, which once revealed the country's biased and lop-sided development. Growth has been characterized by typical core–periphery patterns with the majority of economic activity and subsequent higher Human Development Index concentrated in urban governorates and Lower Egypt (Nile Delta area). Upper Egypt (the south) instead lags seriously behind the rest of the country with disproportionate levels and numbers of people living in conditions of poverty and extreme deprivation (66 per cent of the country's extreme poor).

This situation accurately illustrates that without specific policies that target the poor and ensure a more equitable distribution of the national GDP, benefits stemming from a growing economy are enjoyed by only a portion of the Egyptian people. In fact, over a five year period between 2000 and 2005, absolute poverty[1] levels have increased from 16.7 per cent to 19.6 per cent at a time when the country boasts net growth (World Bank, 2007). Levels of extreme poverty[2] have practically doubled in some areas (particularly urban) and the emergence of 'pockets of extreme poverty' in rural areas has increased, both a direct reflection of augmented social exclusion.

When put within the overall framework of the MDGs the country's general growth trends and improvement in human development are reflected in Egypt's proximity to achieving the majority of the MDG goals. Yet, despite the optimism, Egypt's MDG reports and latest analysis expose the emergence of worrying gaps in income levels and living standards between Lower and Upper Egypt, pointing to the use of averages in measuring achievement as a deceiving mask for a less attractive reality (MDGR, 2004).

The question therefore is not only if Egypt will achieve the Millennium Goals, but also, will all Egyptians? It has been recognized that although it is mainly the responsibility of national governments to enable their country to reach basic MDG targets, the role of civil society can play a major role in boosting these efforts where they exist and/or pressuring for them where they do not. Although the Egyptian government has, in rhetoric, recognized and committed to increasing levels of citizen participation and adopting a more decentralized political structure, the reality remains quite controlled and restrictive.

Egyptian politics are characterized by the domination of the National Democratic Party, which has ruled the country for over 25 years. Although presidential elections are held every six years, in reality, few shifts in power have occurred since the 1952 Revolution. This has instilled a widespread sense of disassociation and passivity vis-à-vis public power, with most Egyptians feeling they have little say or control over the future of their country. Many NGOs and civil society organizations exist but their activities are limited by a restrictive NGO law that tends to control rather than empower.

The project

It is within this general social, political and economic context that 'Sailing the Nile for the Millennium Development Goals' was adopted as a creative way to transplant the dialogue on MDGs out of Cairo to Upper Egypt, where the most serious development issues are concentrated. The main idea is to raise awareness and trigger local action around the MDGs, adopting a human rights-based approach. Research done for the United Nations in 2003 by Zogby International illustrated that only 5 per cent of a sample of the Egyptian population knows about the MDGs. Equipping citizens with basic MDG and human-rights information will increase their propensity to act in relation to these. This rationalizes the emphasis on awareness raising that Sailing the Nile takes. Within this context, NGOs and civil society organizations are called upon to encourage volunteerism among civil society.

Sailing the Nile also seeks to expose Upper Egypt to the various development initiatives that are currently underway, on the one hand to provide examples of potential avenues for activism, but also on the other hand as a means to increase the visibility of the work being done by the UN and its partners. This is particularly relevant at a time when the organization is suffering from a negative image due to regional political turbulences and the less than admired role of the Security Council in these. The UN cannot achieve the purposes for which it was created unless the peoples of the world are informed and agree with its aims and activities.

Goals and objectives

Sailing the Nile is an advocacy-based communication campaign that seeks to reduce developmental disparities in Egypt, working with NGOs and civil society to make relevant information accessible, raise awareness and call upon these sectors to assume a more proactive role in meeting the MDGs.

The overarching goal of the initiative is to promote community participation in efforts to achieve the MDGs, building informed and active communities in Upper Egypt that are sensitive and responsive to ongoing developmental needs and can be mass mobilized to act swiftly and effectively towards the achievement of the MDGs in Egypt.

The main objectives of the project are to raise awareness of the meaning of the MDGs among the youth and children of Upper Egypt, informing them of their rights and responsibilities in relation to these; and to trigger dialogue and local voluntary action that contributes to achieving the MDGs.

Key elements of the project

The main target population in this initiative is the youth (mainly ages 15–24) and children of Upper Egypt who are traditionally excluded from programmes. Special attention is given in order to ensure that approaches are gender sensitive, affording girls concrete opportunities for participation. Secondary targets are NGOs, government representatives at the governorate level and media.

Project area

As illustrated in Figure 20.3, Sailing the Nile covers eight governorates namely Aswan, Luxor, Qena, Souhag, Assiut, Menya, Beni Suef and Cairo. Variations occur each year regarding the order of events (launch and finale of events) and which MDG is celebrated in which location, but the actual campaign takes place between 17 October, the International Day for the Eradication of Poverty and 10 December, International Human Rights Day.

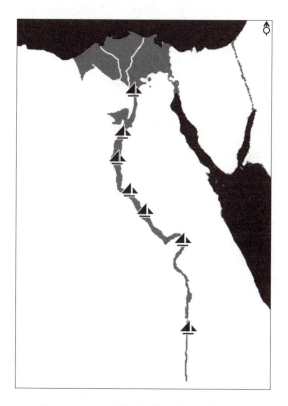

Figure 20.3 *The Sailing the Nile route*

Starting in Aswan, the route sailed north to Cairo to celebrate the final stop

Project activities

The key idea is for eight *feluccas* (traditional Egyptian sailboats), each with an 'Egyptianized' MDG symbol on its 18-metre sail, to stop in eight cities between Aswan and Cairo. These stops are used to launch a series of events celebrating human rights, development and youth volunteerism as they relate to the MDGs. Successful MDG projects involving volunteerism are shared, aiming to guide and inspire local communities to start their own projects and/or to volunteer in UN-led MDG projects. In each city concrete visible results and tools will be left behind benefiting the local community.

Communication for development features heavily in this initiative with the use of various arts culture, sports and media interventions implemented with youth and children. This is done both as a creative means to attract youth and children's participation while providing a channel for expression and dialogue on specific issues. The many arts and media activities are also used to transmit key messages in a non-threatening and easy to understand way. This is particularly relevant given the occasional reluctance to discuss sensitive issues as well as the high levels of illiteracy found in these parts of the country.

Key components and activities

The key components and corresponding activities of the project are grouped as follows and are aligned with the aforementioned four main objectives:

Design and implementation of a media strategy

This includes increasing the visibility of the development work that is being done at the grassroots level with the UN and partners. In the first year of the project an Inter-Agency Communication/Media Task force was created (and remains intact) with wide representation from UN agencies as well as communications experts from key partners. It proved to be highly functional and the agencies represented agreed early on to bypass individual agency branding in favour of coming together as 'One-UN' under the umbrella of the Sailing the Nile logo. This decision was highly symbolic of the cooperation with which this group worked and as a result of this collaboration Sailing the Nile was able to implement the following activities:

- Produce 'Egyptianized' MDG icons that are printed on the *felucca* sails. These were created by different Egyptian artists through a participatory process that involved pre-testing in different Governorates of Upper Egypt.
- Have regular contact with journalists, provide them with relevant material and organize press conferences in almost every location to discuss and draw attention to the particular MDG relevant to that stop.
- Ensure that at the opening event in each of the eight stops a UN representative knowledgeable about the specific MDG in question (for example, gender

empowerment – UNIFEM, maternal health – UNFPA, primary education – UNICEF) would be present to address the crowds alongside the governor of the governorate and a representative from civil society.

- Organize media training for governorate focal points where agreed upon templates/guidelines were given regarding the production and printing of materials in order to have a common feel among the posters and banners set up in the different governorates.
- Collaboratively produce public service announcements using Good Will Ambassadors that were aired through time allocated by private partners.
- Produce youth documentaries: another joint initiative involving two young volunteers from each governorate (one male and one female), who were trained on how to conduct interviews and shoot documentaries. Eight high-quality short documentaries were produced, each about the specific MDG that was covered by Sailing the Nile in their respective governorates. This initiative sought to facilitate and favour the expression of youth's alternative views, while providing them with concrete skills that can be reused to this end.

The 2006 experience regarding communication interventions is being built on to create a more comprehensive communications strategy that integrates targeted awareness raising, participation in global advocacy events (for example, the Stand Up campaign that set an official Guinness World Record last year), exposure to ongoing development initiatives, use of arts and culture to transmit messages and media coverage.

Organization and implementation of events

In each of the eight participating governorates a local committee with a local coordinator was set up in an NGO or civil society organization. They were responsible for organizing and implementing the activities in their location, liaising with other NGOs, local media and government while mobilizing youth to actively participate. These preparations are an essential part of Sailing the Nile and are carried out in a participatory way encouraging multi-sectoral representation.

NGO training

Training is provided on: (1) coordination and implementation of socio-cultural interventions and the use of culture, arts, media and sports as a means of social transformation; (2) MDGs and the role that volunteerism and youth mobilization can play in advancing Egypt's development situation; and (3) on communication interventions and media so as to ensure that key slogans and messages are consistent and that basic know-how on liaising with local media channels, government, NGOs and civil society exists. Publications were produced and distributed to assist local committees in mobilizing volunteers. These include the 'Popular UNDAF' created by the main implementing agency, the Youth Association for

Population and Development (YAPD) and the 'Toolkit for Youth Action for MDGs' by the UN Millennium Campaign.

Follow up

The eight local coordinators continue their work for months after the events ensuring that the synergies produced are followed up on and youth have adequate support so as not to lose their momentum. Each year it is envisaged that local linkages and partnerships are forged so as to create a strong civil society network working on the MDGs.

Key technical inputs

In order to implement the key components and activities of Sailing the Nile, the project relied heavily on the commitment and expertise of the Inter-Agency Communication Task force, specialized agencies who took the lead in conducting parallel training on specific issues (for example, UNAIDS trained all eight local committees thereby mainstreaming MDG 6 throughout the stops); a variety of specified trainers/consultants for particular issues (for example, media, youth documentaries MDGs, volunteerism) and the adaptation of published materials from the UN Millennium Campaign and UN Country Team.

Timeframe

Implementation takes place between August and June with the actual sailing of the *feluccas* occurring approximately between 17 October and 10 December each year.

Impacts and outcomes

A formal evaluation of Sailing the Nile is planned for early 2008 after the 2007 campaign is finalized in December, and will look at both quantitative and qualitative achievements that the initiative has made. To date, several outcomes are already apparent from the activities implemented and can be summarized as follows:

- Inter-Agency Task Force that has succeeded in joining for the first time in Egypt 18 UN agencies (FAO, IFAD, ILO, UNAIDS, UNESCO, UNFPA, UNIDP, UNIFEM, UNHCR, UNIC, UNIDO, UNODC, UNV, WHO and WFP) under the umbrella of 'One UN'. The Task Force is affording UN agencies the opportunity to pilot joint programming, building on experiences gained from one year to the next.
- Establishment of local committees that are developing skills and knowledge on mobilization of young volunteers to address development issues at the local level.

Aswan, Goal 7, Environmental Sustainability
Daytime conference on conservation of clean water and sources of pollution followed by evening football matches between teams representing different MDGs.

 Luxor, Goal 4, Child Mortality
Youth Marath on including over 200 volunteer participants was organized to raise awareness of child mortality. Local schools participated in various theatre and dance performances transmitting key messages on Goal 4.

 Qena, Goal 5, Improve Maternal Health
Events were launched with a big youth parade starting at Municipal Hall involving life size puppets holding messages and moving to the sound of local rhythms. Clear messages on Goal 5 and civil society engagement were transmitted.

 Souhag, Goal 2, Achieve Universal Primary Education
Young volunteers from a 'girl-friendly school' presented plays highlighting some of the main constraints and obstacles that girls face in trying to achieve an education.

 Assiut, Goal 1, Eradicate Extreme Poverty and Hunger
The cross cutting nature of Goal 1 was stressed and exemplary voluntary action was planned mobilizing medical caravans to rural areas where the poorest live offering free consultancies.

 Minya, Goal 3, Gender Equality and Women's Empowerment
Coinciding with the International Day for the Elimination of Violence against Women, this stop saw strong collaboration between UN Agencies and NGOs working to stop the practice of Female Genital Mutilation/Cutting.

 Beni Suef, Goal 6, Combat HIV/AIDS, Malaria and other Major Diseases
Coinciding with International AIDS Day, this stop collaborated with religious leaders to integrate messages on HIV/AIDS prevention.

Cairo, MDG 8, Develop Global Partnership for Development
Coinciding with International Human Rights and Volunteers Days, this stop saw exceptional collaboration with 22 booths set up displaying the work of UN Agencies and NGOs. The UN Millennium Campaign attended and organized 8 workshops on the *feluccas* with Egyptian youth.

Figure 20.4 *Glimpses from the governorates*

Each governorate focused on one MDG. The symbols on the left are the Egiptianized MDGs.

- Egyptian MDG icons have been created through a participatory process and are now the recognizable symbols of the MDGs.
- Increased awareness and dialogue on the MDGs. Although an evaluation will have to present concrete numbers for this claim, there is no doubt that at least all the young volunteers involved in the organization of events as well

as all those who attended last years events have increased the percentage of Egyptians that know about the MDGs. Dialogue has been sparked through several different forums.

- Sailing the Nile has succeeded in obtaining substantive media coverage on the MDGs in a variety of national newspapers for a period of 6 weeks with over 35 articles (of varying lengths) published over that time period in 2007. Sailing the Nile was also covered on local and national television, radio and even reached international media organizations such as Reuters.

- Sailing the Nile with the UN has encouraged private sector companies who contribute through their CSR portfolios to operationalize some of the commitments made when signing up to the Global Compact. In addition, these companies demonstrate how the private sector can support and draw attention to MDG initiatives in the country.

Total project cost

The total budget for Sailing the Nile was US$218,000 in 2006, slightly increased in 2007 to US$250,000. In 2006, the budget was financed heavily by the private sector (US$50,000), the UN(US$100,000) and government in-kind contributions (US$68,000).

Project management

The main implementing partner is YAPD, a national NGO established in 1994 with over 12,000 members. YAPD has local offices in Assiut, Qena, Minya and Alexandria, in addition to its central office in Cairo. The organization strongly believes in mobilizing youth to contribute to their communities by encouraging them to undertake voluntary actions.

The National Council for Childhood and Motherhood (NCCM) took the lead as the main government counterpart for Sailing the Nile. The Council was established in 1988 by a Presidential Decree and is entrusted with policymaking, planning, coordinating, and monitoring and evaluating of activities in the areas of protection and development of children and mothers. NCCM operates through a strong network of NGOs, students, volunteers, community leaders, academia, youth centres and schools and is in partnership with a large number of donors as well as the UN family. In Sailing the Nile, NCCM was instrumental in facilitating all necessary governmental permits and served as a bridge between the local coordinators and the local authorities.

Management arrangements

Sailing the Nile is based on an exemplary and unique partnership that brings together 18 UN Agencies, the government, civil society, NGOs, the private sector, media and academia in an effort to raise awareness and trigger local action around the MDGs. These efforts are increasingly being linked to and build on national initiatives that relate to the MDGs thereby inserting Sailing the Nile into Egypt's overall framework.

Sailing the Nile has thus far proved to be a very promising initiative and has consequently been integrated into the 2007–2011 UN programming cycle. The long-term vision is to create an annual festival of development and youth action managed and implemented by a network of Egyptian civil society organizations that can carry Sailing the Nile beyond 2011 up to 2015.

Figure 20.5 illustrates the management arrangements envisaged for Sailing the Nile to be successful. Most of the elements have already been formalized yet some are in the process of materializing:

- Eight local coordinators hosted in an identified NGO coordinate all planned activities in the selected locations along the Nile basin and report to the National Field Coordinator.
- Nine technical functions at the local level that can be performed by two or three people. These functions include: establishing and maintaining local partnerships; giving sound development advice, with a special focus on gender mainstreaming; coordinating MDG localization processes, such as production of MDG shadow reports; identifying and organizing exemplary voluntary actions; coordinating the volunteer recruitment and monitoring process for local listed projects; liaising with local media; coordinating the local public relations campaign; organizing arts and sports activities; and organizing the logistics for the events.
- National Field Coordinator responsible for the overall management and coordination of the activities on the ground and a member of all eight local committees.
- National Officer whose primary role is to coach the National Field Coordinator and design and implement the capacity building strategy for the implementing agency.
- International UN Officer responsible for overall management and guidance to all staff and for the design of the communications strategy.
- Information and communications specialist responsible for assisting in the implementation of the communications strategy and ensuring that the recommendations of the UN task force are followed up.
- The National Advisory Group will be formed inviting development experts, thinkers, economists, MDG practitioners, NGOs and private sector stakeholders that are familiar with the Egyptian context and the challenges that face the achievement of the MDGs. This group will meet four times a year to review project reports/status and to give strategic direction to the initiative ensuring that it remains linked to the national policy framework and actions are targeted and impact oriented. It is important to balance the guidance of

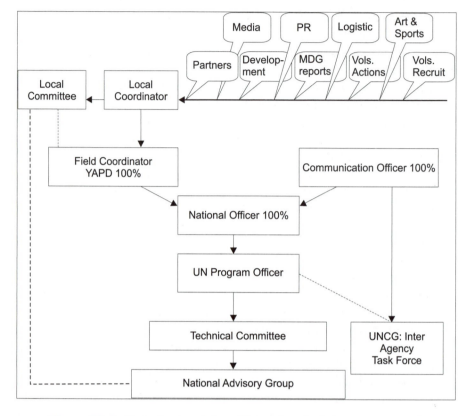

Figure 20.5 *Organizational chart illustrating the bottom-up approach of the project*

the National Advisory Group with the overall decentralized approach where the two coalesce to create a locally driven initiative with strategic direction.
• A technical committee meets every month to review progress in light of the strategic direction it has been given and the objectives it has set out.

Challenges and how they were overcome

Challenges were faced at different stages and on various levels throughout project implementation.

Mobilizing funds is often a challenge and can be a limiting factor regarding the quality and quantity of activities the project can implement. So far this has been overcome by the many in-kind and/or parallel contributions project partners have made, thereby strengthening the substantive components (with added training, conferences and workshops) as well as the level of media coverage (through organized journalist trips to governorates). Also important when mobilizing funds is the existence of strong institutional backing in order to increase the legitimacy of the initiative.

Yet resource mobilization is not the only challenge related to funds, in fact, actual allocations and subsequent management of these funds posed an even greater challenge. These difficulties occurred for various reasons, one being that some partners preferred to channel their contributions directly to the implementing partner (the national NGO), others chose to deposit into the UNDP account (as the managing agent), while still others opted for making direct expenditures on specific activities. This scenario definitely created some level of financial confusion making management quite difficult. Efforts to overcome this include encouraging partners to pool funds against an articulated work plan. Related to these challenges are the administrative obstacles present in UNDP, which lacks a system that accommodates joint programming. With so many partners, attempting to input the project into the ATLAS system was extremely cumbersome. The lack of experience and institutional set up for joint programming is a critical point to highlight, particularly within the context of UN reform. In order to overcome these issues it is imperative to operate with commonsense, creativity and flexibility, ensuring that administrative processes facilitate action and the achievement of project objectives rather than create bottlenecks.

Some difficulties were also encountered due to the bureaucracy and absence of an efficient financial management system within the national NGO. This often resulted in serious expenditure delays in the field and was overcome by offering full support and guidance to their financial department, requesting feedback at all stages, reviewing and following up on payments and sharing financial reports with the steering committee.

At the governorate level, local committees felt that a lot of experience and knowledge was gained and shared among all elements and people in the project and this was very positive.

Organizing and implementing the events was a challenge since committees did not have previous experience. They felt there was little time for preparation, while gathering members all at once to plan the events was difficult. Feedback indicated that dealing with government authorities was often complex and bogged down by bureaucracy and lack of efficiency. Committees learned that it is critical to involve government in event planning and to constantly follow-up with officials to ensure that events unfold as planned.

Partnerships were sometimes difficult to forge at the local level with the already established NGO coalitions showing little support to local coordinators who are not from a coalition NGO. Establishing these linkages has been facilitated by UN staff since both Sailing the Nile and the NGO coalitions are UN initiatives.

Lessons learned

Based on the aforementioned challenges it is important to think carefully how to manage and plan the joint nature of this initiative ensuring that implementation is facilitated. Clarity regarding the roles and responsibilities of collaborating and/or contributing partners is also important so as to avoid confusion and ensure that they are complied with. This can be facilitated through establishing Memorandums (or Letters) of Understanding.

The strong commitment of the implementing agency YAPD and the NCCM was critical for the success of Sailing the Nile. YAPD was active in facilitating knowledge transfer and mobilizing youth in the governorates where they have offices. NCCM played a key role in gaining the governmental support needed at the governorate level in order to facilitate implementation.

The project's decentralized approach through the establishment of eight local committees in each governorate fostered a deep sense of local ownership over the entire organization and implementation of the event. In Assiut, for example, the local committee met 32 times in order to prepare for the event. This translates into young people getting together to discuss MDGs and organizing to raise awareness and plan exemplary volunteer actions, one of the main aims of Sailing the Nile. Many natural synergies also occurred between local coordinators who advised and shared experiences with one another.

The events would not have been possible without the tremendous contribution made by young volunteers who committed themselves and worked enthusiastically to organize the celebrations. Strong coordination, good organization and teamwork proved to be essential for the success of the project with those involved believing in a common goal and putting aside any potential individual interests. Good interaction and communication among team members, persuasion and patience at all levels were also essential.

Another important success factor is the ability to establish and maintain a strong partnership between all stakeholders, ensuring that the contributions complement each other and are in line with the overall aim of the initiative.

Role of champions

Probably the most important thing to say in relation to champions is how Sailing the Nile as an initiative championed an exemplary collaboration across the board, prompting positive behaviour and contributions from all its stakeholders. The UN Volunteers programme was instrumental in this regard due to its creativity and ingenuity but also due to its exceptional placement within the Resident Coordinators Office. This placement combined with its perceived non-threatening nature helped bring other UN agencies on board.

The UN agencies made significant contributions beyond financing, especially through the work of UNAIDS that conducted training and seminars in all eight governorates. The NCCM championed the role of the Egyptian government, playing a pivotal role in bringing governors on board. The private sector stretched beyond mere financial support offering the technical expertise of its advertising staff to help with the MDG icons (Vodafone) and in attending press conferences at the stops (Procter & Gamble). YAPD showed strong conviction and commitment to mobilizing youth and allocating significant volunteer time, and the local coordinators and committees translated all this into wonderful substantive celebrations in the governorates. Undoubtedly this joint effort was able to attract the attention of the media who covered Sailing the Nile for over 45 days.

Good practice

Sailing the Nile has proved to be a very promising initiative that has earned international recognition for its creativity, collaboration and decentralized approach (allocated the 2006 UNDP Administrators Award). The project made use of a traditional and locally relevant way of reaching the people (the use of *feluccas* along the Nile) and its highly visual and colourful presence (through the use of arts and culture) attracted the attention of people who are usually excluded from development programmes.

The 'One UN' approach fuelled by the willingness to coordinate and work together under one flag provides a concrete example of the strength that can be achieved when agencies put their minds together. It is envisaged that this coming together can be mirrored at the government level by increasing the participation of other councils and/or ministries (for example, Youth Council, Ministry of Social Solidarity, National Council for Women, Human Rights Council).

Balancing a decentralized approach that harnesses local capacities and creativity with strong strategic direction provided through the establishment of a National Advisory Group is an important step in linking the local to the national, inserting Sailing the Nile into Egypt's overall framework.

Potential for scaling up and replication

Sailing the Nile has tremendous potential for scaling up both in terms of geographical coverage as well as in relation to its target groups, main goals and messages. Although as the name implies, 'Sailing the Nile' is relevant to the locations that are along the banks of this main waterway, there is no impediment to developing 'sister' campaigns that ensure wider geographical coverage using other means of transport such as trains and caravans (jeeps, trucks, camels). It is worth planning these expansions carefully in order to make them as fruitful as possible, building on experience gained in the initial years. Continuing with Sailing the Nile for more years will allow local coordinators to gain enough expertise in mobilization efforts that they can then share and transfer to new local coordinators in new locations, thereby fostering the development of horizontal linkages between youth in civil society.

When attempting to replicate and/or scale up this initiative it is important to do so with enough creativity and flexibility so as to include what is relevant to a specific country and its people. It is not recommended that the MDGs be separated, as was done in the first year of Sailing the Nile. Although this provides an attractive format it is not in the interest of the MDGs and the overall goals of the project. In 2007, Sailing the Nile made its main message clearer (ending poverty), celebrating all MDGs in each stop.

In terms of increasing and scaling up target groups, goals and messages, the yearly nature of Sailing the Nile should naturally follow this trend, defining more clearly its messages so as to encompass and reach government with the ultimate aim of achieving concrete policy changes that benefit the poor.

Conclusions

Sailing the Nile for the MDGs was conceived as a lively and innovative way of triggering dialogue and activism around the MDGs in Egypt's most developmentally depressed area. Although still in its initial years, the initiative has managed to stimulate enthusiasm among all its partners from young volunteers to high government officials and international partners. Decentralizing and giving space for local decision making in relation to the organizing and implementation of events has contributed to the strengthening of local capacities and fostered national ownership. Allowing for this flexibility at the local level is critical, even if the quality of some interventions is compromised.

One must look at Sailing the Nile with a long-term vision of a yearly campaign that will build on its own lessons as they unfold, strengthening over time and space. The collaborative approach offers many insights into the practicalities of delivering as 'One UN' and the immense opportunity this can afford in reducing fragmented interventions in favour of more holistic and encompassing efforts that build on the comparative advantages of each participant. With innovative and experimental programmes it is imperative to be open and daring enough to learn by doing, keeping in mind what is important.

Notes

1 Absolute poverty as defined by a recent World Bank study consists of 'spending less than needed to cover absolutely minimal food and non-food needs' (World Bank, 2007).
2 Defined as the inability to provide for basic food even if all expenditures are directed towards these needs (World Bank, 2007).

References

World Bank (2007) *Arab Republic of Egypt Poverty Assessment Update*, Report No. 39885, Vol I, Washington DC, World Bank

List of Contributors

Editors

Paul Steele
Environment Advisor, Millennium
   Development Goals Initiative
   (MDG-I)
UNDP Regional Centre in Colombo
No. 23, Independence Avenue
Colombo 7
Sri Lanka

www.undprcc.lk
Email: paul.steele@undp.org
Tel: +94 (11) 4526400
Fax: +94 (11) 4526410

Neil Fernando
Programme Analyst, Millennium
   Development Goals Initiative
   (MDG-I)
UNDP Regional Centre in Colombo
No. 23, Independence Avenue
Colombo 7
Sri Lanka

www.undprcc.lk
Email: neil.fernando@undp.org
Tel: +94 (11) 4526400
Fax: +94 (11) 4526410

Maneka Weddikkara (Ms)
Research/Programme Officer,
   Millennium Development Goals
   Initiative (MDG-I)
UNDP Regional Centre in Colombo
No. 23, Independence Avenue
Colombo 7
Sri Lanka

www.undprcc.lk
Email: maneka.weddikkara@undp.org
Tel: +94 (11) 4526400
Fax: +94 (11) 4526410

Authors

Chapter 1

Va Moeurn
Executive Director, Mlup Baitong
Email: vamoeurn@online.com.kh

Lay Khim
Assistant Resident Representative
and Team Leader, Environment and
Energy Cluster, UNDP Cambodia
Email: l.khim@undp.org

Chhum Sovanny
National Community Learning
Coordinator, Environment and
Energy Cluster, UNDP Cambodia
Email: chhum.sovanny@undp.org

Chapter 2

Anindya Kumar Sarkar
Secretary-cum-Executive Director,
Development Professionals' Forum
Email: aniksarkar@gmail.com

Pradeep Kumar Jena
Assistant Country Director, UNDP
India
Email: pradeep.jena@undp.org

Chapter 3

Andre Alexander
Tibet Heritage Fund
Email: al-iskandar@gmx.net

Pimpim de Azevedo
Tibet Heritage Fund
Email: pemamarpo@yahoo.com.hk

Lundup Dorje
Beijing Minority University
Email: dragondorje@hotmail.com

An Li
Beijing Capital Museum (formerly
Lhasa Cultural Relics Bureau)

Chapter 4

Owais Parray
Technical Advisor, Ministry of
National Planning in Indonesia and
UNDP Indonesia
Email: owaisparray@hotmail.com

Abdurrahman Syebubakar
Programme Manager, MDG Support
Unit, UNDP Indonesia
Email:
abdurrahman.syebubakar@undp.org

Chapter 5

Ramesh Adhikari
Building Local Democracy Thematic
Advisor, MS Nepal
Email: ramesh.adhikari2@gmail.com

Suresh Dhoj Shrestha
Email: sureshdhoj@yahoo.com

Chapter 6

Chudatip Ritruechai
Manager, International Relations
Division, President Office, SME
Development Bank of Thailand (SME
ANK)
Email: chudatip@smebank.co.th

Chaivej Nuchprayoon
Vice President, Ashma Foundation
Email: chaivej@hotmail.com

Octavio B. Peralta
Secretary-General, Association of
Development Financing Institutions
in Asia and the Pacific (ADFIAP)
Email: obp@adfiap.org

Chapter 7

Lutfullah Rlung
National Field Manager of the
dairy projects in Afghanistan, FAO
Afghanistan
Email: Lutfullah.Rlung@fao.org

Chapter 8

Zhao Jinqiu
Associate Professor, International
Communications College,
Communication University of China
Email: zjq_99@yahoo.com

Chapter 9

Ramiro Rodriguez Alcalá
Consultant, UNDP Paraguay
Email: rodalster@gmail.com

Thomas Otter
Economic Development Specialist,
UNDP Paraguay
Email: tho@tigo.com.py

Chapter 10

Tran Dinh Hoa
Deputy Director, Department of
Planning and Investment, Vietnam
Email: hrdp@hn.vnn.vn

Nguyen Thanh Tung
Policy Development Officer, IFAD
Email: tung.ifadvn@vnn.vn

Chapter 11

Pons Batugal
President, Farmers Community
Development Foundation
International (FCDF)
Email: pbatugal@gmail.com

Erlene Manohar
Project Development Officer IV, Field
Services Branch, Philippine Coconut
Authority
Email: ecmanohar@yahoo.com

Maria Luz George
Coordinator, International Coconut
Genetic Resources Network
(COGENT)
Email: m.george@cgiar.org

Chapter 12

Gamini Batuwitage
Chief Executive Officer, Gemidiriya
Foundation
Email: batuwita@sltnet.lk

Neil Fernando
Programme Analyst, Millennium
Development Goals Initiative
(MDG-I), UNDP Regional Centre in
Colombo
Email: neil.fernando@undp.org

Chapter 13

Neela Mukherjee
Director, Development Tracks RTC
Email: neelamukherjee@gmail.com

Chapter 14

Tran Van Thuat
Director, EM Policy Department,
State Committee for Ethnic Minority
Affairs
Email: tranvanthuat@cema.gov.vn

Ha Viet Quan
Specialist, EM Policy Department,
State Committee for Ethnic Minority
Affairs
Email: havietquan@cema.gov.vn

Chapter 15

Sheau Ching Chong
Executive Director, eHomemakers
Email: scchong@ehomemakers.net

Audrey Desiderato
Peace Fellow (Intern), eHomemakers
Email: adesiderato@gmail.com

Chapter 16

Nahleen Zahra
Research Assistant, Economics Group,
Research and Evaluation Division,
BRAC Centre
Email: nahleen.zahra@gmail.com

Naomi Hossain
Coordinator, Governance Research
Group, Research and Evaluation
Division, BRAC Centre
Email: naomih@msbx.net

Chapter 17

Evelyne Rodriguez Ortega
Private Consultant
Email: evelyne_rodriguez@hotmail.com

Chapter 18

Ed Aurelio C. Reyes
Professor, International Academy
of Management and Economics,
Philippines
Email: dingreyes@yahoo.com

Chapter 19

Tara Sinha
Research Coordinator, Self Employed
Women Association (SEWA)
Email: taragsinha@yahoo.co.in

Lionel Siriwardena
Senior Research Officer, Millennium
Development Goals Initiative
(MDG-I), UNDP Regional Centre in
Colombo
Email: lionel.siriwardena@undp.org

Chapter 20

Layla Saad
Consultant
Email: tietasaad@gmail.com

Yasmine Mahmoud
Country Operations Assistant, UN
Volunteers, UNDP Egypt
Email: Yasmine.mahmoud@undp.org

Index